Dualistic Economic Development

Dualistic Economic Development
Theory and History

Allen C. Kelley
Jeffrey G. Williamson
Russell J. Cheetham

The University of Chicago Press
Chicago and London

The University of Chicago Press, Chicago 60637
The University of Chicago Press, Ltd., London
© 1972 by The University of Chicago
All rights reserved. Published 1972
Printed in the United States of America
International Standard Book Number: 0–226–42983–0
Library of Congress Catalog Card Number: 72–75881

Contents

Preface

This book has its origin in the classroom. As teachers and students of growth economics, economic development, and economic history, we have been continually frustrated by the lack of an integrated treatment of the sources and determinants of national development. Growth theory has the great strength of examining the properties of formal models with rigor, but it does so in a framework—long-run balanced growth—only marginally relevant to the analysis of structural change and economic transformation. The development literature offers rich insights in a partial equilibrium framework, but it usually avoids a formal, rigorous, and integrated treatment. The economic historian provides a store of institutional and quantitative data, but he has mined it with relatively weak theoretical tools. In this volume we attempt an integrated use of theory, quantitative analysis, and economic history to bring three subdisciplines to bear on a common economic problem—the determinants of growth and structural change.

Our theory of development is not without precedent. It is most indebted to the pioneering theories of Dale Jorgenson, and John C. Fei and Gustav Ranis. These two theories, one neoclassical and the other classical, both focus on dualistic development and highlight the transition from rural-traditional to urban-modern economies. Ours is an extension of this approach. Drawn from a reading of the development and historical literature, our model is made more general by the incorporation of technological dualism in agricultural and industrial production, sector-specific biased technological progress, dualism in rural and urban household demand for goods and services, and dualism in household preference in family size. By extending the model to a more general characterization of the underdeveloped economy, we have been able to reconcile much of the apparent conflict between the neoclassical and classical formulations of the developing economy.

Our methodological procedure has been to define rigorously an "equilibrium" model, examine its properties with mathematical analysis, and then move toward a quantitative analysis of the system with simulation techniques. The latter approach permits us to move beyond the restrictions of growth theory, since we can identify not only the direction of influences on the development process but also their quantitative dimension. This departs from the growth-development-theoretic literature and allows a more detailed test of the descriptive accuracy of the underlying theoretical framework. Can it reproduce history? In a detailed study of Meiji Japan, we conclude that indeed it can. After establishing the plausibility of the basic model with reference to the historical record, we then proceed to increase its complexity to encompass disequilibrium growth. We capture the notion of disequilibrium growth by imposing restrictions on the operation of factor markets and by inhibiting factor mobility in the system—certainly a "realistic" feature of the developing economies. We then analyze this revised model numerically and compare the results with those obtained from a similar analysis of the equilibrium model.

While the models we have developed are intended to be broadly applicable to the developing nations, the specific empirical descriptions employed in this study draw heavily on the experience of Southeast Asia in general and of the Philippines in particular. The choice of this area derives from our personal interests in this region and research of Kelley and Williamson in Philippine and Asian production technology, sources of growth, demand patterns, and demographic change. An integration of this research into a more formal, interdependent framework was facilitated by Cheetham, whose Wisconsin doctoral dissertation was instrumental in the development of chapters 2 and 3. He is presently a member of the staff of the World Bank, although the work on which this book is based was undertaken while he was in residence at the University of Wisconsin. The World Bank does not necessarily concur with the contents or conclusions of this study. The research venture has been financed by the Graduate School, the Center for Development, and the East Asian Studies Program of the University of Wisconsin and by a grant to Kelley and Williamson from the National Science Foundation (GS 1837).

Acknowledgments must be made to the *Journal of Economic History* and the *Quarterly Journal of Economics,* where early versions of portions of this study appeared. Most helpful in their criticism and encouragement were our colleagues at the University of the Philippines, in particular José Encarnacion; Monash University in Australia, especially Colin Clark, Fred Gruen, and Alan Powell; and the University of Wisconsin, Robert Baldwin, Donald Harris, and Samuel Morley. Additional readings were provided by Jack Dowie, Kenneth Jameson, John Richards, Henry Rosovsky, Joseph Swanson, Kozo Yamamura, and Paul Zarembka. The research aid of Nina Davis, James Matson, Paul Robertson, Robert Schmidt, and Tat-Wai Tan was provided with dispatch and, on occasion, even with enthusiasm. Finally, and most important we're told, our spouses and children sustained the ardor of this undertaking with amazing patience.

A. C. K.
J. G. W.
R. J. C.

1

Toward a Theory of Economic Dualism

1.1. THE PHENOMENON OF GROWTH AND STRUCTURAL CHANGE

The level and expansion of per capita income have always been the central focus of growth and development studies. Indeed, both in terms of the urgency of the development problem—the widening disparity of rich and poor lands—and in terms of national planning objectives, a sustained expansion in per capita consumption of the impoverished third world has been taken as one of the paramount social goals of our time. As economists have turned their attention to this issue, it has become increasingly clear that, while growth and development may be viewed as a rise in per capita income, the process is integrally related to the economy's structural transformation. The shift from rural-agricultural to urban-industrial activity has not only been empirically verified as accompanying growth, but it has been postulated as a major factor explaining economic development.[1] Whether nonproportionate output and employment growth is a cause of development, or merely the effect of rising incomes, remains one of the more important, unresolved issues in the literature on economic development. Some attribute structural change to shifts in final and intermediate demand; others explain it by alterations in supply conditions and comparative costs. There is still no general agreement on the relative importance

1. L. H. Bean, "International Industrialization and Per Capita Income," *Studies in Income and Wealth*; C. Clark, *Conditions of Economic Progress*; H. B. Chenery, "Patterns of Industrial Growth," p. 636; and S. Kuznets, *Modern Economic Growth*, pp. 86–153.

of these two forces. In this book we provide a partial resolution of the debate by examining the causal forces as they flow in both directions and by evaluating their quantitative importance in an interdependent economic system.

The debate over causation has persisted largely because of the analytical methods employed. Explanations of the causes of structural change are frequently based on partial equilibrium analyses of the growth process. While such analyses have been useful in focusing attention on the operation of various forces in this process, partial equilibrium analysis by its very nature cannot contend with the interdependence between factor and product markets. As a result, such analysis cannot satisfactorily identify the relationship between economic growth and structural change. The critical importance of interdependence in the developing economy leads naturally to the use of general equilibrium models in both theoretical and empirical analysis.

There have been numerous attempts to describe the process of economic growth with general equilibrium systems for the higher-income economies. But as Chenery has noted, the general equilibrium models of Walras, von Neumann, and Leontief customarily omit those elements which would lead to persistent differences in sector growth rates.[2] The Leontief dynamic input-output models and the von Neumann framework of an expanding economy imply a proportionate expansion of all sectors in the long run, a pattern observed only when per capita income growth is constant. Furthermore, conventional analysis in neoclassical growth theory focuses primarily on periods of proportional growth. Yet historical evidence suggests that the growth process has been characterized by *non*proportional rates of change in the relevant economic magnitudes, and that the assumption of proportional growth as a description of this phenomenon is at least inaccurate and may be grossly misleading. In an effort to depart from the restrictions of these conventional theoretical descriptions, we have developed in our study a family of growth models capable of generating nonproportionate

2. Chenery, "Patterns of Industrial Growth," pp. 625–30.

sectoral output and employment expansion. Using these models, we have explored the sources of growth and structural change in detail.

1.2. SOURCES OF GROWTH AND STRUCTURAL CHANGE: A SELECTIVE REVIEW

Two basic empirical approaches to the identification of the causes of growth and structural change have appeared in the literature. The first attempts to distribute the contribution of various current factor inputs to current output growth and is commonly referred to as sources-of-growth analysis. The second, drawn from an extensive literature associated with such economists as Chenery, Clark, and Kuznets, represents an effort to quantify in a partial equilibrium framework those factors most important in explaining structural change. We have found both bodies of literature useful in developing our approach to model construction and analysis.

1.2.1. The Sources-of-Growth Methodology

The sources-of-growth methodology, initiated by Solow's pathbreaking paper,[3] relies heavily on the neoclassical conception of an aggregate production function and highlights supply conditions. It examines the contribution of current factor input expansion and technical change to current output growth. More important, the analysis is descriptive; it provides an accounting decomposition of input growth that must totally account for (but not necessarily explain) output expansion. Most of the literature subsequent to Solow's study has expanded on the accounting classifications of input change and the specification of the production function. Some scholars have focused on human capital formation and an appropriate recognition of the heterogeneity of the labor force.[4] Others, like Jorgenson and Griliches, have emphasized the heterogeneity of the capital

---

3. R. M. Solow, "Technical Change and the Aggregate Production Function."
4. E. F. Denison, *The Sources of Economic Growth in the United States.*

stock.[5] The competing specifications have been limited almost exclusively to issues relating to input measurement and technical specifications.

In our study we adopt the position that the more substantive issue relates less to measurement problems and more to the analytical conception and interpretation of this methodology. To what extent can the resulting measures yield insights into the causes of growth and structural change? The answer is straightforward. To the extent that each factor input grows *exogenously* and is completely independent of the growth in other inputs, the sources-of-growth methodology both accounts for *and* explains development. But growth and development theories have been primarily concerned with models in which factor supply growth is determined *endogenously*. While the sources-of-growth literature has improved our conception of the production function, and provides a useful first approximation of factors accounting for development, *causes* of growth and structural change can only be evaluated in a dynamic interdependent model in which factor input growth is determined endogenously. Factor input growth may indeed produce output expansion and thus structural change, but alterations in the structure of economic activity may also have an important impact on the growth of factor inputs.

1.2.2. Determinants of Structural Change

A selective review of the hypotheses purporting to explain the observed patterns of nonproportional growth reveals the economists' uncertainty regarding the sources and effects of structural change. It also provides a list of basic hypotheses that might be incorporated in formal models of economic development.

According to Kuznets, changes in the structure of final demand are likely to assume an important role.[6] This hypothesis is based on the premise that a rise in per capita product or

5. D. W. Jorgenson and Z. Griliches, "The Explanation of Productivity Change."
6. Kuznets, *Modern Economic Growth,* pp. 98–101.

technological change (and thus, relative price changes) may affect various categories of final demand at different rates. Consistent with this observation, Houthakker and others have developed extensive empirical evidence which shows lower income elasticities of demand for primary than for industrial products.[7] While these well-documented demand influences have often been cited as a key explanation of structural change, Kelley has emphasized that demographic factors may systematically attenuate the so-called Engel effects.[8] In general, any model attempting to confront the issue of growth and structural change must contain meaningful demand specifications consistent with the evidence of Engel effects.

Chenery, Shionoya, and others have argued that changes in intermediate demand may also play a fundamental role.[9] They suggest that the rise in the relative importance of intermediate demand for manufactured goods is due to a relative increase in final demand for manufactured goods, the replacement of handicraft by factory production, and the replacement of imports by domestic production. Although these authors have argued that much of the observed change in economic structure can be explained by the growth in intermediate demand, it should be clear that this source of industrialization is "derived" from more fundamental forces operating elsewhere in the system.

The best-known empirical study attempting to explain the patterns of industrialization is that of Chenery.[10] From a cross-sectional analysis of fifty-one countries, he concluded that the major influences affecting industrial patterns are not the determinants of demand but rather those of supply. Because the proportions in which labor and capital can be combined vary

7. H. S. Houthakker, "An International Comparison of Household Expenditure Patterns, Commemorating the Centenary of Engel's Law"; and "The Present State of Consumption Theory."

8. A. C. Kelley, "Demand Patterns, Demographic Change, and Economic Growth."

9. Chenery, "Patterns of Industrial Growth," pp. 639–44; Y. Shionoya, "Patterns of Industrial Development," pp. 93–96.

10. Chenery, "Patterns of Industrial Growth," pp. 624–54.

from sector to sector, changes in factor supplies can shift the sectoral comparative advantage as per capita income rises. Changes in relative factor costs in turn cause a substitution of domestic production for imports (and, to a lesser extent, of factory goods for handicraft goods and services) and thus generate the observed patterns of industrialization. Chenery's empirical results have been confirmed with historical evidence drawn from twentieth-century Japan.[11] However, the 1960 study assumed technology to be fixed across nations; in contrast, the 1962 paper allowed for variations in technology over time. The latter formulation may be especially relevant for developing theories of growth of low-income economies. In fact, the authors found the combined effects of factor substitution and technical progress to be important explanations of structural change. The detailed Japanese study thus suggests the advisability of constructing development models which allow for both technical progress and factor substitution.

A further extension of the supply-technology approach to the analysis of structural change has as its source the pathbreaking contribution of Arrow, Chenery, Minhas, and Solow.[12] These authors have stressed the importance of variations in factor intensity and the ease of capital-labor substitution in production as an explanation for changes in comparative advantage. If the implications of their study are expanded, alterations in factor prices, in turn, affect relative product prices, international trade, and the distribution of employment by sector. Empirical evidence suggests that substitution elasticities are higher in primary production than in secondary and tertiary industries, a hypothesis that might be productively explored in the theoretical description of the low-income economy.

In addition to variations in the possibilities of factor substitution among sectors, development economists have stressed

11. H. B. Chenery, S. Shishido, and T. Watanabe, "The Patterns of Japanese Growth, 1914–1954."
12. K. J. Arrow et al., "Capital Labour Substitution and Economic Efficiency."

the importance of differences in sectoral capital intensities.[13] In low-income economies the production process in secondary industries is far more capital intensive than in agriculture, which, together with differences in elasticities of factor substitution, gives rise to "technological dualism." Leibenstein has persuasively argued that the pattern of industrialization resulting from these features is reinforced by a bias in each sector's technology.[14] He asserts that innovations in secondary industries have been of a labor-saving kind, while those in agriculture have tended to be labor using. This hypothesis is supported by Watanabe and Williamson, who have shown that in Japan and the Philippines technological progress in the industrial sector has been labor saving.[15] Similarly, in explaining American economic growth, Habakkuk and Kennedy have argued that rising wages have induced a labor-saving bias in technological development.[16]

In summary, the literature related to sources of structural change suggests that any model purporting to explain this phenomenon should at a minimum explore differences in income elasticities of demand for consumer goods and sectoral differentials in (1) the bias in production technologies, (2) factor substitution possibilities, (3) capital intensities, and (4) rates of technical change. In the next section this list of hypotheses will be expanded to include demographic dualism as well.

1.3. The Concept of Dualism in Theory and History
Central to developing a formal model of the dualistic economy are the criteria employed in bisecting the economy into ana-

13. R. S. Eckaus, "The Factor Proportions Problem in Underdeveloped Areas."
14. H. Leibenstein, "Technical Progress, the Production Function and Dualism."
15. T. Watanabe, "Industrialization, Technological Progress, and Dual Structure," p. 122; J. G. Williamson, "Dimensions of Philippine Postwar Economic Progress."
16. H. J. Habakkuk, *American and British Technology in the Nineteenth Century*, pp. 41–88; C. Kennedy, "Induced Bias in Innovation and the Theory of Distribution."

lytically and empirically meaningful units. One possible framework for sectoral division is represented by the Uzawa models which specify investment- and consumption-goods sectors. While this dichotomy may be an appropriate characterization of the industrialized economy, it is less useful in studying the low-income economy where the focus is on the relative shift out of agricultural or, alternatively, traditional activity. Following a long tradition in development economics, we shall specify a rural-agricultural and an urban-industrial sector. In addition to the empirical justification, this formulation has the attribute that Engel effects can be explicitly examined, a possibility excluded from the Uzawa models.

Given the rural-agricultural, urban-industrial nexus, we must next specify the relevant characteristics of these two sectors. A brief summary of the literature not only provides useful insights into possible model formulations but also provides a base for comparing our model with the work preceding it.

1.3.1. The Taxonomy of Dualism

There are many views of dualism, ranging from vaguely stated hypotheses regarding sectoral differences in social, political, and economic behavior to formal statements implying well-defined predictions about the course of economic development and structural change. These interpretations usually include hypotheses about differences in the determinants of economic or social behavior as well as hypotheses about differences in the parameter values related to a given set of determinants. The existence of dualism has been argued on the basis of differences in (1) social systems,[17] (2) racial or ethnic backgrounds,[18] (3) production conditions,[19] (4) demographic be-

17. J. H. Boeke, *Economics and Economic Policy of Dual Societies.*
18. J. S. Furnivall, *Colonial Policy and Practice.*
19. R. S. Eckaus, "Factor Proportions Problem"; B. J. Higgins, *Economic Development,* pp. 325–40; D. W. Jorgenson, "The Development of a Dual Economy"; W. A. Lewis, "Development with Unlimited Supplies of Labour"; and J. C. Fei and G. Ranis, *Development of the Labor Surplus Economy: Theory and Policy,* pp. 7–20.

havior,[20] (5) consumer expenditure and consumer savings behavior,[21] and (6) the domestic and foreign sectors.[22]

The scope of dualism in all but the Boeke and Furnivall formulations tends to be narrow. Models emphasizing behavioral or technological parameter differences between sectors appear to constitute the predominant interpretation of dualism, and in fact the notion is typically based solely on differences in production conditions, with little or no hypothesized variation in demand, saving, and demographic parameters. Jorgenson's pioneering model of economic dualism, for example, contrasts two sectors with different production conditions but with identical demand and demographic parameters.[23] In view of the abundant evidence on the *varied* facets of dualism, coupled with the insights generated by the many studies which have examined only one aspect of dualism in isolation from others, the stage is now set for a multidimensional approach to model building of the low-income, growing economy. Indeed, the impact of alternative dualistic features constitutes the next logical advance to the theory of growth and structural change.

At the same time, there is a need to recognize the dynamic nature of dualism. In the highly criticized paper by Boeke as well as the studies by Baldwin, Eckaus, and Higgins, dualism is attenuated or eliminated through time as the differentials in parameter values describing sectoral behavioral and production conditions diminish or disappear. Since a complete disappearance is unlikely at any stage of development, "some degree of dualism exists in virtually every economy. Even the most advanced countries, such as Canada and the United States, have areas in which techniques lag behind those of the most advanced sectors, and in which standards of economic and social

20. B. J. Higgins, "The 'Dualistic Theory' of Underdeveloped Areas."

21. Boeke, *Dual Societies*; Higgins, " 'Dualistic Theory' of Underdeveloped Areas."

22. R. E. Baldwin, *Economic Development and Export Growth: A Study of Northern Rhodesia, 1920–1960*; Furnivall, *Colonial Policy and Practice*.

23. Jorgenson, "Development of a Dual Economy."

welfare are correspondingly low."[24] This conception is in marked contrast to the Fei-Ranis and Jorgenson formulations, to which dualism is eliminated when "traditional" (agricultural and industrial) production becomes "commercialized." In their models, dualism is no longer part of economic growth and development when agricultural or industrial production units employ significant amounts of purchased capital goods.

Spatial characteristics of dualism have assumed a minor role in the theoretical literature. While the traditional, or indigenous, sectors and the modern, or enclave, sectors may in fact correspond to a rural-urban dichotomy, this spatial distinction has rarely been introduced into the analysis. Indeed, the rural plantation enterprise is analytically treated as a modern industry; the farmer utilizing improved seeds, fertilizer, insecticides, or advanced irrigation techniques is likewise considered part of the modern sector. Similarly, the urban handicraft and putting-out industries are often classified as traditional. Since factor flows between the traditional-indigenous and modern-enclave sectors are typically treated with considerable abstraction— with migration costs, adjustment lags in migrant decision making, and market imperfections ignored—spatial aspects of economic dualism are largely minimized.

In summary, the mainstream of literature on economic dualism has (1) focused almost exclusively on differences in production conditions and, in particular, on differential parameter values in production processes; (2) emphasized in any given formal model only a single feature of dualism; and (3) abstracted from the spatial features of structural change.

1.3.2. Economic Dualism in Our Basic Model

Our approach to the formulation of a theory of the dualistic economy has several distinguishing features. First, dualism is viewed as being multidimensional. Differing sectoral characteristics are postulated for production, consumption, and demographic behavior.

24. Higgins, " 'Dualistic Theory' of Underdeveloped Areas," p. 106.

Second, not only are there many dimensions to economic dualism, but these enter both individually and in concert to influence the course of development. Explicit recognition of the *interaction* of dualistic behavior in consumption, demographic change, and production represents a significant extention of the traditional formulation of two-sector models.

Third, our formulation is developed in a spatial framework. The empirical literature supports the existence of rural-urban differences in consumer behavior, demographic behavior, and production conditions. While neither of these sectors is homogeneous in character, the three aspects of differing sectoral behavior, *when taken together,* provide the empirical basis for the rural-urban dichotomy and provide a geographic-specific interpretation of dualism. Moreover, one of the most important aspects of economic development is the migration of capital and labor. The movement of factors from sectors of low productivity to those of higher productivity is one of the primary means by which economic progress takes place. An explicit investigation of intersectoral migration, including an examination of adjustment lags, information costs, and market imperfections, constitutes a potentially fertile area of analytic inquiry. Even though the basic model presented in chapter 2 incorporates only simple hypotheses on the determinants of intersectoral factor migration, it does provide a geographic-specific interpretation of dualism which lays the theoretical foundation for the more complex model presented in chapter 7.

Fourth, our approach to dualism falls within the mainstream of the economic literature focusing on differing sectoral *parameter* values in behavioral and production conditions. There is some historical evidence to suggest that these parameters change systematically as development takes place. Accordingly, an evaluation of the impact of changing parameter values on the course of economic growth constitutes a primary focus of our analysis. For example, chapter 6 presents an extensive examination of "structural elasticities"—changes in endogenous variables in response to changes in parameter values and, hence, the model structure.

Finally, our model includes capital and labor in the agricultural production function, in contrast to the Fei-Ranis and Jorgenson formulations, which characterize "traditional" production (either agricultural or industrial) as based on land and labor. While the reasons for the omission of land are examined in detail in chapter 2, we consider briefly here the role capital plays in the agricultural process. First, the inclusion of industrial capital in the agricultural production function is based in part on the historical evidence of early application of nonfarm inputs (such as fertilizer, insecticides, and machinery) to agriculture.[25] The extent to which this type of capital is substituted for traditional inputs depends on the relative profitability of each input. Not only has industrial capital been a substitute for labor in agriculture, but, equally important, it has been a substitute for traditional capital and land. Second, in contrast to most formal development models, this study highlights the role of labor-saving biases in industrial technological change and labor-using biases in agricultural technological change. We accomplish this by appealing to a divergence in the elasticity of substitution between labor and capital in the two sectors. Finally, contemporary dualistic models rely heavily on *exogenous* determinants of labor productivity in traditional agriculture (for example, fixed endowment of land and exogenously determined levels of efficiency). In our approach agricultural productivity is *endogenously* determined, since purchased capital inputs can be accumulated, albeit from very low initial levels. In our view, the dualistic model must be able to confront explicitly the problem of investment allocation between agriculture and industry. Descriptions of the agricultural production process which exclude capital omit an important part of the production technology and oversimplify the phenomenon of structural change.

25. B. Hansen, "The Distributive Shares in the Egyptian Agriculture, 1897–1961"; J. I. Nakamura, "Growth of Japanese Agriculture, 1875–1920"; and T. Shukla, *Capital Formation in Indian Agriculture.*

1.4. EQUILIBRIUM GROWTH AND THE TIME DIMENSION OF ANALYSIS

In examining the long-run dynamic properties of equilibrium models, the typical approach has been to inquire whether a steady state solution exists and, assuming it exists, to determine its properties. Steady state, or balanced, growth is usually defined as a situation in which the rate of growth of all relevant magnitudes is constant over time.[26] Comparative dynamic analysis is then undertaken to establish the required values of the variables if the steady state equilibrium is to be achieved, and to determine how these values are affected by the model's parameters. An inherent feature of steady state growth is that relative prices remain constant over time and production in each sector grows at the same rate. For our purposes an exploration of the steady state properties of our models (if a steady state exists) is of limited value for at least three reasons. First, most definitions of steady state that are mathematically tractable provide inadequate descriptions of the historically observed patterns of growth and structural change. Balanced growth is usually characterized by constant levels of industrialization and urbanization. Yet one of the important characteristics of low-income economies—and a characteristic of primary interest in this study—is the phenomenon of *non*proportional growth. Second, while perhaps simplifying the qualitative analysis of model properties, the behavior of the model in steady

26. The concept of balanced growth has been discussed extensively in relation to the choice of criteria for resource allocation in low income economies by R. Nurske (*The Problems of Capital Formation in Underdeveloped Countries*), W. A. Lewis (*The Theory of Economic Growth*), T. Scitovsky ("Two Concepts of External Economies"), P. N. Rosenstein-Rodan ("Problems of Industrialization of Eastern and South-Eastern Europe"), and others. Nurske does not define his concept of balanced growth in a precise manner. Lewis suggests that balanced growth implies that relative product prices should remain constant. R. M. Solow ("A Contribution to the Theory of Economic Growth") defines balanced growth as an equilibrium growth path determined independently of output proportions.

state may not be any guide to its dynamic properties in other than steady state. The possibility that a model may exhibit disequilibrium behavior that is markedly different from that in steady state is illustrated by Jorgenson's pioneering work on economic dualism. Whereas Jorgenson's analysis and conclusions were based on a particular definition of steady state in his model, Dixit has recently shown that the model displays very different properties if the frame of reference is shifted away from the steady state; Zarembka, employing simulation analysis, reaches a similar conclusion.[27] Third, not only does empirical evidence suggest that the concept of steady state provides an inadequate description of observed patterns of growth and structural change, but also there is very little evidence to suggest that the speed of adjustment to balanced growth is rapid. In most empirical applications of growth theory the period being studied is likely to fall far short of the time required to reach steady state from a position of disequilibrium. Moreover, if adjustment to a steady state is indeed slow, then it is probably unrealistic to assume constant parameters and a stable model structure, which, in turn, may dictate a somewhat different approach to model construction and analysis than that required if the concept of steady state were used.

It should be noted that, despite its limitations, the concept of steady state growth may be a useful means for investigating the conditions (if any) under which an economy may stagnate at a low level of income per capita. Its importance for this purpose has been stressed by Leibenstein, Nelson, Tsiang, Jorgenson, and others.[28] A central issue in any development model capable of generating a low-level stationary state is the conditions under which stagnation is transformed into sustained

27. A. Dixit, "Growth Patterns in a Dual Economy"; P. Zarembka, "Introduction and a Basic Economy Model."
28. H. Leibenstein, *Economic Backwardness and Economic Growth*; R. R. Nelson, "A Theory of the Low-level Equilibrium Trap in Underdeveloped Economies"; S. C. Tsiang, "A Model of Economic Growth in Rostovian Stages"; Jorgenson, "Development of a Dual Economy"; Jorgenson, "Surplus Agricultural Labor and the Development of a Dual Economy."

growth. While it is possible that our model may possess such a low-level trap, the properties of the model in this state and the conditions required for escape from it are not investigated, since we are primarily concerned with a description and analysis of sources of growth and structural change when per capita income is rising.

In the growth conception utilized in this study the economy moves through a sequence of static, short-run positions from a given set of initial conditions. For the first two models examined these short-run positions are also equilibrium states; the third model characterizes an economy in short-run disequilibrium. Consider briefly the growth mechanism of the equilibrium models. An instantaneous and costless adjustment to price differentials is assumed in both the factor and the product markets. For any given point in time, the stocks of labor and capital are given, while production and consumption levels and commodity and factor prices are endogenous variables. The static model may therefore be regarded as a miniature Walrasian system. Equilibrium values of endogenous variables are determined from the simultaneous solution of the equations for demand, factor use, and price formation. A static equilibrium exists when there is no excess demand in any market, all prevailing market prices are nonnegative, and factor returns are equalized between uses. For each static equilibrium solution, the distribution of labor between sectors determines the increment to the labor force and net investment determines the increment to the capital stock. The addition of these increments to factor supplies disturbs the existing static equilibrium, and, given a stable, short-run, dynamic adjustment mechanism, a new static equilibrium is sought. This conception of the growth process is akin to the position taken by Bruton, who argues that development is both a short-run and a long-run problem.[29] For Bruton and us, the problem is to explain why and how an economy grows in a given short-run interval, since the economy is always in a short-run situation.

29. H. J. Bruton, *Principles of Development Economics*, pp. 4–5.

1.5. DISEQUILIBRIUM GROWTH AND PUTTY CLAY IN THE DUAL ECONOMY

Neoclassical analysis in both growth theory and development theory has been under attack for some years. Cambridge growth theorists have argued that capital goods are heterogeneous and therefore cannot be aggregated; moreover, capital goods cannot be transferred from one activity to another. To put it differently, machines are different in vintage and in sector specificity. We do not examine the issue of vintage in this study, since the assumption of disembodied (but nonneutral) technical progress is maintained throughout. However, the issue of sector specificity is explicitly confronted. These model specifications will have particular significance to appraising the development economists' argument that factor markets are so imperfect in developing economies that models employing restrictive hypotheses of instantaneous adjustments to factor-price differentials are of limited usefulness.

In chapters 7 and 8 we examine the quantitative relevance of these criticisms. There we relax the assumptions that wage and rental rates must be equated throughout the economy and that the movement of factors is instantaneous and costless. Explicit hypotheses are introduced to describe how factors respond to price differentials. Growth is characterized by a sequence of short-run equilibria in the commodity markets; in factor markets, however, continuous disequilibrium prevails. The dualistic economy is therefore transformed into a disequilibrium system of economic growth.

This approach is inspired by the views of Hirschman, Scitovsky, and others, who take the position that, in analyzing growth at low levels of income, theories based on a search for equilibrium rates of growth may be inappropriate.[30] Instead, development must be conceived as a disequilibrium process. They further argue that, even in the short run, where in equilibrium models the speed of approach to (static) equilibrium is abstracted from by assuming instantaneous adjustment, the devel-

30. A. O. Hirschman, *The Strategy of Economic Development;* Scitovsky, "Two Concepts of External Economies."

opment process is inadequately described. According to Higgins, for example, cumulative movements away from dynamic equilibria or from balanced growth are typical of low-income economies. Higgins notes that the cumulative movements away from a stable equilibrium in models of advanced economies are important in the theories of fluctuations in which movements are limited by floors and ceilings, as in Hicks's model of the trade cycle.[31] He argues, however, that, where concern is with trends, there are no such limits, at least over very long periods. Acceptance of this view requires the development of theories describing behavior in disequilibrium situations where mistakes are not corrected instantly, or markets are not always cleared. While arguments for these types of models have a priori appeal, the crucial test of their significance involves comparing the predictions of the growth process described by equilibrium and disequilibrium economies so that the contributions of added complexity through incorporating market frictions and lags can be appraised. When we undertake this exercise in our study, somewhat surprising results emerge.

1.6. QUALITATIVE VERSUS QUANTITATIVE ANALYSIS

Modern growth theory has maintained a safe distance from quantitative analysis. If a relatively complex system generates ambiguous qualitative results, the usual modus operandi is to revise and simplify the model structure rather than to restrict the values parameters may assume. Our study departs from this approach. While the basic model we formulate in chapter 2 is subjected to extensive mathematical analysis, which produces many significant insights into the behavior of the dual economy, certain ambiguities remain. Simplifying the model in the interests of obtaining unambiguous mathematical results is discarded as too costly a solution. Our basic dualistic model incorporates as many concessions to abstraction as we feel are acceptable. To simplify the model still further—for example, to eliminate capital goods from agricultural activity—would completely sup-

31. J. R. Hicks, *A Contribution to the Theory of the Trade Cycle.*

press the interesting and relevant development problems we wish to confront. Alternatively, we could have assumed that the model can be approximated by a linear framework through the use of a Taylor series expansion, thereby eliminating the ambiguities. In our view, however, linearization of models is appropriate only when small perturbations are considered; this may not be the case in the study of long-run growth. The existence of non-linearities in production and consumption may, in fact, be central to an understanding of the process of long-run development. As a result, when ambiguities in qualitative analysis have arisen, we have chosen instead to restrict the parameter and initial conditions and to utilize numerical analysis. While the model simulations represent special economies, these have been taken as representative of contemporary Southeast Asia and Meiji Japan in terms of both initial conditions and parameter values. How much generality has been lost in the process? Very little. Our objective has been to explain successful development from low-income levels. The concern is, not with all conceivable growth paths, but only with historically relevant growth paths. The quantitative representation of the dualistic economies developed in this study comprises a significant portion of that relevant set.

There is yet another compelling reason for quantitative analysis. Theorists typically evaluate the *sign* of a variable's response to parameter shifts. But the problems and issues surrounding economic development are largely *quantitative* in nature. It is instructive to know, for example, that capital accumulation or increased rates of technical change positively affect per capita expansion, but the relevant issues require insight into the relative *importance* of alternative factors influencing growth and structural change. Development economics is largely an applied area of economic theory. Although rigorous theoretical analysis is required to untangle complex interactions, quantification is mandatory if progress is to be made toward developing frameworks useful for the study of economic history and policy. We attempt in this study to move toward bridging this gap between abstract growth theory and empirical analysis, including economic history.

It has been customary in growth and development theories to treat lightly, if at all, the predictive power of the modeled economy. Economic theory can certainly be viewed as a necessary aid to thinking about complex problems. But at some point model predictions must be confronted with historical evidence. Our study is devoted not only to the development and analysis of theoretical structures but also to the provision of models which describe the development process. Accordingly, Japanese data drawn from the Meiji period have been used to evaluate the degree to which the simulated growth trajectories broadly conform to an observed and well-documented historical growth pattern. We shall find that our neoclassical model has "predicted" well indeed. While neither theory nor history can be confidently used to "predict" the future, a central theme of this study is that, when the two are used in *conjunction,* the forecasting capabilities of either approach are increased. For this reason we view this book as a treatise on economic dualism in theory and history.

1.7. AN OVERVIEW

The theoretical focus of this study is that useful insights into growth and structural change can be obtained through the analysis of simple abstract models incorporating various factors hypothesized to be important in the development process. These factors include the possibility of production and consumption sectors of widely differing characteristics, postulates about consumption and investment under risk and uncertainty, the role of innovation and technological progress, and market adjustment lags and imperfections. The list could be significantly expanded, but it is necessary to begin with a model incorporating only the most basic features of the growth process. Such a framework is developed in chapter 2, and it is used as a norm for assessing the more complex, alternative descriptions of the developing economy that are progressively introduced.

In chapter 3 a qualitative analysis of the static and dynamic properties of this "basic" dual economy model is undertaken. An attempt is made to determine the conditions under which growth will occur, and to provide qualitative insights into the conditions under which one set of factors rather than another is responsible for a given pattern of structural change. The complexity of the basic model limits the extent to which general statements can be made. To overcome this difficulty we could significantly simplify the basic model, but to do so would eliminate several theoretical features that make the model potentially useful.

Accordingly, in chapter 4 we turn to numerical methods to analyze the properties of a model slightly more complex than that developed in chapter 2. From a given set of initial conditions and parameters, characterizing a representative low-income economy, the time paths of the endogenous variables are obtained by simulation. In the initial period most of the labor force is located in the agricultural sector, agriculture accounts for a larger share of aggregate output than does industry, there is a relatively low aggregate savings rate and a high population growth rate, technical change is labor saving in industry and labor using in agriculture, and the real wage is close to the minimum subsistence level. The results of the simulation are analyzed in conjunction with the qualitative analysis of chapter 3. In chapter 5 Japanese data from the Meiji period are used to evaluate in much greater detail the degree to which the simulation results conform to a case from economic history.

The investigation of the equilibrium models is concluded in chapter 6 with a sensitivity analysis of key variables to changes in parameter values. There is ample evidence to suggest that certain parameters, such as those describing tastes, production, and family size, change systematically as development takes place. Thus, in addition to permitting an assessment of the model's generality, sensitivity analysis enables us to identify the impact of changes in parameters on the rate and direction of growth and structural change. This exercise provides the basis for explicitly considering several key hypotheses in development economics: the sources of economic growth, the relative importance of demand and supply factors in determining the course of structural change, an interpretation of the export-technology hypothesis, and the response of the economy to biased technical progress and demographic change.

In chapter 7 we turn to the specification of the disequilibrium model. The regional and dualistic elements of the equilibrium model are integrated by adding several hypotheses relating to intersectoral factor movements. We find in chapter 8 that the resultant analytical framework is particularly useful for capturing regional disparities in factor prices and for analyzing structural change under conditions of disequilibrium growth. We are also able to compare the ability of the equilibrium and disequilibrium models in describing the Japanese experience of growth and structural change.

The study concludes in chapter 9 with a summary of the findings together with suggested directions for future theoretical development. The movement toward a theory of economic development does not involve the initial construction of "the" seminal model, but rather the evolution of simple constructs. Model features which add complexity and appear to contribute little to explaining key variables should be discarded. Further postulates of the development process should then be considered, in addition to the interaction of newly incorporated theoretical features with those discarded. It is therefore appropriate to conclude our study with a number of research suggestions for moving toward improved models of economic development—suggestions based both on the findings of the study itself and, equally important, on the heuristic insights inevitably developed in a theoretical undertaking of this kind.

2

A Basic Model of Economic Dualism

2.1. THE THEORETICAL APPROACH

One approach to the construction of a formal model of the developing economy is to capture in a single framework the many features the literature deems critical to the development process: these might include "dualism" (somehow defined), market adjustment lags and imperfections, production and consumption sectors of widely differing characteristics, a foreign trade sector, and postulates about consumption and investment behavior under risk and uncertainty. Such a description would not only result in a highly complex system, but it would also provide a framework which would be difficult, if not impossible, to relate to the models presented in the development and growth literature or to derive analytically general properties, predictions, and theorems.

We adopt the view that, while the economic system is admittedly complex, it is necessary to begin with a model structure that incorporates only the most basic features of the growth process. The theoretical description of the developing economy formulated in this chapter is called our "basic model" of economic dualism. It incorporates perhaps the most elementary features which development economists generally consider important in describing the growth process. An explicit statement of the static and dynamic elements of the basic model is developed in section 2.2. Because of its simplicity, the basic model can be related to the existing literature on growth and development. Thus, we conclude with a comparison of the features of the basic model with those highlighted in the growth-development literature and, in particular, in the Jorgenson model of dualistic development.

2.2. THE BASIC MODEL

2.2.1. Production Conditions

We shall consider the case of a closed economy consisting of an agricultural and industrial sector, each of which produces a single homogeneous commodity.[1] The output of the agricultural sector can be used only as a consumption good. Industrial output may be consumed or invested, or both. The latter assumption distinguishes our model from those developed by Uzawa and others, who assume that one sector produces capital goods (the industrial sector) and the other produces consumption goods (the agricultural sector).[2] The Uzawa dichotomy has not always been maintained in the development-theory literature. Fei and Ranis, and Jorgenson, for example, admit the possibility that industrial output may be used for both consumption and investment purposes.[3]

Our two-sector economy is assumed to consist of laborers who supply only labor services for employment in each sector and capitalists who supply no labor services but are the owners of the productive units in the economy. They provide the entrepreneurial services required for the operation of these units and determine the optimal method of producing firm outputs.

2.2.1.1. *Production Technology.* It is assumed that the production process in each sector can be described by a con-

1. By restricting our attention to the analysis of a closed two-sector economy we forego the possibility of examining the impact of international trade and expansion of intermediate demand on industrial patterns, the importance of which has been stressed by H. B. Chenery ("Patterns of Industrial Growth") and others.

2. H. Uzawa, "On a Two-Sector Model of Economic Growth, I"; and "On a Two-Sector Model of Economic Growth, II."

3. J. C. Fei and G. Ranis, *Development of the Labor Surplus Economy: Theory and Policy*, chap. 2; D. W. Jorgenson, "The Development of a Dual Economy"; and idem, "Surplus Agricultural Labor and the Development of a Dual Economy."

tinuous, twice-differentiable, single-valued function. It will be convenient to regard sector 1 as the "industrial sector" and sector 2 as the "agricultural sector." Output in each sector is produced by two homogeneous factors, namely, labor and capital.[4] Production in each sector is subject to constant returns to scale, and diminishing marginal rates of substitution are assumed to prevail.[5] Joint products are excluded and external economies (diseconomies) do not exist. It is assumed that factor-augmenting technical change applies to both capital and labor. Thus, each sector is analogous to a large firm or industry having a production function and exhibiting optimal behavior. Such behavior implies cost minimization with respect to inputs and revenue maximization with respect to outputs.

The production functions can be written as:

$$Q_i(t) = F^i\,[x(t)K_i(t), y(t)L_i(t)] \quad (i = 1, 2),[6] \qquad (2.1)$$

where $Q_i(t)$ is the quantity of the ith good currently produced; $K_i(t) > 0$ and $L_i(t) > 0$ are, respectively, the amounts of capital and labor currently employed in the ith sector; and $x(t) > 0$ and $y(t) > 0$ are the respective variables of technical progress. Hereafter, we shall refer to $x(t)K_i(t)$ as "efficiency capital" and $y(t)L_i(t)$ as "efficiency labor."

The production process in the industrial sector is considered to be more capital intensive than that in agriculture. The importance of the capital intensity of the production process in various sectors has been stressed by Eckaus.[7] He has argued that in underdeveloped economies the production process in secondary industry is more capital intensive than in agriculture,

4. A defense of our omission of land is considered below in this section.
5. The choice of linearly homogenous production functions precludes an examination of the role of nonconstant returns to scale in the growth process. (For an example of the treatment of nonconstant returns in a neoclassical growth model, see J. Conlisk, "Nonconstant Returns to Scale in a Neoclassical Growth Model".)
6. Unless noted otherwise, it can be assumed throughout this study that subscript $i = 1, 2$.
7. R. S. Eckaus, "The Factor Proportions Problem in Underdeveloped Areas."

which, together with the differences in elasticities of factor substitution, gives rise to the phenomenon of "technological dualism." However, the choice of continuous production functions to describe the technology of the economy eliminates the possibility of "technological dualism" as defined by Eckaus. We impose alternate restrictions consistent with his view, namely, that in the industrial sector the current elasticity of substitution of efficiency labor for efficiency capital is less than one and that in the agricultural sector it is equal to or greater than one. Symbolically, these restrictions can be stated as $0 < \sigma_1(t) < 1$, and $1 \leqq \sigma_2(t) < \infty$.[8] There is abundant empirical evidence supporting this view for the advanced economies. Griliches's research on American agriculture suggests high substitution elasticities, at least with $\sigma_2(t) \geqq 1$, and in general none of the evidence drawn from developing economies conflicts with Griliches's results.[9] The successful application of the constant elasticity of substitution (CES) production function in manufacturing, where $\sigma_1(t) < 1$, is reviewed in Nerlove.[10] The most recent support for the hypothesis, $0 < \sigma_1(t) < 1$, comes from Ferguson and Moroney, who utilize a factor-augmenting model that estimates simultaneously the elasticity of substitution and the bias of technological progress.[11] The Ferguson and Moroney result has been supported by Williamson in an analysis of Philippine manufacturing where the elasticity of substitution was found to be less than one and technical progress biased

---

8. We define the current elasticity of factor substitution in the *i*th sector to be $\sigma_i(t) = F_K^i F_L^i / F^i F_{KL}^i$, where

$$F_K^i = \frac{\partial F^i}{\partial[x(t)K_i(t)]} ,$$

$$F_L^i = \frac{\partial F^i}{\partial[y(t)L_i(t)]} , \quad F_{KL}^i = \frac{\partial^2 F^i}{\partial[x(t)K_i(t)] \, \partial[y(t)L_i(t)]} .$$

9. Z. Griliches, "Research Expenditures, Education, and the Aggregate Agricultural Production Function."

10. M. Nerlove, "Recent Empirical Studies of the CES and Related Production Functions."

11. C. E. Ferguson and J. R. Moroney, "The Sources of Change in Labor's Relative Share: A Neoclassical Analysis."

against labor.[12] On the other hand, Zarembka's finding that the Cobb-Douglas production function is the most appropriate description of recent American secondary production appears, at first glance, to be at variance with our basic production hypothesis.[13] However, there is evidence to believe that, as development takes place, substitution elasticities in industry systematically increase. Indeed, as reported in chapter 6 below, Chetty's extensive analysis of substitution possibilities in a large number of developed and underdeveloped economies provides strong support for this view.[14] Thus, Zarembka's findings are not necessarily inconsistent with our conception of the industrial production technology of a growing economy.

In much of the literature on development theory, the conventional assumption is that agricultural output is a function of labor and land inputs.[15] In these theories the essential distinction is between a "commercialized" agricultural sector using capital produced in the advanced sector and a peasant agricultural sector using only traditional forms of capital. Jorgenson, for example, argues that, in principle, commercialized agriculture can be included in the modern sector of the economy.[16] Since we are interested in explicit treatments of the impacts of both demand conditions and supply conditions in the growth process, and since we assume that consumers regard agricultural output as different from industrial output, the distinction emphasized by Jorgenson and others is inappropriate for our purposes.

12. J. G. Williamson, "Capital Accumulation, Labor Saving, and Labor Absorption Once More."

13. P. Zarembka, "On the Empirical Relevance of the C.E.S. Production Function."

14. V. K. Chetty, "International Comparison of Production Functions in Manufacturing."

15. W. A. Lewis, "Development with Unlimited Supplies of Labour"; J. C. Fei and G. Ranis, "A Theory of Economic Development"; idem, "Innovation, Capital Accumulation, and Economic Development"; idem, *Labor Surplus Economy: Theory and Policy*, chap. 2; Jorgenson, "Development of a Dual Economy"; idem, "Surplus Agricultural Labor."

16. Jorgenson, "Surplus Agricultural Labor."

Inclusion of industrial capital in the agricultural production function is based on the considerable historical evidence of the relatively early application of nonfarm inputs (such as fertilizer, insecticides, and machinery) in agriculture.[17] The extent to which this type of capital is substituted for traditional inputs depends on the relative profitability of each input. Not only has industrial capital historically been a substitute for labor in agriculture, but, equally important, it has been a substitute for traditional capital and land.

There are two conflicting views on the role of land in growth.[18] Fei and Ranis, Jorgenson, Tsiang, and others attribute a major role to it; still others consider its importance to be relatively minor, if omission of the argument can be taken as a test of its significance.[19] We recognize that the quality and character of land in a low-income economy may have an important effect on the pattern of production and on the rate of increase in per capita output. Yet economic theory provides few guidelines explaining either the rate of land expansion or the rate of land improvement.[20] The common treatment of the land variable in two-sector models has it fixed and unaugmented.[21] While a fixed land stock provides diminishing returns to other factors of production, this feature could be ensured simply by assumption. Moreover, the history of innovation in agriculture has cast some doubt on the long-run empirical relevance of diminishing

17. B. Hansen, "The Distributive Shares in the Egyptian Agriculture, 1897–1961"; J. I. Nakamura, "Growth of Japanese Agriculture, 1875–1920"; and T. Shukla, *Capital Formation in Indian Agriculture*.

18. For a comprehensive discussion of the role of natural resources in the growth process, see T. W. Schultz, *Economic Growth and Agriculture*.

19. Fei and Ranis, *Labor Surplus Economy*, chap. 2; Jorgenson, "Development of a Dual Economy"; and S. C. Tsiang, "A Model of Economic Growth in Rostovian Stages."

20. See, however, P. B. Kenen, "Nature, Capital and Trade," for an example.

21. Fei and Ranis, *Labor Surplus Economy*, chap. 2; Jorgenson, "Surplus Agricultural Labor," p. 294.

returns to labor and capital attributable to a fixed supply of unaugmented land. Tokugawa and Meiji Japanese agriculture is an excellent case in point.[22]

Finally, theoretists have questioned the importance of diminishing returns in studies of economic growth, in view of the attenuating influence of such alternative possibilities as complementaries in factors, external economies, and increasing returns to scale. On the demand side, inclusion of land can influence savings and consumption patterns only if these are specific to property income. Here again, however, the available empirical literature to guide our specification is meager.[23] In sum, since we cannot identify a specification of land augmentation or hypotheses relating to savings out of land rents that command significant empirical support, we have elected to omit land as an argument in the production function at this point. If our model predicts poorly or if subsequent evidence provides us with additional insights on the role and nature of land in growth, there may be a better case for its inclusion.

2.2.1.2. *Nature of Technological Progress.* With factor-augmenting technical progress assumed, it is of interest to define more precisely the nature of the change in factor efficiency in our economy. The neoclassical growth literature typically assumes exogenously determined and Harrod-neutral rates of technical change. Recent work by Phelps retains the neutrality feature but relaxes the assumption of exogenous intensity of technical change by introducing a technology sector.[24] Samuel-

22. T. C. Smith, *The Agrarian Origins of Modern Japan,* pp, 87–123, 201–14; K. Ohkawa and H. Rosovsky, "The Role of Agriculture in Modern Japanese Economic Development"; and H. Rosovsky, "Rumbles in the Ricefields: Professor Nakamura vs. the Official Statistics," pp. 357–59.

23. Both the Fei-Ranis and the Jorgenson models assume that the marginal propensity to save out of property income is zero. This is consistent with the Lewis hypothesis in "Unlimited Supplies of Labour" but at variance with limited empirical findings (see A. C. Kelley and J. G. Williamson, "Household Saving Behavior in the Developing Economies: The Indonesian Case").

24. E. Phelps, "Models of Technical Progress and the Golden Rule of Research."

son, Drandakis, and Phelps, on the other hand, introduce a trade-off function between capital-augmenting and labor-augmenting technical change (a technical change frontier) but still assume the trade-off function to be exogenously fixed in position.[25] Conlisk has broken new ground by developing a model with an endogenously positioned technical change frontier.[26] Nevertheless, an acceptable endogenous treatment of technical change is still in primitive stages of development, and, as a result, we have retreated to the standard practice which assumes that the rates of factor-augmenting technical change are exogenously given and stable.

The two characteristics of technical progress that are important for our purposes are: (1) the current rate or intensity of technical progress in the ith sector, $R_i(t)$, which measures the output-raising effect of technical change, holding the inputs of capital and labor constant; and (2) the factor-saving bias or direction of progress in the ith sector, $B_i(t)$, which traces the output-raising effect to the specific inputs. We define

$$R_i(t) = \frac{\partial Q_i(t)}{\partial t} \frac{1}{Q_i(t)}.$$

Differentiating formula (2.1) with respect to t, for fixed $K_i(t)$ and $L_i(t)$, and dividing through by $Q_i(t)$, we obtain

$$R_i(t) = \frac{F_K{}^i x(t) K_i(t)}{Q_i(t)} \frac{\partial x(t)}{\partial t} \frac{1}{x(t)} +$$
$$\frac{F_L{}^i y(t) L_i(t)}{Q_i(t)} \frac{\partial y(t)}{\partial t} \frac{1}{y(t)}.$$

We assume that $x(t)$ and $y(t)$ grow at exogenously given rates, λ_K and λ_L, respectively, and are the same in the two sectors. That is:

25. P. A. Samuelson, "Rejoiner: Agreements, Disagreements, Doubts, and the Case of Induced Harrod-Neutral Technical Change"; E. M. Drandakis and E. S. Phelps, "A Model of Induced Invention, Growth, and Distribution."
26. J. Conlisk, "A Neoclassical Growth Model with an Endogenously Positioned Technical Change Frontier."

$$x(t) = x(0)e^{\lambda_K t},$$ (2.2)

$$y(t) = y(0)e^{\lambda_L t}.$$ (2.3)

By an appropriate definition of units, we can set $x(0) = 1 = y(0)$. It follows from the above expressions that the rate of technical progress in each sector is a weighted average of the rates of factor augmentation, the weights being the output elasticities of inputs;[27] that is,

$$R_i(t) = \lambda_K \, \alpha_i(t) + \lambda_L \, [1 - \alpha_i(t)],$$ (2.4)

where the current elasticity of output with respect to the capital input in the ith sector is given as

$$\alpha_i(t) = \frac{F_K{}^i x(t) K_i(t)}{Q_i(t)}.$$

The nature of the bias in technical progress can be analyzed conveniently in terms of the Hicksian concept of neutrality.[28] According to this definition, technological progress is neutral if it leaves the capital-labor ratio unaltered at a constant ratio of factor prices. The Hicksian factor-saving bias of technical progress in the ith sector, $B_i(t)$, is defined to be the proportionate rate of change in the marginal rate of factor substitution in that sector.[29] That is,

$$B_i(t) = \frac{\partial F_K{}^i}{\partial t} \frac{1}{F_K{}^i} - \frac{\partial F_L{}^i}{\partial t} \frac{1}{F_L{}^i},$$

where $F_K{}^i = F_K{}^i x(t)$ and $F_L{}^i = F_L{}^i y(t)$ are the marginal products of capital and labor, respectively. Thus, for any given

---

27. A. Amano, "Neoclassical Biased Technological Progress and a Neoclassical Theory of Economic Growth"; Fei and Ranis, "Innovation," pp. 307–10; and idem, *Labor Surplus Economy,* chap. 3.

28. J. R. Hicks, *The Theory of Wages.*

29. The marginal rate of substitution used here refers to natural units of capital and labor and not efficiency units. Furthermore, it is the reciprocal of that used in the previous definition of the elasticity substitution.

capital-labor ratio in the ith sector at time t, technical progress is labor saving in the Hicksian sense if $B_i(t) > 0$, Hicks neutral if $B_i(t) = 0$, and capital saving if $B_i(t) < 0$.

Given expressions for the proportionate rates of change over time in the marginal products of capital and labor,[30]

$$B_i(t) = \frac{(\lambda_L - \lambda_K)\,[1 - \sigma_i(t)]}{\sigma_i(t)}. \tag{2.5}$$

Thus, the nature of the bias in the ith sector depends on the difference between the rates of factor augmentation and on the magnitude of the current elasticity of factor substitution.

There is considerable empirical evidence to support the view that technical progress is nonneutral. The evidence obtained in recent years from lower-income economies suggests that technological progress in industry has tended to be labor saving while in agriculture it has tended to be labor using.[31] An explanation for these results is readily forthcoming. It is frequently the case that in present day low income economies agricultural technologies are endogenously developed, and with their labor-using bias they tend to reflect the relative abundance of labor in these economies. The industrial technologies, on the other hand, are more likely to be imported from higher income economies where labor-saving innovations have been precipitated by historically rising wage-rental ratios. The latter is, of course, the "induced innovation hypothesis" recently extended by Kennedy,

30. This derivation can be found in a number of sources. See Fei and Ranis, *Labor Surplus Economy*, chap. 3; K. Kotowitz, "On the Estimation of a Non-neutral CES Production Function"; and for a summary, J. G. Williamson, "Capital Accumulation, Labor Saving, and Labor Absorption Once More," pp. 42–46.

31. H. Leibenstein, "Technical Progress, the Production Function, and Dualism." We have said nothing about the nature of the bias for the economy as a whole, which, presumably, could be investigated for any given commodity-price ratio (see J. G. Williamson, "Capital Accumulation, Labor Saving, and Labor Absorption: A New Look at Some Contemporary Asian Experience," pp. 9–17, for an investigation of these "compositional" effects in the Asian case).

Samuelson, and others.[32] A recent historical application to nineteenth- and twentieth-century Japanese and American agriculture lends support to the thesis of induced innovation.[33]

We accept these arguments that in many of the present day low income economies technical progress is labor saving in industry and labor using in agriculture; that is to say, we assume that $B_1(t) > 0$ and $B_2(t) < 0$. Given the restrictions already imposed on the elasticities of factor substitution, it follows from equation (2.5) that for all t $\lambda_L > \lambda_K$ and therefore, that $y(t) > x(t)$ when $t > 0$ in view of our assumption that $x(0) = 1 = y(0)$.

There is an important consequence of our assumptions on technical change bias and on factor substitution. Namely, when the output elasticity of capital is greater in industry, then the rate of technical change in agriculture exceeds that in industry. From the definition of $R_i(t)$ it follows that $R_1(t) - R_2(t) = (\lambda_K - \lambda_L)/[\alpha_1(t) - \alpha_2(t)]$. Given that $\lambda_K - \lambda_L < 0$, it follows that $R_1(t) - R_2(t) < 0$ when $\alpha_1(t) - \alpha_2(t) > 0$. As will become evident in the analysis in chapter 3, $\alpha_1(t) - \alpha_2(t)$ is indeed positive in our model because we require that the efficiency capital-labor ratio in industry exceed that in agriculture. This result may appear to conflict with some historical evidence. For example, Ueno and Kinoshita have estimated that in Japan, during the period 1919–36, the annual rate of technological progress was 0.4 percent in agriculture, 4.4 percent in the textile industry, and 1.6 percent in the metal and machinery industry.[34] Similar results have been obtained by Watanabe for the Japanese economy in the period 1952–62 and by Massel for the American economy in the period 1950–57, although the time periods spanned by these studies may be too short to adequately

32. C. Kennedy, "Induced Bias in Innovation and the Theory of Distribution"; P. A. Samuelson, "A Theory of Induced Innovation along Kennedy Weisacker Lines."

33. Y. Hayami and V. Ruttan, "Factor Prices and Technical Change in Agricultural Development: The United States and Japan, 1880–1960."

34. H. Ueno and S. Kinoshita, "A Simulation Approach with a Modified Long-term Model of Japan."

reveal long-run trends.[35] Nevertheless, recent contemporary experience with the "Green Revolution" appears consistent with our specification, and as we shall note in chapter 5, Japanese experience during the Meiji period appears, from the limited evidence available, to suggest a similar result.

2.2.2. Factor Markets

2.2.2.1. *Factor Supplies.* We define $K(t)$ and $L(t)$ as the respective stocks of capital and labor available for employment in the economy at time t. When these factors are fully employed,

$$K(t) = K_1(t) + K_2(t), \tag{2.6}$$

$$L(t) = L_1(t) + L_2(t). \tag{2.7}$$

At any given time, the total stock of capital in the economy is determined by the past levels of net investment undertaken by capitalists. Thus,

$$K(t) = K(0) + \int_0^t [I(\tau) - \delta K(\tau)] \, d\tau, \tag{2.8}$$

where $I(\tau)$ is the gross investment in period τ and δ is the fixed rate of replacement of the capital stock.

It is convenient to distinguish between rural and urban households. Rural households supply labor to the agricultural sector, and urban households provide the industrial labor force. This, of course, does not exclude the possibility of rural-urban migration. It only excludes the possibility of joint employment in both sectors. We assume that the labor force resident in the ith sector grows at an exogenously given rate, $n_i > 0$. If $u(t) = L_1(t)/L(t)$ is defined to be the current proportion of the total labor force resident in the industrial sector, then

$$n(t) = \frac{\partial L(t)}{\partial (t)} \frac{1}{L(t)} = n_1 u(t) + n_2[1 - u(t)]. \tag{2.9}$$

The parameter n_i can be viewed as deriving from the natural increase in the population and from changes in the participation

35. B. F. Massel, "A Disaggregated View of Technical Change."

rates in the labor force. Given the widely observed phenomenon of higher fertility rates in rural than in urban areas and the lack of appreciable differences in the sectoral mortality rates, we assume that $n_2 > n_1$.[36] It should be emphasized that such evidence on demographic dualism is far less abundant for advanced economies. Indeed, most of the interesting aspects of dualism eventually are minimized after considerable historical success with industrialization, urbanization, and growth.

In chapters 3 and 6 it will become evident just how critical "demographic dualism" is to growth in our economy. Surprisingly, there has been little or no serious treatment of demographic dualism in the growth and development literature. In view of the importance of this specification, an important assumption implied by equation (2.9) must be emphasized. Recent immigrants to the expanding urban sector are unlikely immediately to adjust their family size and marriage (or expenditure) behavior to the "typical" behavior of urban households. It seems more likely that the migration process will modify the natural demographic conditions of the population in the two regions.[37] Since immigrants tend to be relatively young and of marriageable age, migration would increase (decrease) the birth rate in urban (rural) regions. We ignore this possibility as well as the possibility of habit persistence in our model. In any case, the empirical evidence drawn from economies where rural-urban migration is extensive suggests high natural population growth rates in rural areas even when unadjusted for differences in age structure.

2.2.2.2. *Factor Mobility.* A fundamental proposition of the theory of general equilibrium and the theory of the competitive market is that discrepancies in factor payments lead to appropriate reallocations of productive factors until equilibrium is restored. Interindustry or interregional factor mobility is a

36. United Nations, *The Determinants and Consequences of Population Trends.*
37. V. Galbis, "Dualism and Labor Migration in the Process of Economic Growth: A Theoretical Approach."

force which tends to equalize prices for homogenous factors between markets.

In the basic model we assume that capital and labor adjust instantaneously to any price differentials between sectors and that there are no costs associated with the transfer. The usefulness of these assumptions depends on the observation that the time required for factor markets to adjust to discrepancies in factor payments is short relative to the time period implicit in the study of growth. Justification for the assumption that no resources are used in effecting the transfer of factors between sectors must rest on a belief that, relative to the resources available in the economy, the costs associated with the transfer are small and therefore can be ignored for the purposes of the analysis. This assumption is reexamined in chapters 7 and 8.

2.2.2.3. *Pricing of Factors.* We assume that efficiency factors are paid their marginal value products, provided that at each point in time the marginal product of efficiency labor in each sector is sufficient to allow every member of the labor force to consume a certain quantity of agricultural output, which we define as γ. We interpret γ to be a "subsistence" level of consumption of agricultural output per capita considered by the society to be essential for the welfare of its members. This minimum bundle of agricultural goods, which is the same for all laborers in the economy, is assumed to be above the caloric level at which starvation occurs.

Defining $w_i(t)$ to be the current wage per efficiency labor unit in the ith sector, we can state the wage functions as

$$w_1(t) = P(t)F_L^1, \tag{2.10}$$

$$w_2(t) = F_L^2, \tag{2.11}$$

where $P(t)$ is the current price of industrial goods in terms of agricultural goods.

Given the requirement that efficiency factor payments in the ith sector exhaust the output of that sector at each point in time,

$$r_1(t) = P(t)F_K^1, \tag{2.12}$$

$$r_2(t) = F_{K^2}, \qquad\qquad\qquad (2.13)$$

where $r_i(t)$ is the current rental rate of efficiency capital in the ith sector.

With perfect mobility of capital and labor and no transfer costs, common wage and rental rates will prevail in the economy. Moreover, in view of our assumption of constant returns to scale, capitalists maximize their profits by equating the marginal rates of substitution of efficiency capital for efficiency labor between sectors. Under conditions of full employment such profit-maximizing behavior determines the allocation of factors between sectors. However, if the marginal value product of efficiency labor implied in this distribution of factors does not permit a per capita consumption of γ, our model is undefined. We have therefore imposed an important restriction on the model by requiring that $w_i(t) \geqq \gamma/y(t)$ for all t. That is, the wage per laborer must be equal to or greater than γ. Given that $r_i(t) > 0$, then $Q_2(t) \geqq \gamma L(t)$ is satisfied by the wage constraint. This inequality is equivalent to Jorgenson's phase of dualistic development with the appearance of an agricultural surplus.

An issue arises concerning the treatment of the case in which the market wage is less than the minimum subsistence bundle. Given the assumption of full employment, it is necessary to specify an alternative distribution scheme for the economy in this situation. Cheetham has considered a model in which laborers are paid the subsistence wage by being subsidized by capitalists.[38] Alternative approaches range from permitting unemployment to treating the growth of the labor force as endogenous so that starvation below γ precludes the wage from violating the caloric minimum subsistence floor.[39] Fei and Ranis specify a wage-fixing mechanism in the agricultural sector in which the average productivity of labor forms a floor under

38. R. J. Cheetham, "Growth and Structural Change in a Two-Sector Economy."
39. Jorgenson, "Surplus Agricultural Labor," pp. 301–2.

rural wages.[40] While each of these several approaches has merits and weaknesses, we have elected to focus solely on the case in which the income of wage earners exceeds γ.

Since so much debate has been aroused by the merits of alternative factor-pricing schemes in theorizing about developing economies, some discussion of the so-called classical and neoclassical frameworks might be useful at this point. The classical approach, emphasized by Lewis, and Fei and Ranis, assumes that at least one sector (typically agriculture) is characterized by overt or disguised unemployment of labor such that the prevailing wage is less than labor's marginal product.[41] In extreme versions of this model labor is redundant; labor's marginal product is zero. Since the theory of marginal productivity cannot explain the distribution of income under the assumed classical conditions, an alternative framework of income distribution (an "institutionally" determined wage) is offered as a substitute. When the marginal product of labor rises above the institutionally determined wage, the classical and neoclassical models merge.

A choice between the classical and the neoclassical framework can be made on either empirical or theoretical grounds. The empirical relevance of the models has occupied the center of attraction in discriminating between the theories. As in all tests of model veracity, quantitative investigation may focus on the model assumptions—and, in this case, the existence and nature of unemployment—or on the model's predictions. The relative failure of the empirical investigations to discriminate between the two competing models can be illustrated by comparing the conclusions of those supporting the classical inter-

40. Fei and Ranis, *Labor Surplus Economy*, chap. 2. A continuing controversy has surrounded the empirical and theoretical implications of the assumption (for recent studies, see S. Wellisz, "Dual Economies, Disguised Unemployment, and the Unlimited Supply of Labour"; and B. Hansen, "Employment and Wages in Rural Egypt").

41. Lewis, "Unlimited Supplies of Labour"; and Fei and Ranis, *Labor Surplus Economy*, chap. 2.

pretation of development with the neoclassical protagonists. Lewis, the earliest modern exponent of the classical dualistic model, asserts, "More than half of the world's population (mainly in Asia and in Eastern Europe) lives in conditions which correspond to the classical and not the neoclassical assumptions."[42] Adding to this inventory of countries, Fei and Ranis conclude that "the empirical support of both our theory and policy conclusions draws heavily on the experience of nineteenth century Japan and contemporary India."[43] The Lewis-Fei-Ranis interpretation of the empirical record is in sharp contrast to Jorgenson's reading. He forcefully argues that "the scope and applicability of the classical approach to the development of a dual economy is severely limited. More specifically, the classical assumptions do not apply to Latin America, Africa, Southern Europe, India, China, or the remainder of Southeast Asia."[44] In our review of the debate, we find that neither side has provided persuasive evidence to support its view. Jorgenson and others, for example, have shown that the annual marginal productivity of labor (adjusted for seasonality of employment) is positive in almost all areas, and thus the *extreme* version of the classical model, which assumes redundant labor, is at variance with the historical record.[45] However, the most relevant case of the classical framework, where the marginal productivity of labor is positive but less than the institutional wage, is also consistent with the Jorgenson findings. Furthermore, as Marglin has correctly pointed out, "the relevant question . . . is whether or not the industrial wage reflects the product foregone by adding another man to the ranks of the employed in industry."[46] While there may be *seasonal* unemployment, the average *annual* return to labor in agriculture may be less than, equal to, or greater than the institutional wage. In any case, as Sen has

42. W. A. Lewis, "Unlimited Labour: Further Notes," p. 1.
43. Fei and Ranis, *Labor Surplus Economy,* p. 6.
44. D. W. Jorgenson, "Testing Alternative Theories of the Development of a Dual Economy," p. 53.
45. H. T. Oshima, Review of *The Growth Rate of the Japanese Economy since 1878* by Kazushi Ohkawa and Associates.
46. S. Marglin, "Comment," p. 63.

shown, the existence or nonexistence of disguised unemployment is neither a necessary nor a sufficient test of the appropriateness of the classical theory.[47] Nor is it even a sufficient test of some neoclassical models.[48]

The classical model possesses an illusive defense, since the determinants of the "institutional" wage are seldom articulated rigorously. Similarly, the neoclassical theorist can always fall back upon a modified theoretical formulation where unemployment in the labor force is due to adjustment lags in the labor market, which permit temporarily underutilized factors; the theory of marginal productivity is still operative in explaining factor returns. Only the extreme formulations of either model have been successfully utilized for empirical testing of the issue of factor unemployment, and, even in these cases, the empirical results are inconclusive.

Similar ambiguity in empirical findings relates to the testing of predictions of alternative models. Jorgenson argues that "the hypothesis of a constant real wage in the agricultural sector where disguised unemployment exists is the most important assumption underlying the classical approach. . . . The classical approach stands or falls on this hypothesis."[49] Partly because of his finding that Japanese development shows rising real per capita labor income in agriculture during the so-called classical period of growth, Jorgenson asserts that "the classical approach must be rejected."[50] But as Marglin has shown, the Jorgenson conclusion rests on a restrictive assumption that production in the agricultural sector is characterized by a Cobb-Douglas function. Since this is not a necessary assumption in the classical model, and since, for example, a CES production function yields predictions similar to those found by Jorgenson for Japan, the evidence is again inconclusive. It might also be noted that, even if production in the agricultural sector were described

47. A. K. Sen, "Peasants and Dualism with or without Surplus Labor."
48. J. Conlisk, "Unemployment in a Neoclassical Growth Model: The Effect on Speed of Adjustment."
49. Jorgenson, "Testing Alternative Theories," p. 54.
50. Ibid., p. 60.

by a Cobb-Douglas function, constancy of real wages would not be sufficient to reject the theory of marginal productivity. This empirical result may reflect a phase characterized by a constant capital-labor ratio and, hence, no change in the output per laborer.

In summary, our evaluation of the controversy about the relative applicability of the classical and neoclassical models parallels that of Marglin, who cannot subscribe to the spirit of a debate which views "simple highly aggregate economic models as contestants, with oblivion the penalty for those which are inconsistent with observed data and survival the reward of the more fit. . . . simple models [are] a means of distilling one's assumptions into an essence sufficiently tractable that one can derive and examine their policy implications. To *test* the assumptions one must go beyond simple aggregative models."[51] We would interpret Marglin's argument to urge that both the classical and neoclassical models require expansion and more rigorous specification before the historical record can usefully provide a basis for discriminating between the theories.

In our study we have therefore chosen to develop a model of economic dualism within the tradition of neoclassical economics; in our notation, we analyze only those cases where the income of wage earners exceeds γ. This decision was based on several considerations. First, we have yet to identify persuasive theoretical arguments or empirical findings which reject the validity of marginal product pricing as being applicable to at least a large group of developing countries. Second, marginal product pricing is founded on well-established postulates of economic behavior. In contrast, formulations of the determinants of the institutional wage equally well founded in theory have not yet emerged in the economic literature. We recognize that there is an abundant set of plausible hypotheses of institutional-wage determinants. Neither theory nor empirical evidence has permitted us to discriminate among these competing hy-

51. Marglin, "Comment," p. 64.

potheses.[52] In short, while we admit that the institutional wage is a plausible notion, we are reluctant to discard one of the most powerful weapons in the economic arsenal—the theory of marginal productivity of distribution—until a theory can be derived to establish the analytical foundations of this formulation, and/ or until this theory is established to conform with fact. Second, and more important, our focus is on the low-income, *growing* economy in which stagnation and below-subsistence conditions are not key features in the analysis.

Finally, our approach to an analysis of the dualistic economy parallels that of all who engage in the construction of formal models—protagonist and adversary alike. The predictions of our formulation will be confronted by evidence; the relative success or failure of our model will be judged, in part, by the historical record. While such a comparison of a simple dualistic model with the historical record will not be sufficient to establish its validity, we feel that at this point an empirical appraisal of our model's predictions is more productive than entering further into an already muddled classical-neoclassical debate.

2.2.3. Commodity Markets

2.2.3.1. *The Relative Importance of Demand.* As indicated at the outset, there has been considerable debate over the role of commodity demand and demand parameters in the growth process. Interest has centered on the role of investment demand, consumer demand, and the demand for intermediate goods. While we do not investigate here the impact of changes in intermediate demand, Chenery, Shionoya, and others have stressed its importance.[53] An increase in intermediate demand for manufactured goods relative to total production is regarded as a consequence of the evolution of the interindustry structure.

52. For a recent theoretical and empirical examination of the validity of the marginal productivity theory in a developing economy, see B. Hansen, "Employment and Wages in Rural Egypt."

53. H. B. Chenery, "Patterns of Industrial Growth"; Y. Shionoya, "Patterns of Industrial Development."

As Shionoya points out, this phenomenon may be considered evidence of an increase in the degree of interrelatedness among sectors and of roundabout production in the process of economic growth. Chenery suggests that the rise in the relative importance of intermediate demand for manufactured goods is due to a relative increase in final demand for manufactured goods, replacement of handicraft by factory production, and replacement of imports by domestic production, all of which cause manufacturing output to rise more rapidly than total demand.[54]

At the same time there has been controversy over the relative importance of investment demand in growth. The extensive discussion about the impact of changes in the savings rate is one example. Emphasis has ranged from the demand-oriented models of the Keynesian type to the supply-oriented, neoclassical models. Since there is no explicit treatment of supply in the former,[55] the long-run growth of output is a function of demand parameters (assuming the model is capable of sustained growth). In the standard neoclassical model,[56] only supply parameters influence long-run growth rates. Demand always adjusts to supply as relative factor prices change to clear markets. Nevertheless, there are conflicting results within the neoclassical models. Whereas the Solow and Swan models lead to the conclusion that, in the long run, the rate of growth in output is unaffected by changes in the savings rate, Conlisk has obtained the opposite result with the introduction of endogenous augmentation of labor supply.[57] Within the context of two-sector growth models, however, there has been relatively little attention given to the impact of changes in the savings rate.

54. H. B. Chenery, "The Use of Interindustry Analysis in Development Programming."
55. For example, J. S. Dusenberry, *Business Cycles and Economic Growth.*
56. R. M. Solow, "A Contribution to the Theory of Economic Growth"; and T. W. Swan, "Economic Growth and Capital Accumulation."
57. J. Conlisk, "A Modified Neoclassical Growth Model with Endogenous Technical Change," pp. 199–208.

The above results, relating to the behavior in steady state or long-run equilibrium, deal with the possibility that changes in the parameters of investment demand will *permanently* change the growth rate. There is little disagreement that changes in demand parameters can have an important temporary effect on the growth of output. The difficulty lies in distinguishing between the short run and the long run. A once-over change in demand parameters that has an effect over many periods may be of great significance for a low-income economy, despite the fact that its effect is not permanent. Alternately, if demand parameters tend to change systematically over time, their cumulative effect may be quite important even though the impact of a once-over change is short-lived.

In the formulation of our basic dualistic model we make the simplifying assumption that capitalists invest all rental income while laborers consume all wage income. (In chapter 4 this assumption is relaxed to allow capitalists to consume and invest.) This permits an examination of the consequences of a change in the propensity to save, that is, the impact of a change in the demand for investment goods. At this stage, however, we focus solely on the impact of consumption demand on the growth process. According to Kuznets, changes in the structure of final demand may be due either to the rise in per capita product or to technological changes that do not affect all categories of final goods at the same rate.[58] In stressing the importance of a rising per capita income, Houthakker and others have cited empirical evidence suggesting that the income elasticity of demand for primary products is low compared with that for industrial or secondary products.[59] These elasticities, in turn, tend to be lower than those for services.[60]

Despite such empirical evidence, there has been surprisingly little attention given to the role of consumer demand and ex-

58. S. Kuznets, *Modern Economic Growth*, pp. 114–15.
59. H. S. Houthakker, "The Present State of Consumption Theory."
60. H. S. Houthakker, "An International Comparison of Household Expenditure Patterns, Commemorating the Centenary of Engel's Law."

penditure allocation decisions in formal analyses of the growth process. To a large extent, the development and growth literature either ignores parameters of final demand entirely while focusing on supply conditions[61] or makes model specifications which leave little room for consumer expenditure decisions to assume an interesting role.[62] The Uzawa models, for example, do not confront expenditure allocation issues, since there is only a single consumer-goods sector. The Jorgenson models, on the other hand, make the limiting assumption that per capita consumption of agricultural products is constant. We wish to show that with a simple extension of the familiar neoclassical model consumer expenditure decisions can be introduced; moreover, that they play an important role in determining the growth of output by influencing the allocation of goods between urban and rural residents, on the one hand, and between consumption and investment, on the other.

2.2.3.2. *Consumption Demand.* When a meaningful demand system is introduced into our simple economy, the demand equations must encompass all commodities and must satisfy the "adding-up criterion." Three demand models which meet these criteria have attained considerable popularity: Houthakker's indirect addilog system, Stone's linear expenditure system, and a modified "Rotterdam" version of the double logarithmic system developed by Theil and Barten.[63] For analytical reasons presented below, we utilize the Stone-Geary system. There is considerable empirical support for this choice. The most recent is the research of Parks and Yoshihara.[64] Following earlier work

61. Chenery, "Patterns of Industrial Growth."
62. Uzawa, "Two-Sector Model of Economic Growth, I"; idem, "Two-Sector Model of Economic Growth, II"; Jorgenson, "Development of a Dual Economy"; and idem, "Surplus Agricultural Labor."
63. H. S. Houthakker, "The Influence of Prices and Income on Household Expenditures"; H. Theil, "The Information Approach to Demand Analysis"; idem, *Economics and Information Theory*; and A. Barten, "Consumer Demand Functions under Conditions of Almost Additive Preferences."
64. R. Parks, "Systems of Demand Equations: An Empirical Comparison of Alternative Functional Forms"; K. Yoshihara,

by Stone, Parks introduces greater flexibility into the linear expenditure system by allowing the demand parameters to vary systematically with exogenous variables; for example, the demand parameters are given a linear time trend.[65] In his empirical analysis of Swedish consumption patterns, 1861–1955, Parks finds the linear expenditure system superior to the competing models for the two commodity groups (agricultural and manufactured goods) of interest to the present study. The superiority of the linear expenditure system is also shown by Yoshihara's examination of Japanese consumption behavior during the period 1902–60.

Our model assumes that each laborer possesses a utility function of the Stone-Geary form.[66] At each point in time the consumer allocates his budget so as to maximize the utility he derives from the consumption of agricultural and industrial goods. The function is the same for each member of the labor force in the economy. As Goldberger has pointed out, the Stone-Geary expenditure system aggregates perfectly over individuals in a group, if each group member has the same utility function.[67] The utility function for laborers in the jth sector is given by

$$U_j(t) = \sum_{i=1}^{2} \beta_{ij} \log \left\{ \frac{D_{ij}(t)}{L_j(t)} - \gamma_{ij} \right\} \quad (j = 1, 2),^{[68]}$$

where $U_j(t)$ is the utility derived from consumption by a mem-

"Demand Functions: An Application to the Japanese Expenditure Pattern."

65. R. Stone, "Linear Expenditure Systems and Demand Analysis: An Application to the Pattern of British Demand."

66. R. C. Geary, "A Note on a Constant-Utility Index of the Cost of Living"; R. Stone, ed., *A Programme for Growth*, vol. 1, *A Computable Model of Economic Growth*; Stone, "Linear Expenditure Systems and Demand Analysis"; Stone, ed., *A Programme for Growth*, vol. 5, *The Model in its Environment: A Progress Report*; and Stone, *Mathematics in the Social Sciences and Other Essays*.

67. A. S. Goldberger, "Functional Form and Utility: A Review of Consumer Demand and Theory."

68. Unless noted otherwise, it can be assumed throughout this study that the subscript $j = 1, 2$.

ber of the labor force in the jth sector and $D_{ij}(t)$ is the total amount of the ith good consumed by the labor force in the jth sector at time t. The parameters β_{ij} and γ_{ij} are fixed over time.

We require that $0 < \beta_{ij} < 1$ and $\Sigma_{i=1}^{2} \beta_{ij} = 1$. We further assume that there is a difference in consumption behavior in the two sectors. Dualism in consumption behavior is reflected in the specification that $\beta_{11} - \beta_{21} > \beta_{12} - \beta_{22} > 0$. Recent work by Kelley and Williamson suggests that, in the Philippines, consumption behavior in rural and urban areas is significantly different. Their study suggests a greater preference for urban goods among urban households than among rural households.[69] The existence of substantial differences in consumer preferences is implicit in the notion of dualism. Like demographic dualism, dualism in demand may not persist into very high stages of industrialization and urbanization. We do assume, however, that urban immigrants adopt the behavior of urban consumers immediately, with no "habit-persistence" lags. Kaneda's recent historical research on Japan over the period 1878–1964 shows a gradual elimination of dualism in demand; nevertheless, sectoral differences in demand parameters persisted during most of the first half-century of modern Japanese development.[70]

The parameter γ_{ij} is the minimum acceptable amount of the ith commodity per capita required by laborers in the jth sector. In keeping with the interpretation of industrial output as a nonessential consumer good, $\gamma_{1j} = 0$ and $\gamma_{2j} = \gamma > 0$.[71]

We adopt the interpretation provided by Goldberger for the parameters of the system.[72] Given wage income per capita in the jth sector, $y(t)w_j(t)$, and the commodity price ratio, $P(t)$, each member of the labor force first purchases the minimum

69. This result is also highlighted by Kuznets (*Modern Economic Growth,* pp. 271–74).

70. H. Kaneda, "Long-Term Changes in Food Consumption Patterns in Japan, 1878–1964."

71. Work by A. S. Goldberger and T. Gamaletsos ("A Cross Country Comparison of Consumer Expenditure Patterns") gives an indication of the relative importance of the "minimum bundle" of various categories of consumer goods in some thirteen countries.

72. A. S. Goldberger, "Functional Form and Utility."

required quantity of agricultural output, γ. At the given relative price this costs γ, which may be termed "subsistence income." He is left with $y(t)w_j(t) - \gamma$, which may be called "supernumerary income"; this he distributes among the goods in the proportions β_{ij}.[73] Because the utility function is defined only for $D_{ij}(t)/L_j(t) - \gamma > 0$, it makes no predictions about the behavior of a consumer for whom $y(t)w_j(t) - \gamma < 0$, since he cannot purchase γ at the prevailing prices.

The laborers' demand system can now be summarized as follows:[74]

$$\frac{D_{1j}(t)}{L_j(t)} = \frac{\beta_{1j}}{P(t)} \; [y(t)w_j(t) - \gamma], \qquad (2.14)$$

$$\frac{D_{2j}(t)}{L_j(t)} = \beta_{2j}y(t)w_j(t) + [1 - \beta_{2j}]\gamma. \qquad (2.15)$$

Now define the current elasticity of demand for the ith good with respect to per capita income of laborers in the jth sector to be

$$\eta_{ij}(t) = \frac{\partial[D_{ij}(t)/L_j(t)]}{\partial[y(t)w_j(t)]} \; \frac{y(t)w_j(t)}{D_{ij}(t)/L_j(t)} \; .$$

73. This treatment is not inconsistent with the arguments advanced by R. Roy ("La hierarchie des besions et la notion de groupes dans l'economie de choix") and J. Encarnación ("Two-Sector Models of Economic Growth and Development"), who suggest a scheme based upon the notion of lexicographically ordered preferences. Roy assumes that there is a hierarchy of needs satisfied by different classes of commodities and that at very low levels of income only the most basic commodities are purchased. Only at higher levels of income is there any expenditure on higher-category goods.

74. The general form of the Stone-Geary demand system, is

$$\frac{D_{1j}(t)}{L_j(t)} = \frac{\beta_{1j}}{P_1(t)} \; y(t)w_j(t) + [1 - \beta_{1j}]\gamma_1 - \beta_{1j}\gamma_2 \; \frac{P_2(t)}{P_1(t)},$$

$$\frac{D_{2j}(t)}{L_j(t)} = \frac{\beta_{2j}}{P_2(t)} \; y(t)w_j(t) + [1 - \beta_{2j}]\gamma_2 - \beta_{2j}\gamma_1 \; \frac{P_1(t)}{P_2(t)} \; .$$

However, assuming $\gamma_1 = 0$, $\gamma_2 = \gamma$, and $P_2 = 1$ (agricultural output is the numeraire), the formulation collapses to the demand system reported in the text.

It follows from equations (2.14) and (2.15) that

$$\eta_{1j}(t) = \frac{y(t)w_j(t)}{y(t)w_j(t) - \gamma},$$

$$\eta_{2j}(t) = \frac{\beta_{2j}y(t)w_j(t)}{\beta_{2j}y(t)w_j(t) + (1 - \beta_{2j})\gamma},$$

from which it is clear that $0 < \eta_{2j}(t) < 1 < \eta_{1j}(t) < \infty$ for all t, irrespective of the value of β_{ij} and $\gamma > 0$.[75] Significantly, the model exhibits behavior consistent with that attributed to "Engel effects" for any combination of theoretically feasible parameter values. This result, which is somewhat surprising, follows solely from the assumption that $\gamma_1 = 0$. The role of demand in our model will be discussed at length in chapter 6.

2.2.3.3. *Investment Demand.* There is both empirical and theoretical justification for focusing on sources of income and occupation as a basis for considering savings behavior in a growing economy. Analysis of data from low-income countries in Southeast Asia indicates that savings functions which ignore long-run changes in the distribution of functional income will invariably be inaccurate.[76] Lewis has argued that the profit-making entrepreneurs are the significant savers in society and that landlords, wage earners, peasants, and members of the salaried middle class contribute relatively little.[77] Furthermore, the savings of these nonentrepreneurs typically are channeled into relatively unproductive investment. According to Fei and Ranis, the essence of the difference between agrarianism and dualism lies in the motivation of the owners of the surplus in

75. In general, it can be shown that $\eta_{ij}(t) \gtreqless 1$ when $P(t) \gtreqless \beta_{ij}\gamma_2/[1-\beta_{ij}]\gamma_1$, provided that $\gamma_1 > 0$ and $0 < \beta_{ij} < 1$. Of course, in taking $\gamma_1 = 0$, attention is restricted to a special case of the more general formulation of the model.

76. J. G. Williamson, "Personal Savings in Developing Nations: An Intertemporal Cross-Section from Asia."

77. Lewis, "Development with Unlimited Supplies of Labour," pp. 156–66.

agriculture.[78] In this connection, Fei and Ranis have placed considerable emphasis on the savings behavior of the landlord as a crucial determinant of the extent to which an economy will grow.

The theoretical justification for the distinction between the entrepreneurial household and all other households lies in the recognition that, for the entrepreneurial group, the firm and the household are no longer separable.[79] For the wage-earning household, which offers only its labor services to the factor market, the determination of savings involves, in addition to an allocation between present and future consumption, a decision regarding the maintenance of the existing stock of human capital and the increments in that stock. The self-employed entrepreneur, on the other hand, receives income for labor services, for the use of his nonhuman earning assets, and for managerial abilities. To the extent that household savings decisions are determined simultaneously with those based on entrepreneurial earning assets, consumption behavior different from that of other occupational households is to be expected.

Models stressing source of income as a determinant of savings behavior take several forms. The simplest of these postulate a two-factor growth framework which yields a differential response of savings to income from capital and from labor.[80] Assuming that the propensity to consume out of wage earnings is less than that out of profits, and in the extreme zero, aggregate savings rates are uniquely determined by the source distribution of income.

In our basic model we make the assumption that capitalists invest all rental income; this assumption equates the savings and investment decisions. (This assumption is relaxed in chap-

78. J. C. Fei and G. Ranis, "Agrarianism, Dualism, and Economic Development," pp. 3–7.

79. Kelley and Williamson, "Household Saving Behavior."

80. F. H. Hahn, "The Share of Wages in the National Income"; N. Kaldor, "Alternative Theories of Distribution"; and J. Robinson, *The Accumulation of Capital.*

ter 4.) As Drandakis has pointed out, this kind of savings assumption in effect separates each market from all successive markets.[81] As a result, price expectations and interest rates do not play an independent role in the model.

We make no distinction between industrial and agricultural capitalists: all capitalists behave in an identical manner, and they allocate their investment goods to both sectors. Thus, investment demand is given by

$$P(t)I(t) = x(t) \ [r_1(t)K_1(t) + r_2(t)K_2(t)].\qquad(2.16)$$

We assume that current net investment in the economy is equal to total investment minus replacement, where replacement is proportional to the aggregate capital stock. Thus, current net investment is given by

$$\frac{\partial K(t)}{\partial t} = I(t) - \delta K(t),\qquad(2.17)$$

where δ is the fixed rate of replacement. Jorgenson and Stephenson provide a justification for this specification.[82]

2.2.4. Market Equilibrium

In the static version of the model the stocks of capital and labor are given, and there is no technological progress; that is, $K(t) = K$, $L(t) = L$, $x(t) = x$, and $y(t) = y$. Equilibrium in the static economy occurs when all "individuals" are choosing those quantities they prefer to produce and consume. As noted above, equilibrium in the factor markets implies that wage and rental rates are equated throughout the economy, and in the commodity markets the quantity of the ith good supplied is equal to the quantity demanded. This requirement precludes the possibility of factor unemployment due to underutilization

81. E. M. Drandakis, "Factor Substitution in the Two-Sector Growth Model."
82. D. W. Jorgenson and J. A. Stephenson, "Investment Behavior in U.S. Manufacturing, 1947–1960."

of the capital stock and the labor force as a result of deficient demand.[83] The equilibrium conditions thus become

$$w_1(t) = w_2(t) = w(t), \qquad (2.18)$$

$$r_1(t) = r_2(t) = r(t), \qquad (2.19)$$

$$Q_1(t) = D_{11}(t) + D_{12} + I(t), \qquad (2.20)$$

$$Q_2(t) = D_{21}(t) + D_{22}(t), \qquad (2.21)$$

where $w(t)$ and $r(t)$ are the equilibrium wage and rental rates, respectively. The static equilibrium is therefore one in which there is no excess demand in any market and all prevailing market prices are nonnegative. If we assume that there is at least one positive value for the terms of trade that will satisfy the equilibrium conditions, it is a simple matter to show that equilibrium in the two factor markets and in either commodity market necessarily implies equilibrium in the remaining commodity market. Thus, one of the two commodity market equations can be ignored; the model then becomes a system of fourteen equations and fourteen variables.

2.2.5. The Basic Model Summarized
After making use of the equilibrium factor price conditions (equations [2.18] and [2.19]), the static model is composed of fourteen endogenous variables: $Q_i(t)$, $K_i(t)$, $L_i(t)$, $w(t)$, $r(t)$, $P(t)$, $D_{ij}(t)$, *and* $I(t)$; and four exogenous variables: $K(t) = K$, $L(t) = L$, $x(t) = x$, and $y(t) = y$. The basic model can be summarized in the following equations:

83. Relaxing this requirement—the clearance of the commodity market—to allow for deficient demand would, for example, necessitate including an additional asset, money, and an additional price, the money wage. Unless this is done there is no explanation for the behavior of excess savings, for without the addition of some stores of value, capitalists (if they were allowed to consume) and laborers (if they were allowed to hold assets) would simply increase consumption whenever capital accumulation became unattractive.

Production:

$$Q_i(t) = F^i[xK_i(t), yL_i(t)] \tag{2.1a}$$

Commodity demand:

$$\frac{D_{1j}(t)}{L_j(t)} = \frac{\beta_{1j}}{P(t)} [yw(t) - \gamma] \tag{2.14a}$$

$$\frac{D_{2j}(t)}{L_j(t)} = \beta_{2j}yw(t) + (1 - \beta_{2j})\gamma \tag{2.15a}$$

$$I(t) = \frac{x}{P(t)} r(t)K \tag{2.16a}$$

Factor demand:

$$w(t) = P(t)F_L^1 \tag{2.10a}$$

$$w(t) = F_L^2 \tag{2.11a}$$

$$r(t) = P(t)F_K^1 \tag{2.12a}$$

$$r(t) = F_K^2 \tag{2.13a}$$

Full-employment conditions:

$$K = K_1(t) + K_2(t) \tag{2.6a}$$

$$L = L_1(t) + L_2(t) \tag{2.7a}$$

Market-balancing equations:

$$Q_1(t) = D_{11}(t) + D_{12}(t) + I(t) \tag{2.20a}$$

$$Q_2(t) = D_{21}(t) + D_{22}(t) \tag{2.21a}$$

Four equations summarize the dynamic properties of the model:

$$x(t) = x(0)e^{\lambda_K t}, \tag{2.2a}$$

$$y(t) = y(0)e^{\lambda_L t}, \tag{2.3a}$$

$$\dot{K}(t) = I(t) - \delta K(t), \tag{2.17a}$$

$$\dot{L}(t) = \{n_1 u(t) + n_2[1 - u(t)]\} L(t). \tag{2.9a}$$

2.3. THE BASIC MODEL AND THE JORGENSON ECONOMY

Before we explore the static and dynamic properties of the model, it is useful to relate it to one portion of the literature on development theory and, in particular, to the Jorgenson framework.[84] The similarities and contrasts between Jorgenson's neoclassical economy and the classical Lewis-Fei-Ranis models have been developed in detail above in this chapter, and elsewhere.[85]

Our basic model is a generalization of Jorgenson's in the sense that our framework, with two exceptions, can be reduced to Jorgenson's by making restrictive assumptions on specific parameter values. We shall consider, first, the two structural features in which the two models diverge, after which we shall indicate the restrictions on the parameter values that reduce our system to Jorgenson's.

The distinguishing feature of economic dualism in the Jorgenson model is that the "traditional" sector produces output with land and labor alone; the "modern" sector employs capital and labor. This treatment is in contrast to our model in which production in both sectors utilizes labor and capital, although the specific manner in which these inputs are combined is different between sectors. While Jorgenson's "traditional" sector produces many commodities, including agricultural and industrial goods, peasant agriculture is considered its primary activity. However, as soon as agricultural enterprises in this sector become commercialized (that is, utilize capital goods produced in the "modern" sector, as distinct from traditional forms of capital), they are no longer analytically different from firms in the "modern" sector: capital and labor then become the sole inputs to the production process. In effect, then, the extent of dualism in the Jorgenson model depends on the pervasiveness with which enterprises utilize industrially produced capital in their production process. This result coincides with his premise that "the special character of the theory of development of a

84. Jorgenson, "The Development of a Dual Economy."
85. Jorgenson, "Surplus Agricultural Labor."

dual economy is a certain asymmetry in the production relations."[86] Our approach, which is consistent with but somewhat
broader than the Jorgenson interpretation of dualism, is that
differential technical and behavioral features between rural-
agricultural and urban-industrial activities form the primary
dualistic asymmetry. As we shall discover in this study, this
broader treatment of dualism has significant implications for
the interpretation of the development process.

A second structural difference between the two models lies
in the labor supply function. In the case where the wage rate
exceeds the caloric minimum subsistence level required for survival, labor supply in Jorgenson's model is exogenously determined and constant. Below this level population grows at a
rate sufficient to maintain the wage at subsistence. Since his
model (like ours) is not designed to describe an economy in
which unemployment is present, his theory of population growth
effectively maintains the economy in a neoclassical world; the
supply of labor is always inelastic, and all factors are scarce.
By contrast, our labor supply function, while exogenous in the
n_i parameters, endogenously determines the rate of population
growth as a weighted function of the differential rates of population growth in the rural and urban sectors. As development
takes place, rural-urban migration diminishes the overall rate
of population growth. However, with demographic dualism absent, our model reduces to Jorgenson's during the neoclassical
growth phase; furthermore, both models effectively guarantee
that neoclassical conditions will be maintained—Jorgenson's
through his labor supply function, ours by assumption.

The remaining differences between the models lie in assumptions on the parameter values. In several aspects our framework
is more general. First, Jorgenson assumes a Cobb-Douglas production function in both sectors. We require that the elasticity
of substitution between capital and labor in industry be less
than one; in agriculture it is equal to or greater than one. Second, Jorgenson assumes that demand parameters are identical

86. Jorgenson, "Development of a Dual Economy," p. 311.

between sectors and, further, that all consumer expenditures above subsistence are devoted to goods produced in the "modern" sector, that is, produced with industrial capital. If wages fall below subsistence, all consumption expenditures are channeled toward goods produced by "traditional" forms of capital. In contrast, we assume that demand parameters are different in the rural-agricultural and the urban-industrial sectors and that "subsistence" consumption is tied to a commodity—in our case, food products—rather than to the output of a sector utilizing a particular form of capital. It appears that the basic structural features distinguishing Jorgenson's "traditional" and our "agricultural" production processes is critical to the interpretation of the differences in demand behavior of the two economies.

A third difference in parameter assumptions relates to the different wage rates of the sectors. Since Jorgenson's peasant laborer in the "traditional" sector is an owner-operator, he obtains rents from land. The income of the peasant household in this sector is the per capita product, composed of returns to both labor and land. Therefore, the "wage" rate in the traditional sector need not equal that prevailing in the modern sector. In the Jorgenson model the urban wage and the peasant's opportunity cost are equated.[87] In our formulation, capital returns and labor returns are both equalized between sectors in equilibrium. Finally, in the Jorgenson model the depreciation rate is zero; in our formulation it is positive.

A comparison of our model with those of Lewis, Fei, and Ranis is straightforward. The phases of growth highlighted by their (labor-surplus) economies, which Jorgenson denotes as the "classical" description of growth, are not considered in either our model or Jorgenson's. When the agricultural wage exceeds subsistence requirements, the economy is basically similar to Jorgenson's. Our interpretation of "subsistence" require-

---

87. For a similar treatment in an advanced economy, see L. Johansen, *A Multi-sectoral Study of Economic Growth.* The Jorgenson assumption appears to us far more relevant to the advanced economy than the peasant economy, where the landlord assumes greater relevance as an owner of assets.

ments is analytically similar to the labor-surplus treatment in which this minimum consumption level is "behaviorally" determined. This is in contrast to Jorgenson's interpretation, which corresponds to a biological determination of subsistence as that level below which population cannot survive.

In the analyses of Jorgenson, Fei and Ranis, and others[88], attention has also been given to the concept of marketable surplus. One characterization of this problem is that the economy must increase its output of agricultural products at a rate sufficient not only to feed a rapidly growing rural population but also to provide food for a growing urban population. If we define the current agricultural surplus to be the difference between total agricultural output and that consumed by the agricultural labor force, the marketable surplus is $D_{21}(t)$ in our formulation. It is usually argued that in order to obtain this marketable surplus the terms of trade must be favorable to agriculture or direct taxation of the agricultural sector may be required. We do not consider the possibility of taxation in our model, but the terms of trade certainly have a bearing on the outcome. If efficiency factors are paid their marginal products, agricultural laborers exchange some (food) income for industrial goods; the amount depends on the demand parameters *and the terms of trade*. At prevailing commodity prices, all property income of agricultural capitalists is exchanged for industrial (capital) goods produced by industrial laborers. Given the restriction that the wage must be sufficient to meet subsistence requirements, our model does not address itself to the question of ensuring sufficient food for the industrial sector. As already indicated, to explore this issue the model would have to be extended with an alternative theory of distribution, and perhaps of population growth.

In conclusion, it is apparent that our model may be characterized as a more general formulation of the existing models of dualism which focus on a neoclassical description of growth.

88. W. H. Nicholls, "An 'Agricultural Surplus' as a Factor in Economic Development"; B. F. Johnston and J. Mellor, "The Role of Agriculture in Economic Development."

It is, however, similar to models presented in the literature on economic dualism. As noted above, the strategy of being able to relate our basic analytic framework to the mainstream of growth-development theory was considered in our model construction. On the other hand, our model departs significantly from models in the literature by treating dualism as primarily a difference in the technical and behavioral characteristics of the rural-agricultural and urban-industrial sectors. This dualism is found not only in production conditions but also in consumption and demographic behavior. On the production side, we conceive of the rural-agricultural sector as possessing commercialized and noncommercialized elements, that is, as using both traditional capital and investment goods produced by industry. The two production sectors possess quite different production processes. Since capital is employed in agriculture, our model further includes rural capitalists who accumulate and contribute to output expansion. On the demand side, differential consumer behavior between the rural and urban sectors is hypothesized. Finally, economic dualism extends to the formulations of population growth. Thus, our model of dualism permits us to incorporate a spatial dimension into the analysis. The coincidence of a geographic characterization of dualism with the analytical distinction based on sectors with differential technical and behavioral conditions enrichs our interpretation of the disequilibrium model presented in chapters 7 and 8.

3

Analysis of Growth and Change in a Basic Dualistic Economy

3.1. INTRODUCTION

In analyzing the model of economic dualism constructed in chapter 2 our focus will be on model predictions regarding growth and structural change. While insights into such behavior can best be derived from dynamic analysis, the comparative static properties of the economy are considered first. In section 3.2 and appendix A we ascertain whether the system possesses a solution and, if it does, whether this solution is unique and stable. This discussion is followed by a detailed review of the operation of the static economy. The analysis provides considerable insight not only into the workings of the economy but, more important, into the role of the dualistic specifications in influencing the course of development. The differing sectoral demand, production, and demographic conditions enter conspicuously into the determination of resource allocation, of sectoral output mix, and of the aggregate rate of growth and structural change. (The reader who is prepared to accept our conclusions of existence, uniqueness, and stability of the basic static model may wish to move directly to section 3.3, where the more important issues relating to growth and structural change are examined.)

The dynamic properties of the model are examined in section 3.3, where the main focus is on the course of output growth, urbanization, and industrialization. In some instances the use of mathematical techniques alone is not sufficient to completely characterize the development process. A case is therefore established for the numerical experiments—simulation analysis—

58

utilized in subsequent chapters. The chapter concludes with a comparison of our dualistic economy's predictions with those implied by the pioneering works on two-sector development models by Dale Jorgenson and by John Fei and Gustav Ranis.

3.2. RESTATEMENT AND PROPERTIES OF THE STATIC ECONOMY
The static version of the model can be regarded as a miniature Walrasian system consisting of four goods (labor, capital, industrial output, and agricultural output) and four markets. In such a general equilibrium model there is a question whether an equilibrium always exists for arbitrary initial conditions and, if it exists, whether it is unique. The problem is essentially one of determining, for any given combination of capital and labor, the conditions under which there exists a set of nonnegative prices that clear these four markets. Whether such equilibrium values exist and, if they exist, whether they are unique will be considered in sections 3.2.2 and 3.2.3. Multiplicity of short-run equilibria can complicate both the comparative static and the long-run dynamic analysis of an economy. It is therefore important to know whether there exist plausible sufficient conditions for uniqueness. A sufficient condition may be obtained by considering the short-run dynamic behavior of the economy. In section 3.2.4 a simple model of short-run market adjustment is described; it is shown that a necessary condition for stability is that the wage-rental ratio be an increasing monotonic function of the capital-labor ratio.

Given our conception of the growth process as a movement by the economy through a series of short-run equilibria, we have a further interest in the stability of the economy in the short run. While comparative static theorems can be derived independently of any stability analysis (since such theorems are concerned solely with changes in the equilibrium values of variables in response to changes in the exogenous variables or parameters), the theorems are of limited usefulness unless equilibrium positions are stable. That is, if an equilibrium is not stable, a change in the environment may lead to time paths for the variables that do not approach a new equilibrium position. Consequently, the predictive value of comparative statics theorems derived without attention to the stability question is severely limited. Moreover, as Samuelson has pointed out, the stability conditions may impose restrictions on the values that can be assumed by the parameters of the dynamical system and, hence, on the values assumed by the "corresponding" parameters of the static model.[1]

3.2.1. Restatement of the Basic Dualistic Model

For purposes of analyzing the properties of the static dualistic economy it is convenient to transform the model into per capita terms. This transformation is made possible by the assumption of constant returns to scale in production. For i, $j = 1, 2$ and for any given t, we define:

$$q_i(t) \equiv \frac{Q_i(t)}{y(t)L_i(t)}$$ The output of the ith good per efficiency unit of labor employed

$$k(t) \equiv \frac{x(t)K(t)}{y(t)L(t)}$$ The ratio of the efficiency capital stock to the efficiency labor force

$$k_i(t) \equiv \frac{x(t)K_i(t)}{y(t)L_i(t)}$$ The ratio of the efficiency capital stock to the efficiency labor force employed in the ith sector

$$u(t) \equiv \frac{L_i(t)}{L(t)}$$ The proportion of the labor force resident in the industrial sector

$$\omega(t) \equiv \frac{w(t)}{r(t)}$$ The equilibrium wage-rental ratio in the economy

$$\omega_i(t) \equiv \frac{w_i(t)}{r_i(t)}$$ The wage-rental ratio in the ith sector of the economy

$$z_{ij}(t) \equiv \frac{D_{ij}(t)}{L_j(t)}$$ The per capita consumption of the ith good by laborers in the jth sector

$$\phi(t) \equiv \frac{I(t)}{K(t)}$$ The ratio of investment demand to capital stock

1. P. A. Samuelson, *Foundations of Economic Analysis*.

The static equilibrium model can be restated as follows:

$$q_i(t) = f_i(k_i), \qquad \text{from equation (2.1);[2]} \qquad (3.1)$$

$$k = uk_1 + (1-u)k_2, \quad \text{from (2.6) and (2.7);} \qquad (3.2)$$

$$\omega = \frac{f_1(k_1)}{f'_1(k_1)} - k_1, \qquad \text{from (2.10a) and (2.12a);} \quad (3.3)$$

$$\omega = \frac{f_2(k_2)}{f'_2(k_2)} - k_2, \qquad \text{from (2.11a) and (2.13a);} \quad (3.4)$$

$$z_{1j} = \frac{\beta_{1j}}{P}[y\omega f'_2(k_2) - \gamma], \qquad \begin{array}{l}\text{from (2.14a)}\\ \text{and (2.11a) (3.5)}\end{array}$$

$$z_{2j} = \beta_{2j}y\omega f'_2(k_2) + (1-\beta_{2j})\gamma, \qquad \begin{array}{l}\text{from (2.15a)}\\ \text{and (2.11a) (3.6)}\end{array}$$

$$\phi = xf'_1(k_1), \qquad \text{from (2.16a) and (2.12a);} \quad (3.7)$$

$$yuq_1 = uz_{11} + (1-u)z_{12} + \frac{y\,k\phi}{x}, \qquad \begin{array}{l}\text{from (2.14a),}\\ \text{(2.16a) and (2.20) (3.8)}\end{array}$$

$$y(1-u)q_2 = uz_{21} + (1-u)z_{22}, \qquad \begin{array}{l}\text{from (2.15a)}\\ \text{and (2.21); (3.9)}\end{array}$$

$$P = \frac{f'_2(k_2)}{f'_1(k_1)} \qquad \text{from (2.12a) and (2.13a) (3.10)}$$

The static model is a system of thirteen equations in twelve endogenous variables. For reasons indicated previously, one of the commodity market clearance equations may be ignored in the subsequent analysis, since the behavior of the static economy is completely described by the remaining twelve equations.

3.2.2. Existence
Briefly, the existence of a solution is demonstrated in the following way. It can be shown (see appendix A) that it is possible to define numbers a and b such that a positive solution to the model is possible for all values of k contained within the

---

2. Since the function F^i is linearly homogeneous, $F^i[xK_i, yL_i] \equiv yL_iF^i[k_i, 1] \equiv yL_if_i(k_i)$, and $q_i = f_i(k_i)$. In view of the restrictions already imposed on the production system, it follows for $0 < k_i < \infty$ that $f'_i(k_i) > 0$ and $f''_i(k_i) < 0$. Note also that $F_K^i = f'_i(k_i)$ and $F_L^i = f_i(k_i) - k_if'_i(k_i)$.

interval $[a, b]$.[3] We then impose lower and upper limits on ω_i (denoted as $\underline{\omega}_i$ and $\bar{\omega}_i$, respectively) as k_i approach zero and infinity, respectively; it is further assumed that the production functions are well behaved, so that $\underline{\omega} = \max [\underline{\omega}_1, \underline{\omega}_2] < \bar{\omega} = \min [\bar{\omega}_1, \bar{\omega}_2]$ holds. An additional restriction on ω is required in view of our constraint that the wage paid to laborers must be equal to or greater than $\gamma(y)^{-1}$. For any choice of $\gamma(y)^{-1}$ there is only one $\omega = \omega^*$ that satisfies the limiting wage condition, and, if it is assumed that $\gamma(y)^{-1}$ is such that $\omega^* \in [\underline{\omega}, \bar{\omega}]$, the model is defined for all ω such that $\omega^* \leq \omega < \bar{\omega}$.

After some manipulation of the equations of the static model, it can be shown that

$$k = \psi(\omega) \equiv k_2(\omega) +$$
$$\frac{\{yf_2[k_2(\omega)] - z_{22}(\omega)\}[k_1(\omega) - k_2(\omega)]}{yf_2[k_2(\omega)] + z_{21}(\omega) - z_{22}(\omega)}. \qquad (3.11)$$

When $k_1(\omega) \neq k_2(\omega)$ we demonstrate that $\psi(\omega) > 0$ for all $\omega \in [\omega^*, \bar{\omega}]$ which, in turn, implies that $k = \psi(\omega)$ has a positive solution for any k such that

$$a = \inf_{\omega \in [\omega^*, \bar{\omega}]} \psi(\omega) < k < \sup_{\omega \in [\omega^*, \bar{\omega}]} \psi(\omega) = b;$$

that is, for any $k \in [a, b]$ there exists at least one $\omega \in [\omega^*, \bar{\omega}]$. It is an easy matter to show that, for any such ω, positive values for the remaining variables can be found.

In the course of the above proof it is shown that for any given ω the remaining endogenous variables are uniquely determined when $k_1 - k_2 > 0$. Because several of these relationships are utilized extensively throughout this study, we briefly report them here and elaborate on their nature and role in the comparative static analysis below.

First,

$$dw_i/dk_i > 0;$$

3. The approach adopted by E. M. Drandakis in "Factor Substitution in the Two Sector Growth Model" is used to demonstrate the existence of an equilibrium for the static model.

the sectoral wage-rental ratio is a monotonic, increasing function of the sectoral capital-labor ratio. As production becomes more (less) capital intensive, the relative reward of labor (capital) increases. This result is forthcoming in all neoclassical models where production functions are well behaved.

Second,

$$d\phi/d\omega < 0;$$

the rate of capital stock growth (including depreciation requirements) is a decreasing function of the wage-rental ratio. Since total investment is determined by the source distribution of income, an increase in the relative reward to labor, the low (zero) savers, will decrease the rate of capital formation.

Third,

$$dP/d\omega \lessgtr 0 \text{ when } [k_1(\omega) - k_2(\omega)] \gtrless 0;$$

the terms of trade is a decreasing (increasing) function of ω when capital intensity in industry is greater (less) than that in agriculture. This result demonstrates that if and when factor reversal occurs the movement in the terms of trade changes direction. As indicated at the outset, however, there is considerable support for the view that the industrial sector is more capital intensive than the agricultural sector, particularly at low levels of per capita income. This specification is adopted throughout our analysis. As labor becomes relatively more expensive, the price of industrial goods declines, since labor is used in relatively smaller proportions in this sector.

Fourth,

$$dz_{ij}/d\omega > 0;$$

per capita consumer demand for both urban and rural goods moves directly with the wage-rental ratio. Since an increase in the wage-rental ratio implies an increase in each consumer's (wage-earner's) income, the demand for all consumption goods receives a positive stimulus.

Fifth,

$$du/d\omega \lessgtr 0 \text{ when } [k_1(\omega) - k_2(\omega)] \gtrless 0;$$

urbanization moves inversely with the wage-rental ratio in the case where urban goods are produced with relatively capital-intensive techniques. As the relative cost of labor increases, substitution against this factor takes place in both sectors. Given the relative ease of substitution in agriculture, more labor is retained and thus the rate of urbanization diminishes. This result holds for any given k. When k and, hence, ω change, it can be shown that u moves in the same direction.

3.2.3. Uniqueness

We now wish to consider how many short-run equilibrium values for the economy are possible for a given capital-labor ratio. It has already been demonstrated that for any given wage-rental ratio the endogenous variables are uniquely determined for $k_1(\omega) - k_2(\omega) > 0$. However, $k = \psi(\omega)$ need not be monotonic, and if ω is not uniquely determined, the remaining endogenous variables are not uniquely determined.

After differentiating equation (3.11) with respect to ω and rearranging the result, we can show that, when $k_1(\omega) - k_2(\omega) > 0$, a sufficient condition for uniqueness is that $\sigma_2(\omega) \geqq 1$ (see appendix A), an assumption made earlier which we think is consistent with reality.

This result points up an important qualitative difference between the properties of our dualistic model and the Uzawa type of two-sector framework which utilizes the same assumption about savings behavior. Uzawa has found that a sufficient condition for uniqueness of the static equilibrium is that the consumption-goods (agricultural) sector be more capital intensive than the capital-goods (industrial) sector.[4] At least when applied to low-income economies, this assumption seems to be somewhat artificial, although work by Gordon suggests that it may not be unreasonable for higher-income economies.[5] The issue, of course, is not whether capital-goods activities are less

4. H. Uzawa, "On a Two-Sector Model of Economic Growth, I."
5. R. A. Gordon, "Differential Changes in the Prices of Consumers' and Capital Goods."

labor intensive than manufactured consumption-goods activities but whether the industrial sector is less capital intensive than agriculture. Drandakis, however, has shown that a sufficient condition for uniqueness in the Uzawa static model is that the elasticity of substitution in either of the production functions be equal to or greater than one.[6] Our analysis shows that in the dualistic model, where industrial output can be used as a consumption good as well as a capital good and the consumption behavior is described by a linear expenditure system, a sufficient condition for uniqueness is that $k_1 - k_2 > 0$ and $\sigma_2 \geqq 1$. This is in contrast with the result in the models of the Uzawa type, where uniqueness is ensured by either of these conditions.

3.2.4. Stability

In considering whether the economy, if disturbed from equilibrium by some change in the environment, tends to return to a new equilibrium position, it is necessary to specify something about reactions to (static) disequilibrium. We adopt a specification that is within the spirit of the Walrasian *tâtonnement* process. On the one hand, given excess demand in the industrial-goods market, the relative price of industrial goods rises. On the other hand, if the industrial sector is more capital intensive than the agricultural sector and there is instantaneous adjustment of the firm's capital-labor ratios to the prevailing ratio of factor returns, excess demand for agricultural goods tends to increase the demand for labor relative to capital and thereby to raise wages relative to rentals. The rate of increase in P and ω is assumed to vary monotonically with the level of excess demand in the industrial-goods and agricultural-goods markets, respectively. Under these conditions, it can be demonstrated (see appendix A) that the sufficient conditions for local stability of static equilibrium are that $k_1(\omega) - k_2(\omega) > 0$ and $\sigma_2(\omega) \geqq 1$. As already shown, these are also sufficient conditions to ensure a unique static equilibrium in our dualistic economy.

6. Drandakis, "Factor Substitution."

3.3. Sources of Growth in the Basic Dualistic Economy

3.3.1. A Comparative Static Analysis of Change

From any given static equilibrium position, the actual pattern of change depends upon the way in which the dualistic economy responds to changes in the stocks of capital and labor and in the efficiency of these factors as a result of technical progress. While the rate of change in technical knowledge is determined exogeneously, alterations in the capital stock and the labor force depend upon the economy's short-run activities. The rate of capital accumulation is determined by the level of net saving in each time period, whereas the growth in the labor force depends upon changes in the sectoral distribution of labor.

In this section the short-run effects of changes in factor supplies and factor efficiency are examined with the technique of comparative static analysis.[7] This technique permits an identification of the *direction* of change in the endogenous variables —for example, structure of demand, urbanization—induced by an arbitrarily specified change in one of the exogenous vari-

---

7. The static model described by $\Psi[\mathbf{X}; k] = 0$ can also be stated as $\Psi[\mathbf{X}; \mathbf{A}] = 0$, where $\mathbf{A}$ is a vector of exogenous variables and parameters; that is, $\mathbf{A} = [\hat{k}, x, y, \beta_{ij}, \gamma]$, where $\hat{k} = K/L$. For a given change in $\mathbf{A}$ the effects on $\mathbf{X}$ can be determined from the relationship

$$d\Psi_i = \sum_{j=1}^{n} \Psi_{ij} d\mathbf{X}_i + \sum_{s=1}^{m} \Psi_{is} d\mathbf{A}_s = 0 \quad (i = 1, \ldots, n),$$

where

$$\Psi_{ij} = \frac{\partial \Psi_i}{\partial \mathbf{X}_j} \quad \text{and} \quad \Psi_{is} = \frac{\partial \Psi_i}{\partial \mathbf{A}_s}.$$

The total derivative $d\Psi_i = 0$ for every i, since the system must be in equilibrium before and after the change in $\mathbf{A}$. We define $\mathbf{J} = [\Psi_{ij}]$ to be the $n \times n$ matrix of partial derivatives and $\mathbf{b} = [\sum_{s=1}^{m} \Psi_{is} d\mathbf{A}_s]$ to be an $n \times 1$ vector of the derivatives of the elements of $\mathbf{A}$ as they appear in Ψ. Thus, $\mathbf{J}d\mathbf{X} = -\mathbf{b}$. By restricting attention to the case in which a unique equilibrium exists ($k_1 - k_2 > 0$ and $\sigma_2 \geqq 1$), the Jacobian matrix $\mathbf{J}$ is nonsingular; so $d\mathbf{X} = -\mathbf{J}^{-1}\mathbf{b}$. After considerable manipulation it can be shown that most of the signs of Ψ_{is} can be identified by using the restrictions required for stability of the static equilibrium.

ables or parameters. The objective here is to reveal the behavior of the dualistic economy at any point in time, but it will also provide the basis for analyzing the long-run patterns of change in the economy undertaken in section 3.3.2 and the investigation of the relationship between growth and structural change reported in section 3.3.3.

In chapter 6 the comparative statics are expanded in much greater detail to lay bare the role of consumer demand, investment demand, biased technological progress, population growth, and production conditions in the economy. All these important development issues, as examined in chapter 6, deal with *parameter* changes and the response of the dualistic economy to them. *Variables* exogenous to the static model are the physical stocks of capital and labor, and their efficiency levels. The analysis in this section is limited to these exogeneous variables. Furthermore, since the long-run path of the economy analyzed in sections 3.3.2 and 3.3.3 are related to changes in the *efficiency* capital-labor ratio, $k = xK/yL$, it is convenient to explore the influence of changes in each of these components individually: that is, $d\hat{k} = d(K/L)$, dx, dy. Table 3.1 summarizes some results of the comparative static analysis.

TABLE 3.1 Results of comparative static analysis

dA	dX: change in endogenous article									
Increase in	$d\omega$	dk_1	dk_2	dP	du	dz_{11}	dz_{12}	dz_{21}	dz_{22}	$d\phi$	dv
$d\hat{k}$......	+	+	+	−	+	+	+	+	+	−	?
dx......	+	+	+	−	+	+	+	+	+	?	?
dy	−	−	−	+	−	?	?	?	?	+	?

Consider first the consequences of an increase in the supply of capital relative to labor, that is, an increase in $\hat{k}$. The excess supply of capital per capita tends to decrease the price of capital services relative to labor services; that is, the wage-rental rate rises. Firms in both sectors respond to the increase in the relative price of labor by substituting capital for labor. Accord-

ingly, the degree of capital intensity increases in both agriculture and industry. But since the elasticity of substitution is
higher in agriculture, the rise in the wage-rental ratio increases
capital intensity in agriculture more rapidly than in industry.
Although the agricultural sector remains the more labor intensive, even in the low-income economy the increase in ω
generates a more rapid rate of mechanization in agriculture
than in industry, so that in the new equilibrium position the
difference between sectoral capital-labor ratios is reduced.
Furthermore, the price of agricultural goods rises relative to
urban goods, given the comparatively greater utilization there
of the now more expensive factor of production (labor). Note
that urbanization also receives a positive stimulus from this
increase in capital supply. Differences in the possibilities of
factor substitution result in a net inflow of labor into the industrial sector, since industry finds it more difficult to econo-
mize on labor than agriculture. In effect, the increase in u
offsets the tendency for a relatively large increase in ω_1 as
k_1 increases. The increased rate of in-migration to the cities
is, in fact, just sufficient to ensure that factor prices are
equalized between the two sectors. Indeed, with no frictions
and lags to inhibit factor mobility, the simple classical theory
of migration implied by our model guarantees equilibrium in
factor markets.

To determine the impact on demand, information is required on both income and price movements. As shown
above, higher capital-labor ratios give rise to an increase in
output per efficiency unit of labor in each sector and to a relative decline in the price of industrial goods. Since wage incomes
rise throughout the economy, consumption per capita rises as
well. There will, of course, be an additional stimulus to the
consumption of urban goods in response to the fall in the
prices of industrial goods. The increase in consumption of agricultural output per capita is given by

$$\beta_{2j} y a_2 f'_2(k_2) \frac{\partial \omega}{\partial k} > 0.$$

Although the price of industrial goods falls, the value of industrial output consumed per laborer increases; that is, the income effect outweighs the price effect, since

$$z_{1j} \frac{\partial P}{\partial \omega} + P \frac{\partial z_{1j}}{\partial \omega} = \beta_{1j} y a_2 f'_2(k_2) > 0.$$

Furthermore, given our assumption that $\beta_{1j} > \beta_{2j}$, per capita *consumption* of industrial goods rises relative to agricultural goods; that is

$$z_{1j} \frac{\partial P}{\partial \omega} + P \frac{\partial z_{1j}}{\partial \omega} > \frac{\partial z_{2j}}{\partial \omega}.$$

The final component of demand, purchases of investment goods by capitalists, diminishes with the decline in the marginal productivity of capital. The ratio of gross investment demand to the capital stock, ϕ, declines as well. Furthermore, the reduction in investment demand may be large enough to offset the increase in workers' consumption demand for industrial goods. Accordingly, the final impact on the *production* of urban goods, and thus on the level of industrialization, is ambiguous.

The impact of changes in factor efficiency on the endogenous variables in the economy, reported in the last two lines of table 3.1, is now relatively easy to analyze. An increase in x has an effect similar to an increase in $\hat{k}$, since it augments the efficiency capital stock relative to efficiency labor. Its effect on investment demand, however, is ambiguous, since the increased efficiency of the capital stock is offset by the lower marginal productivity of the larger stock. It can be seen from formula (3.7) that the rise in x implies a rise in k_1 as well, and thus an offsetting decline in $f'_1(k_1)$.

With an increase in y alone, the effect is to lower k and, hence, lower ω and k_i and raise P. Whereas output per efficiency laborer falls in each sector, the effect on consumption demand is ambiguous. The fall in the marginal productivity of efficiency labor tends to lower the wage paid to laborers, but this is offset by the rise in y, so that the net change in the wage,

$yf'_2(k_2)$, is ambiguous. On the other hand, the rise in the marginal productivity of efficiency capital gives rise to an increase in capitalists' income and a corresponding increase in investment demand per unit of capital.

The impact of a bias in technical change on the course of development might be considered briefly at this point, although the issue is explored in greater detail in chapter 6. This is accomplished by varying both x and y while holding $\hat{k}$ constant. Recall that the assumption of labor-saving technical change in industry and labor-using technical change in agriculture implies that $\lambda_L > \lambda_K$, and therefore $dy/y > dx/x$. It follows that technical change will decrease both the efficiency capital-labor ratio and the wage-rental ratio.[8] These results, reported in table 3.2,

TABLE 3.2 Impact of a decrease in x/y with a constant $\hat{k}$

$d\omega$	dk_1	dk_2	du	dP	dz_{11}	dz_{12}	dz_{21}	dz_{22}	$d\phi$	dv
−	−	−	−	+	?	?	?	?	+	?

are of particular interest, since the predicted decline in the laborer's relative price due to technical change is the opposite of the finding reported by some economists in the recent literature.[9]

The fall in ω results in a decline in $\hat{k}_i$ which, together with the decline in x/y, leads to a fall in k_i. Thus, the marginal productivity of efficiency labor declines in each sector, but the change in the marginal productivity of labor is ambiguous, since the decrease in the former is offset by the increase in y. Generally, the net effect cannot be determined. This explains in part why the crucial impact on per capita consumption cannot be identified with certainty. It is clear, however, that the

8. We have $k \equiv x\hat{k}/y = \Psi(\omega)$ so that $dk = k\,(dx/x - dy/y) < 0$ when $d\hat{k} = 0$. But $dk = (\partial\Psi/\partial\omega)\,[(\partial\omega/\partial x)dx + (\partial\omega/\partial y)dy]$. We have already shown that $\partial\Psi/\partial\omega > 0$ when $(k_1 - k_2) > 0$. Thus, $[(\partial\omega/\partial x)\,dx + (\partial\omega/\partial y)dy]$ is negative.

9. B. F. Johnston and J. Cownie, "The Seed-Fertilizer Revolution and Labor Force Absorption."

rise in x and in the marginal productivity of capital combine to raise investment demand per unit of capital.

The separate investigation of the impact of technical change yields a crucial analytical result. With the exception of u, the decline in x/y has an effect on the dualistic economy opposite to that due to an increase in $\hat{k}$. As a result, the actual behavior of an economy in which $\hat{k}$ is rising—overall capital deepening, the typical course of development—can only be determined by reference to the behavior of $k(t)$, a topic to which we now turn.

3.3.2. Feasible Patterns of Growth

Consider now the alternative long-run growth paths that are possible in our dualistic economy. In all cases the economy is analyzed only when the agricultural sector is less capital intensive than the industrial sector. Because the model does not consider the question of *optimal* intertemporal behavior for producers and consumers, the analysis that follows is concerned with *feasible* patterns of long-run growth.

Before examining the feasible growth paths, however, we shall consider briefly the behavior of the economy at the lower bound of the system. Income per laborer has been assumed equal to or greater than the minimum consumption bundle, γ; that is, $y(t)w(t) \geqq \gamma$. We can define

$$k^*(t) = \psi[\omega^*(t)]$$

such that

$$y(t)\omega^*(t)f'_2\{k_2[\omega^*(t)]\} = \gamma; \qquad (3.12)$$

$k^*(t)$ is that efficiency capital-labor ratio at which the per capita income of laborers is equated with the minimum bundle, γ, when marginal product pricing prevails.

When $k(t) < k^*(t)$, the resource endowment per capita is so low at the given technology that the marginal value product of efficiency labor does not permit the per capita consumption of γ, the minimum bundle of agricultural goods. Although our model is not defined for this regime, extensions are relatively simple. Cheetham has considered the case in which the current wage per efficiency laborer is set equal to $\gamma/y(t)$ when $k(t) < k^*(t)$; laborers are able to consume the minimum amount of food by being subsidized by capitalists.[10] Alternately, a variant of the approach adopted by Jorgenson could be introduced such that the population growth in each sector is endogenously determined when primary production does not grow at least as fast as total population.

The point $k(t) = k^*(t)$ is somewhat analogous to the "commercialization point" identified in the Fei and Ranis model. In their treatment, the commercialization point is synonomous with the elimination of disguised unemployment in agriculture, whereas in the model considered by Cheetham it signifies the end of a "tax" imposed on capitalists to support labor at the minimum consumption level. To determine the time path of $k^*(t)$, it is first necessary to identify the behavior of the wage-rental ratio, $\omega^*(t)$. By differentiating equation (3.12) with respect to time and rearranging terms, we obtain

$$\frac{\dot{\omega}^*(t)}{\omega^*(t)} = \frac{-\lambda_L}{\alpha_2{}^*(t)}, \tag{3.13}$$

where $\alpha_2{}^*(t)$ is the elasticity of output with respect to capital in agriculture. Note that $\alpha_2{}^*(t)$ varies with the capital-labor ratio and thus with the wage-rental ratio itself.[11] Since the elasticity

10. R. J. Cheetham, "Growth and Structural Change in a Two-Sector Economy."

11. To obtain this result note that

$$\dot{\omega}^*(t)\{f'_2 k_2[\omega^*(t)]\} + \omega^*(t)f''_2\{k_2[\omega^*(t)]\}\frac{\partial k_2[\omega^*(t)]}{\partial \omega_2{}^*(t)} = \frac{-\gamma\dot{y}(t)}{[y(t)]^2}.$$

But

$$f''_2\{k_2[\omega^*(t)]\}\frac{\partial k_2[\omega^*(t)]}{\partial \omega^*(t)} = \frac{-(f'_2\{k_2[\omega^*(t)]\})^2}{f_2\{k_2[\omega^*(t)]\}}$$

and

$$\omega^*(t)f'_2\{k_2[(\omega^*(t)]\} = f_2\{k_2[\omega^*(t)]\} - k_2[\omega^*(t)]f'_2\{k_2[\omega^*(t)]\},$$

so

$$\dot{\omega}^*(t)\alpha_2[\omega^*(t)]f'_2\{k_2[\omega^*(t)]\} = \frac{-\gamma\lambda_L}{y(t)}.$$

Thus,

$$\frac{\dot{\omega}^*(t)}{\omega^*(t)} = \frac{-\lambda_L}{\alpha_2[\omega^*(t)]} = \frac{-\lambda_L}{\alpha_2{}^*(t)}.$$

of output with respect to capital is always positive, the wage-rental ratio will remain constant if λ_L is zero, or it will fall with positive rates of labor-augmenting technical progress. This result has a common sense interpretation: if technical progress augments labor, the *efficiency* wage required to satisfy minimum consumption needs declines. Given the positive relationship between $\omega^*(t)$ and $k^*(t)$, the capital-labor ratio also decreases over time when $\lambda_L > 0$ and is stable over time when $\lambda_L = 0$. The latter case is similar to the low-level-trap predictions of Leibenstein, Nelson, and others where there is a stable equilibrium level of per capita income at (or close to) subsistence requirements.[12]

Now let us turn to the behavior of the system when $k(t) > k^*(t)$. It is convenient to begin the discussion under the assumption of no technical progress, that is, where $\lambda_L = 0 = \lambda_K$. In this case the behavior of the efficiency capital-labor ratio is described by

$$\frac{\dot{k}(t)}{k(t)} = f'_1[k_1(t)] + (n_2 - n_1)u(t) - (\delta + n_2). \quad (3.14)$$

The first term in equation (3.14) is nothing more than the ratio of gross investment to the capital stock, $\phi(t)$, which was defined in equation (3.7). Note that when $n_1 = n_2 = n$, (3.14) collapses to

$$\frac{\dot{k}(t)}{k(t)} = f'_1[k_1(t)] - (\delta + n),$$

the familiar differential equation describing the behavior of the Uzawa two-sector models. Subject to the somewhat different conditions required for uniqueness in the static model, an analysis of this differential equation in our dualistic economy would parallel that reported by Uzawa, Drandakis, Inada, and others.[13]

12. H. Leibenstein, *Economic Backwardness and Economic Growth;* R. R. Nelson, "A Theory of the Low-Level Equilibrium Trap in Underdeveloped Economies."
13. Uzawa, "Two-Sector Model of Economic Growth, I"; idem, "Two-Sector Model of Economic Growth, II"; Drandakis, "Factor

Since $f'_1[k_1(t)]$ and $(n_2 - n_1)$ are always positive, the sign of equation (3.14), and hence the behavior of $k(t)$ over time, depends on the magnitude of the first two terms relative to the negative influence of $(\delta + n_2)$. In general, we shall see that in our low-income economy the capital-labor ratio may increase without limit, decrease to $k^*(t)$, and thus enter a wage-fixing (labor-surplus) phase, or follow an irregularly moving path or limit cycle.

To illustrate this point, consider first the behavior of the system when the growth of $k(t)$ is positive and hence the capital-labor ratio is rising. It can be shown that, when $k(t)$ increases, the level of urbanization increases and thereby exerts a positive influence on the growth of the capital-labor ratio. However, as $k(t)$ rises, so too does the capital-labor ratio in the industrial sector; hence, $f'_1[k_1(t)]$, the marginal product of industrial capital, falls because of the assumption of diminishing marginal rates in substitution between capital and labor.[14] In general, it is not possible to determine which of these opposing forces dominates; we can only delineate the various possibilities.

It is possible that $k(t)$ may increase continuously through time because the increasingly positive influence of $(n_2 - n_1)u(t)$ may be sufficient to offset the decreasing positive influence of $f'_1[k_1(t)]$ together with the negative effect of $(n_2 + \delta)$. Another possibility is that $k(t)$ will increase up to the point where factor reversal occurs at, say, $k(t) = \bar{k}(t)$, and agriculture becomes the more capital intensive of the two activities—a case

---

Substitution"; and K. I. Inada, "On a Two-Sector Model of Economic Growth: Comments and a Generalization."

14. By differentiating equation (2.1) with respect to t and rearranging, we obtain

$$\frac{\dot{f}'_1[k_1(t)]}{f'_1[k_1(t)]} = \frac{-[1 - \alpha_1(t)]}{\sigma_1(t)} \frac{\dot{k}_1(t)}{k_1(t)}.$$

When $k(t)$ increases, $k_1(t)$ increases, which implies that $f'_1[k_1(t)]$ decreases.

we dismiss as uninteresting.[15] On the other hand, $f'_1[k_1(t)]$ may decrease sufficiently rapidly to offset the increasingly positive influence of $(n_2 - n_1)u(t)$ so that eventually the growth of $k(t)$ will become negative at some $k(t) = k_u(t) < \bar{k}(t)$.

When the growth rate of the capital-labor ratio becomes negative, two possible cases can be distinguished. On the one hand, $f'[k_1(t)]$ may become sufficiently large at some $k(t) = k_l(t) > k^*(t)$ to reverse the downward trend in $k(t)$. Alternately, the decline in $k(t)$ may continue until $k(t) = k^*(t)$, beyond which the model is undefined. Thus, we conclude that while the value of $k(t)$ may change continuously the behavior of the system may be described by an irregularly moving time path. Cyclical behavior would *not* constitute a business cycle, since full employment is assumed. But as Stiglitz has noted, the properties of the business cycle may be observed: fluctuations in the distribution of income, the output per man, the growth of output, and the investment-output ratio.[16]

For completeness, it should also be noted that it is possible for the economy to enter a phase in which the aggregate capital-labor ratio is constant over time, for there may exist some $k(t) = k^e(t)$ such that

$$\phi(t) + (n_2 - n_1)u(t) - (\delta + n_2) = 0.$$

Of course, if by chance $k^*(t) = k^e(t)$ were a solution, the economy could stagnate in this low-level equilibrium trap.

In summary, we have thus far not been able to identify unambiguously the growth path of $k(t)$. *As a result, it is not possible to determine the conditions under which one time path rather than another prevails without more restrictive*

15. Since $\dfrac{\dot{\omega}(t)}{\omega(t)} = \dfrac{1}{\sigma_i(t)} \dfrac{\dot{k}_i(t)}{k_i(t)}$,

it follows that $\dot{k}_2(t)/k_2(t) > \dot{k}_1(t)/k_1(t)$ when $\sigma_2(t) > \sigma_1(t)$. Thus, $k_1(t) - k_2(t)$ must decrease when $k(t)$ increases.

16. J. E. Stiglitz, "A Two Sector Class Model of Economic Growth."

*assumptions about production conditions and the relative mag-
nitudes of other parameters in the dualistic economy.*

Now consider the long-run behavior of the economy in the
presence of technical progress. The dynamic behavior of the
system is now described by

$$\frac{\dot{k}(t)}{k(t)} = \phi(t) + (n_2 - n_1)u(t) - (\delta + n_2 + \lambda_L - \lambda_K),$$
$$\text{(3.15)}$$

$$\frac{\dot{x}(t)}{x(t)} = \lambda_K, \tag{3.16}$$

$$\frac{\dot{y}(t)}{y(t)} = \lambda_L. \tag{3.17}$$

The qualitative behavior of $u(t)$ and its positive influence on
the growth of $k(t)$, of course, remains unchanged. However,
in the present case, $\phi(t) = x(t)f'_1[k_1(t)]$. As before, the behavior of $\phi(t)$, the ratio of gross investment to the capital
stock, is central to analyzing the long-run growth of the model.
Growth under technical progress can best be explored by differentiating equation (3.7) with respect to time, using equation (3.16) and rearranging terms, to get

$$\frac{\dot{\phi}(t)}{\phi(t)} = \lambda_K - \frac{[1 - a_1(t)]}{\sigma_1(t)}\frac{\dot{k}_1(t)}{k_1(t)} = \lambda_K - [1 - a_1(t)]\frac{\dot{\omega}(t)}{\omega(t)},$$
$$\text{(3.18)}$$

since $\dot{\omega}(t)/\omega(t) = [1/\sigma_1(t)]\,[\dot{k}_1(t)/k_1(t)]$. Unfortunately, the
behavior of $\phi(t)$ cannot be determined with certainty now that
we introduce the possibility of capital-augmenting technical
progress.

When the efficiency capital-labor ratio rises it does not
necessarily follow that $\phi(t)$ will decrease, since the rate of decline in $f'_1[k_1(t)]$ may be smaller than λ_K, in which case $\phi(t)$
would also increase. Thus, there are even more possibilities
when $k(t)$ is increasing. When $k(t)$ is decreasing, however,
$\phi(t)$ must rise, and depending on its magnitude, the decline in
$k(t)$ may be reversed at some $k(t) = k_l(t) > k^*(t)$; alternatively, $k(t)$ may decline continuously to $k^*(t)$ again. Of

course, it was already shown that $k^*(t)$ itself declines when $\lambda_L > 0$. It is therefore possible that $k(t)$ may decline continuously at a rate less than that of $k^*(t)$. In this case the economy would not violate the minimum wage constraint.

Thus, with positive rates of technical progress the economy may display an even broader range of feasible time paths for the capital-labor ratio than would be displayed in the absence of technical progress. Once again, we conclude that it is not possible to determine in general the conditions under which one time path rather than another will prevail. More restrictive assumptions regarding production conditions and parameter values are required if the behavior of our dualistic economy is to be fully delineated. This critical step is taken in chapter 4.

3.3.3. Structural Change and the Growth Process

Rising per capita incomes have generally been accompanied by a redistribution of the labor force from agriculture to industry and by an increase in the share of industrial output (in value terms) in gross national product. We now consider (1) the relationship between these two aspects of structural change and increases in the value of output per capita in our basic dualistic model, and (2) the impact on this relationship that follows from changes in the supply and demand characteristics incorporated within the model. In examining the causes of structural change it is useful to distinguish conceptually between (1) structural change arising from variations in endogenous variables for any given set of parameter values (the changes engendered by shifts in $k(t)$), and (2) structural change arising from variations in the parameters themselves. In reality, the actual pattern of structural change probably results from simultaneous changes in both endogenous variables and parameters.

From among the many influences advanced to explain these observed patterns of structural change, the present model highlights sectoral differences in factor intensity, elasticity of factor substitution, consumption demand, and population growth. However, as may be expected from the preceding analysis of the behavior of $k(t)$, not all time paths for the economy produce growth, even though structural change may be taking place. It is important, therefore, to distinguish conceptually between the set of all feasible time paths along which the economy may move and that subset of time paths along which *growth* occurs. The former was the theme of section 3.3.2. The latter, considered here, depends upon an identification of the conditions that must be fulfilled in order for growth to take place.

3.3.3.1. *Conditions for growth.* We follow the usual convention in considering a growing economy to be an economy in which per capita income is increasing over time and a stagnant economy one in which per capita income is constant or declining. If $G(t)$ is defined as the value of current output (in terms of agricultural goods) in the economy,

$$G(t) = P(t)Q_1(t) + Q_2(t). \tag{3.19}$$

The value of current gross output per laborer is given by $g(t) = G(t)/L(t)$, which can be restated as

$$g(t) = y(t)[k(t) + \omega(t)]f'_2[k_2(t)]. \tag{3.20}$$

Growth occurs when $g(t)$ is increasing over time. It follows from equation (3.20) that

$$\frac{\dot{g}(t)}{g(t)} = \lambda_L + s^*(t) \left\{ 1 - \frac{k(t) - k_2(t)}{k_2(t) + \omega(t)} \frac{\partial \omega(t)}{\partial k(t)} \right\} \frac{\dot{k}(t)}{k(t)}$$

$$= v(t) \left\{ \frac{\dot{P}(t)}{P(t)} + \frac{\dot{Q}_1(t)}{Q_1(t)} \right\} + [1 - v(t)] \frac{\dot{Q}_2(t)}{Q_2(t)} - \frac{\dot{L}(t)}{L(t)},$$

$$\tag{3.21}$$

where $s^*(t)$ is the (variable) gross savings rate in the economy. When $k_1(t) - k_2(t) > 0$, it is not possible to derive any general statements about the conditions under which growth takes place that are particularly useful to our analysis.

A relatively restrictive sufficient condition for growth is that $[\partial\omega(t)/\partial k(t)][k(t)/\omega(t)] \leqq 1$ when $k(t)$ is increasing.[17] This condition has a straightforward interpretation: $k(t)/\omega(t) = r(t)x(t)K(t)/\omega(t)y(t)L(t)$ is simply the ratio of capital income to wage income in the economy. Consequently, given an increase in $k(t)$, capitalists' income must rise relative to wage income, a result well-documented in developing economies. Rising capitalists' income share is also consistent, of course, with an increase in the gross savings rate in the economy.[18] While the most empirically relevant case is clearly that in which $g(t)$ increases with a rising $k(t)$, we cannot generally determine the nature of the relationship. This result complicates the analysis of the relationship between growth and structural change to be undertaken in the next section.

3.3.3.2. *Labor Redistribution: Urbanization.* The rate of labor redistribution to the industrial sector in the dual economy has received considerable attention in the development literature, particularly in view of the fact that such a redistribution has normally accompanied a growth in income per capita. Fei and

17. With some rearrangement it follows that

$$1 - \frac{k(t) - k_2(t)}{k_2(t) + \omega(t)} \frac{\partial k(t)}{\partial \omega(t)} = -\frac{1}{k_2(t) + \omega(t)} \left\{ k_2(t) \left\{ 1 + \frac{\partial \omega(t)}{\partial k(t)} \right\} + \omega(t) \left\{ 1 - \frac{k(t)}{\omega(t)} \frac{\partial \omega(t)}{\partial k(t)} \right\} \right\}.$$

When $[\partial\omega(t)/\partial k(t)][k(t)/\omega(t)] \leqq 1$ the expression is positive, which, in turn implies that $\dot{g}(t)/g(t) > 0$ when $\dot{k}(t)/k(t) > 0$. The range of plausible values for $[\partial\omega(t)/\partial k(t)][k(t)/\omega(t)]$ depends upon whether $\omega(t)$ approaches $\tilde{\omega}(t)$ asymptotically or whether it intersects $k_1(t) - k_2(t) = 0$ at $\bar{k}(t)$. In the former case $[\partial\omega(t)/\partial k(t)][k(t)/\omega(t)]$ becomes increasingly large as $k(t)$ increases, whereas in the latter case, $[\partial\omega(t)/\partial k(t)][k(t)/\omega(t)]$ may approach zero as $k(t)$ approaches $\bar{k}(t)$ if, for example, there is an inflexion in $\omega[k(t)]$ at $\bar{k}(t)$.

18. It can be shown that
$$\frac{ds^*(t)}{dk(t)} = \frac{1 - s^*(t)}{k(t) + \omega(t)} \left\{ 1 - \frac{k(t)}{\omega(t)} \frac{\partial \omega(t)}{dk(t)} \right\},$$
so that when $ds^*(t)/dk(t) > 0$, $[k(t)/\omega(t)][\partial\omega(t)/\partial k(t)] < 1$.

Ranis believe it to be the prime concern of development theory. In our model the rate of urbanization is given by

$$\frac{\dot{u}(t)}{u(t)} = \frac{k(t)}{u(t)} \frac{\partial u(t)}{\partial k(t)} \frac{\dot{k}(t)}{k(t)}. \tag{3.22}$$

Since $\partial u(t)/\partial k(t) > 0$, it follows that sign $[\dot{u}(t)/u(t)] = $ sign $[\dot{k}(t)/k(t)]$; that is, the degree of urbanization increases when the overall efficiency capital-labor ratio increases. However, an increase in urbanization does not necessarily coincide with growth in the economy, since it was shown above that growth does not necessarily occur when the efficiency capital-labor ratio is rising. The general relationship between growth and urbanization cannot therefore be determined. This, in turn, prevents an examination of the manner in which changes in the various characteristics of supply and demand jointly influence $u(t)$ and $g(t)$. Nevertheless, in view of the importance generally attached to labor redistribution in the development process, it is useful to review the relationship between some of these demand-supply characteristics and the urbanization level.

The response of the level of urbanization to changes in the capital-labor ratio is determined in part by the relative factor intensity of the sectors. Given $k_1(t) - k_2(t) > 0$ and the relative ease of factor substitution in agriculture, an increase in $k(t)$ results in a transfer of labor from agriculture to industry. But an increase in $k(t)$ leads to a reduction in $k_1(t) - k_2(t)$, so that as $k(t)$ increases (decreases) the economy approaches (recedes from) the point where factor reversal takes place. Obviously, at the point of factor reversal, $\partial u(t)/\partial k(t) = 0$ and $\dot{u}(t) = 0$. Here the implications of growth on the rate of labor redistribution are fairly straightforward. With positive rates of growth in the economy-wide ratio of efficiency capital to efficiency labor, positive rates of urbanization are assumed at low-income levels. As long as $\dot{k}(t) > 0$, then $\dot{u}(t) \geqq 0$, but at higher values for $k(t)$, the value of $\partial u(t)/\partial k(t)$ diminishes to the extent that sectoral capital intensities converge. Acceleration in the rate of capital formation in early growth phases should produce acceleration in the rate of urbanization. At higher levels of urbanization, however, two forces appear to dampen the rate of urbanization. First, $k(t)$ *may* increase more slowly, and, second, $\partial u(t)/\partial k(t)$ is certain to diminish as the economy approaches the point at which factor reversal occurs. In short, when the efficiency capital-labor ratio is rising, the dual economy should pass successively through phases of increasing rates of urbanization, stability in urbanization rates at a high level of $u(t)$, and declining urbanization rates if factor reversal occurs, although this is not guaranteed. If factor reversal occurs, the qualitative behavior of many variables in the model, including $u(t)$, is likely to change. Our analysis, however, is restricted to the case of greater industrial capital intensity.

The influence of different sectoral elasticities of factor substitution on labor redistribution can be readily determined. (The impact of different sectoral elasticities is explored in more detail in chap. 6, sec. 2.5.) A decrease in the ease of substitution of capital for labor in agriculture relative to that in industry means that with an increase in $k(t)$ the agricultural sector substitutes relatively less capital for labor than before. As a result, less labor must be transferred from agriculture to industry in order for a new equilibrium to be attained. Thus, ceteris paribus, a reduction in $\sigma_2(t) - \sigma_1(t)$ diminishes the extent to which labor will be transferred from agriculture as $k(t)$ increases. We have so far implied that the elasticity of factor substitution has been held constant; nothing has been said about the way in which it might vary over time. In the long run, changes in $\sigma_i(t)$ are likely to be determined by the evolution of technical knowledge. While such an argument is difficult to maintain in a model where capital is homogeneous and perfectly mobile and technical change is an exogenously given force, it may have applications in an extension to the basic framework presented here. If, for example, the capital stock is immobile, the technology embodied in the capital stock may be such that $\sigma_1(t)$ increases over time. Ceteris paribus, the effect would be to retard the rate of urbanization in the economy. Alternatively, the "export technology hypothe-

sis" could be employed.[19] This literature appeals to the variation in production parameters between alternative export commodities in explaining the character of growth in developing
economies. To the extent that the composition of agricultural
output changes markedly with the introduction and expansion
of the export sector in early growth stages, secular variations
in $\sigma_2(t)$ are a relevant possibility. We return to this issue in
chapter 6.

It has been suggested that differences in the rate and bias of
technical change also have an important influence on labor redistribution. Consider first the implications of the bias in technological progress. There is a labor-saving bias in the industrial
sector and a labor-using bias in the agricultural sector.[20] As indicated in table 3.2, the impact of technical progress alone is
to transfer labor from industry to agriculture. Other things
being equal, biased technical progress results in the adoption of
a more labor intensive technique in agriculture. It may be

19. S. C. Tsiang, "A Model of Economic Growth in Rostovian
Stages"; R. E. Baldwin, *Economic Development and Export Growth:
A Study of Northern Rhodesia, 1920–1960.*

20. At this stage, it is convenient to point out one of the shortcomings of the assumptions about technological change in the
model. In equilibrium, $\omega_1 = \omega_2 = \omega$. But

$$\omega_i = \frac{f_i(k_i)}{f'_i(k_i)} - k_i = \frac{k_i}{\alpha_i}(1 - \alpha_i), \text{ so that } \frac{k_1}{k_2} = \frac{\alpha_1(1 - \alpha_2)}{\alpha_2(1 - \alpha_1)}.$$

It follows, therefore, that $\alpha_1 - \alpha_2 > 0$ when $k_1 - k_2 > 0$. These
two restrictions are generally considered to be consistent with the
rather limited empirical evidence available for low-income economies. But as we have pointed out elsewhere, when $\alpha_1 - \alpha_2 > 0$
and $\lambda_L - \lambda_K > 0$, it follows that the rate of total factor productivity
growth is higher in agriculture than in industry; that is, the rate of
technological progress in agriculture is greater than that in industry,
a result generally considered inconsistent with the empirical evidence
(at least prior to the appearance of the "Green Revolution"). Thus
the model does not admit the simultaneous existence of restrictions
on factor intensities and on the rate and bias of technological progress in the economy that are consistent with the limited amount of
empirical evidence that is available. Having said this, we shall note
below in chapter 5 that Japanese experience during the Meiji period
appears, from the limited evidence available, wholly consistent with
our theory.

noted, however, that the size of the bias in each sector depends upon the extent to which the elasticity of substitution diverges from one. Any tendency for $\sigma_1(t)$ to increase over time, for example, would reduce the relative capital-using bias in industry and, hence, reduce the tendency for technical change to retard urbanization as $k(t)$ increases. These issues are developed more fully in chapter 6.

3.3.3.3. *Composition of Output: Industrialization.* The other key aspect of structural change that has long interested development economists and economic historians is the rate of industrialization. We define $v(t)$ to be industry's share in the gross value of output at time t:

$$v(t) = \frac{P(t)Q_1(t)}{P(t)Q_1(t) + Q_2(t)} = \frac{P(t)Q_1(t)}{G(t)}. \tag{3.23}$$

One of the most commonly observed characteristics of modern economic growth is a decline in the share of agriculture and related industries in aggregate output as per capita income increases. A frequent explanation for this relationship is the change in the composition of demand, of which the decline in the share of food (Engel's law) is the most notable feature. It is therefore of interest to explore the behavior of $v(t)$ over time, particularly when $g(t)$ is increasing, as well as the influence of the differential income elasticities on the behavior of $v(t)$.

It follows from the definition of $v(t)$ that the rate of industrialization can generally be decomposed into price and quantity effects:

$$\frac{\dot{v}(t)}{v(t)} = [1 - v(t)] \left\{ \frac{\dot{P}(t)}{P(t)} + \frac{\dot{Q}_1(t)}{Q_1(t)} - \frac{\dot{Q}_2(t)}{Q_2(t)} \right\}.$$

Recall that

$$\frac{\dot{P}(t)}{P(t)} = [a_2(t) - a_1(t)] \frac{\dot{\omega}(t)}{\omega(t)}.$$

Since industry is more capital intensive than agriculture, $a_1(t) > a_2(t)$ and thus, with rising wage-rental ratios the rela-

tive price of industrial products *always* declines, contrary to
the Singer-Prebisch thesis popular in the 1950s. As a result,
even if the growth of industrial output exceeds the growth of
agricultural output, the decline in industrial prices may offset
this quantity effect. Furthermore, it is not unambiguously the
case that with increases in $k(t)$ the rate of industrial output
growth will exceed that of agriculture.

Sectoral output growth can be written as

$$\frac{\dot{Q}_i(t)}{Q_i(t)} = \lambda_L + a_i(t)\frac{\dot{k}_i(t)}{k_i(t)} + \frac{\dot{L}_i(t)}{L_i(t)},$$

and thus

$$\frac{\dot{Q}_1(t)}{Q_1(t)} - \frac{\dot{Q}_2(t)}{Q_2(t)} = [a_1(t)\sigma_1(t) - a_2(t)\sigma_2(t)]\frac{\dot{\omega}(t)}{\omega(t)}$$

$$+ \frac{\dot{L}_1(t)}{L_1(t)} - \frac{\dot{L}_2(t)}{L_2(t)},$$

since $\dot{\omega}(t)/\omega(t) = [1/\sigma_i(t)]/[\dot{k}_i(t)/k_i(t)]$. Increases in $\omega(t)$ always produce a labor redistribution to industry, so that the
last two terms in the equation of relative output growth sum
to some positive number. But the expression $[\alpha_1(t)\sigma_1(t) -
\alpha_2(t)\sigma_2(t)]$ *can* assume negative values in general. Thus, even
the behavior of relative output growth is ambiguous.

Only in the special case of $\sigma_1(t) = 1 = \sigma_2(t)$ can the relationship between $v(t)$ and $k(t)$ be identified. It is easy to
show that, when $\sigma_1(t) = 1 = \sigma_2(t)$, sign $\dot{g}(t)/g(t) =$
sign $\dot{k}(t)/k(t)$. Furthermore, sign $\dot{v}(t)/v(t) =$ sign $\dot{g}(t)/g(t)$.
Except for this particular case, we are unable to draw any
general conclusions about the nature of the relationships between changes in $k(t)$ and $v(t)$ over time; moreover, there
remains the unresolved problem of relating the behavior of $g(t)$
to $k(t)$ and hence the behavior of $v(t)$ to $g(t)$. Thus, we are
unable to derive any useful statements about the way in which
the various characteristics of supply and demand influence the
behavior of $v(t)$ through their impact on $k(t)$.

The ambiguity between $v(t)$ and $k(t)$ may at first seem
inconsistent with trade theory and the so-called "Rybczynski

effect." The Rybczynski theorem states that increases in $k(t)$ should generate a relative expansion in that sector which utilizes capital most intensively. In our model increases in $k(t)$ do not *necessarily* produce a relative expansion of the share of industrial output. The apparent conflict can be easily resolved. The Rybczynski theorem is derived assuming "small-country" conditions, that is, constant and exogenously determined commodity prices. In our model, commodity prices are determined endogenously.

The small-country assumption is very strong indeed. With it commodity prices *and* ω are assumed constant; the latter result is more familiarly known as the "factor price equalization theorem." This strong assumption, normally made by trade theorists, yields

$$\frac{\dot{v}(t)}{v(t)} = [1 - v(t)] \left\{ \frac{\dot{Q}_1(t)}{Q_1(t)} - \frac{\dot{Q}_2(t)}{Q_2(t)} \right\} > 0,$$

since

$$\frac{\dot{Q}_1(t)}{Q_1(t)} - \frac{\dot{Q}_2(t)}{Q_2(t)} = \frac{\dot{L}_1(t)}{L_1(t)} - \frac{\dot{L}_2(t)}{L_2(t)} > 0.$$

As long as commodity prices are determined endogenously, industrialization is not assured by increase in $k(t)$. Comparative static theorems from trade theory may have only very limited application to the broader problems of the sources of industrialization in low-income societies.

Moreover, when the necessary condition for $\dot{g}(t) > 0$ is fulfilled it is not possible to derive any plausible sufficient conditions for $\dot{v}(t) > 0$ despite the fact that $0 < \eta_{2j}(t) < 1 < \eta_{1j}(t)$ for all t. In view of the importance some analysts attach to the role of Engel effects in explaining this pattern of industrialization, it seems reasonable to expect that the requirement $0 < \eta_{2j} < 1 < \eta_{1j}$ would provide a plausible sufficient condition for $\dot{v}(t) > 0$ when $\dot{g}(t) > 0$. Apparently, even this requirement is not sufficient to ensure a rising industrial share in aggregate output.

In a sense, the apparent unimportance of Engel effects in providing sufficient conditions for industrialization is of our own making. By this we mean that we have, to date at least, regarded wage income per laborer, $y(t)w(t)$, as the relevant measure of income in defining income elasticities. This has been done because of our assumption that there is no consumption out of rental income—it is all invested. If, as in the next chapter, we allow consumption out of rental income, then aggregate income per capita, $g(t)$, would be the relevant measure of income for the purposes of defining income elasticities. We then find that the income elasticity of demand for agricultural goods, when constrained within quite plausible limits, provides sufficient conditions for $g(t)$ and $v(t)$ to increase when $k(t)$ increases. Nevertheless, it is useful to illustrate the point with respect to the simple model being analyzed here.

We can define $d_i(t)$ as the per capita consumption of the ith commodity; that is,

$$d_i(t) = \sum_{j=1}^{2} \frac{D_{ij}(t)}{L(t)}.$$

We also define the elasticity of demand per capita for the ith good with respect to changes in *aggregate income per capita* as

$$\eta^*_i(t) = \frac{\partial d_i(t)}{\partial g(t)} \frac{g(t)}{d_i(t)};$$

but $[\partial d_i(t)/\partial g(t)] = [\partial d_i(t)/\partial \omega(t)] \, [\partial \omega(t)/\partial k(t)] \, [\partial k(t)/\partial g(t)]$, and it can be shown that $[\partial d_2(t)/\partial \omega(t)] > 0$, so that $[\partial d_2(t)/\partial g(t)] > 0$ implies that $[\partial k(t)/\partial g(t)] > 0$.[21] (We have already

21. By definition

$$d_2(t) = \sum_{j=1}^{2} \frac{D_{2j}(t)}{L(t)} = \frac{Q_2(t)}{L(t)} = y(t) \, [1 - u(t)] f_2 \, [k_2(t)].$$

Thus,

$$\frac{\partial d_2}{\partial \omega} = y[1 - u] f'_2 \frac{\partial k_2}{\partial \omega} - y f_2 \frac{\partial u}{\partial \omega};$$

but

$$\frac{\partial u}{\partial \omega} < 0 \text{ and } \frac{\partial k_2}{\partial \omega} > 0, \text{ so that } \frac{\partial d_2}{\partial \omega} > 0.$$

indicated the conditions under which $\partial\omega(t)/\partial k(t) > 0$.) Thus a sufficient condition for $[\partial g(t)/\partial k(t)] > 0$ is that $\eta^{*}{}_{2}(t) > 0$.

Now consider the relationship between the level of industrialization and aggregate income per capita. By definition we know that

$$v(t) = 1 - \frac{d_2(t)}{g(t)},$$

from which we find that

$$\frac{dv}{dk} = -\frac{\partial g}{\partial k}\frac{d_2}{g^2}\left\{\frac{\partial d_2}{\partial k}\frac{\partial k}{\partial g}\frac{g}{d_2} - 1\right\} = -\frac{\partial g}{\partial k}\frac{d_2}{g^2}(\eta^{*}{}_2 - 1).$$

Clearly if $0 < \eta^{*}{}_2 < 1$, then $dv/dk > 0$ because of the fact that $\eta^{*}{}_2 > 0$ is sufficient to ensure that $\partial g/\partial k > 0$; that is to say, $0 < \eta^{*}{}_2 < 1$ is a sufficient condition for both $g(t)$ and $v(t)$ to increase with increases in $k(t)$.

Of course, wage income per laborer rather than aggregate income is the relevant measure of income for defining income elasticities because there is no consumption from rental income in the model analyzed here. While this may be so, we shall find in chapter 4 that when we allow consumption from rental income and, hence, $g(t)$ is the relevant measure of income, the above restriction is still sufficient to obtain an unambiguous relationship between $k(t)$, $g(t)$ and $v(t)$.

3.4. SUMMARY: THE NEED FOR SIMULATION

In the preceding analysis it was argued that the nature of the relationship between growth and structural change is influenced by both supply and demand characteristics of factor and product markets, but that only within a general equilibrium framework could a more adequate understanding of the relative importance of these characteristics be developed. The problem of evaluating the influence of these characteristics on growth and structural change is dependent upon the development of a framework that allows an unambiguous statement of the relationship between gross national product per capita and the elements of structural change that are of interest. We have not been able to derive such a general statement from the basic dualistic model. We have found that the long-run behavior of variables in our two-sector economy can be described by the long-run behavior of the economy-wide ratio of efficiency capital to efficiency labor, and that there are several feasible time paths for $k(t)$ which are likely to yield widely differing patterns of growth and structural change. We have, however, demonstrated that when $k(t)$ is rising there does exist a plausible set of restrictions such that the qualitative nature of the relationship between growth and structural change is in accord with the historically observed experience of a large number of the present-day higher income economies; that is to say, when the efficiency capital-labor ratio is rising then

(a) $\sigma_2(t) \gtreqless 1,$

(b) $k_1(t) - k_2(t) > 0,$

and

(c) $0 < \eta^*_2(t) < 1,$

are sufficient to ensure that aggregate income per capita increases and that the level of urbanization and industrialization also increase. Nevertheless, the fact that for any given set of parameter values and initial conditions, $k(t)$ is capable of a variety of time paths severely limits the scope for further qualitative analysis of the influence of the various characteristics of supply and demand on the pattern of growth and structural change in the economy.

To identify fully these key relationships, yet still maintain the basic dualistic features of our model, it will be necessary to employ numerical analysis. Simulation of the model is therefore undertaken in chapter 4. We do not consider the utilization of simulation techniques as a "defeat" in our theoretical development, but rather as a logical methodological development of the model's analysis.

Despite its inconclusiveness, at least in relation to the patterns of growth and structural change in our simple model, the qualitative analysis has been useful insofar as it has allowed a detailed statement of the static properties of the economy. At the same time, it has provided a basis for relating our approach to the existing two-sector growth and development literature.

3.5. Patterns of Change in the Jorgenson and Fei-Ranis Models

In contrast to our findings, the models of Fei and Ranis (the classical model) and Jorgenson (the neoclassical model) display a smaller range of time paths by virtue of their more restrictive assumptions. At this stage it is convenient to review briefly some of the analytic results and predictions that can be obtained from these two models.[22]

Jorgenson specifies a Cobb-Douglas production function in manufacturing in his review of the classical model:[23]

$$Q_1(t) = e^{\lambda t} K_1(t)^{\beta_1} L_1(t)^{1-\beta_1}. \tag{3.24}$$

This is a special case of our framework where $\sigma_1 = 1$, $\lambda/(1-\beta_1) = \lambda_L$, and $\lambda_K = 0$. Additionally, Fei and Ranis adopt the classical assumption of constancy in the real wage, although the classical models generally do not specify exactly how this real wage is set. Given the classical assumptions that the terms of trade and the real wage in agricultural goods are fixed, Jorgenson shows that average labor productivity in manufacturing must also be constant, since, from the *special* form of the production function in equation (3.24),

$$\frac{\partial Q_1(t)}{\partial L_1(t)} = (1-\beta_1) \frac{Q_1(t)}{L_1(t)} = w. \tag{3.25}$$

---

22. It should be noted that the Fei-Ranis model is "classical" in only one of its phases, the labor-surplus phase. When it passes out of this growth stage, the economy effectively enters a neoclassical world. However, because the labor-surplus phase is the one they have highlighted and the one around which most discussion and controversy has centered, it is not unfair to describe their theory as "classical."

23. D. W. Jorgenson, "Surplus Agricultural Labor and the Development of a Dual Economy."

Manufacturing output growth can be expressed as

$$\frac{\dot{Q}_1(t)}{Q_1(t)} = \lambda + \beta_1 \frac{\dot{K}_1(t)}{K_1(t)} + (1-\beta_1)\frac{\dot{L}_1(t)}{L_1(t)},$$

and, with constant average labor productivity assumed, it follows that

$$\frac{\dot{K}_1}{K_1} - \frac{\dot{Q}_1}{Q_1} = \frac{-\lambda}{\beta_1}. \tag{3.26}$$

As long as $\lambda > 0$, the capital-output ratio in manufacturing must decline over time at the constant rate λ/β_1. Finally, the classical labor-surplus model predicts increasing rates of growth for $Q_1(t)$, $L_1(t)$, and $K_1(t)$ as development takes place. This follows if we invoke the hypothesis that all property income is saved. Using equations (3.24) and (3.25) and the classical savings hypothesis that $K_1(t) = \beta_1 Q_1(t)$, we obtain

$$\frac{\dot{K}_1(t)}{K_1(t)} = \beta_1 \left(\frac{1-\beta_1}{w}\right)^{\frac{1-\beta_1}{\beta_1}} e^{\frac{\lambda t}{\beta_1}}. \tag{3.27}$$

Thus, capital stock growth increases over time, and, as a result, output and employment growth in manufacturing increase over time as well.

It follows from equations (3.25) and (3.26) that

$$\frac{\dot{k}_1(t)}{k_1(t)} = \frac{-\lambda}{\beta_1(1-\beta_1)} < 0.$$

The rate of change in the capital-labor ratio in manufacturing declines at a fixed rate over time, this rate being a function of parameters λ and β_1. One of the consequences of this formation is that fluctuations in the behavior of k_1 over time can be explained only by appealing to changes in these parameters. In general, we can say that *the classical model is capable of generating changes along only one time path and that the success or failure of the development effort depends critically upon the size of the parameter values rather than upon any endogenously determined forces in the model.*

The neoclassical model of Jorgenson, on the other hand, makes less restrictive assumptions and consequently is capable of generating a variety of time paths. However, his predictions are derived from an analysis of the long-run (or steady state) behavior of the model, where it is assumed that $\dot{k}_1(t)/k_1(t) = 0$. Under the assumption of steady state growth—a condition this book rejects as uninteresting—the rate of capital stock and output growth are equal in the long run. In contrast with the classical result (the capital-output ratio declines at a constant rate) and with the neoclassical assumption of constancy, our model allows for a constant, an increasing, or decreasing ratio. In our economy,

$$\frac{\dot{K}_1(t)}{K_1(t)} - \frac{\dot{Q}_1(t)}{Q_1(t)} = [1 - \alpha_1(t)] \frac{\dot{k}_1(t)}{k_1(t)} - \lambda_K. \tag{3.28}$$

The industrial capital-output ratio is constant in our dualistic economy only when $[1 - \alpha_1(t)][\dot{k}_1(t)/k_1(t)] = \lambda_K$. In the absence of capital-augmenting technical progress, the constancy holds only when $\dot{k}_1(t)/k_1(t) = 0$ or when $\alpha_1(t) = 1$. It is the former restriction which Jorgenson invokes in his analysis. We made no such restriction in the analysis in section 3.3.2. Furthermore, since the growth rate of employment in manufacturing in the long run approaches that of total population in Jorgenson's model, he shows that

$$\frac{\dot{Q}_1(t)}{Q_1(t)} = \frac{\lambda}{1 - \beta_1} + n. \tag{3.29}$$

Whereas the classical model assumes fixed wages and thus a constant average labor productivity in manufacturing, the Jorgenson framework implies that wages increase at a constant rate, $\lambda/(1 - \beta_1)$.[24] Since

---

24. In our model and under the neoclassical regime, the growth in wages is given by
$$\frac{\dot{w}(t)}{w(t)} = \alpha_2(t) \frac{\dot{\omega}(t)}{\omega(t)}.$$

$$\frac{\partial Q_1(t)}{\partial L_1(t)} = (1 - \beta_1) \frac{Q_1(t)}{L_1(t)} = w(t),$$

the growth in wages is given by

$$\frac{\dot{w}(t)}{w(t)} = \frac{\dot{Q}_1(t)}{Q_1(t)} - \frac{\dot{L}_1(t)}{L_1(t)} = \frac{\lambda}{1 - \beta_1}. \tag{3.30}$$

Thus, under neoclassical assumptions, Jorgenson's special case of dualism predicts that, in steady state, manufacturing employment will grow at a slower rate than both output and the capital stock. It appears, therefore, that there are appreciable differences in the predictions of these competing models about the behavior of output per laborer in industry and about the industrial capital-output ratio. Our model, on the other hand, employs less restrictive assumptions and as a result is capable of a generating a wider range of behavior in these ratios. The relative usefulness of these competing models for explanation and prediction of economic growth becomes an important empirical matter, a question we shall take up in chapter 5.

In part, these differences result from the various limiting assumptions used in each model. But as Dixit has shown, the Fei-Ranis-Jorgenson models do not necessarily yield conflicting results when the behavior of the Jorgenson model is analyzed in other than the steady state.[25] He shows that under Jorgenson's assumptions the manufacturing labor force can be determined as a residual where

$$L_1(t) = L(0) \ (e^{nt} - e^{vt})$$

and $n > (n - \alpha)/(1 - \beta_2) = v$. It follows that

$$\frac{\dot{L}_1(t)}{L_1(t)} = \frac{ne^{nt} - ve^{vt}}{e^{nt} - e^{vt}}, \tag{3.31}$$

so that manufacturing employment follows a short-run path as in figure 3.1. Now let the rate of capital stock growth be de-

25. A. Dixit, "Theories of the Dual Economy: A Survey."

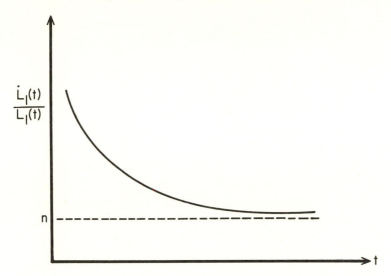

Fig. 3.1. Short-run Manufacturing Employment Growth in Jorgenson's Model

noted by ϕ. (This corresponds to ϕ in our model where $\delta = 0$, an assumption explicit in the Jorgenson framework.) Thus,

$$\frac{\dot{K}_1(t)}{K_1(t)} = \phi(t) = \beta_1 \frac{Q_1(t)}{K_1(t)}$$

and

$$\frac{\dot{\phi}(t)}{\phi(t)} = \frac{\dot{Q}_1(t)}{Q_1(t)} - \frac{\dot{K}_1(t)}{K_1(t)} = \lambda + (1 - \beta_1) \left\{ \frac{\dot{L}_1(t)}{L_1(t)} - \frac{\dot{K}_1(t)}{K_1(t)} \right\}$$

Let the rate of technical change in labor-augmenting form be $\mu = \lambda/(1 - \beta_1)$; then

$$\frac{\dot{\phi}(t)}{\phi(t)} = (1 - \beta_1) \left\{ \frac{\dot{L}_1(t)}{L_1(t)} + \mu - \phi(t) \right\}.$$

The rate of employment augmentation in manufacturing, $\dot{L}_1(t)/L_1(t) + \mu$, and the rate of capital stock growth are exhibited in figure 3.2. Two paths of $\phi(t)$ are feasible, and both rise over time. The first, $\phi_1(t)$, continues to increase until $\phi_1(t) = \dot{L}_1(t)/L_1(t) + \mu$ where $\dot{\phi}_1(t) = 0$ and $\phi_1(t) = n + \mu$. The second, $\phi_2(t)$, rises more rapidly

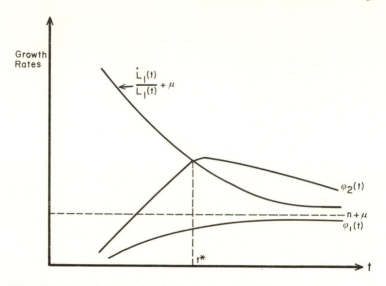

Fig. 3.2. Growth Rates in the Jorgenson Model

until $\phi_2(t) = \dot{L}_1(t)/L_1(t) + \mu$ where $\dot{\phi}_2(t) = 0$ and $\dot{L}_1(t)/L_1(t) > n$. Up to $t = t^*$, the capital-output ratio is *declining* and rates of capital stock growth are *rising*. Thus, up to t^*, *Jorgenson's neoclassical model makes the same predictions as the classical model*. Dixit estimates that the period up to t^* falls into range of from two to six decades. Since most of the "historical tests" of the dualistic models, including our own in chapter 5, tend to focus on periods within two to six decades of economic history, clearly the short-run, rather than the asymptotic properties of the Jorgenson model are the appropriate frame of reference for empirical tests. Accordingly, we conclude that the predictions derived from steady state properties of the neoclassical model are inappropriate, and the simulated behavior in other than steady state is the growth phase relevant for historical testing.

It is useful to conclude our discussion by highlighting a key feature of the qualitative predictions of the Fei and Ranis, and Jorgenson models as well as ours. The striking feature of the qualitative results is *not* the differences between the classical and neoclassical versions, but rather the precision of the Fei-Ranis-Jorgenson predictions in contrast to our inability to obtain general predictions on several variables when the restrictive assumptions regarding technology and consumer behavior are relaxed. We do *not* consider this result compelling evidence of a weakness in our basic model. General solutions to these types of models represent a desirable theoretical attribute, but this feature may be obtained at considerable cost. There is no adequate resolution to this "trade-off" between the generality of description and the generality of assumptions other than by appeal to an alternative, and overriding, criterion for judging theory—its descriptive power.

The descriptive power of our model is the focus of chapters 4, 5, and 8 of this book. At this stage we can, however, summarize our "theory" as one which develops a general "structure" of the development process but admits, even *postulates,* that the behavioral and technical parameters of the system may vary from country to country and through time. Thus, to obtain precise model predictions it will be necessary to select a country or group of countries and define a point in time—a phase of development—so that the properties of our model may be fully revealed. This we do by making restrictive assumptions on parameter values rather than by simplifying the model structure. In chapter 4 we utilize the characteristics of several present-day Southeast Asian countries as our prototype and generate the growth path of the "typical" country using simulation techniques. These forecasts should characterize the future growth experience from these initial conditions of a typical Southeast Asian country if our model and assumed parameter values have validity. A test of the framework can be made, however, by examining the *past* record of one of the countries in the region which was *not* used in obtaining parameter values but has passed through the growth phases under description—Meiji Japan. This exercise, undertaken in chapter 5, provides us with a preliminary appraisal of our model in terms of the historical record.

4

Numerical Analysis of Growth and Change in a Dualistic Economy

4.1. THE SIMULATION MODEL

While more explicit results about the determinants of industrialization could be obtained by means of a major simplification of the theoretical structure, this would involve a significant modification of the key dualistic characteristics of the economy. The dualistic demographic specification could be eliminated, for example, but in our view this would remove an important element of the modeled economy. Alternatively, we could follow Jorgenson, Fei and Ranis, and others and omit capital as an argument in the agricultural production function. However, this would rob the model of a key allocation decision relevant to a current policy debate in the developing economies; that is, should investment be made in agriculture or in industry? The alternative approach is to initiate a more complete exploration of the model with the aid of numerical analysis. While such an approach has less generality—it requires specific assumptions regarding functional form, parameter values, and initial conditions—the approach represents the only viable method for exploring the modeled process of economic growth short of retreating to a simpler framework with less interesting characterizations of economic development. As a result, throughout the remainder of this book we rely heavily on simulation analysis to explore further the determinants of growth and structural change.

To provide a suitable link with the more complex model developed in later chapters, several modifications to the basic equilibrium model are introduced in section 4.1.1. In section 4.1.2 the estimation procedures for obtaining parameter values

96

and the rationale for the choice of initial conditions are presented. Section 4.2 outlines the results of the simulation in detail and compares the patterns of growth and structural change in our economy with those of a number of low-income economies. Of the many features of economic development, only a few may be considered well-established empirical generalizations. The most commonly cited generalizations are the tendency for both labor shares and output shares in the primary sector to decline secularly as growth takes place.[1] This prediction constitutes a minimum test for any development model.[2] While this broad trend is in fact revealed in the simulated economy, we also consider whether the *rate* of sectoral shift is consistent with that of other developing countries at similar *levels* of development. The latter permits an appraisal of the model's temporal dimension. Even though a period in the simulation is designed to correspond to a calendar year, an investigation of the rates of change produced by the simulated economy provides the basis for establishing whether a fifty-period simulation corresponds to the "typical" country's experience over, say, 25, 50, or 100 years.

4.1.1. Revisions to the Basic Dualistic Model
We now revise the basic model analyzed in chapter 3 to allow capitalists to consume as well as to accumulate. It is assumed

1. Kuznets, "Industrial Distribution"; H. B. Chenery, "Patterns of Industrial Growth"; and C. Clark, *The Conditions of Economic Progress*.
2. In his excellent survey of dualistic development models, "Theories of a Dual Economy: A Survey," A. Dixit expresses skepticism over the ability to discriminate empirically between alternative models, or even to appraise the descriptive power of the key sectoral trends in these models. Using the above-cited sectoral shifts as a starting point, he notes, "These are merely the broadest facts of development, but further generalizations seem difficult and perhaps even dangerous. I shall consider a model *prima facie* useful if it accounts for these observations" (p. 6). On the use of Japanese data for more detailed empirical testing, Dixit comments that "we do not believe that the crude and dubious data warrant our passing such judgments on such simple and basically qualitative models" (p. 33). Obviously we do not agree.

that capitalists continue to save a fixed portion of their income but that this savings parameter is less than one. Clearly, there is considerable scope for further extension of the savings function. No distinction is made, for example, between industrial and agricultural property income recipients; yet savings behavior may be quite different for the two groups. This assumption will be modified in chapters 7 and 8, but for the present we postulate that all capitalists behave in an identical manner and allocate their investments to both sectors.

Many plausible assumptions could be introduced regarding the size distribution of property income within and between sectors. We assume that recipients of property income constitute a fixed proportion, Φ, of the total labor force.[3] The value of Φ uniquely determines per capita property income, given the distribution of a fixed stock of resources, and thus has an explicit influence on demand composition. It is clear that the assumption of a single capitalist would be unacceptable, since γ is likely to be very small relative to the capitalist's income; thus, the subsistence demand parameter in the linear expenditure system would have a negligible impact on the allocation of expenditures between urban and rural goods. In the numerical analysis we select a value for Φ consistent with the evidence that per capita property income is greater than per capita wage income in developing economics. This specification results in the plausible hypothesis that the subsistence consumption requirement is a much smaller component of capitalists' income than of workers' income.

Capitalist consumption demand is described by

$$\frac{D_1^k(t)}{\Phi L(t)} = \frac{\pi_1}{P(t)} \frac{[(1-s)Y(t) - \gamma]}{\Phi L(t)}, \tag{4.1}$$

$$\frac{D_2^k(t)}{\Phi L(t)} = \pi_2(1-s)\frac{Y(t)}{\Phi L(t)} + (1-\pi_2)\gamma, \tag{4.2}$$

3. With this specification, total population, call it $N(t)$, is in fact composed of both laborers and recipients of property income, $N(t) = [1 + \Phi]L(t)$.

The Simulation Model

where π_1 and π_2 represent capitalist demand parameters for urban and rural goods, respectively; $D_i^k(t)$ is the quantity of the ith good consumed by capitalists, $\Phi L(t)$, all of whom reside in the urban sector; and $0 \leq s < 1$ is the fixed share of capitalists' income, $Y(t)$, that is set aside for investment purposes. It is convenient to assume that the demand parameters for non-wage-earning households are the same as those for the urban wage earners; that is, $\pi_1 = \beta_{11}$, and $\pi_2 = \beta_{21}$. It should be noted that, even when $\gamma = 0$, the demand equations still retain the basic flavor of the Stone-Geary hypothesis, although the "minimum bundle" then becomes $sY(t)$. This variable might be interpreted as that minimum amount of savings the recipient of property income considers necessary, quite apart from his minimum consumption requirements.

In equilibrium,

$$Y(t) = x(t)r(t)K(t), \tag{4.3}$$

and investment demand is given by

$$P(t)I(t) = sY(t) = sx(t)r(t)K(t). \tag{4.4}$$

After transformation to per capita terms, the revised static equilibrium model is described by equations (3.1)–(3.6), (3.10), and

$$c_1 = \frac{\beta_{11}}{P} \left[\frac{(1-s)}{\Phi} ykf'_2(k_2) - \gamma\right], \tag{4.5}$$

$$c_2 = \beta_{12} \frac{(1-s)}{\Phi} ykf'_2(k_2) + (1 - \beta_{12})\gamma, \tag{4.6}$$

$$\phi = sxf'_1(k_1), \tag{4.7}$$

$$yuq_1 = uz_{11} + (1-u)z_{12} + \Phi c_1 + sykf'_1(k_1), \tag{4.8}$$

and

$$y(1-u)q_2 = uz_{21} + (1-u)z_{22} + \Phi c_2. \tag{4.9}$$

The revised static equilibrium model is a system of fifteen equations, one of which is redundant, and fourteen endogenous variables, namely, q_i, k_i, u, ω, P, z_{ij}, c_i and ϕ where $i, j = 1, 2$.

By allowing consumption of a fixed share of rental income, we do not change the properties of the static model in any essential way. It can be shown that $\sigma_2 \geqq 1$ and $k_1 - k_2 > 0$ are still sufficient to ensure uniqueness and stability.[4] It can also be shown that $\partial c_i/\partial \omega < 0$ when $k_1 - k_2 > 0$.[5] Of course, in the

4. From equations (3.1), (3.2), (3.9) and (4.9) we have

$$k = k_2 + \frac{[yf_2 - z_{22} - \Phi c_2][k_1 - k_2]}{yf_2 + z_{21} - z_{22}}$$

Differentiating this expression with respect to ω and rearranging the result, we have

$$\frac{dk}{d\omega} [1 + \frac{\beta_{21}(1-s)yf_2(k_1 - k_2)}{yf_2 + z_{21} - z_{22}}] = u\frac{\partial k_1}{\partial \omega} + (1-u)\frac{\partial k_2}{\partial \omega}$$

$$+ \frac{yf_2 + z_{21} - z_{22}}{(k_1 - k_2)H^*}$$

where

$$H^* = H - \beta_{21}(1-s) ykf''_2 \frac{\partial k_2}{\partial \omega},$$

and where H is the expression defined in A.13 of appendix A.

We have already shown that when $\sigma_2 \geqq 1$, $H > 0$ and in view of the fact that $f''_2 < 0$, it follows that $\sigma_2 \geqq 1$ is also a sufficient condition for $H^* > 0$. It follows that $k_1 - k_2 > 0$ and $\sigma_2 \geqq 1$ are sufficient conditions for $dk/d\omega > 0$, thus ensuring uniqueness in the model. It can also be shown that these two restrictions are sufficient for the stability of the static model.

5. Differentiating c_1 with respect to ω in (4.5) we have

$$\frac{\partial c_1}{\partial \omega} = \frac{\beta_{11}}{P}(1-s)\frac{ykf''_2}{\Phi}\frac{\partial k_2}{\partial \omega} - \frac{c_1}{P}\frac{\partial P}{\partial \omega}.$$

But

$$f''_2 \frac{\partial k_2}{\partial \omega} = -\frac{f'^2_2}{f_2} \text{ and}$$

$$\frac{1}{P}\frac{\partial P}{\partial \omega} = \frac{(k_2 - k_1)}{(\omega + k_1)(\omega + k_2)} = \frac{(k_2 - k_1)f'_1 f'_2}{f_1 f_2},$$

so that

$$\frac{\partial c_1}{\partial \omega} = -\frac{\beta_{11}}{P}\{(1-s)\frac{yk}{\Phi}\frac{f'^2_2}{f_2}[1 + (k_2 - k_1)\frac{f'_1}{f_1}]\frac{\gamma}{P}\frac{\partial P}{\partial \omega}\}$$

$$= -\frac{\beta_{11}}{P}[\frac{(1-s)ykf'_2}{\Phi(\omega + k_1)} - \frac{\gamma}{P}\frac{\partial P}{\partial \omega}].$$

But $\frac{\partial P}{\partial \omega} < 0$ when $k_1 - k_2 > 0$, so that also $\frac{\partial c_1}{\partial \omega} < 0$ in this case.

Differentiating c_2 with respect to ω in (4.6) we have

$$\frac{\partial c_2}{\partial \omega} = \beta_{21}(1-s)\frac{yk}{\Phi}f''_2 \frac{\partial k_2}{\partial \omega}.$$

Thus, $\frac{\partial c_2}{\partial \omega} < 0$ in view of the fact that $f''_2 < 0$.

dynamic model the variety of time paths for $k(t)$ remains, and without further restrictions the ambiguity between $k(t)$, $g(t)$, and $v(t)$ also remains. Restrictions on the elasticity of demand for agricultural goods with respect to changes in aggregate income per capita are sufficient to eliminate the ambiguity when $k(t)$ is rising. We define $d_i(t)$ to be the per capita consumption of the ith good in a manner similar to that in chapter 3 except that the total population is now given by $(1 + \Phi)L(t)$. As before, $\partial d_2/\partial \omega > 0$ so that $\eta_2{}^*(t) > 0$ is a sufficient condition for $\partial g(t)/\partial k(t) > 0$ where $g(t) = G(t)/(1 + \Phi)L(t)$. Moreover, following the procedure used in chapter 3 we can easily show that $0 < \eta_2{}^*(t) < 1$ is sufficient to ensure that $dy(t)/dk(t) > 0$; that is to say, when $k(t)$ is increasing $\sigma_2(t) \geqq 1$, $k_1(t) - k_2(t) > 0$, and $0 < \eta_2{}^*(t) < 1$ are sufficient to ensure that $g(t)$ also increases and that the levels of urbanization and industrialization increase. Having established the correspondence between the model presented in this chapter and the one analyzed in chapter 3, we now use numerical analysis for a more detailed exploration of the model.

4.1.2. Choice of Parameter Values and Initial Conditions

In choosing the method of estimating parameter values for our model we have rejected an econometric approach for two reasons: first, the data drawn from developing economies are sufficiently questionable to cast doubt on the likelihood that econometric procedures would result in satisfactory parameter estimates of the system; second, because of the limited number of observations available in most cases, and the relatively large number of parameters to be estimated (a total of twenty), the degrees of freedom remaining may be so few that we would have very little confidence in the accuracy of any parameter estimates obtained from such an econometric exercise. Thus, our general approach is to develop parameter estimates, not by using detailed econometric analysis, but rather by drawing liberally from the existing literature providing quantitative descriptions of the structure of developing economies. (A detailed discussion of the procedure is given in appendix B.)

These parameter values are then utilized in a simulation to ascertain whether the resulting initial conditions conform to our preestablished constraints. (Chapter 6 considers the importance of alternative parameter values through the technique of sensitivity analysis.)

In choosing the initial conditions for simulation, we sought to depict a low-income economy that was "representative" with respect to such characteristics as composition of sectoral output, relative factor productivities, factor distribution, and intensity of factor utilization. The nature of the constraints on initial conditions, together with the procedures for incorporating them in the simulations, is also discussed in appendix B. It is useful, however, to summarize here the six key initial conditions that describe our economy. First, since most low-income economies have a predominantly rural population engaged in agriculture and a relatively small modern industrial sector located in urban centers, an initial figure of 30 percent is taken as the degree of urbanization. Second, the initial conditions imply that the capital-labor ratio in industry is more than three times that in agriculture, a result which conforms with the relatively low agricultural capital intensities in developing economies. Third, the economy-wide capital-output ratio is slightly less than twice, while the capital-output ratio in industry is almost one and a half times, that of agriculture. Although there is little concrete evidence on capital-output ratios in developing economies, these initial conditions appear reasonable and are consistent with assumptions frequently made in macro-models of the developing economies. Asian macro-models, for example, commonly assume the capital-output ratio in nonagricultural production to be in the neighborhood of three and the economy-wide figure to be two. Furthermore, our figures are almost the same as those reported by Sicat, Tidalgo, and Williamson for the Philippines.[6] Fourth, the implied differentials in sectoral labor productivity appear repre-

6. G. Sicat and R. Tidalgo, "Output, Capital, Labor, and Population: Projections from the Supply Side"; J. G. Williamson, "Dimensions of Philippine Post-War Economic Progress."

sentative of low-income Asian and Latin American economies. Kuznets, for example, reports that average labor productivity in Philippine nonagriculture was 2.4 times that in agriculture in 1948, after excluding unpaid family labor;[7] our initial conditions yield a figure of roughly 1.8. Fifth, the initial conditions imply that nonagricultural output accounts for about 43 percent of aggregate output. This feature is consistent with the general observation that, at low levels of per capita income, with most of the labor force engaged in agriculture, the output share of the nonagricultural sector is substantially less than that of agriculture. Demand for industrial output, of course, derives from four competing sources; the demand of urban and rural wage earners for industrial consumption goods, the demand of capitalists for industrial consumption goods, and the demand for capital goods. The initial structure of demand in the simulation model is similar to that prevailing in most low-income economies. By far the largest share of urban output goes to satisfy the demands of urban workers and recipients of property income for consumption goods. Only one-third of industrial output is allocated to the combined uses of capital formation and agricultural consumption of urban goods. These results are consistent with the oft-observed weaknesses of intersectoral linkages in developing economies; only 4 percent of industrial output goes to farm consumption.

Finally, the savings parameter of the recipients of property income has been set at 0.31 in the simulation. This implies that the aggregate savings rate, which is uniquely determined by the property income recipients' savings parameter and the distribution of income, has an initial value of 0.15. In a recent study of low-income economies covering the period of 1957–62, Chenery and Strout found the following figures for the aggregate savings rate: median, 0.17; upper quartile, 0.20; and lower quartile, 0.14.[8] Our interest is restricted to a growth

7. S. Kuznets, "Quantitative Aspects of the Economic Growth of Nations, II: Industrial Distribution of National Product and Labor Force."
8. H. B. Chenery and A. M. Strout, "Foreign Assistance and Economic Development."

trajectory rising from relatively low levels of economic development; there is, therefore, conformity between the simulation model's initial aggregate savings rate and that of the lower quartile of developing nations.

One further point needs clarification before we discuss the results of the simulation. Since it is well established that rates of sectoral change vary with the level of per capita income, the initial level of output per capita represented by the model must also be identified.[9] This will permit the utilization of cross-sectional data in comparisons between results from our model and the experience of a number of low-income economies. As noted in appendix B, the basic parameter values used in the simulations are drawn from Southeast Asia, although in most dimensions they have much wider applicability. Accordingly, the initial period's per capita output level is taken at $150 (1960 dollars), the average output per capita prevailing in Asia in the fifties.[10]

4.2. NUMERICAL ANALYSIS OF TIME PATHS

Given the parameter values and initial conditions, the time paths of the endogenous variables are obtained with a computer simulation of the dynamic model. The behavior of individual variables in the simulation will be examined in detail in the following sections (but see appendix C for the numerical results of the simulation). In brief, we find that the time paths of key variables appear reasonable as judged by a comparison with the historical record. Labor's share declines throughout, although in industry it reverses this trend at later stages of development; the overall rate of technical change is relatively constant; the level of urbanization and industrialization initially rises rapidly but approaches an asymptote in late phases of

9. H. B. Chenery and L. J. Taylor, "Development Patterns: Among Countries and over Time," pp. 393–403.

10. The countries included in the average are Burma, Cambodia, Thailand, Taiwan, South Korea, the Philippines, Malaya, and Japan (ibid., p. 414).

development; production becomes more capital intensive overall, although agriculture experiences an early period of increasing labor intensity; and output growth, while rising throughout,
decreases its rate of increase over time. The model exhibits
characteristics somewhat representative of long-run balanced
growth only after about one hundred periods of simulation.

4.2.1. Output and Population Growth

The central focus of development and growth theory is the
path of per capita output growth. As indicated in table 4.1,
output per capita grows at an increasing rate in our modeled
economy. Since the rate of population growth is high but fairly
stable over time (falling from only 2.7 to 2.6 percent a year
in the first five decades), we focus on output growth. The
growth of GNP increases from 3.5 percent a year in the first
decade to just under 4 percent a year by the fifth decade of
development. There does appear to be a long-run tendency
toward balanced growth in the last half of the century when
sectoral output growth rates begin to converge, but over
the first five decades unbalanced growth is maintained and
the sectoral differentials continue to rise, though at a continually slower rate. Since the economy generates only small
increases in the gross savings rate, per capita output growth
never exceeds 1.5 percent a year. While this result will be
analyzed at greater length in chapters 5 and 6, we should
emphasize here that an acceleration in output growth rates is
forthcoming without dramatic increases in savings rates. Needless to say, "Golden Ages" do not intrude into this century of
dualistic development: the growth rate of output per laborer
exceeds the rate of increase in labor force efficiency by far,
even in late phases of growth.

The growth of GNP per capita constitutes the most aggregative comparison of the model's performance with the historical record, and in table 4.2 we compare the average per capita
GNP growth rate over ten simulation periods with the average
decennial growth rates for those countries having sufficient

TABLE 4.1 Average annual growth of population and output from the simulation model

Decade	Population (1)	Aggregate output (2)	Agricultural output (Valued) (3)	Industrial output (Valued) (4)	Aggregate output per capita (5)	Agricultural output per laborer (6)	Industrial output per laborer (7)	Col. 7/Col. 6 (8)
1–10.........	0.0269	0.0346	0.0305	0.0399	0.0075	0.0047	0.0096	0.835
11–20........	.0268	.0366	.0312	.0427	.0104	.0075	.0109	2.043
21–30........	.0266	.0380	.0318	.0443	.0113	.0097	.0112	1.453
31–40........	.0264	.0390	.0324	.0450	.0136	.0117	.0111	1.155
41–50........	.0260	.0395	.0327	.0450	.0146	.0133	.0111	0.949
Average (1–50)......	0.0265	0.0375	0.0317	0.0435	0.0107	0.0086	0.0099	1.151

TABLE 4.2 Average decennial growth rates for GNP per capita

Sample	Period	Rate per decade
Simulation	1–50	11.0
Argentina, Brazil, Chile[a]	1925/29–1950/54	11.9
Philippines[b]	1955–65	14.0
Kuznets sample[c] "less economically developed areas"	1885–1950	10.4
Japan[d]		
Ohkawa	1883/87–1908/12	31.4
LTES	1883/87–1908/12	25.4
Nakamura	1883/87–1908/12	21.9

NOTE: Kuznets's average decennial growth rates represent the average of the individual decade rates for the intervals indicated. For each decade the initial period is used as the denominator in the calculation. Since our interest is in comparisons between entries, the conclusions are not sensitive to the particular computational procedure employed.

a. The Latin American data (from S. Kuznets, *Six Lectures on Economic Growth*, p. 22) represent the arithmetic average of the decadel ratio for the three countries.

b. The Philippines growth rates are computed from data in United Nations, *Yearbook of National Income Accounts*, 1967 (New York: United Nations, 1968), and United Nations, *Economic Survey of Asia and the Far East* (New York: United Nations, 1968).

c. Kuznets's total sample includes the United Kingdom, France, Germany, Switzerland, Netherlands, Denmark, Norway, Sweden, Russia and U.S.S.R., United States, Union of South Africa, Australia, New Zealand, Japan, Ireland and Eire, Spain, Hungary and Italy. The latter four are identified by Kuznets as being "less economically developed areas."

d. See chap. 5, sec. 2.

historical documentation.[11] An interesting picture emerges. The model's growth of 11.0 percent per simulation decade corresponds very closely to both the long-run decennial growth

11. The Philippine time series is much too short to qualify as "sufficient historical documentation." It is included in table 4.2 only because so many of the parameters and initial conditions assumed in the numerical analysis are estimated from Philippine data.

performance for Argentina-Brazil-Chile (11.9 percent)[12] and Kuznets's sample of "less economically developed areas" (10.4 percent).[13] In contrast, Japanese growth averaged an astounding 22.7–35.1 percent per decade. Japan is clearly an outlier as judged by our model's performance, the historical record of the low-income countries, and even the long-term growth rate of Kuznets's total sample (15.9 percent).[14] Taking the expansion of GNP per capita as the norm, we may conclude that the simulation produces aggregate growth rates roughly identical with those observed for low-income countries historically.

Systematic variations in the shares of sectoral output constitute the most widely investigated facet of structural change in the kind of low-income economies that our model purports to represent. In our economy industrial output growth exceeds that of agriculture throughout the entire first half-century of growth, so that the level of industrialization rises without interruption to 57 percent. Table 4.3 compares the rate at which the dualistic economy is shifting out of primary production with the rates derived from time series studies and from a cross-

12. The average long-term growth rate of the smaller Latin American countries has been somewhat more rapid. Since the two-sector model most directly corresponds to those nations where foreign trade is relatively less important, only the three largest Latin American countries are considered here.

13. S. Kuznets, *Six Lectures on Economic Growth*, p. 20.

14. Kuznets has also broken the period into two parts, using World War I as the dividing point (ibid, pp. 33–35). The first and second periods yield average growth rates of 19.7 and 16.9, respectively. He concludes that growth rates tend to decline at later stages of development, largely as the result of the slower rate of development and diffusion of science and technology. The higher growth rates of early development in the countries Kuznets examines are still less than those in Japan. This theme is also developed by J. I. Nakamura, in *Agricultural Production and the Economic Development of Japan, 1873–1922* (p. 21): "The Japanese experience, however, differed from that of the Western economies in many important respects, at least in *degree* where not in kind. Growth was assured within twenty years after the Meiji Restoration. . . . Her development from a feudal to an industrial economy of the 1930's was crowded into a *shorter span of years*" (italics ours).

TABLE 4.3 Rates of change in the primary-output share

Country or sample	Period or income range	Rate of decline per year (period)[a] (%)
Simulation	1–50	−0.48
Chenery[b]	$150–$250	−0.44
Kuznets's cross-sectional sample[c]	$150–$250	−0.46
Kuznets's time series[d] ...	1850–95	−0.52
Japan[e]		
Ohkawa	1883/87–1908/12	−1.06
LTES	1883/87–1908/12	−1.31
Nakamura	1883/87–1908/12	−1.49

a. The computational formula, where $A(t)$ = primary output share at initial year (period) t, is as follows: rate of change (in percent) = $([A(t+n) - A(t)]/A(t)/n)$ 100, where n = number of years in interval. When considering cross-sectional data, n = 50, corresponding to the assumed fifty years required for a "typical" developing country to increase its per capita income level from $150 to $250.

b. Chenery and Taylor, "Development Patterns," p. 394. This represents the case of large-country patterns typical of most countries under consideration. Of the Southeast Asian countries, these regressions include Burma, Thailand, Korea, the Philippines, and Japan.

c. S. Kuznets, *Modern Economic Growth*, p. 402. The Kuznets data correspond to two income groupings, $100–$199 and $200–$349. The estimates for $150–$250 assume that Kuznets's figures apply to the mean of the income groupings and that between these means the share changes linearly.

d. The sample includes all countries in Kuznets's table for which data were available for the period before 1900. These countries are the United Kingdom, France, Germany, Denmark, Norway, Sweden, Italy, United States, and Australia. Japan is excluded and treated as a separate observation. The periods and initial and concluding levels represent an unweighted average of the nine countries included in the sample.

e. See chap. 5.

section of countries. The model produces shifts out of agricultural production at an average rate of −0.48 percent a period. This compares very closely with the cross-sectional studies of both Chenery-Taylor and Kuznets. For their samples over similar variations in per capita output, primary production shares decline at rates of —0.44 and —0.46 percent, respectively. Of equal significance, for a wide range of presently developed areas, Kuznets's investigation shows historical rates of —0.52 percent. In contrast, Japan attained rates of structural change between two and three times those found in both the "typical" developing case and the model forecasts. As compared with most countries, Japan appears to have halved the time needed to accomplish these changes. With the exception of Japan, the model appears to conform very closely to both the historical and the contemporary cross-sectional record.

While increasing industrialization in our model is partly explained by the increased share of labor resources allocated to nonagricultural activity, it also derives from an increasing divergence in average labor productivity between the two sectors in early development phases. It is frequently observed that average labor productivities are higher in nonagricultural activity in developing economies. These differentials also appear in our neoclassical model in which sectoral factor prices are equalized. It is also emphasized in the literature that these differentials may even increase with development. This is only partially the case in the simulation (table 4.1, col. 8), since growth of labor productivity in agriculture surpasses that in industry by the fourth decade of development. This reversal is explained by the combined effects of more rapid increases in capital intensity (mechanization) in agriculture *during the development phases*—the opposite is true in early growth phases —and of more rapid rates of technological progress in agriculture throughout. The simulation model therefore appears to exhibit an "agricultural revolution" with the generation of increasingly greater capital intensity in the agricultural sector in the late phases of growth. These issues are discussed at greater length in chapter 5.

4.2.2. Technical Change
The production functions of constant elasticity for agriculture and industry yield a constant bias in technical change in each

sector. Given our choice of parameter values, it follows that the biases in technical change for industry and agriculture are, respectively, $B_1 = 0.0070$ and $B_2 = -0.0023$. The overall rate of technical change is quite stable with $0.006 < R(t) < 0.007$ for all simulation periods (table 4.4); $R(t)$ seems reasonably consistent with the quantitative evidence from Asia. Although *abrupt* "agricultural revolutions" are not revealed in our model, rapid rates of technical improvement are. In fact, consistent with the Japanese experience reported in chapter 5, agriculture undergoes somewhat more rapid technological improvement than industry.[15] An attempt is made in chapter 6 to isolate the sensitivity of the model's growth patterns to assumptions regarding technical change in agriculture. It will be shown that a lower rate in agriculture would inhibit industrialization and diminish the terms of trade.

Before leaving the discussion of technical change, an experiment applying the much criticized "sources-of-growth" methodology[16] to our simulated model merits reporting. Criticism of the method has taken several forms: (1) the specification of a Cobb-Douglas production function, (2) the assumption of disembodied and neutral technical progress, and (3) the assumption of competitive factor markets. The following prob-

---

15. Y. Ho, *Agricultural Development of Taiwan, 1903–1960*; T. C. Liu, "The Tempo of Economic Development of the China Mainland, 1945–1965"; T. Watanabe, "Economic Aspects of Dualism in the Industrial Development of Japan"; idem, "Industrialization, Technological Progress, and Dual Structure"; and K. Ohkawa and H. Rosovsky, "The Role of Agriculture in Modern Japanese Economic Development." Recall from chapter 2, equation (2.4), that

$$R_i(t) = \lambda_K \alpha_i(t) + \lambda_L [1 - \alpha_i(t)].$$

If $(\lambda_L - \lambda_K) > 0$ and the output elasticity of capital is greater in industry than in agriculture, $R_2(t) > R_1(t)$.

16. E. F. Denison, *The Sources of Economic Growth in the United States*; R. M. Solow, "Technical Change and the Aggregate Production Function"; A. C. Harberger and M. Selowsky, "Key Factors in the Economic Growth of Chile: An Analysis of the Sources of Past Growth and of Prospects for 1965–1970"; and J. G. Williamson, "Philippine Postwar Economic Progress."

TABLE 4.4 Average annual growth rate in technical change and sources of growth calculations compared

Decade	$R(t)$ (1)	$R_1(t)$ (2)	$R_2(t)$ (3)	Economy-wide sources of growth			Industry sources of growth		
				$\alpha(t)\dfrac{\dot{K}(t)}{K(t)}$ (4)	$[1-\alpha(t)]\dfrac{\dot{L}(t)}{L(t)}$ (5)	Residual $(\hat{R}(t))$ (6)	$\alpha_1(t)\dfrac{\dot{K}_1(t)}{K_1(t)}$ (7)	$[1-\alpha_1(t)]\dfrac{\dot{L}_1(t)}{L_1(t)}$ (8)	Residual $(\hat{R}_1(t))$ (9)
1–10........	0.0066	0.0055	0.0075	0.013	0.014	0.0076	0.021	0.011	0.0069
11–20........	.0066	.0054	.0076	.016	.014	.0066	.024	.013	.0057
21–30........	.0065	.0054	.0076	.017	.014	.0070	.026	.013	.0053
31–40........	.0064	.0054	.0076	.020	.013	.0060	.028	.013	.0040
41–50........	.0064	.0054	.0076	.021	.013	0.0055	.029	.014	0.0020
Average (1–50)........	0.0065	0.0054	0.0076	.....	.....	.....	.....	.....	.....

NOTE: Cols. 6 and 9 are calculated under the assumption of Cobb-Douglas production functions. Thus, $\hat{R}(t) = \dot{G}(t)/G(t) - [1 - \alpha(t)]\,\dot{L}(t)/L(t) - \alpha(t)\,\dot{K}(t)/K(t)$. Output growth rates are taken from table 4.1. Factor shares are decade midpoint observations produced by the simulation model. Factor stock growth rates, also taken directly from the model's simulated figures, are average annual growth rates per decade.

lem is posed to illustrate the implications of this methodology. Given our model structure and its simulated growth experience, what would the description of the economy's rate of technical progress be had it been *inferred* from the simulated historical data and the sources-of-growth methodology? In our model, competitive conditions are satisfied by assumption. Moreover, we know precisely the "true" rate of technical change. Given the simulated data on factor shares, physical input series, and deflated output growth, and applying the sources-of-growth methodology, we can derive the estimated residual, $R(t)$. Assuming neutral and disembodied technical progress and unitary elasticity of substitution, it follows that

$$R(t) = \frac{\dot{G}(t)}{G(t)} - [1 - \alpha(t)]\frac{\dot{L}(t)}{L(t)} - \alpha(t)\frac{\dot{K}(t)}{K(t)}.$$

A comparison of the estimated $R(t)$ and its "true" value reveals striking discrepancies (table 4.4). There is a sharp decline in $R(t)$ over time, while the true $R(t)$ is constant! In some cases the discepancies are very large indeed: for example, $R_1(t)$ is less than one-half of $R_1(t)$ by the fifth decade of development. In chapters 5 and 6 the impact of technical progress is analyzed in much greater detail, and our results shed further doubt on the relevance of the sources-of-growth literature.

4.2.3. Sectoral Capital-Labor Ratios and Factor Prices

Even though the simulated economy is characterized by a high rate of population growth, over a period of five decades the economy-wide unaugmented capital-labor ratio increases by almost 50 percent. Because of the negative effects of technical change, however, the ratio of efficiency capital to efficiency labor declines during the first decade and then increases steadily as the effects of rising rates of capital accumulation dominate. The behavior of the efficiency wage-rental ratio reflects the lower rate of capital accumulation (and high population growth) in early growth phases, coupled with high rates of labor aug-

mentation compared with capital.[17] Since the rate of growth
of $y(t)$ exceeds that of $x(t)$—that is, $\lambda_L > \lambda_K$—technical
change tends to lower the wage-rental ratio for a given capital-
labor ratio. Low rates of capital accumulation are thus consistent with a declining wage-rental ratio, while more rapid rates
in later years reverse this trend. (see figs. 4.1 and 4.2).

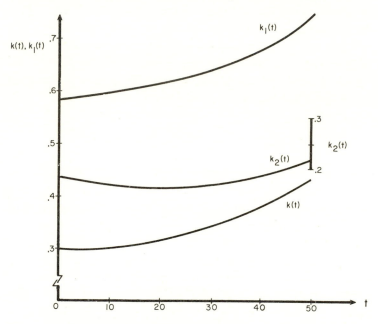

Fig. 4.1. Augmented Capital-Labor Ratios

The secular behavior of the unaugmented capital-labor ratio
is unusually interesting (table 4.5). The rate of growth of the
manufacturing capital-labor ratio is positive throughout. In
spite of the decline in the efficiency wage-rental ratio in early
growth phases, the substitution of capital for labor continues
unabated in manufacturing as labor-saving technical change
takes place. This result is consistent with, and possibly explains,

17. From our CES production functions, it follows that $\omega_i(t) =$
$k_i(t)^{1/\sigma_i}$ and therefore,

$$\frac{\omega(t)}{\omega(t)} = \frac{1}{\sigma_i} \frac{\dot{k}_i(t)}{k_i(t)} = \frac{1}{\sigma_i} \left\{ \lambda_K - \lambda_L + \frac{\dot{k}_i(t)}{k_i(t)} \right\} .$$

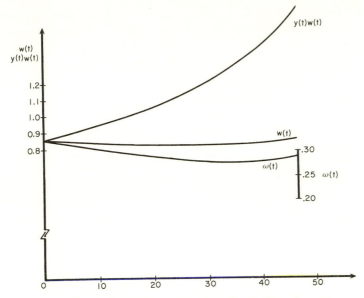

Fig. 4.2. Actual Wage Paid, $y(t)w(t)$, Real Wages, $w(t)$, and Efficiency Wage-Rental Ratio, $\omega(t)$

Asian experience with persistent increases in industrial capital intensity in the face of apparently low and stable per unit labor costs (and even *declining* efficiency wage-rental ratios), a trend that has been of great concern to Asian economists.[18] Moreover, as the rate of capital accumulation accelerates, so the rate of growth in the manufacturing capital-labor accelerates. The fourth and fifth decades exhibit much higher rates of capital-labor substitution in industry as the efficiency wage-rental ratio reverses and begins to rise.

Production in industry is relatively capital intensive over the entire simulation period. This is consistent with the arguments advanced earlier about relative factor intensities. Although there is little evidence of convergence in sectoral capital-labor

18. W. Baer and M. Hervé, "Employment and Industrialization in Developing Countries"; M. P. Todaro, "A Model of Labor Migration and Urban Unemployment in Less Developed Countries"; and J. G. Williamson, "Capital Accumulation, Labor Saving, and Labor Absorption Once More."

TABLE 4.5 Average annual growth rates and annual values of efficiency capital-labor ratios

	Annual growth rates		
	$k(t)$ (1)	$k_1(t)$ (2)	$k_2(t)$ (3)
Decade			
1–10.........	(neg.)	0.0021	(neg.)
11–20.........	0.0043	.0040	(neg.)
21–30.........	.0084	.0058	0.0036
31–40.........	.0107	.0074	.0086
41–50.........	.0143	.0089	.0128
Average			
(1–50)........	0.0076	0.0057	0.0031
	Value		
	(4)	(5)	(6)
Year			
1...........	0.302	0.571	0.186
10..........	.300	.582	.174
20..........	.312	.605	.170
30..........	.339	.641	.176
40..........	.381	.690	.191
50..........	0.438	0.754	0.217

ratios, the growth rate of the capital-labor ratio of agriculture surpasses that of industry by the fourth decade of development. Thus, rapid rates of capital deepening in agriculture are predicted by the simulation model, but only at a late stage in the development process.

The experience of agriculture with capital intensity is quite different from that of industry. The early phase of industrialization and growth produces a *reduction* in the capital-labor ratio. This result is consistent with the importance that those concerned with "unemployment" in the less developed economies place on agriculture as a potential labor-absorbing sector. With the rapid rates of labor-using technical change in agriculture—the introduction of new seed varieties, intensive soil preparation, and the use of pesticides—increases in labor intensity play a major role in absorbing increments of the labor force in early growth phases when capital accumulation is less rapid (and thus, when the efficiency wage-rental ratio is declining). This phase of agricultural development is relatively brief, but it may be critical.

In the above discussion attention has been focused on real factor prices as they are perceived by the decision-making units in the economy as distinct from the behavior of workers' "living standards" during the development process. Partly because this simple conceptual distinction is rarely made in the empirical literature, the extensive debate over the behavior of real wages in development has continued.[19] In view of the emphasis real wage behavior has received in the literature in an attempt to discriminate between alternative models of factor pricing, a discussion of figure 4.2 is appropriate. Unfortunately, much of the confusion surrounding "tests" of the labor-surplus model is attributable to the naïve observation that real wages *have* remained constant over long historical time periods. Yet the periods studied may be periods in which the capital-labor ratio is also constant! In the simulated economy, however, the capital-labor ratio initially declines although positive growth rates for GNP per capita are obtained. Note the behavior of "real wages" for this growing low-income economy. Real *efficiency* wages, $w(t)$, decline consistently over three to four decades of impressive economic growth. Yet the real wage bill per laborer, $y(t)w(t)$, rises systematically throughout. In summary, the neoclassical model is able to generate stable or falling efficiency real wages for even a growing economy. These trends are therefore not exclusive to the labor-surplus model, nor do they imply that workers' living standards are constant. We return to this issue in chapter 5 when the Japanese historical record is examined.

19. The economic history literature abounds with examples. For discussions of American experience, see P. A. David, "The Growth of Real Product in the United States before 1840: New Evidence, Controlled Conjectures"; and S. Lebergott, *Manpower in Economic Growth: The American Record since 1800.* For English experience during the Industrial Revolution, see E. Hobsbawm, "The Standard of Living during the Industrial Revolution: A Discussion"; R. M. Hartwell, "The Standard of Living"; and J. E. Williams, "The British Standard of Living, 1750–1850."

4.2.4. Factor Shares

Before we consider the behavior of factor shares in the simulation model, we shall review briefly the available evidence. Quantitative historical data on factor shares is notoriously poor, which perhaps explains the persistence of the Great Ratio Debate over their behavior. This makes an examination of our model's predictions all the more difficult, especially since the model generates phases of factor share movements.

A relevant historical case study is Japan from the Meiji Restoration. But as we shall see in chapter 5, the work of Ohkawa on national income distribution in Japan suggests only tentative insights into the behavior of factor shares after 1920.[20] The problem is made especially complex because of the requirement that the data be reported by sector. The research by Fei and Ranis, for example, relates only to the industrial sector.[21] Their work suggests that the Japanese industrial-urban sector passed through two stages of changes in factor shares from the 1880s to the 1930s. The word "stages" is used advisedly, since they rely on a changing specification of wage determination to explain a reversal in movements of factor shares. Fei and Ranis, using what we believe are questionable capital stock estimates (see chap. 5), argue that Japanese industry experienced a declining labor share up to World War I and a rise thereafter. Ohkawa's evidence suggests that the economy-wide wage share was relatively stable, although it declined during the 1920s and 1930s. However, lack of information on the agricultural sector makes generalization difficult.

The only developing agricultural economy for which reliable data are available is nineteenth-century United States. Haley's and Budd's studies reveal that over the period 1850–1910, when the United States was passing through her intermediate growth phase, the following patterns are exhibited: (1) Labor's share declined sharply in agriculture up to 1910. (2) Labor's

20. K. Ohkawa, "Changes in National Income Distribution by Factor Share in Japan."
21. J. C. Fei and G. Ranis, *Development of the Labor Surplus Economy: Theory and Policy.*

share rose modestly in the nonagricultural sector. (3) Labor's share *declined* for the economy as a whole as American industrialization took place.[22] These patterns are consistent with Japanese experience *after* World War I.

The one-sector growth literature makes singularly uninteresting predictions regarding factor shares. In most cases the share of property income is constant. Since aggregate savings is determined only by income distribution, stability in the savings ratio is assured.[23] However, Kaldor has developed a model which generates two stages of capitalistic growth.[24] In the first stage, with the economy close to subsistence, the profit share is low but rises as growth takes place. In the second stage the profit share stabilizes.

Marx has predicted a rising capitalist share and in a two-sector framework; Lewis, Fei, Ranis, and Jorgenson make similar forecasts. The labor-surplus models generate a rising profit share in manufacturing and then stability after the turning point when neoclassical conditions are satisfied. Jorgenson's framework predicts an improvement in the overall share of property income even in the neoclassical case, since the larger share in manufacturing produces an overall increase as industrialization takes place.[25] In the long run, however, balanced growth ensures stability in labor's share in the Jorgenson model.

The simulation results are broadly consistent with the historical evidence of phases in capitalist development. A declining overall labor share is evident throughout a century of historical experience, although most of this decline takes place in the first half-century. Labor's share, as seen in figure 4.3, declines from an initial value of 52 percent to 48 percent in fifty periods,

22. B. F. Haley, "Changes in the Distribution of Income in the United States"; E. C. Budd, "Factor Shares, 1850–1910."
23. F. H. Hahn and R. C. O. Mathews, "The Theory of Economic Growth: A Survey."
24. N. Kaldor, "A Model of Economic Growth"; idem, "Capital Accumulation and Economic Growth," pp. 177–222.
25. D. W. Jorgenson, "The Development of a Dual Economy"; and "Surplus Agricultural Labor and the Development of a Dual Economy."

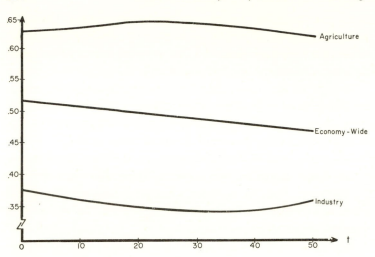

Fig. 4.3. Labor's Share

and to 46 percent by $t = 100$. Perhaps of greater interest is the behavior of factor shares *within* sectors. The first three decades of early growth from low levels of income and urbanization are decades of declining labor share in manufacturing. This corresponds to the predictions of Lewis, Fei, Ranis, Jorgenson, and Kaldor, but it is the dominance of labor saving technical change, rather than a special wage-fixing mechanism, that explains this behavior. In contrast to most forecasts, but consistent with the limited evidence from economic history, labor's share in industry then reverses its trend and rises after this early development phase. The turning point appears in $t = 32$, after which labor's share improves. Beyond this point increasingly rapid rates of capital accumulation dominate, and labor's share increases (decreases) in manufacturing (agriculture), since the elasticity of substitution is less (greater) than one. To summarize, our model predicts results which appear consistent with the historical record: (1) distinctive phases of factor share growth; (2) a rising, then falling capital share in the urban-industrial sector; and (3) relative stability in overall factor shares in the later phase of development. The significant feature of this model, in contrast to the labor-surplus formulation and Kaldor's framework, is that these predictions are generated under assumptions of parameter stability. Many models rely on a changing specification of wage determination to yield this result, whereas our result derives instead from the endogenously determined sectoral divergence in output growth.

4.2.5. Terms of Trade

The terms of trade in the simulation moves in favor of industry during the early periods, but after the third decade of development the relative price of urban goods declines. Consistent with the result derived in our static analysis, the terms of trade improves in the early growth period because the stock of efficiency labor is growing more rapidly than that of efficiency capital in the industrial sector. Although the industrial capital-labor ratio increases throughout, it is only after the third decade that the rate of accumulation of the physical stock of capital increases enough to offset the more rapid rate of labor-aug-

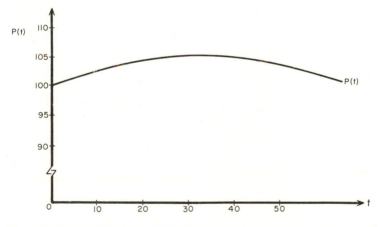

Fig. 4.4. Index of Terms of Trade

menting technical change. Jorgenson's model makes the opposite prediction. Zarembka has shown that the terms of trade deteriorates (for industry) in Jorgenson's model, since productivity increases are more rapid in industry than in agriculture.[26] As in our model, however, in industry the terms of trade deteriorates all the more rapidly as the accumulation of capital accelerates.

In any case, the net effect in our economy is only a mild upward trend in industrial goods prices until the end of the third decade when the overall capital-labor ratio begins to rise and the terms of trade undergoes a mild secular decline. The stability of the terms of trade in the simulation is notable. A large share of the burden of market adjustment in response to a changing demand composition and differential rates of technical change is placed upon factor mobility rather than upon commodity price variation and factor substitution possibilities.[27]

4.2.6. The Savings Rate, Capital Accumulation, and Capital-Output Ratios

We have assumed a constant savings rate in the neighborhood of 30 percent for all recipients of property income; labor income is entirely consumed. Thus the overall savings rate, which is uniquely determined by the economy-wide factor shares, rises only slightly (as does the capital share) over the fifty years from an initial value of 15.0 percent to 16.2 percent (table 4.6).

TABLE 4.6 Share of savings in aggregate output

Year	Net savings (1)	Depreciation allowance (2)	Gross savings (3)
1.............	0.063	0.087	0.150
10.............	.069	.082	.151
20.............	.075	.079	.154
30.............	.080	.077	.157
40.............	.084	.076	.160
50.............	.087	.075	.162
Average.....	0.076	0.080	0.156

26. P. Zarembka, "Introduction and a Basic Dual Economy Model."

27. With the introduction of greater supply rigidities in chapter 7, greater secular variability in the terms of trade seems likely. In any case, demand conditions will be shown to play a greater role.

There are no abrupt increases in the gross savings rate, and the model may be weaker for it. Nevertheless, it is clear that no *dramatic upward shift in the savings function is required to generate a "take-off" in our model.* Rapid and accelerating urbanization, industrialization, and per capita income growth is forthcoming without the Rostovian drama in savings behavior and without an appeal to W. A. Lewis's famous dictum that the central problem in development theory is to explain an increase in net domestic savings from 5 to 12 percent of national product.[28]

However, stability in the savings rate does not imply stability in capital stock growth. Depreciation requirements decrease as a share in gross saving over time (table 4.6), and given the overall savings rate, the rate of capital accumulation is most critically influenced by the capital-output ratio (table 4.7). To see the analytical basis for this conclusion, recall the simulation model's dynamic equation for the growth of the efficiency capital-labor ratio.

$$\frac{\dot{k}(t)}{k(t)} = sx(t)f'_1[k_1(t)] + (n_2 - n_1)u(t) - (\delta + n_2 + \lambda_L - \lambda_K).$$

The technical change parameters, the depreciation rate, the savings parameter, and the rates of population growth are all

TABLE 4.7 Trends in capital-output ratios

Year	Industry (K_1/Q_1) (1)	Agriculture (PK_2/Q_2) (2)	Aggregate (PK/G) (3)	Ratio (Col. 1/Col. 2) (4)
1.........	2.455	1.402	1.853	1.751
10.........	2.352	1.286	1.765	1.829
20.........	2.259	1.198	1.704	1.886
30.........	2.183	1.144	1.671	1.908
40.........	2.122	1.117	1.657	1.900
50.........	2.072	1.111	1.656	1.865
Average...	2.241	1.210	1.718	1.852

28. W. A. Lewis, "Development With Unlimited Supplies of Labour."

constant, although rising urbanization slightly lowers the overall rate of population growth (since $n_1 < n_2$). Thus, the values
of $x(t)$ and $f'_1[k_1(t)]$ become critical in determing the rate of
accumulation. Apparently the impact is strongly positive in our
model, since the rate of accumulation rises from 2.4 percent a
year to 4.1 percent a year after five decades. The behavior of the
growth rates of sectoral capital stock is equally interesting. The
rate of growth in industry exceeds that in agriculture in *all*
decades, but the differential diminishes as the economy approaches balanced growth.

4.2.7. Urbanization, Labor Absorption, and Labor Migration
The rate of labor redistribution in the dual economy has been
an issue of central interest in the development literature. In
chapter 3 it was shown that labor redistribution to industry is
guaranteed by a rising efficiency capital-labor ratio.[29] But we
were able to say much more than this. An increase in the
capital-labor ratio leads to a reduction in the sectoral divergence in capital intensities, since agriculture has higher substitution elasticities than industry. As the economy-wide capital
intensity increases, the economy approaches a factor reversal
point. In section 4.2.3 it was shown that factor reversal was
absent in a century of growth experience in our economy.
Nevertheless, the tendency was evident. Clearly, as the differentials in sectoral capital intensity diminish, the impact of
capital-labor growth on urbanization also diminishes. In short,
the numerical analysis confirms our prediction that early
acceleration in the rate of capital formation should produce an
acceleration in the rate of urbanization as well. At higher levels
of per capita GNP, the rate of urbanization declines as the
rate of capital-labor growth diminishes; moreover, the pace

29. The rate of urbanization was shown (eq. [3.22]) to be
given by

$$\frac{\dot{u}(t)}{u(t)} = \frac{k(t)}{u(t)} \frac{\partial u(t)}{\partial k(t)} \frac{\dot{k}(t)}{k(t)} .$$

But $\partial u(t)/\partial k(t)$ is positive when $k_1(t) - k_2(t) > 0$.

diminishes with the reduction in sectoral capital-labor differentials. Apparently the increasing rate of industrial capital-labor growth offsets the positive influence of urbanization at later stages of growth. Thus, *the dualistic economy produces phases of development reminiscent of Rostovian stages, but once again it does not rely on parameter shifts or changes in model structure to yield such historically observed behavior.* The rate of urbanization accelerates from low levels to very high levels by the third decade of simulation, after which it stabilizes. The level of urbanization rises from 0.30 to 0.41 over the five decades. Less than half of that increase occurs in the first three decades. More than half of the increase in the level of industrialization occurs in the same period, however, because the positive rate of increase is somewhat higher for industrialization than for urbanization.

The rate of urbanization in the dual economy is far less dramatic than the rate of industrialization in early growth phases, but the rate of urbanization accelerates more noticeably in later growth phases (figs. 4.5 and 4.6). Because of the greater substitution possibilities in agriculture, labor tends to

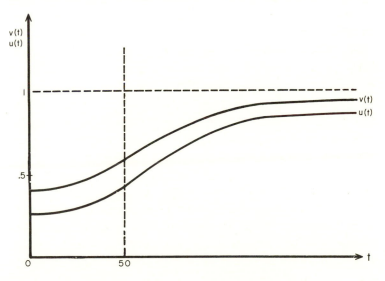

Fig. 4.5. Levels of Urbanization and Industrialization

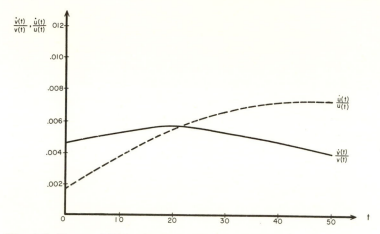

Fig. 4.6. Rates of Urbanization and Industrialization

be retained in agriculture in early phases of development but to be repelled in later stages. The reason for this behavior is that the early growth stages are periods of declining efficiency wage-rental ratios; only in the fourth decade does this trend reverse itself. The impact of industrialization on urbanization is restrained still further by the character of technical change: it is assumed to be labor saving in industry and labor using in agriculture.

The rate of decline in agriculture's share of the labor force tends to vary positively with the level of per capita income.[30] Because of the nonlinear trend in the level of "urbanization," the predicted rate is presented in table 4.8 for both the first fifty periods (−0.32 percent per period) and the subsequent half-century of per capita output expansion (−0.56 percent). Kuznets's cross-sectional study reveals a similar pattern, where the rate of decline increases from −0.27 to −0.40 percent over comparable levels and ranges of development. These trends must be taken into account in analyzing Kuznets's time series estimates, where, at relatively high levels of per capita income, the rate advances to approximately −0.68 percent a year. We infer that rates of decline exceeding approximately

30. S. Kuznets, *Modern Economic Growth*, pp. 106–7.

TABLE 4.8 Rates of structural change in the primary labor force share

Country sample	Period or income range	Level (%)		Percentage rate of decline per year (period)[a]
		Initial	Concluding	
Simulation	1–50 ($150–$250)	70.1	58.8	−0.32
	51–100 ($250–$500)[b]	58.7	42.2	−0.56
Kuznets's cross-section[c]	$150–$250	55.7	48.1	−0.27
	$250–$500	48.1	36.5	−0.40
Kuznets's time series[d]	1860–97	44.8	33.5	−0.68
Japan[e]	1872–1925	85.0	52.0	−0.73

a. For the computational formula, see table 4.3.

b. From period 51 to period 100, GNP per capita in the simulation model increased by 96 percent, which corresponds to the income range of $250–$500 in Kuznets's cross-sectional sample.

c. Kuznets, *Six Lectures on Economic Growth*, p. 45. For a discussion of the computational procedure, see n. c, table 4.3.

d. Kuznets, *Modern Economic Growth*, pp. 106–8. The eight countries included in Kuznets's sample are the United Kingdom, France, Belgium, Switzerland, Norway, Sweden, Italy, and the United States.

e. The individual rates of decline for the periods 1880–90, 1890–1900, and 1900–10 are −0.75, −0.81, and −0.99 percent, respectively (Ohkawa et al., *Growth Rate of the Japanese Economy*, p. 145).

—0.50 percent a year correspond to relatively advanced levels of development. Thus, the model's forecasts correspond quite closely both to the historical record and to changes within comparable ranges of per capita output expansion. But again, in terms of *rates* of change, Japan must be considered an outlier compared with the empirical record of most countries for which data are available. From 1872 to 1925, the rate of decline in agricultural employment in Japan is not only about twice that of the model, Kuznets's cross-sectional study, and Italy,[31] but it even exceeds that of the relatively more developed areas represented in Kuznets's grouping of countries by time series.

The implications for the rate of labor migration and the rate of labor absorption in industry are interesting and conform to the present concern over these issues in the low-income countries (table 4.9). Because of rapid labor-saving technical

TABLE 4.9 Trends in employment and migration

Year	Employment index[a]			Rate of migration to industry[b]	Labor absorption rate[c]
	Agriculture	Industry	Total		
0....	69.992	30.008	100.000	0.0037	0.0285
10....	87.894	39.168	127.060	.0050	.0312
20....	111.660	53.947	165.600	.0064	.0334
30....	140.010	75.389	215.400	.0077	.0344
40....	173.450	105.990	279.440	.0089	.0347
50....	212.490	148.940	361.430	0.0100	0.0344

a. The index sets $L(0) = 100.0$.
b. The rate of migration is defined as the ratio of the net number of laborers moving into industry to the total agricultural labor force.
c. The rate of growth of industrial employment.

change and initial low rates of capital accumulation in industry, the rate of labor absorption is singularly unimpressive. Al-

31. Italy is the only country in Kuznets's sample which he denotes as an "economically less developed area." For Italy the rate of decline in the agricultural labor force share is −0.29 percent a year.

though the growth of capital stock in the initial decades approaches 5 percent, the rate of labor absorption is only about 3 percent, barely above the overall rate of population growth (2.7 percent). These results appear to justify concern with "low" rates of labor absorption and urban "unemployment" problems. Yet "disappointing" rates of labor absorption in industry appear to be an inevitable result of early development and hardly seem to be uniquely related to contemporary policy in less developed economies. Note, however, that the rate of labor absorption increases over time. By the end of the fourth decade the rate approaches 3.5 percent, although this trend reverses after the retardation in the growth of the industrial capital stock.

Not surprisingly, the *rate* of labor migration off the farm increases continuously as industrialization proceeds. We have seen how our growing economy generates increasingly rapid rates of urbanization and labor absorption in industry over time. Clearly the rate of in-migration from agriculture must increase as well to satisfy labor demands. In the simulation the *rate* of labor migration triples over the first half-century of growth. By the end of the fifth decade, 1 percent of the rural labor force migrates annually. This rate should continue to increase as the relative stock of potential migrants (the agricultural labor force) diminishes.

In summary, we judge the model to have passed the minimum test. It appears to replicate the quantitative historical record on aggregate growth and structural change quite effectively. It remains now to examine its ability to predict the behavior of movements of factor prices and commodity prices, average labor productivity by sector, income distribution, aggregate savings behavior, and other key variables critical to our understanding of the development process. This is the task of chapter 5.

5

Dualism in Historical Perspective: Japan and Modern Economic Growth

5.1. INTRODUCTION

Having found in chapter 4 that our model reproduces the most aggregative features of growth and structural change, we now turn to a more detailed excursion into the economic history of Japan. Following the transition subsequent to the Meiji Restoration, Japanese experience provides an excellent case study of the development process for at least three reasons. First, Japan experienced sustained economic growth, rising from low levels per capita income to a modern economy in all key attributes. From this point of view it is a relevant case to compare with our theory.[1] Second, thanks to the pioneering efforts of Ohkawa, Rosovsky, Nakamura, Taeuber, and others, quantitative data documenting Japan's development process are now available.[2] Finally, Japan has often been selected as a prototype of the labor-surplus theory of development.[3] Confronting the model with the evidence used to support the labor-surplus theory will provide a useful basis for comparing our framework with others.

1. Recall that our model is not designed to analyze low-level equilibrium traps or factors initiating modern economic growth. Our economy is expanding; the analytical focus is on the relationships of key variables contributing to and interacting in this process.
2. K. Ohkawa et al., *The Growth Rate of the Japanese Economy since 1878*; H. Rosovsky, *Capital Formation in Japan, 1868–1940*; J. I. Nakamura, *Agricultural Production and the Economic Development of Japan, 1873–1922*; and I. Taeuber, *The Population of Japan*.
3. In particular, consult D. W. Jorgenson, "Testing Alternative Theories of the Development of a Dual Economy."

130

On the other hand, Japanese history poses several limitations for model testing. Japan was either in a state of war preparation or actually engaged in conflict during the period under study.[4] Moreover, after a long period of isolation, its foreign trade sector played an increasing role in development.[5] Furthermore, Japanese growth was characterized by moderate price inflation and monetary expansion.[6] Finally, natural disasters, major deflations, and exogenous shocks (for example, World War I) all played a role in shaping Japanese growth. These features are not captured by our model, and there is no way of factoring them out of Japanese history. In view of these difficulties the analysis can only indicate the relationships between the broad outlines of historical experience and the predictions of the modeled economy. One could abstract from these "unique" features specific to Japan by considering a wide range of additional countries, but this alternative is beyond the scope of the present inquiry, and perhaps even impossible with the data constraints.

In this chapter we proceed by comparing the predictions of the economy simulated in chapter 4 with the Japanese historical record. While some of the initial conditions and parameter values are somewhat different in the Japanese case, we have elected not to resimulate the model to take account of these differences. Japanese experience will thus be compared with a "representative" developing economy as it has been modeled. Fine tuning the parameter estimates and initial conditions would represent pseudoprecision, especially in the light of the data limitations previously considered.

Leontief has offered a somewhat intriguing alternative justification for utilizing contemporary evidence in confronting theories and hypotheses with the historical record.

4. H. T. Oshima, "The Meiji Fiscal Policy and Agricultural Progress."
5. B. Baba and M. Tatemoto, "Foreign Trade and Economic Growth in Japan: 1858–1937"; W. W. Lockwood, ed., *The Economic Development of Japan*, chaps. 6, 7.
6. K. Ohkawa, M. Shinohara, and M. Umemura, *Estimates of Long Term Economic Statistics of Japan since 1868*, vol. 8.

> In following the paths of historical development . . . the analyst finds himself . . . engaged in the rather thankless task of trying to derive known from unknown or, at least, better-known from less well-known facts. Would it not be much more efficient to reverse this procedure? By establishing the base of his operations, that is, the principal store of primary factual information in the present or a very recent past, and then moving on backward with the help of theoretical weapons step by step toward the more and more distant past, the analytical historian could make most effective use of the limited amount of direct factual information to which he usually has access.[7]

Thus, even though our specific objective in this chapter is to compare a contemporary modeled economy with the historical record, the decision to maintain current parameters and initial conditions in this test may also be interpreted as an exercise in writing economic history *backward.* A criticism of this interpretation might be that parameters may have changed through time. But if this is true, how can the lessons of economic history be relevant to contemporary problems? If the interest of the economic historian is to generalize from the past, clearly the research process may, indeed must, be considered in reverse. This can be accomplished by estimating parameters from *contemporary* Southeast Asia and then examining the ability of the numerical model to replicate Meiji Japanese economic history. If this attempt is successful, Japanese economic history may be utilized with greater confidence as a "relevant" application to contemporary Asian development problems.

Section 5.2 considers the quality of the data used in the analysis. Section 5.3 examines the similarity between the model predictions in three variables—output growth per capita, urbanization, and industrial composition—and Japan experience. We also review the results of chapter 4, where the primary objective was to ascertain the extent to which the simulation model was typical of the development process. Our interest now is also to evaluate the extent to which Japanese experience is typical of the development process. Given these results, section

7. W. W. Leontief, *Essays in Economics: Theories and Theorizing,* p. 16.

5.3 then considers the relationship between a *period* in the simulation framework and a *year* of Japanese economic growth. A comparison of the initial conditions of the model and Japan is examined in section 5.4. This provides the criteria for selecting beginning and terminal dates for examining Japanese economic history. Section 5.5 compares the model's forecasts and the Japanese historical record in detail. We conclude in section 5.6 with observations on the relative correspondences of our model and the Fei-Ranis framework to the Japanese experience with growth and development.

5.2. THE CONTROVERSY OVER FACT: A JAPANESE MIRACLE?
5.2.1. Competing Theories and the "Japanese Model"
The statistics on early historical experience with industrialization and growth are fragmentary and of doubtful quality. This generalization holds for many contemporary developing nations, for American growth in the antebellum period, for British industrialization experience in the late eighteenth century, and for Meiji Japan as well. Indeed, the attempts to reconstruct modern Japanese economic history have been shrouded in an unusually intense data controversy. This debate has been concerned even with such fundamental facets of Japanese development as the role of agriculture in modern economic growth. The history of Western economies suggests that an agricultural revolution and a subsequent rise in agricultural productivity may often be viewed as prerequisites for modern economic growth and industrialization.[8] This has been termed the "prerequisite" hypothesis. With the appearance of quantitative Japanese research by such scholars as Ohkawa and Rosovsky, the prerequisites thesis has been vigorously challenged. Using official agricultural statistics, Johnston, Ohkawa, Rosovsky, and others have argued that the Japanese experience was unique. Not only did the Japanese record in the Meiji period suggest "miraculous" growth performance, but the rapid expansion of

8. Much of the following paragraph is taken from the excellent summary in Y. Hayami and S. Yamada, "Agricultural Productivity at the Beginning of Industrialization," pp. 105–6.

agricultural productivity from levels comparable to those of
contemporary monsoon Asia took place simultaneously with
industrialization. This thesis diminishes the importance of agricultural revolutions as a prerequisite to modern economic
growth and stresses instead the *concurrent* growth of agriculture and industry. An index of the widespread acceptance of
the Johnston-Ohkawa-Rosovsky characterization of Meiji economic history is the frequent reference to the "Japanese model"
of development.

Nakamura and Oshima have sharply questioned the uniqueness of the Japanese growth experience, in relation to both the
"miraculous" overall rates of progress and the Johnston-
Ohkawa-Rosovsky interpretation of agriculture's role in Asian
development.[9] Nakamura has argued that the Ohkawa estimates

9. J. I. Nakamura, "Growth of Japanese Agriculture, 1875–
1970"; idem, *Agricultural Production*; H. T. Oshima, "Survey of
Various Long-term Estimates of Japanese National Income"; idem,
Review of *The Growth Rate of the Japanese Economy since 1878*
by Kazushi Ohkawa and Associates; idem, "Meiji Fiscal Policy."
A comprehensive review of the unresolved issues relating to Japanese economic history resulting from the controversy over the
growth rate of agricultural output is compiled by R. P. Sinha,
("Unresolved Issues in Japan's Early Economic Development").
From an extensive examination of the qualitative evidence, together
with a study of population caloric requirements and foreign trade
data, Sinha concludes, "Whether or not Nakamura's estimates of
a 1 percent rate of growth is nearer the truth is highly conjectural,
but if the circumstantial evidence is assigned some weight, it would
seem that his margin of error is not excessive" (p. 119). An important analytic result of the Ohkawa estimates is that agriculture
provided sufficient food and savings out of "surplus" production
to permit rapid expansion in the secondary-tertiary sector. In an
examination of food imports and tax receipts, Sinha concludes that
"however fast the sector grew, it did not provide 'sufficient' food to
feed the growing population in the secondary and tertiary sectors,
nor did it meet the growing financial needs (including foreign exchange) of the emerging nation" (p. 112). Central to explaining
the rapid expansion in agricultural output implied by the Ohkawa
estimates is a hypothesized high rate of agricultural productivity
increase, largely resulting from an adoption of new techniques and
the increased utilization of improved fertilizer and seeds. Sinha's
review of the evidence suggests that the rate of acceptance of new

greatly understate the level of agricultural production beginning in the period 1878–82; moreover, this understatement, resulting from biases in official government statistics due to tax evasion, diminishes over time.[10] The result is a significant over-

---

ideas was not as fast as believed (p. 116). It took twenty years after the discovery of a high-yield rice variety in 1887 for it to be commonly accepted; salt-water sorting of paddy seed, discovered in 1882, was not widely used by the end of the century; governments passed laws to force acceptance of new procedures. Regarding fertilizer usage, Sinha notes that its financing by relatively poor farmers, who assumed all the risks, likely acted as a major constraint to large-scale adoption (p. 117). (This theme has also been developed by H. T. Oshima in "A Strategy for Asian Development," p. 298.) Furthermore, in appraising the usual evidence cited to support wide-scale fertilizer usage, Sinha argues, "It is not clear to what extent the magnitude of the increase suggested by the Shishido fertilizer-input index . . . represents an overall increase in fertilizer use rather than just a shift from domestically produced to commercially produced fertilizer" (p. 118). He concludes that "subsequent institutional reforms were not adequate to achieve a rapid increase in agricultural productivity, while the situation regarding the availability of agricultural inputs—similarly a major constraint on improvements—did not materially improve until towards the end of the century" (p. 119).

10. The land tax was computed on the basis of the value of gross agricultural output minus taxes and intermediate inputs of seeds and fertilizers. Land tax evasions, taking the form of concealment, misclassification, and undermeasurement of arable land, together with underestimates of yields, were common. The most important factor in Nakamura's revisions is his bench-mark estimates of rice yield for 1878–82 of 1.6 *koku* per *tan*. As he underscores, the precise figure of 1.6 is not well supported (J. I. Nakamura, "The Nakamura vs. the LTES Estimates of the Growth Rate of Agricultural Production," p. 359). Indeed, he clearly notes that "much of the revision undertaken is based on assumptions guided by judgments built on historical evidence and understanding of agricultural techniques and practices" (idem, "Growth of Japanese Agriculture," p. 252). Key evidence takes several forms. (1) Average rice yields recorded in official documents for the Bunroku period, 300 years before the Restoration, were 1.3 *koku* per *tan*; Ohkawa's estimates are 1.166, yet Thomas C. Smith (*The Agrarian Origins of Modern Japan*, chap. 7, p. 211) and others (E. S. Crawcour, "The Tokagawa Heritage") have documented an increase in agricultural productivity during the period. (H. Rosovsky, in "Rumbles in the Ricefields: Professor Nakamura vs. the Official Statistics,"

statement in the growth rate of Japanese agriculture. Nakamura's estimates show agricultural output expanding at an
annual rate of approximately 1 percent from the years 1878–82
to the years 1913–17; a comparable figure compiled from the
Ohkawa series is 2.4 percent.[11] Even though Nakamura has
not assembled new estimates for secondary and tertiary production, he asserts that the growth rate in these sectors is also
overstated because of the widespread monetization of produc-

---

p. 352, questions the veracity of economy-wide estimates of rice
yields before 1873–74, the year national production statistics commenced. He further argues that the wide variation in regional yields
made aggregate calculations by government officials impossible
[p. 354].) (2) Nakamura finds little correlation between fertilizer
indexes and yields during the period when major productivity increases were to have taken place (Nakamura, "Growth of Japanese
Agriculture," pp. 791–93). (3) He proposes that the Ohkawa
estimates are implausible in view of the experience of other countries. Japan was a peasant agricultural economy with limited land
supply, yet "net product per worker growth ranked among the
highest of any nation including nations where farming was highly
commercialized and took place under virtually unlimited land
supply conditions" (ibid.). H. Rosovsky ("Rumbles in the Ricefields," pp. 355–56), in contrast, challenges Nakamura's assumption
of a rice yield in the mid-1870s which shows Japanese agriculture
more productive than that of present-day Taiwan or Korea). (4)
Nakamura also cites the level of food imports and implied calorie
levels to support the plausibility of his, and the implausibility of
the Ohkawa, estimates ("Growth of Japanese Agriculture," pp. 791–
93). Referring to the calories per person implied by the Ohkawa
estimates (1,663 per person a day in 1874–77, 1,802 in 1878–82,
1,879 in 1883–87), he concludes, "These are consumption levels
that could not have maintained the Japanese in that state of vig-
orous health and energy that carried him to sustained growth"
(Nakamura, "The Nakamura vs. the LTES Estimates," p. 361).
Oshima, in "Meiji Fiscal Policy," emphasizes that the implied
calorie level per day of 1,400–1,600 from the official data is less
than the current level of 2,000 per day for India. An alternative
interpretation of the calorie debate is provided by Colin Clark,
Review of *Agricultural Production and the Economic Development
of Japan, 1873–1922*, by James I. Nakamura. Rosovsky ("Rumbles in the Ricefields," pp. 355–56) counters that the *growth* of
calorie intake implied by Nakamura's estimates suggests a zero
income elasticity of demand for rice.
    11. Nakamura, *Agricultural Production*, p. 12.

tion during the Meiji period.[12] Given the importance of the agricultural sector, Nakamura's competing estimates reduce the Ohkawa aggregate annual growth rate for Japan, from 1878–82 to 1913–17, from 4.0 to 2.8 percent.[13] If possible biases in secondary and tertiary production are also taken into account, the aggregate growth rate would be even lower, perhaps as low as 1 or 2 percent.[14]

Yet the debate over measurement may have obscured many theoretical issues which are critically important to the economic historian and the development economist. The motivation of this chapter is *not* to add further fuel to the data debate but instead to evaluate our dualistic model, where the results are less dependent on the outcome of that debate.

5.2.2. Competing Facts and the Japanese Miracle

Since the pioneering research by Ohkawa, there have been significant efforts to improve on the agricultural output series. The results have recently appeared in the *Estimates of Long*

12. Oshima was an early critic of the Ohkawa output estimates for the secondary and tertiary sectors. In his review of Ohkawa's *The Growth Rate of the Japanese Economy since 1878* he estimates the national income for 1881 as 25 percent higher than Ohkawa, mainly because of biases in secondary and tertiary production. Oshima questioned Ohkawa's output statistics on the basis of the low per capita incomes in the late 1930s and mid-1950s. He speculated that the levels may have been lower than expected because military activities dissipated the growth or because per capita income at the end of the Tokugawa period may have been extremely low. The appearance of the Nakamura study has strengthened Oshima's criticisms of the Ohkawa secondary and tertiary estimates. The tertiary estimates are tied directly to those of the agriculural sector. Furhermore, as Ohkawa himself notes, "our estimates . . . of new product in manufacturing . . . should be understood as being far weaker than that of primary industry" (Ohkawa et al., *Japanese Economy since 1878*, p. 94).

13. While impressive, aggregate output growth rates of 4 percent a year are not uncommon. These rates have been found, for example, in postwar Philippines, Thailand, Malaya, Taiwan, and India during the 1950s. However, per capita output growth rates of about 3 percent a year over sustained periods (for example, one-half century) are rare.

14. Oshima, "Meiji Fiscal Policy," p. 356.

Term Economic Statistics of Japan since 1868.[15] All partici-
pants in the debate agree that the LTES estimates are an improvement over the early Ohkawa series. The LTES growth
rates are lower, and the initial agricultural productivity levels
are higher. Yet Nakamura's initial critique has not been entirely blunted, since the LTES estimates are still based on
official data of questionable quality and downward bias. There
remains considerable uncertainty regarding the magnitude of
error.[16]

A recent paper by Hayami and Yamada attempts to offer
a defense of the new LTES agricultural series.[17] That the
revised LTES are an improvement over Ohkawa's early efforts
is clear. Between the periods 1878–82 and 1898–1902 the
compound annual growth rates for gross agricultural production are 2.8 (Ohkawa), 1.8 (LTES), and 0.9 (Nakamura).
The rates over the same period for (gross) agricultural labor
productivity are 3.0 (Ohkawa), 2.0 (LTES), and 1.1 (Nakamura). However, the tests which Hayami and Yamada feel
make the LTES series more "plausible and consistent" than
the Nakamura series are not entirely convincing.[18]

15. Ohkawa, Shinohara, and Umemura, *Long Term Economic
Statistics*, vol. 8.
16. K. Ohkawa and H. Rosovsky, in "A Century of Japanese
Economic Growth" (p. 69), acknowledge the *direction* of the bias,
but not its magnitude: "We are quite prepared to concede that
there may have been some underestimation in the early government
statistics, but we do not accept either Nakamura's assumptions or
the highly inflated output figures which result. . . . Our reading of
the evidence (indicates that) official yield figures perhaps contain
a slight downward bias (we would suggest in the magnitude of
10–12%), but they are far closer to the mark than the alternative
proposed by Nakamura." Ohkawa and Rosovsky also note that
the high growth rates are not "impossible," as is often implied.
Goldsmith's calculations on Tsarist Russia between 1860 and 1913
showed 1.75–2.0 percent per year; postwar growth in the ECAFE
region was also above 2 percent.
17. Hayami and Yamada, "Agricultural Productivity."
18. The LTES estimates have been appraised in detail by Nakamura ("The Nakamura vs. the LTES Estimates") and Hayami
and Yamada ("Agricultural Productivity"). The LTES series cor-
rects official statistics for per-*tan* rice yields before 1890, since

Based on our detailed examination of the estimation procedures and the debate over measurement, our commitment is
to the position that the Ohkawa agricultural output series is
unsatisfactory, and that there are not yet sufficient grounds to
ascertain the relative veracity of the Nakamura and LTES
estimates. However, because we intend to evaluate the descriptive accuracy of the model simulated in chapter 4, it is important that we guard against inadvertently "selecting" estimates
which fail to give a completely objective presentation of the
range of alternative quantitative interpretations of Japanese
economic history. In some cases the conclusions derived from
a comparison of Japanese growth and our model may depend
on the choice of series. Accordingly, all three series will be
presented below with the understanding that we will focus on
the Nakamura and LTES versions. The main reason for presenting the latter two series is the absence in the literature of
a clear resolution of the data controversy.[19]

---

many experts agree that the official data are relatively accurate
thereafter. The LTES series relies on the same data base utilized
by Ohkawa, but rice yields are 9 percent higher for the base period
1878–82 after defects are corrected and the coverage is enlarged.
Hayami and Yamada argue that Nakamura's higher yields are implausible, since they exceed the yields of every Asian nation (except
Japan) in 1953–62. Nakamura rejects this "plausibility test," since
crop underreporting is the rule for contemporary developing nations as well. Furthermore, the modern period used for comparison
(1953–62) includes years when many Asian countries were recov-
ering from wartime and postwar lows in output. As a further test
of plausibility, Nakamura has asserted that the equivalents in calorie consumption implied by the LTES figures are much too low
for 1878–82. Hayami and Yamada do not present an entirely
convincing rebuttal to this criticism. On the other hand, they show
that the Nakamura figures implied an "income elasticity of calorie
consumption" of zero. Although Hayami and Yamada do not find
this result credible, Nakamura supports it with both 1957–59 Food
and Agricultural Organization cross-sectional data and Japanese
data from 1918–22 to 1965. In short, "It is not likely that the final
word on the controversy . . . will ever be written due to data defi-
ciency" ("The Nakamura vs. the LTES Estimates," p. 361).
    19. Another volume of the LTES series will appear shortly,
presenting revisions for other sectors and for aggregate output as
well. These estimates were not available to us at the time of writing

Nakamura has challenged not only the Ohkawa-LTES output series but also the Rosovsky investment estimates and the Ohkawa figures on capital stock and the gainfully employed labor force.[20] Here Nakamura's case is based less on an extensive examination of the quantitative record than on plausible conjectures and qualifying assumptions. While errors and biases may be present in these input series, the magnitude of the errors has not been established with the same degree of confidence as that in agricultural production. We shall utilize the Ohkawa and Rosovsky estimates of investment, capital, and the labor force, qualifying the analysis only when existing alternative estimates would alter our basic comparisons or conclusions.

A final point should be noted. The above controversy, arising almost a decade after an "accepted" interpretation of both the description and the analysis of Japanese development had been completed, should underscore the tentative nature of our own efforts to compare the historical record with the model forecasts presented in chapter 4.[21] Dixit has argued that the

this chapter. The aggregate output series appearing below represent our own efforts to derive aggregate output series from the LTES agricultural data and the existing estimates on other sectors.

20. Rosovsky (*Capital Formation in Japan*), Ohkawa et al. (*Japanese Economy since 1878*), and Ohkawa, Shinohara, and Umemura (*Long Term Economic Statistics*, vol. 8) have been very careful to present important qualifications to their investment and capital stock estimates. Another estimate of capital stock has been compiled by John C. H. Fei and Gustav Ranis (*Development of the Labor Surplus Economy: Theory and Policy*, pp. 125–31, 146–48). A crucial assumption in their calculation is that capital stock depreciates at an annual rate of 15–20 percent. Their tests relating to the historical analysis of the labor reallocation process uses capital stock estimates based on the 20 percent rate. We feel that qualitative histories do not justify such high rates of capital consumption. Thus we reject the Fei and Ranis estimates and their resulting empirical analysis. A critique of the Fei and Ranis analysis and estimates is provided by E. P. Ruebens ("Capital Labor Ratios in Theory and History: Comment"); see also R. Minami, "The Turning Point in the Japanese Economy," pp. 397–98.

21. An index of the widespread acceptance of the Johnston-Ohkawa-Rosovsky characterization of Meiji economic history is

simplicity of the dualistic models, coupled with the weaknesses in historical quantitative data, make empirical testing of competing formulations an unfruitful exercise.[22] While we share his concern, recall that our methodology involves the formulation of models which employ progressively richer theoretical specifications, even at the expense of failing to identify completely the general properties of these models through qualitative analysis. Simulation *requires* a complementary investigation of the descriptive accuracy of the predictions. Testing the sensitivity of the model forecasts to parameter estimates (chap. 6) and initial conditions will always yield inconclusive results; only the historical record can provide the final judgment. Thus, on the one hand, we underscore our own qualms regarding the quality of the quantitative evidence describing Japanese economic history: the analysis below will accordingly be considered as only a required beginning to our evaluation of the model. On the other hand, we accept Oshima's challenge: "Under the circumstances, a re-examination of the period from a different point of view may be worthwhile. . . . The interpretation of the Meiji period has influenced the construction of theories of

the frequent reference to the "Japanese model" of development. Rosovsky ("Rumbles in the Ricefields," p. 360) has recently termed this interpretation of Japanese growth as the "standard version" of the analysis. For a sampling of the literature which focuses on the prominent role and potential of small-scale, but productive, agriculture in supplying labor, savings, and food for industrial development, consult J. C. Fei and G. Ranis, "Innovation, Capital Accumulation, and Economic Development"; idem, *Labor Surplus Economy*; B. F. Johnston, "Agricultural Productivity and Economic Development in Japan"; B. F. Johnston and J. Mellor, "The Role of Agriculture in Economic Development"; B. F. Johnston and G. S. Tolley, "Strategy for Agriculture in Development"; B. F. Johnston and J. Cownie, "The Seed-Fertilizer Revolution and Labor Force Absorption"; K. Ohkawa, Review of *Capital Formation in Japan* by Henry Rosovsky; K. Ohkawa and H. Rosovsky, "The Role of Agriculture in Modern Japanese Economic Development"; idem, "Century of Japanese Economic Growth"; idem, "Postwar Japanese Growth in Historical Perspective: A Second Look"; H. Rosovsky, *Capital Formation in Japan*; and idem, "Japan's Transition to Modern Economic Growth, 1868–1885."

22. A. Dixit, "Theories of the Dual Economy: A Survey."

underdevelopment . . . we need to know much more about the period than we do at present."[23]

5.3. TEMPORAL COMPARISONS OF JAPAN AND THE SIMULATED ECONOMY

5.3.1. The Rate of Japanese Economic Growth

In chapter 4, our model's predictions and the empirical record of many developing countries were compared. Specific attention was focused on broad indices of economic development and structural change—per capita output growth and changes in shares of sectoral output and the labor force. Two main conclusions were reached. First, the pattern and rate of change of the variables generated by our model conformed very closely to those of the developing countries as a group. Second, and most important for the present purposes, Japanese growth and structural change appeared to progress at a pace approximately twice the rates of both our model and the remaining countries in the sample. Both the developing countries and our model, for example, achieved rates of per capita output growth ranging from 11.0 to 15.9 percent per decade; for Japan the estimates span 22.7 to 33.1 percent (table 4.2). Similarly, the annual rate of decline of the primary output share approximated −0.50 percent in both our model and the Chenery-Kuznets studies; Japan's rate of structural change was −1.31 percent (table 4.3). Japan's rate of structural change in the sectoral labor force share was also significantly different from our model's rate.

The rapid and sustained character of economic growth has been cited by many as possibly the most distinguishing characteristic of Japanese development.[24] What we have established, however, is the *magnitude* by which the rate of Japanese progress appeared to surpass that of the "typical" country undergoing growth at roughly similar levels of development. Appealing both to cross-sectional and time series data drawn from

23. Oshima, "Meiji Fiscal Policy," p. 356.
24. Ohkawa and Rosovsky, "Century of Japanese Economic Growth," p. 43.

a wide range of currently developed and underdeveloped nations, our comparisons suggest that the rate of Japanese progress was about *twice* that experienced elsewhere and in our model. These observations suggest that we compare *one* year of Japanese experience with *two* periods in the simulated economy. The *interrelationships* between key variables in our model—rates of change in commodity prices, capital-labor ratios, population and output redistribution, and so forth—are of course completely independent of the time dimensionality. Thus, the comparison of one year's experience in Japanese economic history with two periods of the simulated economy in no way interferes with a meaningful evaluation of our model's ability to reproduce the patterns and *structural* characteristics, if not the pace, of economic change.

5.3.2. The Growth of Population and the
Demographic Revolution

An equally important argument for altering the basic dimensions between a period in the model and a year of Japanese growth is based on differences in labor force or population growth. The current "population explosion" is well known and in fact will be discussed at length in chapter 6. Perhaps the magnitude of the demographic revolution is less appreciated. Much of contemporary Southeast Asia has population growth rates three times the rate of Meiji Japan: the growth rates of the Japanese labor force prior to 1915 were fairly stable at 0.9 percent a year, while our simulation assumes an initial rate of 2.7 percent. Not only is this difference large in absolute terms, but unlike so many other parameters for Japan, demographic experience is documented by extensive empirical evidence.[25] Moreover, in the comparative static analysis of chapter 3 and in the sensitivity analysis reported in chapter 6, the impact of population growth on the economy has been found to be both important and pervasive.

25. Ohkawa et al., *Japanese Economy since 1878*, p. 27; and Taeuber, *Population of Japan*.

Two techniques may be utilized to take into account the differing population growth rates. We could resimulate the model, using the same initial conditions but changing only the population growth parameters. One disadvantage of this approach is that the results would not be comparable with those extensively analyzed in chapter 4. More important, the simulated model represents a characterization of a currently developing nation in which high population growth rates are a salient feature: Japan constitutes an exception to this "typical" growth pattern. Finally, it would be somewhat arbitrary to change only two parameters (n_i) and not the remaining parameters and initial conditions characteristic of Meiji Japan. The latter would constitute an attempt to rewrite Japanese economic history, not to utilize Japanese experience by comparing it with contemporary developing economies.[26] Accordingly, we shall employ the second technique, which attempts to qualify the analysis to account for the markedly lower population growth rates in Japan.

A simple means of qualifying the analysis is to alter the dimensionality of the period-year correspondence in the same direction and magnitude as proposed above: equating one year of Meiji Japanese experience with two years in the simulation. One rationale for this procedure can be illustrated by considering the impact of changes in n_i on two key measures of development: the rate of per capita output growth and the rate of urbanization. Suppose, for example, that the natural rate of *rural* population growth has been reduced from 3 to 1 percent a year. (This is consistent with reducing aggregate population growth from 0.027 to 0.009 while at the same time maintaining the dualistic demographic properties of the model.)[27] What would the resulting impact on per capita output growth and the level of urbanization be? In period 50 the level of urbanization

26. Two of the authors of this book are engaged in this effort (A. C. Kelley and J. G. Williamson, *A New Economic History of Japan: Meiji Japan Revisited* [manuscript in preparation]).
27. Recall that $n(t) = n_1 u(t) + n_2 [1 - u(t)]$. If $n(t) = 0.009$, $u(t) = 0.3$, and with $n_2/n_1 = 1.5$, the values of n_1 and n_2 are 0.0067 and 0.0101, respectively.

would increase from 41.2 percent (if $n_2 = 0.03$) to 51.5 percent (if $n_2 = 0.01$).[28] Since the initial level of urbanization is 0.30, the downward adjustment of the population parameter to conform to Japanese conditions *doubles* the rate of population redistribution in the simulation model.

A similar impact on the rate of per capita output growth (g) is produced by this experiment. By altering n_2 alone, per capita output growth increases from 11.7 to around 16.1 percent per decade; g increases further to 17.9 percent when both sectoral population parameters are altered.[29] We conclude that a simple way of adjusting the simulation results to conform to Japanese experience is to assume that one year of Japanese progress corresponds to roughly two periods of the simulated economy. Indeed, *these results are consistent with the hypothesis that the unusual rapidity of Japanese development was the result of low population growth rates.* Of course, this simple period-year adjustment is not sufficient to capture the full impact of altering $n(t)$, since its influence on alternative measures of development is different (see chap. 6). On the other hand, the direction and magnitude of change is roughly the same for the key measures of aggregate growth and structural change. Major deviations from this pattern for specific variables will be individually taken into account in the analysis which follows.

5.4. INITIAL CONDITIONS: THE SIMULATION MODEL AND JAPAN
The period of Japanese economic history examined is roughly from 1882–87 to 1908–13. Several factors point to these years as an appropriate span of historical evidence with which to

---

28. While this experiment can be carried out by resimulating the model, a simpler method is to use the structural elasticity results presented in tables 6.6 and 6.7. In chapter 6 it is also shown that the direction—although not the magnitude—of the effects for n_1 are the same as those for n_2. We therefore consider in detail only the results for n_2.

29. Period 30 was used in this calculation. Here $g = 1.7$ percent (decadal rate of about 11.7 percent), and the structural elasticity is -1.372. As above, $11.7(-1.372)(-1) = 16.1$. The sign change is required, since the parameter is altered in the opposite direction from those shown in the table of elasticities.

confront the model's predictions. First, the year 1885 corresponds quite closely to the sectoral patterns of the simulation
model, the sectoral distribution of output and labor force in
terms of two key initial conditions of economic development.
By the mid 1880s, 54 percent of Japanese output was produced in the primary sector while utilizing approximately 71
to 79 percent of the total labor force.[30] Similar initial conditions
for the simulation model are 57 and 70 percent, respectively.[31]
Second, the model describes a development phase in which
economic progress is both continuous and sustained. Kuznets
has termed this phase Modern Economic Growth (MEG).[32]
Rosovsky has argued persuasively that for Japan MEG begins
in about 1885.[33] This year ended a transition in which the
joint priorities of industrialization and growth were elevated

30. Ohkawa et al., *Japanese Economy since 1878*, pp. 26–27.
Nakamura (*Agricultural Production*, p. 147) argues that the Ohkawa labor force series overstate the percentage of the work force
in the agricultural sector. For 1885 two separate estimates by Nakamura yield 71.1 and 72.1 percent. For the same period the Ohkawa
estimates yield 79.2 percent.
31. Ohkawa and Rosovsky ("Century of Japanese Economic
Growth," p. 65) conclude from an examination of the absolute
levels of land and labor productivity of Japan around 1880 that
"Japanese economic development was similar to the current levels
of Southeast Asia."
32. In Kuznets's framework MEG is characterized by four conditions: (1) the application of modern scientific thought and technology to industry; (2) a sustained and rapid increase in real
product per capita, usually accompanied by high rates of population growth; (3) rapid rates of transformation of the industrial
structure (changing sectoral output, labor force and entrepreneurial
distributions); and (4) the emergence of or expansion in international contacts (S. Kuznets, *Six Lectures on Economic Growth*,
Lecture 1).
33. While marked economic, political, and social change occurred in Japan beginning with the Meiji Restoration of 1868,
these events established the necessary, but not the sufficient condition, for MEG. Namely, the Restoration is a period during which
MEG becomes a national *objective*, not a revealed occurrence as
identified by Kuznets's empirically verifiable criteria. Rosovsky
thus characterizes the period 1868–85 as Japan's "transition" to
modern economic growth. During this period the banking system
was developed, fiscal and monetary reform were undertaken, social
barriers to progress were attenuated, political power in the central

to national objectives and modern economic growth actually commenced. The Matsukata Deflation in 1885 marked a period when currency reform, banking development, and government political and economic structure were all consolidated toward the ends of modern economic growth.[34]

Third, World War I represented an unusually strong exogenous shock to stimulate aggregate production, but it also gave a marked impetus to foreign trade, thereby moving the Japanese economy even further away from the closed framework.[35] While the period 1885–1910 constitutes the main period in which Japanese economic history is compared with the predictions of fifty simulation periods, a *precise* correspondence of 1885 with period 1 in the simulation is not implied. Furthermore, while World War I marks the terminal point in the analysis, we shall extend our comparisons, where trends in the Japense time series are not clear, by examining only twenty-five years of data.

A comparison of Japan's and the simulated economy's rates of sectoral output and labor force redistribution is presented

---

government was consolidated, and so forth (see Rosovsky, "Japan's Transition"; see also Ohkawa and Rosovsky, "Century of Japanese Economic Growth").

34. Ohkawa and Rosovsky, in "Role of Agriculture" (p. 43), divide their examination of long-term change in the Japanese economy into three periods: period I, from the Meiji Restoration to World War I; period II, from World War I to World War II; and period III, from World War II to the present. Justifying the demarcation at World War I, they note, "In spite of the sustained character of growth in Japan, the relative position of major sectors in the economy changed considerably . . . World War I marked a distinct structural change, especially pronounced in the relations between agriculture and industry." In a later study (Ohkawa and Rosovsky, "Century of Japanese Economic Growth") the authors consider the period 1886–1905 the initial phase of modern economic growth. From 1906 to 1930 a different economic structure is created which sets the pattern for the second phase of modern economic growth.

35. For a detailed discussion of the role of foreign trade in Japanese development, see W. W. Lockwood, ed., *The Economic Development of Japan*, chap. 6. During the war the exports as a percentage of net national product more than doubled (ibid., p. 315).

in table 5.1. The close correspondence of these two key measures of structural change (from the Ohkawa series) supports our choice of the period-year adjustment discussed above.[36]

5.5. JAPANESE GROWTH AND THE SIMULATED ECONOMY COMPARED IN DETAIL

The detailed comparison of the simulated economy with the Japanese historical record focuses on eight measures of per-

TABLE 5.1 Change in agriculture's share of the labor force and output in the simulated economy and Japan

		Labor force		Output			
						Japan[b]	
Period	(Year)	Simulation	Japan[a]	Simulation	Ohkawa	LTES	Nakamura
1	(1885)...	100.0	100.0	100.0	100.0	100.0	100.0
10	(1890)...	98.9	96.1	96.5	99.1	94.7	93.5
20	(1895)...	96.5	92.3	91.8	94.1	83.1	83.1
30	(1900)...	92.9	88.3	86.3	87.4	74.5	72.6
40	(1905)...	88.7	84.0	81.1	83.8	74.2	71.1
50	(1910)...	84.0	79.5	75.8	77.8	67.1	62.6

a. The labor force shares are from Ohkawa et al., *Growth Rate of the Japanese Economy*, p. 27.
b. In combining the LTES and Nakamura (medium-yield) primary output series with the Ohkawa nonprimary output series, we assumed that the primary output series grew at their own respective rates and that each series was equal in level to the Ohkawa figure in 1900.

36. Nakamura's revisions of labor force shares reveal almost identical rates of decline (Nakamura, *Agricultural Production*, p. 148). We cannot appraise the impact of Nakamura's adjustments to agricultural output on this sector's share, since Nakamura did not revise the output figures of the nonprimary sector. He notes, however, that similar error trends are likely evident in the nonprimary sector (p. 135). If the degree of understatement of production is invariant to sector, the changes in the share will be unaffected by his adjustments. This may argue for utilizing Ohkawa's unadjusted series for this particular comparison. Alternatively, if understatement of production is relatively greater in the primary sector, the rate of sectoral shift in production will be overstated in the Ohkawa figures.

formance: capital-labor ratios, the rate of capital accumulation, savings rates, factor shares, capital-output ratios, labor productivity, the terms of trade, and real wage behavior. What is the relative correspondence of the simulated economy and Meiji Japan?

Before we examine each variable in detail some general remarks on the relevant criteria for evaluating our success in reproducing Japanese economic history might be helpful. Our quantitative model belongs to a general class of simulation models which pose special difficulties in the evaluation of performance. In contrast with conventional systems of simultaneous equations, the usual R^2 and "t" statistics simply cannot be applied. Goodness of fit must be inferred in other ways. Several methods are available, including Theil's statistic of information loss and the National Bureau of Economic Research indices of conformity and diffusion. Each of these methods must deal with the temporal dimension of prediction (for example, month, year, or decade), the unit of prediction (for example, turning points or rates of change), and the relative weights attached to each variable in evaluating the overall performance of the model. Clearly, the "test" is sensitive to the choice of temporal dimension, unit of prediction, and relative weights; these can only be selected (often somewhat arbitrarily) with reference to the specific problem at hand.

The focus of this chapter is the *changing structure* of an economy through time, rather than the levels of prices, outputs, or inputs at any point in time. Indeed, given the differences between the initial conditions which prevailed in Meiji Japan and those assumed in the simulation, comparisons of levels of performance would be inappropriate and misleading. Rather, we shall focus on the direction of change in economic variables and the variability in those rates of change over time. Furthermore, our interest is in long-term performance rather than in annual variations, and, as a result, only decadal changes in the variables are considered.

While formal tests are not presented in the discussion of each variable below, it might be useful to summarize our findings in terms of a simple index of conformity. In particular, the signs of the first and second derivatives of comparable series produced by our model and drawn from Meiji Japan were compared. We then computed the percentage of the total comparisons in which the series directly conform. The overall conformity of our model to Japanese historical experience appears to be high; the model predicts accurately 75–81 percent of the time, depending on whether the official or the Nakamura agricultural output series is utilized. With only those results which include the Nakamura series considered, the first derivatives conform about 90 percent of the time, while the second derivatives conform seven times out of ten. Yet there is considerable variation by series. On a priori grounds, the capital-labor ratio should receive special weight. It is, after all, the key variable explaining economic performance over time; furthermore, the historical data relating to this variable are less subject to controversy. The model predicts the behavior of the capital-labor ratio with an especially high level of accuracy: 100 percent, first derivative; 88.9 percent, second derivative; and 95.2 percent, overall.

The second-derivative comparisons are clearly sensitive to short-run variations in Japanese development; for example, the Sino-Japanese War, depression, and natural disasters. Since the model focuses on long-term trends, it would have been more appropriate to smooth the Japanese figures. Our use of the unsmoothed data presumably implies a lower bound on our indices of conformity. Finally, the discussion which follows will indicate that our model predicts turning points in the Japanese data very well. An interesting case in point is the brief period of capital shallowing in agriculture early in the Meiji period which the model also predicts. Whether examining turning points, trends or rates of trend changes, the model's overall conformity to Japanese historical experience appears to be high.

5.5.1. The Capital-Labor Ratio
Since the behavior of the capital-labor ratio has been shown in

chapters 3 and 4 to be critical in interpreting growth performance, we begin our detailed inquiry with an examination of
this variable's trajectory. The upper panel of table 5.2 (cols.

TABLE 5.2 Annual growth rate of $\hat{k}$: the simulated economy
and Japan

Period (Year)	Simulation (%)			Japan (%)		
	$\hat{k}$ (1)	$\hat{k}_1$ (2)	$\hat{k}_2$ (3)	$\hat{k}$ (4)	$\hat{k}_1$ (5)	$\hat{k}_2$ (6)
0–10 (1885–90)....	0.6	0.9	−0.1	0.6	1.0	−0.3
10–20 (1890–95)....	1.1	1.1	+0.5	1.6	2.3	+0.2
20–30 (1895–1900)..	1.7	1.3	+1.1	2.5	3.2	+0.9
30–40 (1900–05)....	1.8	1.4	+1.5	2.2	1.8	+2.0
40–50 (1905–10)....	2.1	1.6	+2.0	4.3	4.3	+2.3
Average	1.5	1.3	1.0	2.2	2.5	1.0

NOTE: The Japanese data for 1885–90 correspond to data for
1882/87–1888/92. Subsequent years are similarly aligned. The
capital stock figures, representing net capital stock (1934–36
prices) minus residential buildings, are found in Ohkawa, Shinohara, and Umemura, *Long Term Economic Statistics*, vol. 3, tables
2, 5. The labor force figures are gainfully employed population,
from Ohkawa et al., *Growth Rate of the Japanese Economy*, p. 27.

1–3) provides the base for the following summary of the simulated sectoral capital-labor ratios: (1) $\hat{k}_1$ increases throughout
at an increasing rate; (2) $\hat{k}_2$ decreases initially and then increases at an increasing rate; (3) $\hat{k}_1$ exceeds $\hat{k}_2$ throughout;
(4) the growth of $\hat{k}_1$ exceeds that of $\hat{k}_2$, although the trend
reverses at higher levels of development; (5) $\hat{k}$ increases
throughout at an increasing rate (with the exception of the
first two periods). The similarity between these predictions
and the Japanese historical record is striking.[37]

37. An issue arises regarding the choice of capital and labor
variables in our model which correspond to Japanese historical
stocks. Since the Japanese labor series reflect employed labor unadjusted for quality variations, the unaugmented labor stock in our
model is the appropriate representation of Japanese figures. Japanese capital stock series, on the other hand, have been derived as
an aggregate of several forms of physical capital "weighted" by
capital prices. If these prices captured variations solely in capital
quality, the simulated quality-adjusted capital stock series would

Of particular interest is the early period of capital shallowing in Japanese agriculture. The simulation model has been able to capture even this phase of Meiji agricultural development. In these years, capital-saving (labor-using) technical change in agriculture, taking the form of increased utilization of improved techniques, fertilizers, and seeds, played an important role in raising agricultural productivity.[38] Indeed, both the bias and the rate of technical change in agriculture have often been cited as *the* key to explaining the success of Japanese economic development. This historical experience has been quite effectively captured in the simulation model.

In addition to the trend comparisons, note also the generally close correspondence of *levels* of $\hat{k}$ growth. While the average growth in Japanese $\hat{k}$ is somewhat higher (2.2 versus 1.5 percent), the differences are small when the total variation of the series is used as the norm. Furthermore, the average growth of $\hat{k}_2$ is the same in the two economies. This is in contrast to the Japanese experience of capital deepening in industry where both the level (2.5 percent) and its size relative to agriculture (2.5 versus 1.0 percent) are significantly greater than those in the simulated economy.[39] Differentials in Japanese sectoral

---

be the appropriate focus. However, measured capital goods' prices also capture variations in the relative demand for alternative forms of capital as derived from the altering composition of final and intermediate demand. Because this latter influence has not been separately captured in the Japanese series, we have elected to utilize the simulated raw stocks as our measure of capital stock growth. If a capital stock series for Japan becomes available which satisfactorily captures quality change, we will have to modify our treatment to obtain a more appropriate comparison of our model with Japanese growth. (For the American case, see D. W. Jorgenson and Z. Griliches, "The Explanation of Productivity Change.")

38. Ohkawa and Rosovsky, "Role of Agriculture"; idem, "Century of Japanese Economic Growth"; Y. Hayami and S. Yamada, "Technological Progress in Agriculture"; Johnston and Tolley, "Strategy for Agriculture in Development"; and Johnston and Cownie, "Seed Fertilizer Revolution."

39. While the possible understatement of agricultural capital stocks and investment due to the exclusion of land improvement must qualify this observation, the conclusion is not likely to be

productivity, which appear to have been pronounced and persistent over time, represent a notable feature in the country's development.[40] Furthermore, Japan is frequently characterized as a labor-surplus economy during this period. In interpreting the relevance of the labor-surplus framework, it is significant to note that the high rate of labor absorption in the primary sector, through its apparent bias in technical change, went hand in hand with the capital-using trends in nonprimary production.[41]

While capital deepening proceeded at higher rates in Japanese nonprimary production, it appears that in all other respects—aggregate and sectoral levels, trends, and rates of trend changes—the Japanese trajectory of capital-labor ratios is remarkably similar to the trajectories revealed in the simulation.

5.5.2. Capital Accumulation, Savings, Factor Shares, and the Capital-Output Ratio

With labor force expansion relatively constant in both the simulated economy and Japan,[42] the rate of capital accumulation explains most of the variation in $\hat{k}$ growth. The rate of capital accumulation in our model, in turn, depends on the joint be-

---

overturned (on measurement biases see Nakamura, *Agricultural Production*, p. 172; Ohkawa, Review of *Capital Formation in Japan* by Henry Rosovsky, p. 100; and Rosovsky, *Capital Formation in Japan*, p. 6).

40. T. Watanabe, "Economic Aspects of Dualism in the Industrial Development of Japan"; H. Kaneda, "Long-Term Changes in Food Consumption Patterns in Japan, 1878–1964"; and Rosovsky, *Capital Formation in Japan*, chap. 4.

41. In subjecting an element of their model to empirical test, Fei and Ranis have found significant capital shallowing over the entire period 1888–1916 in the *industrial* sector (Fei and Ranis, "Innovation"; and *Labor Surplus Economy*, pp. 125–31, 146–48). For reasons stated above, we cannot accept their estimates and conclusions.

42. For Japan, $n_{1885} = 0.8$ percent, $n_{1910} = 1.2$ percent; in the simulation the comparable rates are 2.7 and 2.6 percent, respectively. Thus, Japanese population trends exerted a downward pressure on k relative to the experience of the modeled economy.

havior of the capital share and the capital-output ratio. This can be seen from the definition

$$\frac{\dot{K}(t)}{K(t)} = \frac{I(t)}{K(t)} - \delta \quad \text{and} \quad P(t)I(t) = sG(t)\alpha(t),$$

so that

$$\frac{\dot{K}(t)}{K(t)} = s\alpha(t)\left\{P(t)\frac{K(t)}{G(t)}\right\}^{-1} - \delta = s^*(t)\left\{P(t)\frac{K(t)}{G(t)}\right\}^{-1} - \delta.$$

The model assumes s to be constant. Since the capital share, $\alpha(t)$, constitutes the only force altering the economy-wide savings ratio, it is also convenient to analyze Japanese rates of capital accumulation within the same framework. In fact, however, $\alpha(t)$ represents the share of income going to "savers" (not necessarily capitalists), and s may be variable or constant. Rates of capital accumulation can therefore be explored by examining the savings rate, factor shares, and the capital-output ratio.

A comparison of the rates of capital accumulation in the simulated economy and Japan is presented in table 5.3. The simulated model predicts that (1) total and sectoral rates of capital accumulation increase at an increasing rate, (2) the

TABLE 5.3 Annual growth rate of K: the simulated economy and Japan

Period	(Year)	Simulation (%)			Japan (%)[a]		
		Primary	Non-primary	Total	Primary	Non-primary	Total
1–10	(1885–90)..	1.6	2.9	2.3	0.2	5.1	1.9
10–20	(1890–95)..	2.2	3.6	3.1	0.4	5.6	2.7
20–30	(1895–1900)	2.7	4.0	3.5	0.4	6.2	3.2
30–40	(1900–05)..	3.1	4.2	3.8	0.6	4.6	2.8
40–50	(1905–10)..	3.4	4.3	4.1	1.2	6.7	4.4
Average		2.6	3.8	3.4	0.6	5.6	3.0

a. The Japanese capital stock series, representing net capital (1934–36 prices) minus residential structures, are from Ohkawa, Shinohara, and Umemura, *Long Term Economic Statistics*, vol. 3, tables 2, 5.

primary sector has accumulation rates substantially lower than those of the nonprimary sector, and (3) the relative pace of the primary sector's capital accumulation increases over time as the economy approaches balanced growth. Like the capital-labor ratios, the trends of capital accumulation in Japan are the same as those forecast by the model. On the other hand, the magnitudes of the growth rates differ considerably. While the overall rates of capital accumulation are similar in the two economies (3.4 versus 3.0 percent), they are considerably higher in Japanese industry and much lower in Japanese agriculture. These low accumulation rates in agriculture in the face of the phenomenal expansion of Japanese agricultural output require explanation, although in part they may simply be the result of undermeasurement.[43]

The economy-wide net and gross savings rates for the two economies are presented in table 5.4. Again, the modeled economy and Japan generate comparable trends. Both the net and

43. The Japanese capital series represents the value (in constant 1934–36 million yen) of gross stocks less residential structures. While net stocks are theoretically more appropriate, Ohkawa feels this series tends to be less accurate because of difficulties in the estimation procedure. Furthermore, the net and gross series are almost a fixed proportion of one another during this period of inquiry. Accordingly, the growth rates, of primary interest here, will be largely unaffected by the choice of series. The exclusion of residential structures is an attempt to obtain a better measure of the nation's productive capacity. If biases are introduced by this procedure, they lie in the understatement of rural productive capacity, since residential structures are used relatively more in this sector for production of economic goods. Nakamura (*Agricultural Production*, p. 172) has also argued that, given the rapid expansion of agricultural land in Hokkaido in the last two decades of the Meiji era, the growth of rural residential capital formation is understated. The primary sector includes agriculture, forestry, and fisheries; the nonprimary sector combines mining, manufacturing, transportation, services, and government. The average lifetime of durable equipment, estimated by the perpetual inventory method, is seventeen years. The estimates exclude all stocks attributable to the military. A potentially significant shortcoming of the agricultural capital stock series is the exclusion of land improvement projects. At this stage we can only point to the direction of the bias; its magnitude cannot be assessed with the available data.

TABLE 5.4 Net and gross savings rates: the simulated economy and Japan

Period	(Year)	Simulation (%)		Japan (%)	
		Net (NDCF/ NNP)	Gross (GDCF/ GNP)	Net (NDCF/ NNP)	Gross (GDCF/ GNP)
1–10	(1887–96)....	6.6	15.1	8.0	12.3
10–20	(1892–1901)..	7.2	15.3	8.0	12.4
20–30	(1897–1906)..	7.8	15.5	7.2	11.9
30–40	(1902–11)....	8.2	15.8	8.8	13.6
40–50	(1907–16)....	8.5	16.1	8.8	13.8

a. The savings figures include government investment in military durables (Rosovsky, *Capital Formation in Japan, 1868–1940*, p. 9).

the gross savings rates increase very slowly through time. As emphasized in chapter 4, the model, and now Japan, experienced impressive (and accelerating) economic progress and structural change without a major increase in the savings rates, which are sometimes cited as being crucial for modern development.[44] While there appears to have been a substantial upward shift in Japanese savings subsequent to the period considered here, the stability of this variable is clearly a notable feature of the early phase of Japanese modern economic growth.

The gradual increase in the savings rate is explained in our model by a change in factor shares. Unfortunately, as yet there is very little evidence on trends in capital shares in Meiji Japan.[45] While not specifically explaining the rising trend in savings during the early stages of Japanese growth, Ohkawa and Rosovsky[46] conclude that the expansion subsequent to 1905 was due to a movement away from traditional production and toward the more capital-intensive techniques in the modern sector. In the early period they emphasize the rate of agricultural surplus

44. W. A. Lewis, *The Theory of Economic Growth*, p. 226.
45. Ohkawa finds a decrease in both the economy-wide and the industrial sector's labor share from 1920 to 1942 ("Changes in National Income Distribution by Factor Share in Japan").
46. Ohkawa and Rosovsky, "Century of Japanese Economic Growth," pp. 77–79.

creation which, through government taxes (primarily the land tax), was channeled into nonprimary production.[47] The economy-wide savings rate thus depended upon a rapidly growing agricultural surplus.

Nakamura's interpretation of aggregate savings behavior is quite different.[48] He places much greater emphasis on the distribution of income as a determinant of aggregate savings. In his model the agricultural sector remains the primary source of investment resources; however, savings growth depends primarily on capturing an increasing share of the existing surplus. This contrasts with the Ohkawa–Rosovsky interpretation, where the increase in savings is based mainly on obtaining a share of a rapidly expanding surplus product.[49]

According to Nakamura, the Restoration transferred income from the high-consuming ruling class (including the *samurai* and the *daimyo*)[50] to a new group of lower-consuming landowners. Decreases in the Meiji land tax coupled with the erosion of the tax burden through inflation distributed income to the relatively higher savers. The landowners not only saved, but "the rural landlord-merchant played a major role in early Meiji financing by establishing and operating banking institutions and industrial and commercial enterprises."[51] Sinha supports the Nakamura interpretation.[52] He qualifies the primacy of govern-

---

47. Rosovsky, *Capital Formation in Japan*; idem, "Rumbles in the Ricefields," p. 360; Ohkawa and Rosovsky, "Role of Agriculture"; idem, "Century of Japanese Economic Growth"; and Sinha, "Japan's Early Economic Development," p. 110.

48. Nakamura, *Agricultural Production*, pp. 151, 155–69.

49. Rosovsky, "Rumbles in the Ricefields," p. 360.

50. Forced consumption by the *daimyo* was implemented by the practice of alternate attendance (*sankin kotai*) where the Tokugawa Shogunate required the *daimyo* to spend time in court, leaving his wife and children behind as permanent hostages. The low savings potential of the samurai is explained by his relative poverty: "The extent of samurai poverty may be judged from the great number of middle and lower class samurai who turned to farming or other occupations in order to subsist or pay off their debts, despite their abhorrence of employment which was associated with commoners" (Nakamura, *Agricultural Production*, p. 158).

51. Ibid., p. 167.

52. Sinha, "Japan's Early Economic Development," pp. 125–27.

ment-taxed agricultural surplus, noting that "in the land tax the
Meiji rulers did not find a new source of revenue, they merely
rationalized it," and "the land tax was not even adequate to
meet the armament expenditures of the regime." On the other
hand, while Sinha feels that the Nakamura thesis of increased
savings based on changes in the income distribution is substantially true, he notes that landowners probably invested some of
their earnings in land improvements and other forms of agricultural enterprise.

In sum, the savings mechanism which Nakamura and others
find supported by qualitative evidence is consistent not only
with our own theoretical framework and with Japanese savings
trends but also with the hypothesis that the labor share in Japan
was declining over time. Even though the members of the
Tokugawa ruling class can be considered early capitalists, the
income distribution relevant to the present discussion took place
after the Meiji land reforms. In this case the capitalists were the
landowners to whom a lower tax burden and inflation conveyed
substantial windfall gains. If this is the case—and we find this
a plausible interpretation of Meiji Japan—an overall decline in
the labor share, causing a gradual rise in the economy-wide
savings rate, appears consistent with the historical record. We
should hasten to emphasize, however, that while the descriptive
literature appears to lend some support to this interpretation,
the relevant quantitative evidence is as yet much too fragmentary for forming definite judgments on these issues.

The trend toward economizing on capital in production, both
economy-wide and by sector, is a feature of the simulation
model critically contributing to the gradually rising rates of
capital accumulation. Indeed, as shown in chapter 4, over one-
half of the increase in the rate of capital stock growth can be
attributed to the decline in the capital-output ratio. On the other
hand, this ratio declines very slowly over time; moreover, its
trend reverses at later phases of development.

Similar trends in the capital-output ratio are found for Japan.
Whether we use the LTES or the Nakamura output series,
table 5.5 shows an economizing on capital, although the Naka-

TABLE 5.5 Capital-output ratios for the simulated economy and Japan

| | Simulation | | | Japan | | | | | | |
| | | | | Ohkawa series | | | LTES series | | Nakamura series | |
Period (Year)	Aggregate	Secondary	Primary	Aggregate	Secondary	Primary	Aggregate	Primary	Aggregate	Primary
1 (1885)...	1.9	2.5	1.4	2.5	1.9	3.0	2.2	2.4	2.1	2.2
10 (1890)...	1.8	2.4	1.3	2.2	1.9	2.5	2.1	2.2	2.1	2.1
20 (1895)...	1.7	2.3	1.2	2.1	1.9	2.4	2.1	2.2	2.0	2.1
30 (1900)...	1.7	2.2	1.1	1.9	1.9	2.0	1.9	2.0	1.9	2.0
40 (1905)...	1.7	2.1	1.1	2.1	2.1	2.0	2.0	1.9	2.1	2.0
50 (1910)...	1.7	2.1	1.1	2.1	2.2	1.8	2.1	1.8	2.1	2.0
Average	1.8	2.3	1.2	2.1	2.0	2.3	2.1	2.1	2.1	2.1

NOTE: The capital series, representing net capital minus residential structures, are found in Ohkawa, Shinohara, and Umemura, *Long Term Economic Statistics*, vol. 3, tables 3, 5. Output estimates are compiled by K. Ohkawa et al., *Growth Rate of the Japanese Economy*. A description of the procedures for constructing the LTES and Nakamura output series is found in n. b, table 5.1.

mura figures show this trend to be much weaker; indeed, according to the LTES figures, the capital-output ratio in agriculture declines from 2.4 to 2.0 in a period of only fifteen years.[53]

Table 5.6 compares the percentage change of the accumulation rate, the capital-output ratio, and the savings rate for the

TABLE 5.6 Changes in the rates of capital accumulation, savings, and the capital-output ratio: the simulated economy and Japan

	Simulation (%)	Japan (%)
Capital accumulation	46	44
Savings rate	5	3
Capital-output ratio	−11	−24 (Ohkawa)
		−14 (LTES)
		−10 (Nakamura)

NOTE: For the first thirty periods (fifteen years), the specific calculations for each designated variable v *are* $[(v_{1900}/v_{1885}) - 1]$ 100. The average savings rate for Japan in the terminal year is taken as the average of the overlapping decades 1897–1906 and 1902–11.

model and for Japan, using the Ohkawa, the LTES, and the Nakamura output estimates. The rate of capital accumulation increases by about 45 percent in both the simulated economy and in Japan. Previous analysis (chap. 4) of the simulation has shown that over one-half of this increase in $\dot{K}/K$ is explained by the 11 percent decrease in the capital-output ratio; the remainder is attributed to an increased aggregate savings rate. Since the aggregate savings rate increased less markedly in Japan than in the simulation, the decrease in the capital-output ratio must have assumed an even greater role in the Japanese case. Indeed, our Asian prototype has an initial aggregate net savings rate of only 0.066, which over five decades increases to only 0.085. Yet the rate of capital accumulation rises from 2.3 percent a year in the first decade to 4.1 percent in the fifth! Dramatic shifts in the savings rates were not required in "take-

53. Throughout this section we use *net* capital stock minus residential structures, since we wish to compare also the absolute levels with those in the simulation.

off"; moreover, Meiji Japan did not find this necessary either.[54] The share of net domestic capital formation in net national product rises only from 0.080 to 0.088 between 1887–96 and 1907–16, while the rate of capital accumulation increases from 1.9 to 4.4 percent a year between 1885–90 and 1905–10. As we have already noted, table 5.6 shows that the rate of capital stock growth rises by 46 percent in the simulation and by 44 percent in Japanese history. Most of the explanation is found in the behavior of the capital-output ratio: in the simulation the rates decline by 11 percent; in Meiji Japan it declined by 24 (Ohkawa), 14 (LTES), or 10 (Nakamura) percent.

Finally, we have already indicated that whether one utilizes the LTES or the Nakamura series, economizing on capital proceeds at a mild rate throughout Japanese development. The rate proceeds somewhat faster in agriculture. Not only is Japanese agriculture more capital intensive than assumed in the simulations, but it also uses relatively more capital per unit of output than does the secondary sector (at least prior to 1900). Nevertheless, an important feature of the simulation *and* Japanese development, as emphasized by Ohkawa, Johnston, and Rosovsky, is the relatively low rate of capital accumulation in agriculture. While we feel this rate of accumulation may have been underestimated, their general conclusion appears to command empirical support.

In summary, with very few exceptions the trends in Japanese rates of capital accumulation, aggregate savings, and capital-output ratios are very similar to those of the simulated economy.

5.5.3. Labor Productivity

Economic development is normally characterized as a process in which there are sustained increases in labor productivity over extended periods of time. This is revealed in the simulation results presented in table 5.7 (cols. 1, 5, 9, and 11), where

---

54. This does *not* imply that savings are potentially unimportant to growth. Chapter 6 investigates in considerable detail the sources-of-growth methodology and the impact of capital formation on development.

TABLE 5.7 Average labor productivity for the simulated economy and Japan

Period (Date)	Primary				Secondary		Total				Relative sectoral productivities (nonprimary/primary)			
	Simulation Ohkawa (1)	Ohkawa (2)	LTES (3)	Nakamura (4)	Simulation Ohkawa (5)	Ohkawa (6)	Simulation Ohkawa (7)	Ohkawa (8)	LTES Ohkawa (9)	Nakamura Ohkawa (10)	Simulation (Col. 5/Col. 1) (11)	Ohkawa (Col. 6/Col. 2) (12)	LTES Ohkawa (Col. 6/Col. 3) (13)	Nakamura Ohkawa (Col. 6/Col. 4) (14)
1 (1885)	100.0	100.0	100.0	100.0	100.0	100.0	100.0	100.0	100.0	100.0	100.0	100.0	100.0	100.0
10 (1890)	104.3	114.3	105.6	102.3	109.0	104.9	106.9	114.5	107.3	104.9	104.6	91.7	99.3	102.5
20 (1895)	111.7	124.6	107.1	105.0	120.2	115.3	117.4	130.0	119.1	116.9	107.6	92.5	107.6	109.8
30 (1900)	121.8	148.6	120.6	111.5	132.7	135.9	131.0	160.1	142.8	136.1	109.0	91.4	112.7	121.8
40 (1905)	135.2	157.4	133.3	120.1	146.6	130.1	147.9	166.4	151.1	142.3	108.5	82.6	97.5	108.3
50 (1910)	152.2	189.1	153.3	132.5	162.1	151.7	168.5	203.3	181.4	168.3	106.5	80.2	98.8	114.4

NOTE: The labor force series are compiled by Ohkawa et al., *Growth Rate of the Japanese Economy*, p. 27. See also n. b, table 5.1. It will be noted that the simulation produces total labor productivity growth (col. (7)) exceeding that of each of the individual sectors (cols. (1) and (5)). This results from the fact that the series are indexed and do not capture the impact of the intersectoral shift.

several trends may be noted: (1) sectoral and total labor productivity increase monotonically over time; (2) the labor productivity increases in secondary production exceed those in the primary sector in early phases of growth, while this trend is reversed in later phases of growth; (3) absolute labor productivity is always greater in the nonprimary sector (not shown here).

A comparison of these simulated paths with Japanese economic history is complicated by the controversy over the LTES and the Nakamura estimates of agricultural output. Consider first those compiled by Ohkawa. Column 2 of table 5.7 clearly reveals the most prominent feature of the "Japanese model." Labor productivity growth in Japanese agriculture is nothing short of phenomenal in view of the unchanging, small farm which utilized relatively small increases in capital inputs. Over a period of twenty-five years, agricultural output (net of intermediate inputs) per unit of labor increased by 89 percent; the gross output per unit of labor increased by 113 percent.[55] The Nakamura and the LTES estimates provide somewhat different characterizations of Japanese labor productivity growth. Primary labor productivity increases by 33 and 53 percent in the Nakamura and the LTES series, respectively, roughly comparable to the 52 percent of the model and in marked contrast to Ohkawa's 89 percent. The "Japanese miracle" vanishes in the LTES–Nakamura estimates; agricultural development proceeds at a more moderate pace. Furthermore, in contrast to Ohkawa's estimates, but consistent with our model, labor productivity growth in nonprimary production exceeds that of primary activities. Finally, in both Japan and the simulated economy, the relative differentials in productivity growth *increase* in early stages of development, only to *reverse* at a later stage. Differences in the rates of productivity change reach a peak around the turn of the century (and in period 30 of our model),

---

55. All the comparisons utilize net output. These measures were also employed by Ohkawa and Rosovsky in their study of agricultural productivity ("Role of Agriculture"). In contrast, Hayami's examination of fertilizer demand in Japanese agriculture employs gross value produced per factor ("Demand for Fertilizer in the Course of Japanese Agricultural Development").

after which a reversal in the trend is revealed (cf. cols. 11, 13, and 14).

These trends in the simulation model are readily explainable. In early phases of growth the economy-wide efficiency wage-rental ratio declines because of the relatively high rates of labor augmentation (through technical change and labor force growth) compared with the rates of capital augmentation.[56] Labor is substituted for capital more readily in agriculture; furthermore, technical change is labor using. Not only does the agricultural capital-labor ratio grow relatively slowly; it actually *declines* in early periods. Capital-using technical change exerts a strong influence on nonprimary production, and in spite of a declining wage-rental ratio, capital is substituted for labor. In later growth phases, the rising rate of capital accumulation (relative to the rate of labor supply growth) reverses the trend in the wage-rental ratio. Given an increasing wage-rental ratio and the relative ease of substitution of capital for labor in agriculture, the growth of the agricultural capital-labor ratio increases, and the rate of growth of primary labor productivity rises relative to labor productivity in secondary industry. In more familiar terms, the scarcity and the high cost of capital in early stages of development provide agriculture with an incentive toward capital-saving forms of technology—primitive fertilizers, simple tools, double cropping, and land improvements requiring heavy labor inputs. As capital becomes relatively more abundant there is greater use of nonfarm inputs such as machinery, chemical fertilizers, and improved seeds and pesticides.

A key issue in explaining trends in Japanese labor productivity is the behavior of the sectoral rate and the bias of technical change, particularly in agriculture. Since the agricultural labor force grew very slowly if at all, and rates of capital accumulation in agriculture were low as well, the primary explanation of Japanese success must rest with technical change. The implica-

56. Recall $\omega(t) = x(t)y(t)^{-1}k_i(t)^{\sigma_i}$ in equilibrium.

tion is that the rate of technical change was rapid and that it was labor using in bias. These are quantitative statements; a satisfactory study of Japanese technical change is yet to be undertaken, although descriptive accounts are readily available.[57]

One of the outgrowths of the data controversy over the Japanese primary output series has been many studies which attempt to explain Ohkawa's high rates of growth in agricultural output (particularly in the period before 1900). After examining Shishido's index of fertilizer-energy input, household survey data on fertilizer purchase, and Saito's study on fertilizer usage, Ohkawa and Rosovsky conclude that "the increased use of better seeds and commercial fertilizers were most responsible for the rise in output."[58] However, the usefulness of the Shishido index has been seriously questioned, since it does not reveal the extent to which the increased fertilizer usage represents merely a shift from domestically produced to commercially produced nutrients.[59] Sinha, and Oshima before him, has also underscored the severe cash and credit constraints on the expansion of commercial fertilizer inputs before 1900.[60] Finally, Hayami's

57. The best study is by T. Watanabe ("Economic Aspects of Dualism in the Industrial Development of Japan") who finds technical change to be labor saving in manufacturing, 1904–1933. Agriculture, over the period 1887–1936, does not appear to reveal a significant bias. There are, as Watanabe later notes, highly tentative estimates ("Industrialization, Technological Progress, and Dual Structure"). The difficulties in estimating simultaneously the elasticity of substitution and the bias in technical change (P. A. Diamond and D. McFadden, "Identification of the Elasticity of Substitution and the Bias of Technological Change: An Impossibility Theorem"), weaknesses in existing data (output, capital excluding land improvements), and the necessity of making limited assumptions, all plague his empirical study.

58. Ohkawa and Rosovsky, "Role of Agriculture," pp. 50–51.

59. Sinha, "Japan's Early Economic Development," p. 119.

60. Ibid., pp. 109–51; Oshima, "Meiji Fiscal Policy." In examining the requirement that land taxes be paid in cash, Oshima notes, "Above all, the provision that taxes be paid entirely in cash strained the resources of the rural economy. . . . The sudden imposition of cash payments brought severe hardship, especially to the small land peasant" (ibid., pp. 362–63).

study of fertilizer use shows a relatively slow rise in per capita use of commercial fertilizers from 1885 to the turn of the century; around 1900 there was a major expansion in this input.[61]

Subsequent analysis of the data has led to the formulation of alternative hypotheses explaining the impressive agricultural expansion. Rosovsky's most recent position is that "seed selection and the more intensive application of fertilizer cannot satisfactorily explain the vigor of indigenous technological progress. The real key to what happened lies, rather, in the diffusion of better farming techniques."[62] In an examination of the rate of diffusion of rice technology for forty-six prefectures, Hayami and Yamada find support for Rosovsky's hypothesis.[63] Sinha forms a more pessimistic judgment regarding the rapidity of technological diffusion: ". . . new ideas regarding improved agricultural practices were probably not as commonplace as is readily believed."[64] As evidence to support his conclusion, Sinha cites government laws forcing adoption of new procedures, the slow acceptance of high-yield rice varieties, and the surprisingly slow adoption of salt-water sorting procedures.

Whether we utilize the Nakamura or the LTES estimates, the debate has revealed insights on the nature of technical change in both agriculture and industry which give support to our formulation. First, the consensus is that technology in agriculture was

61. Nakamura (*Agricultural Production*) finds very little correlation between commercial fertilizer usage and rice yields before 1900.

62. Rosovsky, "Rumbles in the Ricefields," p. 358.

63. The argument is that while agricultural technology was highly developed at the end of the Tokugawa period, feudal constraints on factor mobility and information diffusion resulted in an enormous "backlog" of knowledge. The Restoration removed the constraints; therefore, output increases, requiring mainly "human capital formation" and little of anything else, resulted in significant outward shifts of the production function. (These ideas are most extensively developed by Hayami and Yamada in "Technological Progress in Agriculture"; for an alternative interpretation, see A. M. Tang, "Research and Education in Japanese Educational Development, 1880–1938.")

64. Sinha, "Japan's Early Economic Development," p. 116.

labor using. Second, consistent with the model predictions, the intensity of technical change in Japanese agriculture was almost certainly greater than that taking place in nonprimary production. A range of 1.0 (Nakamura) to 1.7 (LTES) percentage rates of increase in agricultural output, in the absence of appreciable measured factor growth, can lead us to no other conclusion.

5.5.4. The Terms of Trade

Given the relative stability of the terms of trade, both in the simulated economy and in Japan (1895–1910), it is useful to examine a somewhat longer period so that the secular trends will be revealed. Figure 5.1 presents the results for a 100-period

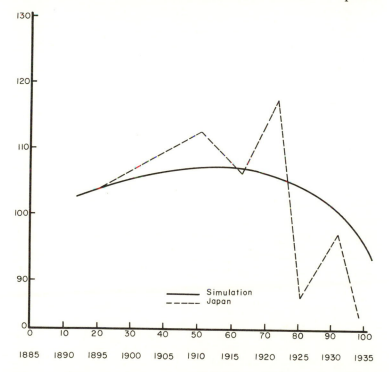

Fig. 5.1. Terms of Trade: The Simulated Economy and Japan (Period 20 = 1895 = 100)

simulation and for Japan, 1885–1935.[65] Since the experience of
the first decade for Japan is clearly atypical, 1895 is taken as
the base year. If we exclude the atypical periods from 1885 to
1895 and during World War I, the terms-of-trade experiences
of the two economies are similar. There is relative stability from
1895 to 1910, after which we observe a long secular decline.
This decline for Japan is most rapid in the postwar period.

As indicated in chapter 4, the terms of trade in the simulation
model is determined by the relative marginal factor productivities of the two sectors. Changes in the terms of trade depend in
turn on variations in the relative growth rates of sectoral productivities. Moreover, the relative changes in sectoral labor
productivities depend upon the relative sectoral rates of capital
deepening (table 5.5); these trends result in the terms of trade
moving in favor of nonprimary production in early stages of
development. The trend is reversed as development proceeds
and the capital-labor ratio increases.

The analysis of Japanese terms of trade is made difficult both
by the availability of competing output series for computing
sectoral productivities and by the increasing role of foreign trade
over time. Ohkawa and Rosovsky conclude that stability in the
terms of trade (roughly until 1910) was due to an approximate
stability in relative sectoral labor productivity changes together
with a balance of agricultural output expansion and demands
generated by population change and income growth.[66] Foreign
competition, increasingly important through time, depressed
agricultural prices. At the level at which their analysis is framed,
it is ironic that the Nakamura revised estimates are also roughly
consistent with the terms-of-trade trends. In the long run, however, both the LTES and the Nakamura series, on the basis of
changing sectoral relative productivities, lend support to a secu-

65. The Japanese data are from Ohkawa, Shinohara, and Umemura, *Long Term Economic Statistics*, vol. 8, tables 10, 15, 33.
They are taken from the Bank of Japan's wholesale price series.
Nonprimary production comprises eight different manufacturing
sectors and mining. The series presented have been smoothed by a
five-year moving average.
66. Ohkawa and Rosovsky, "Role of Agriculture," pp. 44–50.

lar price movement against agriculture, a result consistent with the model's predictions.

5.5.5. Sectoral Real Wage Rates

Two measurement issues arise when the Japanese real wage experience is compared with that in the simulated economy. First, in terms of the available historical data, are wages or annual earnings the relevant variables to compare with the trends in the simulation model? Second, what are the appropriate deflators of "money wages" to yield a real wage index relevant to firm decision making?

In agriculture two types of wage series are available, both constructed by Ohkawa. The first represents a weighted index of wages received by male daily or contract workers. The imputed value of meals received by daily workers is included in the wage. For contract workers the value of board and room is omitted; the series therefore understates the real wage level. Whether the trend in this series is biased depends on whether the value of income in kind changes through time as a proportion of the total real wage. The Ohkawa figures of daily and contract wages represent, with the qualification noted, the wage rate facing the firm. The corresponding series provided by the simulation model is the efficiency wage (see table 5.8). We must recognize, however, that there are significant statistical problems inherent in compiling a composite wage index, because of varying rates of labor augmentation from industry to industry coupled with differential changes in the composition of the labor force through time. These problems plagued Ohkawa in his compilations, and as a result his wage series must be utilized with caution.

The second measurement issue involves the selection of an appropriate price deflator to obtain the real wage facing the firm. The relevant factor price for firm decision making is the efficiency wage deflated by firm output price. Accordingly, the historical wage index must be deflated by the relevant *sectoral* commodity price to obtain an appropriate index of real wages facing the firm. A cost-of-living deflator, while commonly used

TABLE 5.8 Real wages and real annual earnings per laborer: the simulated economy and Japan

Period (Date)	Simulation real wage index[a] (1)	Japanese agriculture male workers[b] Daily (2)	Japanese agriculture male workers[b] Contract (3)	Tussing real daily wage index: Construction workers[c] (4)	Tussing real daily wage index: manufacturing[d] (5)	Simulation real earnings index[e] (6)	Tussing real annual earnings silk reeling[f] (7)
1 (1883–87)	103.2	....	....	91.3	91.2	94.3	86.2
10 (1888–92)	100.0	100.0	100.0	100.0	100.0	100.0	100.0
20 (1893–97)	97.9	122.2	116.2	99.1	103.8	108.2	125.0
30 (1898–1902) ...	97.1	122.7	119.4	79.2	92.3	118.4	121.6
40 (1903–7)	97.4	111.4	114.9	84.9	100.0	131.3	138.8
50 (1908–11)	98.6	112.9	117.5	117.0	103.8	146.8	170.7

NOTE: 10 (1890) = 100. Data are not available on Japanese agricultural male workers' wages before 1890.

a. Efficiency real wage index is $w(t)$.

b. Ohkawa, Shinohara, Umemura, *Long Term Economic Statistics*, vol. 9, table 34. Both wage rates are deflated by agricultural prices (vol. 8, table 10.)

c. Real daily wage for construction workers in Yamanashi Prefecture (A. R. Tussing, "The Labor Force in Meiji Economic Growth: A Quantitative Study of Yamanashi Prefecture," table 7, p. 213).

d. Real daily wage in manufacturing in Yamanashi Prefecture (ibid., table 8, p. 214).

e. Real earnings index is $w(t)y(t)$.

f. Real annual earnings in silk reeling (Tussing, "Yamanashi Prefecture," table 10, p. 215).

in real wage comparisons, is inappropriate, since it relates not to decision making of the *firm* but rather to decisions of the *consumer*. The cost-of-living deflator may yield different results if the sectoral terms of trade and the budget shares vary as development takes place.

Fortunately, the most serious of these estimation problems have been solved by Tussing's recent study, which develops daily real wage *and* real earnings indices for Yamanashi Prefecture. The Tussing series also cover a longer time period, from 1883–87 to 1908–11. The real earnings index is comparable to the simulation $w(t)y(t)$ index, while the real wage series should be compared with the simulated $w(t)$ index. The trends in the simulated and the Tussing series are quite similar (table 5.8). Tussing's real wage index of construction and manufacturing declines to 1898–1902 and rises thereafter. The simulation model produces less dramatic movements, but it, too, declines up to period 30 and rises thereafter (cf. col. 1 with cols. 4 and 5). Declining real wages, however, do *not* necessarily imply deteriorating workers' living standards. Tussing's real *earnings* index and the simulation real earnings index both show impressive gains throughout the Meiji era. The only significant difference between the two series appears in the last half-decade, from 1903–7 to 1908–11. It seems that the simulation model has fairly effectively reproduced Meiji Japanese experience with real wages and earnings.

5.6. COMPETING THEORIES: JAPANESE ECONOMIC HISTORY RECONSIDERED

In a recent article Tussing makes a point worth repeating: "The incomes of the common people rose substantially [during the Meiji era] . . . the Japanese did it mostly by working longer and working harder."[67] Tussing is referring to the large discrepancy between real annual earnings and real wage behavior in Yamanashi Prefecture up to World War I. Tussing's real

67. A. R. Tussing, "The Labor Force in Meiji Economic Growth: A Quantitative Study of Yamanashi Prefecture," p. 220.

wage data, presented in table 5.8, show a decline in real wages up to 1898–1902 and a rise thereafter. His real annual earnings index, on the other hand, exhibits continuous improvement from 1883 to 1887; indeed, the index rises from 86.2 to 170.7! These are the historical facts which competing theories must confront.

The emphasis real wage behavior has received in the literature has been a response to an attempt to discriminate between alternative theories of factor pricing. Much of the confusion surrounding "tests" of the labor-surplus model is attributable to the observation that real wages *have* remained constant over long historical time periods. Yet this is not a sufficient test, since the periods studied may in fact be periods of stability in the overall capital-labor ratio. Nevertheless, real wage stability has also been observed during industrial revolutions. Recall the behavior of real wages in our simulated Asian growing economy. Real wages consistently (but modestly) *decline* over thirty "periods" of impressive growth! The neoclassical economy is therefore able to generate declining or stable real wages for even a growing economy. Those trends are hardly the exclusive property of the labor-surplus model. Moreover, they do not necessarily imply that workers' living standards were constant or declining. In the simulated economy real *earnings* improve, as they did in Japanese economic history, and for the same reasons. In our model we label the cause "efficiency improvements" in labor; in the Japanese case Tussing refers to the phenomenon as "more intensive labor utilization."

The economic history of Meiji Japan has become the chosen battlefield for competing theories of the dualistic economy. In particular, Fei and Ranis have emphasized two key pieces of empirical evidence as support for the labor-surplus formulation of the dualistic economy. First, they cite capital shallowing in industry between 1888 and the end of World War I as "evidence that Japan made maximum use of her abundant factor, surplus agricultural labor."[68] But their data on capital shallow-

68. Fei and Ranis, *Labor Surplus Economy*, p. 132.

ing are based on their own series of industrial capital stock which has not only come under severe criticism but is also at variance with several independent estimates.[69] Second, they emphasize the "virtual constancy before and rapid rise of the real wage after approximately 1918 . . . [as] rather conclusive evidence in corroboration of our theoretical framework."[70] However, in none of the several indexes of real wages for Japan considered in section 5.5.5 were we able to identify constancy during the period they examine. Moreover, considering real wage trends over the classical period they identify as manifesting labor-surplus conditions (from 1888–92 to 1908–11), we find the real wage *increasing* by between 4 and 17 percent. We conclude that the evidence supporting the labor-surplus formulation is highly questionable, *even when the tests Fei and Ranis propose are used and the country and period they select are employed.*

Jorgenson arrives at a similar conclusion when comparing a large number of predictions of the labor-surplus and neoclassical models with the historical evidence from Japan.[71] In addition to real wages and capital intensities, he examines predictions on capital, labor, and output growth, labor productivities, capital-output ratios, and the evidence on disguised unemployment. He concludes that "the neoclassical theory of development of the dual economy is strongly supported by the empirical evidence and that the classical approach must be rejected."[72] His conclusion must be qualified. First, as Marglin has shown, Jorgenson's derived predictions of the labor-surplus model hinge on his assumption regarding the elasticity of substitution (unity) in

---

69. Colin Clark has recently reconstructed a capital stock series using the same procedure as Fei and Ranis (perpetual inventory) but employing different depreciation parameters. Clark's figures show capital deepening throughout the entire period under consideration. We are indebted to Professor Clark for permitting us to utilize his estimates before publication.

70. Fei and Ranis, *Labor Surplus Economy*, pp. 263–64.

71. D. W. Jorgenson, "Testing Alternative Theories."

72. Ibid., p. 60.

the production function.[73] An alternative rendering of the labor-surplus model using a CES production function with nonunitary substitution elasticities could yield quite different results. Second, Jorgenson's predictions are largely based on the *asymptotic* properties of his neoclassical model, an analytical characterization of development which we and Dixit have argued to be of limited applicability both on theoretical grounds and on the basis of numerical analysis.[74] For example, while the neoclassical model reveals constancy in the industrial capital-output ratio and the rate of capital stock growth at the limit, Dixit demonstrates that the behavior of the Jorgenson model is identical with that of the labor-surplus model in the short run. Thus, while Jorgenson has assembled additional evidence buttressing the propriety of the neoclassical formulations and the empirical tenuousness of the labor-surplus version, his "tests" must be qualified.

Our own reconnaissance of Japanese economic history has taken a somewhat different tack. Because our model does not yield the precise qualitative predictions characteristic of the Fei-Ranis and Jorgenson frameworks, our tests have focused on the simulated predictions of chapter 4. These tests, then, are in one sense narrower and in another sense significantly broader than those developed by Fei-Ranis and Jorgenson. On the one hand, the tests may be considered less generally relevant, since they rely on assumed initial conditions and parameter values. But because the values were drawn from a wide range of countries, and because the sensitivity of the predictions to the specific parameters has been investigated in considerable detail (chap. 6), limitations on the generality of the tests may be more apparent than real. On the other hand, our evaluation of the dualistic model is more generally relevant, since in addition to qualitative statements on *signs* of trends and levels of variables, we have explored their quantitative magnitudes. Indeed, the close quantitative correspondence of Japanese economic

73. S. Marglin, "Comment," pp. 60–66.
74. Dixit, "Theories of the Dual Economy."

history with the simulated model using parameters drawn from Southeast Asia as a whole (*excluding* Japan) is notable evidence of our model's veracity.

We have made no bold claims about the overall power of our tests. However, the evidence does yield support for the suitability of our formulation and, at the very least, casts doubt on the labor-surplus description of Meiji Japan. However, sufficient evidence has not yet been assembled for discrimination between Jorgenson's and our neoclassical descriptions of the growth process. The simplicity and similarity of the competing neoclassical models and the severe problems in interpreting the biases in the Japanese quantitative record are persuasive arguments for foregoing further comparison by means of currently available Japanese data. Our excursion into Japanese economic history does provide strong evidence that our model meets minimum empirical tests, and, as a result, we shall continue to expand upon this basic framework in the chapters which follow.

6

Some Development Problems Reconsidered: Sensitivity Analysis and Structural Elasticities

6.1. INTRODUCTION

We have reduced the generality of our dualistic model somewhat by restricting parameter values and initial conditions to represent an economic structure similar to contemporary developing Asian economies. In chapters 4 and 5, however, we found that this model of dualistic growth provided an effective description of both Japanese economic history and the growth experience of low-income countries as a group. Having confirmed the descriptive power of the model, we are now in a position to explore the system's response to various changes in parametric values.

The present chapter has two goals. First, it explores the sensitivity of key variables—for example, output growth, capital accumulation, urbanization, and industrialization—to alternative parameter values—for example, population growth, technical progress, savings rates, and demand parameters. This exercise permits an evaluation of the relative importance of the parameters in the system. Not only does it enable us to identify those parameter estimates which are especially important, and thus may deserve further econometric investigation, but it also eliminates the ambiguities in the qualitative analysis pursued in chapter 3.

Second, this chapter confronts the following six key development issues currently being debated by professional economists:

1. The importance of demand relative to the importance of supply in explaining shifts in the industrial structure remains an unresolved controversy. In section 6.2.2 we conclude that for

176

our economy Engel effects are an important aspect of growth, and that *shifts* in parameters in the expenditure system do indeed have a significant impact on structural change. This confirms the emphasis economic historians have placed on consumption demand in industrial revolutions. It is also shown that the "demonstration effect" exercises a *positive* influence on growth, contrary to the conclusion reached by development theorists in the 1950s. Finally, the analysis isolates the retarding influence of increased subsistence or a minimum wage on the developing economy.

2. The widespread concern over the long-run impact of population growth on economic development, and the intermediate-run influence of the "labor force explosion" expected in the 1970s, is considered in section 6.2.3.1. The simulation model yields insight into the impact of labor force growth. Again, our results are somewhat in conflict with the majority view, since we find some basis for optimism; more accurately, the doom-and-gloom predictions relating to population growth, while still true in direction, appear to hold with less force than is normally believed, at least in an economy undergoing moderately rapid output growth.

3. Labor-saving technical progress in manufacturing induced by the importation of foreign technology has played a conspicuous role in the pattern of urbanization and industrialization. Moreover, biased technological progress has assumed an even greater role with the advent of labor-saving innovations in agriculture, which have generated a "Green Revolution." But to date there have been very few attempts to evaluate the impact of the rate and bias of technical progress in a general equilibrium framework. Section 6.2.3.2 performs this evaluation. There the conflict between output-raising and employment effects of technical progress is stressed. The results appear to conflict with conventional wisdom.

4. The primacy of capital formation in economic development—and the supporting, indeed necessary, role of savings—is examined in section 6.2.4. It was argued in chapters 4 and 5

that an *acceleration* of per capita growth is *not* conditional upon abrupt changes in savings behavior. However, even though aggregate savings rates may be altered through changes in income distribution systematically associated with structural change, they may additionally change exogenously and be influenced directly by public policy. The sensitivity of the economy to shifts in the savings parameter is therefore explored in detail in this section.

5. The model also provides an opportunity to reexamine the sources-of-growth methodology. We find that the "residual" appears to account for as great a proportion of growth in the simulated economy as the empirical studies have found for a wide list of countries. But this result must be reconsidered in terms of its theoretical underpinnings. In particular, we demonstrate in section 6.2.4 that the feedbacks highlighted in a general equilibrium development model, but concealed in the sources-of-growth methodology, in part reconcile the controversy over the relative importance of capital formation, labor force growth, and productivity change to development.

6. Finally, the role of production dualism is examined in section 6.2.5. The findings are reinterpreted within the context of the "export technology" hypothesis. We argue that both this hypothesis and the formulation of production dualism highlighted in this study yield significant insights into the course of structural change.

6.2 SOME DEVELOPMENT PROBLEMS RECONSIDERED

6.2.1. Sensitivity Analysis and Structural Elasticities

Thus far our approach has been to examine the model's time paths by using what we believe to be realistic parameter values and initial conditions. Our interest has been to evaluate analytically and empirically the growth trajectories under assumed *constancy* of parameters. The questions asked in this chapter are somewhat different. Here we seek to identify the impact of *changes* in parameter values on growth. This issue requires both a norm for evaluation and a statistical procedure for summarizing the results. For comparative purposes we have taken as the norm the simulated economy—implicitly, the parameter values and initial conditions presented in chapter 4. The statistical procedure requires the calculation of "structural elasticities" which measure the impact of a change once and for all in a specified parameter on one or more variables of interest.[1]

Let

v_t^* = variable at t (for example, industrial output share, per capita output growth rate, rate of population growth),

θ = parameter being varied;

then

$$\frac{\partial v_t^*(\theta)}{v_t^*(\theta)} \frac{\theta}{\partial \theta} = \epsilon_{v_t^*(\theta)}$$

is the unadjusted structural elasticity measuring the elasticity response of $v_t^*(\theta)$ to a change once and for all in θ. (In practice, $\partial \theta / \theta = 0.01$.) The difficulty with this procedure is that a change in θ implies a change in the initial equilibrium conditions. The growth of the system is therefore affected by a change in θ in two ways: (1) θ influences initial conditions and the resulting growth trajectory; and (2), θ enters explicitly into the dynamic equations, further influencing growth behavior. Since our purpose is to focus on the second way, we require a method of adjusting the structural elasticity $\epsilon_{v_t^*}(\theta)$ so that it measures the second effect while suppressing the impact on initial conditions.

Let the impact of a change in θ on initial conditions be designated by

$$\frac{\partial v_0^*(\theta)}{v_0^*(\theta)} \frac{\theta}{\partial \theta} = \epsilon_{v_0^*(\theta)};$$

then the *adjusted structural elasticity*, which nets out the influence of changing initial conditions, is taken as

$$\epsilon^*_{v_t^*(\theta)} = \epsilon_{v_t^*(\theta)} - \epsilon_{v_0^*(\theta)}.$$

1. In developing our structural elasticity experiments we found helpful the earlier work of J. Vanek, *Estimating Foreign Resource Needs for Economic Development*; and P. Zarembka, "Introduction and a Basic Dual Economy Model."

While the adjusted structural elasticity $\epsilon_{v_t^*(0)}$ is only a first approximation to a measure which completely eliminates the impact of changes in the initial conditions due to changes in θ, we feel that it is superior to a statistic which ignores the effect on initial conditions. To facilitate reporting of results, the sensitivity analyses which follow include values of $\epsilon_{v_t^*(\theta)}^*$ for decadal terminal points; $t = 10, 20, 30, 40, 50$.

A word of caution should be raised in interpreting the structural elasticity measures. While the use of an elasticity statistic permits comparisons of the impacts of various parameter changes on the economic performance of the dual economy, one must avoid interpreting these comparisons as necessarily reflecting the importance of a particular parameter. The total impact of the parameter depends not only on the sensitivity of the system to changes in the parameter's value but also on the rate at which this value is likely to change through time.

The variables and parameters involved in the sensitivity analysis are listed below. Note that the parameters of technical change require special treatment if we are to examine separately changes in the bias, B_i, and changes in the intensity, $R_i(t)$, of technical change.

Variables

v_t^*	Description
$\dot{K}_i(t)/K_i(t)$	Growth rate of sectoral capital stock
$\dot{K}(t)/K(t)$	Growth rate of economy-wide capital stock
$1 - \alpha_i(t)$	Sectoral labor share
$1 - \alpha(t)$	Economy-wide labor share
$\overline{P(t)\dot{Q}_1(t)}/P(t)Q_1(t)$	Growth rate of urban output
$\dot{Q}_2(t)/Q_2(t)$	Growth rate of rural output
$\dot{G}(t)/G(t)$	Growth rate of GNP

$\dot{L}_1(t)/L_1(t)$	Rate of labor absorption
$u(t)$	Level of urbanization
$v(t)$	Industrial output share
$\hat{k}_i(t)$	Sectoral capital-labor ratios
$\hat{k}(t)$	Economy-wide capital-labor ratio

Parameters

θ	*Description*
σ_i	Sectoral elasticity of substitution of capital for labor
n_i	Growth rates of sectoral population
δ	Economy-wide depreciation rate
$\beta_{i1} = \Pi_i$	Demand parameters for urban workers and all property income recipients for urban and rural goods
β_{i2}	Demand parameters for rural workers for urban and rural goods
γ	Minimum-subsistence bundle
s	Marginal savings rate
$\lambda_L - \lambda_K$	Bias in technical change
λ_L, λ_K	Rates of factor augmentation

6.2.2. Consumer Tastes, Engel Effects, and Structural Change in the Dualistic Economy

Economists have long emphasized the role of consumption demand in industrial revolutions and its importance to growth and structural change, but theoretical analysis of this role has been limited. There appear to be two conflicting views concerning the nature and extent of its influence. Challenges to the prime role of demand have developed on two fronts. First, empirical studies have concluded that supply factors occupy the central role in explaining industrial patterns since changes in relative factor supplies associated with growth cause systematic shifts in comparative advantage as per capita income rises.[2] Second, many of the theoretical formulations of the growth process have suppressed or omitted a consideration of the role of consumption demand, focusing almost exclusively on supply conditions. In the literature dealing with two-sector growth models, for example, the approaches range from those which are not designed to confront issues of demand, since only one consumption goods sector is postulated,[3] to those in which demand influences are suppressed through simplifying assumptions.[4]

Support for the view that consumption demand plays an important role in the process of growth and structural change has come mainly from empirical studies establishing the existence of different expenditure and income elasticities for food and non-food goods. It has been argued that Engel effects not only cause a shift in the industrial origin of production, but also induce higher levels of productivity and output.[5] There have, however, been few attempts to explore in a theoretical way the influence of Engel effects within a model framework designed to investigate the relationship between growth and structural change over extended periods of time. The role of consumption demand and the existence of different income elasticities has, of course, been explicitly recognized in those models constructed

2. H. B. Chenery, "Patterns of Industrial Growth."
3. H. Uzawa, "On a Two-Sector Model of Economic Growth, I"; "On a Two-Sector Model of Economic Growth, II."
4. D. W. Jorgenson, "The Development of a Dual Economy."
5. H. S. Houthakker, "The Influence of Prices and Income on Household Expenditures"; S. Kuznets, *Modern Economic Growth*; and A. C. Kelley, "Demand Patterns, Demographic Change, and Economic Growth."

within an input-output framework. However, with few exceptions, these applications have been confined to problems relating to relatively short-run analyses. The role of consumption demand has also been recognized explicitly in the neo-Keynesian literature, but in these models the focus of the inquiry has centered on growth and stability in the short-run rather than on the long-run effects of changes in consumption behavior. Moreover, the level of aggregation in these models frequently is such that there is little scope for changes in the composition of consumption to influence the pattern growth and structural change. Not only has the theoretical literature given comparatively little attention to the role of Engel effects, but also there has been almost no attention given to the role of consumer tastes, despite a growing amount of empirical evidence suggesting that secular changes in consumer tastes have been a part of the process of structural change in many of the present day higher income economies.

The role of demand and supply factors in explaining growth and structural change can only be successfully appraised in a model in which both elements possess meaningful specifications. While our dualistic model contains such specifications, the qualitative analysis in chapter 3 resulted in some ambiguities. In the present section, however, both comparative static analysis and dynamic analysis are utilized to appraise the role of demand on per capita growth and structural change—industrialization, urbanization, and consumption patterns. To gain insight into the dynamic behavior of industrialization, we employ the simulation model developed and analyzed in chapter 4.

In view of the importance attached to Engel effects as an explanation for the historically observed patterns of industrialization, it is useful to begin by reviewing the role of income elasticities of demand in our model. As our analysis in chapter 3 suggested, the measure of income used in defining these elasticities has a bearing on the interpretation of the role of Engel effects. In the simpler model analyzed in chapter 3, where only wage income is used for consumption, we viewed wage income per laborer as the relevant measure of income and defined the income elasticities accordingly. These elasticities may be more accurately thought of as expenditure elasticities for the economy as a whole in view of the fact that aggregate consumption expenditure is equal to total wage income. These income (and expenditure) elasticities were found to be

$$\eta_{1j}(t) = \frac{y(t)w(t)}{y(t)w(t) - \gamma}$$

$$\eta_{2j}(t) = \frac{\beta_{2j}y(t)w(t)}{\beta_{2j}y(t)w(t) + (1 - \beta_{2j})\gamma}.$$

It should first be noted that these elasticities are endogenous variables and not parameters in the model: indeed, the value for each elasticity is uniquely determined for any given efficiency capital-labor ratio. Since these elasticities are determined endogenously, we cannot say that Engel effects are a cause of industrialization because in any given period the values for $\eta_{kj}(t)$ and $v(t)$ are determined simultaneously. However, if we were able to find plausible restrictions on the values of these elasticities such that we could determine the nature of the relationship between growth and industrialization, then in this sense we could say that income elasticities play an important role in the process of development.

However, it is clear from the above definitions of the income elasticities that $0 < \eta_{2j}(t) < 1 < \eta_{1j}(t) < \infty$ for any efficiency capital-labor ratio, and thus $y(t)w(t)$. This result requires only that $0 < \beta_{ij} < 1$ and $0 < \gamma < \infty$. The implication is that the income elasticity of demand for food is *always* less than one, and that for industrial goods it is *always* greater than one.[6] But as we demonstrated in chapter 3, when the efficiency

6. To see this result, note that by differentiating η_{ij} with respect to ω, we obtain

$$\frac{d\eta_{1j}}{d\omega} = \frac{y(1 - \eta_{1j})\alpha_2 f'_2(k_2)}{y\omega f'_2(k_2) - \gamma} < 0,$$

$$\frac{d\eta_{2j}}{d\omega} = \frac{\beta_{2j}y(1 - \eta_{2j})\alpha_2 f'_2(k_2)}{\beta_{2j}y\omega f'_2 + (1 - \beta_{2j})\gamma} > 0.$$

In view of the fact that $d\omega/dk > 0$ (when $\sigma_2 \geqq 1$ and $k_1 - k_2 > 0$) it follows that η_{ij} are uniquely determined for any k. In passing, we also may note that, because ω and k move together, η_{1j} and η_{2j} approach one as k increases without limit.

capital-labor ratio is rising and hence $y(t)w(t)$ is rising, we are unable to determine whether the level of industrialization rises without more restrictive assumptions about production relationships. While we may empirically observe income (or expenditure) elasticities consistent with Engel effects, they are neither necessary nor sufficient for industrialization to occur. On this basis, then, we can conclude that in the simple model Engel effects do not play a role in determining the level of industrialization in our economy.

When we expand the model to allow a fixed share of rental income to be consumed our interpretation of the role of demand elasticities changes. It is still true that when wage income rises a proportionately larger share will be allocated for consumption of industrial goods; likewise, when rental income rises a similar response is observed. However, wage and rental incomes do not necessarily rise together when the aggregate capital-labor ratio is rising.[7] Thus, it is no longer appropriate to conduct the analysis of the role of income elasticities in terms of wage income and rental income. For an analysis of the aggregate behavior of consumers the relevant measure is aggregate income per capita, which we have defined elsewhere as $g(t) = G(t)/(1 + \Phi)L(t)$. On the other hand, if the analysis was in terms of expenditure elasticities, the relevant variable would be

$$e(t) = \frac{y(t)w(t)}{1 + \Phi} + \frac{(1 - s)x(t)r(t)K(t)}{(1 + \Phi)L(t)},$$

where $e(t)$ is the total current consumption expenditure outlay per capita in the economy. We have chosen to conduct our

7. When $\hat{k}$ changes, for example, the change in wage income per laborer is given by $y\alpha_2 f'_2$, which is positive. The change in rental income per capitalist, on the other hand, is ambiguous: it is given by

$$x \frac{f'_2}{\Phi} [\,[1 - \frac{\partial \omega}{\partial \hat{k}} \frac{\hat{k}}{\omega}] + \alpha_2 \frac{\partial \omega}{\partial \hat{k}} \frac{\hat{k}}{\omega}].$$

As noted in our discussion about the ambiguity between changes in $k(t)$ and $g(t)$, a sufficient condition for rental income to rise is that

$$\frac{\partial \omega}{\partial \hat{k}} \frac{\hat{k}}{\omega} \leqq 1.$$

analysis in terms of income elasticities rather than expenditure elasticities, although the same results are forthcoming when the latter concept is used.

By defining $\eta_i^*(t)$ to be the elasticity of demand for the *i*th good with respect to changes in aggregate income per capita; that is,

$$\eta_i^*(t) = \frac{\partial d_i(t)}{\partial g(t)} \frac{g(t)}{d_i(t)},$$

we find that the behavior of the elasticity variables in response to changes in the efficiency capital-labor ratio are ambiguous: the sign of

$$\frac{\partial d_i(t)}{\partial g(t)} = \frac{\partial d_i(t)}{\partial \omega(t)} \frac{\partial \omega(t) \partial k(t)}{\partial k(t) \partial g(t)}$$

cannot be determined because of the ambiguity in the sign of $\partial k(t)/\partial g(t)$. But on the other hand, if we require that $\eta_2^*(t) > 0$, it follows that $\partial g(t)/\partial k(t) > 0$ because $\partial d_2(t)/\partial \omega(t)$ and $\partial \omega(t)/\partial k(t)$ are both positive when $\sigma_2(t) \geqq 1$ and $k_1(t) - k_2(t) > 0$ (see chap. 4). Moreover, we can show that when $\eta_2^*(t)$ is positive but less than one, $v(t)$ necessarily increases when $k(t)$ increases.[8] Thus, when $k(t)$ is increasing, a sufficient condition for growth and increases in the level of industrialization is that the income elasticity of demand for agricultural goods is positive but less than one. The requirement that $0 < \eta_2^*(t) < 1$ does not necessarily imply the existence or absence of Engel

---

8. By definition we know that

$$v(t) = 1 - \frac{d_2(t)}{g(t)}$$

from which we have

$$\frac{dv}{dk} = -\frac{\partial g}{\partial k} \frac{d_2}{g^2} \left[\frac{\partial d_2}{\partial k} \frac{\partial k}{\partial g} \frac{g}{d_2} - 1 \right] = -\frac{\partial g}{\partial k} \frac{d_2}{g^2} [\eta_2^* - 1].$$

If $0 < \eta_2^* < 1$, then $dv/dk > 0$ in view of the fact that $\eta_2^* > 0$ is sufficient to ensure that $\partial g / \partial k > 0$.

effects in the sense that $\eta_1^*(t) > \eta_2^*(t)$.[9] Nevertheless, we can conclude that the existence of Engel effects in the sense that $0 < \eta_2^*(t) < 1 < \eta_1^*(t) < \infty$ is sufficient to ensure growth and industrialization when $k(t)$ is rising, although as we have just seen the restriction on $\eta_1^*(t)$ is unnecessary.

This result highlights an important difference between the two models with respect to the role of income or expenditure elasticities. In the simpler model Engel effects are present for any choice of parameter values and for any efficiency capital-labor ratio. When we admit the possibility of consumption from rental income, restrictions on the value of expenditure elasticities are sufficient to provide an unambiguous interpretation of the relationship between growth and industrialization when the efficiency capital-labor ratio is rising. Moreover, it suggests that, at least in the context of dualistic two-sector models, the extreme assumption of consumption only from wage income can result in a rather misleading interpretation of the role of demand.

Not only do we find an important role for income elasticities of demand, but we also find that changes in tastes (shifts in the individual parameters of the demand system) exert an important influence on growth and structural change in our model. Recent empirical evidence reveals that the assumption of fixed

9. By definition we have
$$g = d_1 + d_2 + d^i,$$
where d^i is the aggregate investment demand per capita, $PI/(1 + \Phi)L$. It follows that
$$\eta_1^* \frac{d_1}{g} + \eta_2^* \frac{d_2}{g} + \frac{\partial d^i}{\partial g} = 1,$$
from which it follows that
$$v < \eta_1^* \frac{d_1}{g} + \frac{\partial d^i}{\partial g} < 1$$
when $0 < \eta_2^* < 1$. When $\partial d^i/\partial g > 0$ then $0 < \eta_1^* < 1$ because $d_1/g < 1$. Even so, η_1^* may still be greater than η_2^*. But if $\partial d^i/\partial g < 0$ then η_1^* may be greater than one, in which case Engel effects definitely would be observed in aggregate consumption behavior.

tastes may be particularly inappropriate in a study of growth and structural change in which the time horizon of analysis may span decades. Using a linear expenditure system similar to that employed in our model, Stone and Brown have identified substantial changes in tastes between 1900 and 1960 in England.[10] Parks has found similar results from Sweden between 1861 and 1955.[11] Moreover, systematic taste changes were also typical of Japan between 1878 and 1964, according to Kaneda's research.[12] Finally, it is well known that there is considerable pressure in developing nations to increase the minimum wage. In view of our interpretation of γ as a behaviorally determined minimum bundle of wage goods,[13] upward pressure on the minimum wage can be reasonably translated into systematic increases in the demand parameter γ.

The impact of taste changes can be explored by considering the consequences of increases in γ and β_{ij}. Since the subsequent analysis is invariant to the consumer's sector of residence, only the results for urban consumers (β_{1j}) are presented. Moreover, the effects of changes in tastes for agricultural commodities (β_{2j}) are merely opposite in sign to those for urban goods. Thus, our analysis will focus primarily on changes in demand for urban goods. The results of the comparative static analysis are summarized in table 6.1.

An increase in β_{1j} leads to a fall in the wage-rental rate as a result of the adjustment to the excess demand for industrial goods in which capital is utilized more extensively than labor. Moreover, because of the increase in the relative cost of capital services, the relative price of industrial goods will be higher than previously. This result can be obtained by noting that, while a decline in the wage-rental ratio will reduce the sectoral capital-

10. R. Stone and A. Brown, "Behavioral and Technical Change in Economic Models."

11. R. Parks, "Price Responsiveness of Factor Utilization in Swedish Manufacturing, 1870–1950."

12. H. Kaneda, "Long-Term Changes in Food Consumption Patterns in Japan, 1878–1964."

13. A. S. Goldberger, "Functional Form and Utility: A Review of Consumer Demand Theory."

TABLE 6.1 Comparative static analysis of demand
parameter changes

Demand change	Key endogenous variable					Structural change variable					
	$d\omega$	dk_1	dk_2	dP	$d\phi$	dz_{11}	dz_{12}	dz_{21}	dz_{22}	dv	du
$d\beta_{11} = -d\beta_{21}$	−	−	−	+	+	?	?	−	−	+	+
$d\gamma$	+	+	+	−	−	?	?	+	+	−	−

labor ratios, this reduction will be less in industry because of
the relative difficulty of factor substitution in this sector. Since
the terms of trade depends on the marginal productivities in
industry relative to those in agriculture, the price of industrial
goods will increase as a result of the increase in the demand
parameter β_{1j}.

The effects of an increase in β_{1j} on the per capita consumption
of agricultural goods may be decomposed into two major influences: one is a decrease in the amount demanded through the
"quantity" effect that results from the increase in β_{1j} and hence,
the allocation of a larger share of any given "supernumerary"
income ($\gamma\omega f'_2 - \gamma$) to industrial goods; the other is the "income" effect that occurs because wage income is lower in the
new equilibrium po ition and hence, a smaller amount of agricultural output is consumed. This "income" effect reinforces
the "quantity" effect of an increase in β_{1j} to yield an unambiguous decline in per capita consumption of agricultural goods.[14]
However, the shift in consumer tastes towards urban goods
results in an ambiguous change in per capita *consumption* of
industrial goods. The "quantity" effect through supernumerary
income is, of course, positive; moreover, in the new equilibrium
position the price of industrial goods relative to agricultural

14. By differentiating z_{2j} with respect to β_{1j} and rearranging,
we have
$$\frac{dz_{2j}}{d\beta_{1j}} = -\left\{ [y\omega f'_2(k_2) - \gamma] - \beta_{2j}y\alpha_2 f'_2(k_2)\frac{\partial\omega}{\partial\beta_{1j}} \right\}.$$
Because of the restriction that $y\omega \geqq \gamma$, it follows that $[y\omega f'_2(k_2) - \gamma] > 0$. Furthermore, $f'_2(k_2) > 0$, while $\partial\omega/\partial\beta_{1j} < 0$. Thus $dz_{2j}/d\beta_{1j} < 0$.

goods is higher, but it is not clear whether the combined influence of the "quantity" and "price" effects is sufficient to offset the above mentioned "income" effect. Should this negative "income" effect be powerful enough, consumption of industrial goods may decline![15] The total demand for industrial goods is our focus, however, and with the rise in the non-wage income share, the demand for investment goods rises as well ($d\phi/d\beta_{1j} > 0$). What is the net effect on the value of industrial *output*?

It can be shown that for any given efficiency capital-labor ratio, an increase in β_{1j} will always result in a higher value of aggregate output per capita in the economy.[16] Since an increase in the preference also lowers the per capita consumption of agricultural goods, the level of industrialization is given a positive stimulus. Similarly, an increase in subsistence requirements in food tends to raise per capita consumption of agricultural goods and lower the value of aggregate output per capita. Urbanization levels increase, because of the additional labor required to produce the newly demanded industrial goods. Even though the decrease in the wage-rental ratio will stimulate the substitution of labor for capital in both sectors, under normal labor supply conditions this substitution effect will never offset the initial positive impact on urban in-migration.

Thus far we have been successful in isolating the determinants

15. By differentiating z_{1j} with respect to β_{1j} and rearranging, we have

$$\frac{dz_{1j}}{d\beta_{1j}} = \frac{z_{1j}}{\beta_{1j}}\left(1 - \frac{\beta_{1j}}{P}\frac{\partial P}{\partial\beta_{1j}}\right) + \beta_{1j}y\alpha_2\frac{f'_2(k_2)}{P}\frac{\partial\omega}{\partial\beta_{1j}}.$$

Now $\partial P/\partial\beta_{1j} > 0$ and $\partial\omega/\partial\beta_{1j} < 0$; thus, when $(\partial P/\partial\beta_{1j})(\beta_{1j}/P) \geqq 1$, it follows that $dz_{1j}/d\beta_{1j} < 0$. When $(\partial P/\partial\beta_{1j})(\beta_{1j}/P) < 1$ the outcome is ambiguous.

16. The value of current output per laborer is given by $g(t) = G(t)/L(t)$, which was restated in chapter 3 as $g(t) = y(t)$ $[k(t) + \omega(t)]f'_2[k_2(t)]$. By differentiating $g(t)$ with respect to β_{1j} and rearranging, we obtain

$$\frac{dg}{d\beta_{1j}} = \frac{-y\alpha_2 f'_2(k_2)(k - k_2)}{k_2}\frac{\partial\omega}{\partial\beta_{1j}}.$$

When $(k_1 - k_2) > 0$, then $(k - k_2) > 0$; if $\partial\omega/\partial\beta_{1j} < 0$, it follows that $dg/d\beta_{1j} > 0$. An increase in the preference for urban goods raises the value of per capita aggregate output.

of the two key aspects of structural change *in the static case*—urbanization and industrialization ratios. The dynamic course of urbanization and industrialization, which have been the prime focus of empirical studies, is far more difficult to analyze. Consider first the impact of shifts in tastes on the long-run behavior of the industrialization rate. This variable has attracted the most attention in the literature on structural change, but in terms of our qualitative analysis of the dynamic model above, the course of the industrialization rate is ambiguous. We expect the proportion of supernumerary income devoted to food to decline over time. (Stone and Brown find that the proportion of supernumerary income spent on food fell at the rate of 0.29 percent a year in Great Britain between 1900 and 1960.[17] The impact of such a change in tastes can be captured by examining the consequences of an increase in β_{1j}. The structural elasticities in tables 6.2, 6.3, and 6.4 show that the shift in tastes in favor of urban goods has a positive initial impact on industrialization in early growth phases, and since the rate of growth in the capital-labor ratio is also raised, the industrial output share receives an *increasingly positive stimulus* over time. In early stages of growth, then, a shift in tastes toward urban goods stimulates industrialization far above the first-order impact stressed in the development literature. This conclusion is the opposite of that reached by development theorists in the 1950s who stressed the inhibiting impact of the "demonstration effect" on growth. Although Nurkse and the others typically focus only on savings behavior, their conclusion was that the demonstration effect inhibited growth.[18] We come to the opposite conclusion. To the extent that the demonstration effect implies a shift out of Z-goods[19] and agricultural goods and into Western urban goods, the effect is to stimulate significantly per capita income

17. Stone and Brown, "Behavioral and Technical Change," p. 208.

18. R. Nurkse, *Problems of Capital Formation in Underdeveloped Countries.*

19. S. Hymer and S. Resnick, "A Model of an Agrarian Economy with Non-agricultural Activities."

Table 6.2 Structural elasticities (demand: capitalists and urban workers, $d\beta_{11} = -d\beta_{21}$)

Variable	$\epsilon_t^*(\theta)$: Value of elasticity at year				
	10	20	30	40	50
GNP growth rate	+0.248	+0.108	+0.065	+0.176	+0.137
Per capita GNP growth rate	+1.306	+0.640	+ .477	+ .819	+ .707
Level of urbanization	+0.127	+0.255	+ .360	+ .469	+ .565
Industrial output share	+0.083	+0.188	+ .221	+ .271	+ .314
Capital-labor ratio (overall) ...	+0.087	+0.189	+ .280	+ .373	+ .452
Capital-labor ratio (urban)	−0.005	+0.030	+ .016	+ .029	+ .046
Capital-labor ratio (rural)	+0.058	+0.035	+ .142	+ .178	+ .217
Capital stock growth (overall) ..	+0.389	+0.025	+ .196	+ .149	+ .067
Capital stock growth (urban) ...	+0.291	+1.178	+ .162	+ .151	+ .087
Capital stock growth (rural)	+0.045	−3.658	− .199	− .284	− .358
Labor factor share (overall)	−0.041	−0.089	− .105	− .131	− .144
Labor factor share (urban)	+0.015	−0.010	+ .035	+ .052	+ .073
Labor factor share (rural)	−0.016	−0.010	− .023	− .035	− .043
Rate of labor absorption	+0.249	+0.510	+0.127	+0.125	+0.058

TABLE 6.3 Structural elasticities (demand: economy-wide joint increase in β_{11}, β_{12} [= decrease in β_{21}, β_{22}])

$\epsilon^*_t(\theta)$: Value of elasticity at year

Variable	10	20	30	40	50
GNP growth rate	+0.154	+0.118	+0.068	+0.020	+0.013
Per capita GNP growth rate	+ .969	+ .732	+ .546	+ .412	+ .419
Level of urbanization	+ .159	+ .319	+ .454	+ .585	+ .700
Industrial output share	+ .107	+ .239	+ .285	+ .345	+ .392
Capital-labor ratio (overall)	+ .107	+ .228	+ .342	+ .455	+ .553
Capital-labor ratio (urban)	− .007	+ .030	+ .017	+ .033	+ .057
Capital-labor ratio (rural)	+ .063	+ .047	+ .159	+ .209	+ .263
Capital stock growth (overall)	+ .484	+ .061	+ .216	+ .119	+ .115
Capital stock growth (urban)	+ .455	+1.216	+ .180	+ .091	+ .112
Capital stock growth (rural)	− .158	−3.758	− .283	− .317	− .315
Labor factor share (overall)	+ .051	− .103	− .131	− .160	− .177
Labor factor share (urban)	+ .015	− .009	+ .038	+ .060	+ .085
Labor factor share (rural)	− .018	− .003	− .025	− .036	− .051
Rate of labor absorption	+0.424	+0.550	+0.145	+0.047	+0.046

TABLE 6.4 Structural elasticities (demand: rural workers, $d\beta_{12} = -d\beta_{22}$)

Variable	$\epsilon_t^*(\theta)$: Value of elasticity at year				
	10	20	30	40	50
GNP growth rate	+0.204	+0.058	+0.004	−0.004	+0.157
Per capita GNP growth rate	+ .905	+ .263	+ .072	+ .051	+ .522
Level of urbanization	+ .088	+ .120	+ .143	+ .161	+ .175
Industrial output share	+ .077	+ .098	+ .111	+ .115	+ .121
Capital-labor ratio (overall)	+ .017	+ .038	+ .062	+ .081	+ .098
Capital-labor ratio (urban)	− .022	− .021	− .017	− .013	− .005
Capital-labor ratio (rural)	− .052	− .047	− .040	− .026	− .005
Capital stock growth (overall) ...	+ .218	+ .146	+ .021	+ .007	+ .047
Capital stock growth (urban)	+ .217	+ .122	+ .019	+ .005	+ .083
Capital stock growth (rural)	+ .095	+ .089	− .084	− .082	− .144
Labor factor share (overall)	− .023	− .032	− .041	− .051	− .049
Labor factor share (urban)	− .011	− .009	− .009	− .007	+ .000
Labor factor share (rural)	+ .002	+ .003	+ .003	− .008	− .003
Rate of labor absorption	+0.178	+0.136	+0.018	+0.001	+0.063

growth in the dual economy. Furthermore, industrialization is fostered beyond the first-order effects, and both urbanization and labor absorption rates in industry are increased.

All these generalizations are reversed in table 6.5, where the results of the long-run impact of an increase in γ are presented. It has long been recognized that increases in subsistence requirements, however defined, have a depressing influence on growth in the dual economy. Normally that analytical result is forthcoming from quite a different model, in which wages are institutionally set equal to some subsistence bundle.[20] In the labor-surplus models, the key analytical focus is the impact of wage setting on available surplus for accumulation. We assume marginal product pricing in our system, and, as a result, γ enters only into the decision on expenditure composition. As table 6.1 suggests, a rise in γ causes a fall in ϕ and $u,$ and hence a fall in the rate of change in $k(t)$. These results are confirmed in table 6.5 and we also find a fall in the growth of per capita output. These conclusions rest on a limiting assumption; γ is composed entirely of agricultural goods. If, as development proceeds, minimum consumption increasingly involves "necessary" expenditures on nonagricultural commodities—a hypothesis at present in vogue in the development literature and confirmed by Parks, Stone, and Yoshihara on Swedish, English, and Japanese historical data, respectively[21]— our conclusions would require appropriate modification.

In summary, three major conclusions are forthcoming from this section. First, we find that the existence of Engel effects is neither a necessary nor a sufficient condition for industrialization to occur in our simple model developed in chapter 2. Engel effects, together with the tendency for demand elasticities to converge toward one as development takes place, will

20. J. C. Fei and G. Ranis, *Development of the Labor Surplus Economy: Theory and Policy.*

21. R. Parks, "Swedish Manufacturing"; R. Stone, ed., *A Programme for Growth,* vol. 5, *The Model in Its Environment: A Progress Report*; and K. Yoshihara, "Demand Functions: An Application to the Japanese Expenditure Pattern."

TABLE 6.5 Structural elasticities (demand: subsistence level, $\theta = \gamma$)

Variable	$\epsilon^*_t(\theta)$: Value of elasticity at year				
	10	20	30	40	50
GNP growth rate	−0.122	−0.118	−0.058	+0.010	−0.105
Per capita GNP growth rate	−.815	−0.673	−.409	−.172	−.492
Level of urbanization	−.052	−0.074	−.057	−.042	−.019
Industrial output share	−.006	−0.018	+.054	+.101	+.143
Capital-labor ratio (overall)	−.107	−0.205	−.277	−.323	−.345
Capital-labor ratio (urban)	−.015	−0.079	−.089	−.117	−.141
Capital-labor ratio (rural)	−.132	−0.200	−.381	−.460	−.508
Capital stock growth (overall)	−.396	−0.048	−.171	−.028	+.018
Capital stock growth (urban)	−.084	−0.940	+.083	+.125	+.119
Capital stock growth (rural)	−.541	2.903	−.504	−.204	−.101
Labor factor share (overall)	+.030	+0.046	+.026	+.008	+.018
Labor factor share (urban)	−.031	−0.024	−.088	−.116	−.139
Labor factor share (rural)	+.032	+0.028	+.052	+.068	+.077
Rate of labor absorption	+0.093	−0.138	+0.250	+0.243	+0.225

always be forthcoming from the simple model for *any* theoretically possible set of demand parameters. Second, we find that when we modify the simple model to allow consumption from both wage and rental income, the existence of Engel effects is a sufficient condition to ensure an increase in the level of industrialization when the efficiency capital-labor ratio is rising. This result leads us to conclude that at least in the context of dualistic two-sector models, the extreme assumption of consumption only from wage income can result in a rather misleading interpretation of the role of demand elasticities. Finally, demand also plays a pervasive and important role in ·the model through changes in consumer tastes. Indeed, the sensitivity of the economy to shifts in tastes toward urban goods may be as stimulatory to structural change in the long run as alterations in savings parameters, the variable of traditional focus in the development literature. Thus the "demonstration effect," commonly a villain in descriptive analyses of growth and development, may turn out to be as much a hero as the touted puritan ethic regarding high savings and spending prudence.

6.2.3. Biased Technological Progress and Labor Force Growth in the Dualistic Economy

6.2.3.1. *Population Explosions and Labor Force Growth.* Asian development in the seventies is likely to take place under conditions quite different from those typical of the past two decades. The population explosion of the 1940s and 1950s experienced by many Asian countries will be transformed into a labor force explosion in the current decade, and without commensurate increases in employment opportunities there is likely to be growing unemployment, or at least widespread underemployment and continued low levels of labor productivity. An extensive literature has developed on problems of urban unemployment and labor absorption in both industry and agriculture,[22] but for the most part this work utilizes par-

22. J. G. Williamson, "Capital Accumulation, Labor Saving, and Labor Absorption Once More"; L. Lau and P. Yotopolous,

tial equilibrium analysis to examine the influence of factors affecting labor absorption. A more productive approach requires a general dynamic framework which specifies explicitly the derived functions of labor demand in the industrial and nonindustrial sectors, the economy-wide labor supply function, and the process of intersectoral migration. Our model is able to capture these interaction effects, and therefore it perhaps provides a better basis for examining the effects of changes in population growth on the development of the economy. While there is, in reality, a long gestation period between changes in population and labor supply growth rates, nevertheless our analysis is able to provide some useful insights into the problems associated with the expected Asian labor force explosion which will manifest itself fully in the present decade.[23] It should be emphasized that in our model labor force growth, contrary to most short-run treatments of demographic elements,[24] affects supply conditions in a very important way but only minimally affects the allocation between consumption and savings, since we assume that only recipients of property income save and that their savings rate is constant. Additionally, we have for simplicity ignored the important impact of family size variations on the household consumption decision. Kelley has found these demographic effects to be potentially quite large.[25] In our demand system, population changes influence the consumption decision only through their effect on wage income and relative commodity prices.

The comparative static analysis of an exogenous augmentation of the labor force is straightforward. An increase in the physical stock of labor relative to that of capital lowers the efficiency capital-labor ratio if there is no change in x and y.

"Micro-functions in a Macro Model: An Application to Agricultural Employment and Development Strategies."

23. B. F. Johnston and J. Cownie, "The Seed-Fertilizer Revolution and Labor Force Absorption."

24. A. J. Coale and E. M. Hoover, *Population Growth and Economic Development in Low-Income Countries.*

25. Kelley, "Demand Patterns."

Per capita consumption levels will fall as a result. Thus, according to our earlier qualitative analysis, an increase in the labor force growth rate (due to an increase in n_i) combined with the increased labor-saving and labor-using character of technological progress in, respectively, industry and agriculture, will result in a decline in the relative price of efficiency labor, a decline in levels of urbanization as labor is redistributed to rural activities, and a rise in the ratio of gross investment to capital stock and in the rate of accumulation. But the positive impact on capital accumulation may partially offset the retarding influence of accelerated labor force growth on $k(t)$ growth. Therefore, the overall effect of the labor force explosion on $\dot{k}(t)/k(t)$ and growth rates unfortunately cannot be determined in a qualitative way, and we again turn to a numerical experiment relevant to those economies.

The results of our sensitivity analysis with the parameters of labor force growth are given in tables 6.6 and 6.7. They provide the basis for two immediate generalizations. First, without exception an increase in the labor force growth rate tends to exert its primary impact during the first two or three decades. In the case of per capita GNP growth, for example, the dramatic and initial adverse impact is significantly dissipated over time; by the middle of the simulation period the structural elasticity has declined from 0.557 to 0.146. The opposite trend, but same pattern, is experienced by urbanization and the industrial output share. Second, growth in the dual economy is far more sensitive to variations in the "natural" rate of labor force growth in rural than in urban areas. This result, of course, will always be produced in an economy with low initial levels of urbanization. Since the signs on the structural elasticities for n_1 and n_2 are always the same, the remaining discussion will focus only on n_2.

The finding that increased rates of population growth will exert a negative impact on per capita output expansion is hardly surprising; this result is forthcoming from most, if not all, models of growth. Of much greater interest and importance,

TABLE 6.6 Structural elasticities (urban population growth, $\theta = n_1$)

Variable	$\epsilon^*_t(\theta)$: Value of elasticity at year				
	10	20	30	40	50
GNP growth rate	+0.043	+0.092	+0.144	+0.173	+0.187
Per capita GNP growth rate	− .557	− .314	− .146	− .091	− .092
Level of urbanization	− .032	− .058	− .074	− .084	− .092
Industrial output share	− .016	− .027	− .027	− .028	− .027
Capital-labor ratio (overall)	− .050	− .096	− .136	− .166	− .192
Capital-labor ratio (urban)	− .021	− .041	− .059	− .075	− .092
Capital-labor ratio (rural)	− .063	− .123	− .176	− .225	− .277
Capital stock growth (overall) ...	− .122	+ .003	+ .104	+ .142	+ .148
Capital stock growth (urban)	− .112	+ .063	+ .089	+ .117	+ .146
Capital stock growth (rural)	− .146	− .154	+ .146	+ .213	+ .150
Labor factor share (overall)	+ .001	+ .005	+ .006	+ .006	+ .004
Labor factor share (urban)	− .016	− .026	− .040	− .050	− .061
Labor factor share (rural)	+ .003	+ .008	+ .018	+ .025	+ .033
Rate of labor absorption	+0.263	+0.096	+0.477	+0.473	+0.537

TABLE 6.7 Structural elasticities (rural population growth, $\Theta = n_2$)

Variable	$\epsilon^*_t(\Theta)$: Value of elasticity at year				
	10	20	30	40	50
GNP growth rate	+0.317	+0.459	+0.420	+0.435	+0.445
Per capita GNP growth rate	−1.178	−0.376	−.372	−.218	−.100
Level of urbanization	−0.110	−0.200	−.234	−.250	−.250
Industrial output share	−0.050	−0.110	−.088	−.082	−.076
Capital-labor ratio (overall) ...	−0.170	−0.321	−.425	−.489	−.521
Capital-labor ratio (urban)	−0.070	−0.160	−.186	−.225	−.249
Capital-labor ratio (rural)	−0.213	−0.335	−.557	−.674	−.752
Capital stock growth (overall) ..	+0.024	+0.400	+.323	+.361	+.389
Capital stock growth (urban) ...	−0.013	−0.749	+.313	+.322	+.384
Capital stock growth (rural)	+0.126	+3.491	+.348	+.465	+.390
Labor factor share (overall)	+0.015	+0.036	+.024	+.023	+.010
Labor factor share (urban)	−0.045	−0.054	−.122	−.145	−.164
Labor factor share (rural)	+0.023	+0.032	+.060	+.080	+.087
Rate of labor absorption	+0.263	+0.096	+0.477	+0.473	+0.537

however, is the observation that this negative influence of population growth may be attenuated through time as the result of the previously mentioned positive impact of labor force growth on factor shares and capital accumulation. In particular, a notable feature of the dualistic model is that a rise in labor force growth also *increases* the rate of accumulation and, as a result, $\dot{k}(t)/k(t)$. Since $d\phi(t) > 0$, the negative impact of a rise in labor force growth rates on $\dot{k}(t)/k(t)$ is somewhat offset. Because of the greater ease of factor substitution in the agricultural sector, the rise in rural population growth has a much smaller impact on the urban than on the rural efficiency capital-labor ratio (table 6.7). Nevertheless, the offsetting influence of $\phi(t)$ increases dramatically in early phases of growth, and the effect of the "labor force explosion" has an *increasingly* positive influence on capital accumulation over time (table 6.7). Thus, *the rate of urbanization (and industrialization) is sharply curtailed in the first two decades of experience with higher rates of labor force growth, but the impact becomes much smaller thereafter.*

The impact of an increase in "natural" labor force growth rates on per capita GNP growth can now be readily isolated. We know that, while urbanization levels will be negatively affected, the magnitude of this influence diminishes over time. Thus, even though the overall population growth rate will rise, its rate of increase will decline significantly. For this reason the adverse impact of an increase in the population growth rate on per capita GNP growth should also diminish. Since per capita GNP is stimulated in the early decades by a rapid rise in $\phi(t)$, it follows that the negative impact of the labor force explosion in the 1970s on labor productivity growth should diminish rapidly after the first decade or so, provided, of course, that the population and labor force explosions do give rise to increased rates of capital accumulation.

These results underscore the utility of our general methodology, which is in contrast to the typical stories of gloom abundant in both partial equilibrium numerical studies and general equilibrium qualitative analyses (where signs alone are considered). It is also necessary to take into account the *quantitative* dimensions of the problem with an explicit consideration of the short and the long run. Thus, while our results are consistent with the prediction of adverse impacts of increased population growth on output expansion, the analysis also suggests that the long-run severity of the problem need not be as great as is commonly alluded; clearly, however, the shorter-run adjustment problems may prove significant indeed, and in the absence of increased rates of capital accumulation the long-run effects may be more severe than implied by the model.

Before leaving this section, we should raise once again an important qualification emphasized early in this chapter. The elasticity statistic permits an evaluation of the marginal impact of a parameter on the dual economy's performance. But the total impact of a given parameter depends both on the sensitivity of the system to changes in a parameter's value and on the magnitude of the parameter's variation. This point can be effectively illustrated by comparing the results of this section with those of chapter 5. Here we argue that increased rates of population growth have a much more modest impact on the performances of low-income economies than is normally assumed. In chapter 5, on the other hand, we suggested that much of Meiji Japan's impressive growth performance can be explained by her unusually low (relative to contemporary Asia's) rates of labor force growth. The apparent inconsistency is easily resolved. The Japanese aggregate labor force growth rate was less than one-third of that prevailing in contemporary Southeast Asia. The impact on Meiji Japanese performance was, as a result, hardly marginal.

6.2.3.2. *The Role of Technical Progress.* The need to create employment, while at the same time raising factor productivity and output with the introduction of new techniques, is widely recognized in low-income countries, faced as they are with the prospect of rapid increases in labor supply. As we have already suggested, the limited empirical evidence suggests that in recent years the output-raising effects of technical change have been substantial. Many Asian nations are introducing high-yielding, fertilizer-responsive seed varieties to an extent reminiscent of earlier Western episodes of agrarian revolution. Important productivity improvements have taken place in industry as well; economy-wide rates of total factor productivity growth have been substantial throughout Asia.[26] However, in introducing innovations many of the low-income Asian countries have faced a conflict between the output-raising effects of technical innovations and the employment effect or labor-saving bias of these techniques. The problem is particularly acute in those countries facing rapid population and labor force growth.

In chapter 2 we reviewed the evidence which has been accumulating, especially for Asian countries, in support of the generalization that technical change is labor saving in industry[27] and labor using in agriculture.[28] Not only is there considerable empirical support for the view of technological progress as nonneutral, but theoretical support for this position is also accumulating. The "induced innovation" hypothesis, recently extended by Kennedy, Samuelson, Ahmed, and others, suggests that under realistic assumptions labor-saving innovations are precipitated by historically rising wage-rental ratios.[29] A recent study of nineteenth- and twentieth-century Japanese and American agriculture lends support to this hypothesis.[30]

The reasons for the nature of the bias confronting low-income economies are not hard to find. The development of

26. J. G. Williamson, "Dimensions of Philippine Postwar Economic Progress."

27. Williamson, "Capital Accumulation, Labor Saving, and Labor Absorption Once More."

28. T. Watanabe, "Economic Aspects of Dualism in the Industrial Development of Japan"; Johnston and Cownie, "Seed-Fertilizer Revolution."

29. C. Kennedy, "Induced Bias in Innovation and the Theory of Distribution"; P. A. Samuelson, "A Theory of Induced Innovation along Kennedy-Weisacker Lines"; and S. Ahmed, "On the Theory of Induced Invention."

30. Y. Hayami and V. Ruttan, "Factor Prices and Technical Change in Agricultural Development: The United States and Japan, 1880–1960"; and "Induced Innovation in Agricultural Development: The United States and Japan."

innovations is expensive in the less developed economies. Thus, it is frequently the case that *industrial* technologies are imported from abroad containing labor-saving biases induced by factor prices prevailing in advanced economies in which these capital goods are produced. On the other hand, agricultural technologies (IR-8, Mexican dwarf varieties) often have been developed locally in successful agricultural areas in Asia, and it has "involved the development of both experimental station and industrial capacity capable of producing the biological . . . and mechanical . . . innovations adapted to factor supply conditions."[31] Finally, we should again emphasize that the factor-saving bias in industry is strengthened by the relatively rapid growth of capital-intensive industrial sectors in the contemporary developing economy. Part of this pattern of unbalanced industrial growth may be explained by policy. In any case, the evidence suggests that the labor-saving bias associated with this "compositional effect" is significant.[32]

The conflict between the output-raising effects and the bias in technical change was, of course, a major concern of Fei and Ranis in their analysis of the labor-surplus economy.[33] Confining their interest to the industrial sector, Fei and Ranis introduce the notion of an innovation frontier which has the properties exhibited in figure 6.1. The frontier is drawn independent of achievable rates of capital formation, since technical progress is disembodied.

The first difficulty with this formulation is that Fei and Ranis use the innovation frontier to explore the conflict between output growth goals and employment- goals *while holding both the rate of capital formation and the rate of population growth constant.* This seems to us a serious error. Any meaningful analysis of the conflict must take account of the impact on

31. Hayami and Ruttan, "Induced Innovation," p. 3.
32. J. G. Williamson, "Capital Accumulation, Labor Saving, and Labor Absorption: A New Look at Some Contemporary Asian Evidence," pp. 9–17.
33. Fei and Ranis, *Labor Surplus Economy*, chap. 4, pp. 111–50.

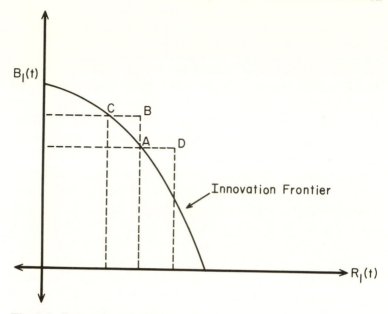

Fig. 6.1. Innovation Frontier

capital accumulation of population growth and the manner in which these variables interact with the improvement of technology.[34] Second, there is no evidence available about the *shape*

34. We should point out that this conflict is closely related to the investment criteria debate of the 1950s, especially to the contributions of A. K. Sen (*Choice of Techniques: An Aspect of the Theory of Planned Economic Development*); M. Dobb (*Economic Growth and Planning*); and W. Galenson and H. Leibenstein ("Investment Criteria and Economic Development"). As T. N. Srinivasan ("On a Two-Sector Model of Growth") has noted, only Sen and Dobb have made an explicit effort to introduce dynamic elements into their models. Yet all these economists emphasized the important feedback effects of current investment choices (technique *or* output mix) on income distribution, factor prices, and thus both on future rates of capital formation and on population growth. These elements are, of course, important building blocks in our own dualistic specifications. Thus, we feel that our dualistic general equilibrium framework offers an opportunity to evaluate the *empirical* relevance of the Sen-Dobb-Galenson-Leibenstein concern.

or *position* of the innovation frontier. Thus, it is not possible to explore the impact of a movement from point A to point C.

Our model does, of course, permit an analysis of the extent to which the rate and bias of technical change influences the dynamic path of the economy both directly and indirectly through feedback effects on population growth and capital formation. We now turn our attention to this analysis. To overcome the difficulty discussed in the preceding paragraph, we explore first the impact of a shift from point A to point B and, second, a shift from point A to point D; that is, we first hold the intensity of technical progress constant while increasing the labor-saving bias in industry (increasing the relative rate of labor augmentation economy-wide); second, we hold the bias constant while increasing intensity. This approach permits a decomposition of technical change into these two key components, thereby facilitating an analysis of the way in which each enters into the dynamic behavior of the growing economy.

To hold the rate constant while increasing the bias involves an increase in $y(t)$ and a *decrease* in $x(t)$.[35] This implies a reduction in the economy-wide efficiency capital-labor ratio and hence a reduction in the wage-rental rate. Thus, the relative price of labor *declines*, contrary to the conclusion some development economists have reached in the recent literature.[36] Moreover, the fall in the wage-rental ratio ω results in a decline in capital-labor ratios in both sectors and, together with $d(x/y) < 0$, a decline in k_i. A reduction in the marginal productivity of *efficiency* labor in each sector follows, but the change in the marginal product of labor is ambiguous. This reduction follows because the fall in the marginal productivity of *efficiency* labor tends to lower the wage paid to laborers, but this tendency is offset by the rise in y; therefore, the *net* change in the wage is ambiguous. On the other hand, the rise in

35. It should be noted that, by holding $R_i(t)$ constant, we mean only that there is no change in $R_i(t)$ in the initial period as a result of changes in the bias.

36. Johnston and Cownie, "Seed-Fertilizer Revolution."

the marginal productivity of efficiency capital gives rise to an increase in property income and a corresponding rise in investment demand per unit of capital. However, since the net effect on wage income cannot be determined, the crucial impact on per capita consumption cannot be identified with certainty. The effect upon labor absorption rates in industry and the level of urbanization is, of course, negative. This results from agriculture's greater success in raising the labor intensity of production. Accordingly, the terms of trade should initially improve for industry. The effect of the increasing labor-saving bias in manufacturing is to diminish both the rate of labor absorption and labor's share in that sector. Without more restrictive assumptions or numerical analysis the impact on $\phi(t)$ is uncertain because $f'_1[k_1(t)]$ rises and $x(t)$ falls, and therefore the impact of the changing bias on the rate of change in the efficiency capital-labor ratio is uncertain. The structural elasticities reported in table 6.8 show the negative impact of the increased bias to be important in our economy. The rate of capital stock growth is diminished throughout (table 6.8, line 8), although the negative impact is much greater in the earlier phases of growth following an "epochal" change in the bias. Since the rate of urbanization is also attenuated by the increased bias, the overall rate of population growth declines at a lower pace: thus the negative impact on $k(t)$ increases in later phases of growth. Surprisingly, the resulting influence on GNP growth rates and the industrial output share is rather small. Nevertheless, the former are affected positively and the latter is affected negatively throughout.

The presence of biased technical change also has important implications for rates of industrialization and capital accumulation in the dual economy. As we have found, increases in the bias may tend to inhibit the rate of industrialization and reduce the rate of capital accumulation without appreciable changes in per capita GNP growth. Related to these results is the extent to which labor absorption in the industrial sector is affected: we observe an important retarding influence that accumulates over time. Most developing economies are faced

TABLE 6.8 Structural elasticities (technical change with overall rate constant and change in bias)

Variable	$\epsilon_t^*(\Theta)$: Value of elasticity at year				
	10	20	30	40	50
GNP growth rate	+0.005	−0.000	+0.056	+0.013	+0.025
Per capita GNP growth rate	− .000	− .036	+ .133	− .021	− .001
Level of urbanization	− .060	− .120	− .169	− .210	− .242
Industrial output share	− .013	− .021	− .024	− .025	− .023
Capital-labor ratio (overall) ...	− .070	− .140	− .202	− .256	− .300
Capital-labor ratio (urban)	+ .008	+ .015	+ .021	+ .025	+ .031
Capital-labor ratio (rural)	− .120	− .257	− .396	− .538	− .675
Capital stock growth (overall) ..	− .245	− .202	− .201	− .115	− .072
Capital stock growth (urban) ...	− .134	− .122	− .133	− .060	− .028
Capital stock growth (rural)	− .545	− .452	− .441	− .336	− .268
Labor factor share (overall)	+ .004	+ .010	+ .008	− .002	− .012
Labor factor share (urban)	− .043	− .088	− .137	− .187	− .231
Labor factor share (rural)	+ .020	+ .049	+ .074	+ .097	+ .126
Rate of labor absorption	−0.060	−0.120	−0.169	−0.210	−0.242

with precisely this bias, and adoption of "modern" industrial techniques is often an explicit policy objective. Yet we find GNP per capita growth rates relatively insensitive to changes in the bias. Presumably, a policy which encourages the adopttion of "modern" techniques is based on the belief that per capita GNP will be raised in the long run. Our analysis suggests that the gains may be minimal.

Very different results are forthcoming if the system maintains a constant bias while the intensity of technical change is accelerated (table 6.9). Initially, of course, the economy-wide capital-labor ratio is unaffected. The rate of capital accumulation responds positively to the increased intensity of technical change, especially in early phases of growth. As a result, the economy-wide capital-labor ratio is higher, and increasingly so as development takes place, than at lower rates of technical change. To summarize, an increased labor-augmenting bias in technical change reduces the rate of capital formation, the rate of urbanization, and, to a lesser extent, the rate of per capita income growth. In contrast, an increased rate (intensity) of technical change has the opposite effect. Furthermore, an increased labor-augmenting bias inhibits industrialization while an increase in the economy's intensity of technical change stimulates industrialization.

The advantage of rapid rates of technical change in developing economies now becomes much clearer. Rapid rates of technical change tend to raise achievable rates of capital accumulation and to lower rates of population growth by stimulating urban-industrial development. Our results also show that for any given $R(t)$ high rates of labor-augmenting technical change are a definite *disadvantage* to developing economies. Furthermore, this disadvantage increases as the degree of dualism increases, that is, as the values of $(\sigma_2 - \sigma_1)$ and $(n_2 - n_1)$ increase. These "dualistic" features of underdevelopment are at the heart of the analysis of the impact of technical change on the process of economic growth. The existence of these features of dualism have important implications for the rate of labor absorption and urban "unemployment."

TABLE 6.9 Structural elasticities (technical change with bias constant and change in the overall rate)

Variable	$\epsilon_t^*(\Theta)$: Value of elasticity at year				
	10	20	30	40	50
GNP growth rate	+0.270	+0.242	+0.300	+0.316	+0.282
Per capita GNP growth rate	+1.143	+ .898	+1.027	+1.042	+ .926
Level of urbanization	+0.054	+ .134	+0.215	+0.297	+ .370
Industrial output share	+0.044	+ .099	+0.134	+0.165	+ .184
Capital-labor ratio (overall)	+0.020	+ .090	+0.202	+0.347	+ .508
Capital-labor ratio (urban)	+0.002	+ .022	+0.059	+0.121	+ .201
Capital-labor ratio (rural)	−0.005	+ .039	+0.178	+0.370	+ .616
Capital stock growth (overall)	+0.156	+ .275	+0.351	+0.375	+ .379
Capital stock growth (urban)	+0.226	+ .303	+0.333	+0.343	+ .334
Capital stock growth (rural)	−0.057	+ .133	+0.339	+0.413	+ .474
Labor factor share (overall)	−0.012	− .027	−0.041	−0.051	− .051
Labor factor share (urban)	−0.002	+ .007	+0.040	+0.080	+ .133
Labor factor share (rural)	+0.001	− .001	−0.020	−0.042	− .071
Rate of labor absorption	+0.224	+0.247	+0.238	+0.209	+0.169

6.2.4. Capital Formation, Savings Behavior, and Sources of Growth

While the key to understanding growth in our dualistic economy is the model's dynamic equation for the growth of the efficiency capital-labor ratio, it is more useful for the present discussion to focus on capital formation alone:

$$\frac{\dot{K}(t)}{K(t)} = sx(t)f'_1[k_1(t)] - \delta.$$

With a fixed savings parameter, the time paths of $x(t)$ and $f'_1[k_1(t)]$ jointly determine the rate of accumulation over time. Since $k_1(t)$ grows at positive rates in the simulation (table 4.3), and the marginal productivity of industrial capital is decreasing, it follows that a reduction in the rate of capital formation can only be forestalled by a rising $x(t)$. Yet this relation may hide more than it reveals. Alternatively, define $\alpha(t)$ as capital's variable share. Recall that gross investment equals savings out of nonlabor income, $P(t)I(t) = sG(t)\alpha(t)$; then

$$\frac{\dot{K}(t)}{K(t)} = \frac{I(t)}{K(t)} - \delta = s\alpha(t) \left\{ \frac{P(t)K(t)}{G(t)} \right\}^{-1} - \delta.$$

Rates of capital formation can therefore be explained by the joint movements in factor shares, the unaugmented capital-output ratio, *and* the savings rate. Should forces in the system produce rising nonlabor income shares and/or falling economy-wide capital-output ratios, rising rates of capital formation are quite consistent with a fixed savings parameter. Furthermore, even a stable *aggregate* savings rate, $s^*(t) = s\alpha(t)$, may be consistent with increasing rates of capital formation, should the capital-output ratio decline through time.

The simulation results presented in chapter 4 and confirmed in chapter 5 with Japanese data make it clear that our model is capable of generating accelerating urbanization, industrialization, per capita income growth, *and rates of capital formation* without changes in savings behavior. Furthermore, these results also indicate that the secular increases in the rate of capital formation are far more dramatic than the increases in the aggregate savings rate. Stability in the savings parameter, *s,* does not imply stability in either the aggregate savings rate, $s^*(t)$, or in capital stock growth, since, as we have seen, the rate of capital accumulation is critically influenced both by shifts in income distribution and by changing capital-output ratios in the economy. It appears, therefore, that the well-known Lewis conclusion that significant growth achievement requires major changes in savings behavior must be significantly qualified. In particular, we are postulating an economy with an initial aggregate *net* savings rate of only 0.063 (table 4.4), which over five decades increases only to 0.087. Lewis has asserted that the central problem in development theory is to explain an increase in net domestic saving from 5 to 12 percent of national income. We do *not* require dramatic shifts such as these to generate a "takeoff" in our model of the developing low-income economy; moreover, the evidence presented in chapter 5 suggests that Japan did not find it necessary either (table 5.7).

Yet the savings propensity, *s,* is a policy parameter of obvious importance which plays a prominent role in all models of growth and development. In the two sections which follow we examine the impact of an increase in the savings parameter on growth and structural change in an attempt to gain insight into its *quantitative* effect. Although increases in *s,* can be viewed as resulting directly from policy, they can also be justified by a hypothesis which has been omitted from our dualistic specification in chapter 2. It should be noted that the efficiency rental rate in the simulated economy increases over time. If the savings decision is responsive (positively) to rates of return, we have further justification for expecting a rise in the level of savings out of property income as growth takes places.[37]

Professional interest in appraising the relative importance of capital formation is revealed in the literature on sources of growth, and section 6.2.4.1 explores this methodology critically and

37. For an interesting discussion of the interest-elastic savings hypothesis in a model of growth, see S. C. Tsiang, "A Model of Economic Growth in Rostovian Stages."

relates it to our own model framework. Section 6.2.4.2 reports our empirical results which isolate the sensitivity of the dualistic economy to variation in the savings parameter.

6.2.4.1. *Sources of Growth and Capital Formation.* A few years ago, Sir John Hicks revealed a very negative reaction to Golden Age models and empirical work with aggregate production functions: "It is very wrong to give the impression to a poor country, which is very far from equilibrium even on a past technology, that capital accumulation . . . is a matter of minor importance."[38] The empirical research referred to is the path-breaking analysis of sources of growth by Abramovitz and Solow, which showed technological progress to be the primary factor "explaining" economic growth in the United States.[39] Not only has this finding stimulated considerable research on the nature of technological progress, but the startling result that capital formation accounted for very little of long-term growth has generated considerable debate. While most of the research on aggregate production functions and technical change has been applied to developed nations, recently the model has been applied to Latin America, particularly Chile, and to Greece, Taiwan, the Philippines, and even Mainland China.[40]

The sources of economic growth may be viewed in two basic dimensions: first, the sources of *aggregate* output growth; and

38. J. R. Hicks, *Capital and Growth,* p. 304. See also J. G. Williamson, "Production Functions, Technological Change, and the Developing Economies: A Review Article."

39. M. A. Abramovitz, "Resource and Output Trends in the United States since 1870"; R. M. Solow, "Technical Change and the Aggregate Production Function."

40. H. J. Bruton, "Productivity Growth in Latin America"; A. C. Harberger and M. Selowsky, "Key Factors in the Economic Growth of Chile: An Analysis of the Sources of Past Growth and of Prospects for 1965–1970"; S. Bowles, "Sources of Growth in the Greek Economy, 1951–61"; T. C. Liu, "The Tempo of Economic Development of the China Mainland, 1945–1965"; J. G. Williamson, "Philippine Postwar Economic Progress"; and R. J. Lampman, "The Sources of Postwar Economic Growth in the Philippines."

second, the rate of average labor productivity growth, a measure sensitive to the rate of labor force expansion. The sources-of-growth literature has focused exclusively on the latter conception. This is justified in part by the concern by development economists with the pace and level of *per capita* output. On the other hand, in the setting of the present model, which is characterized by high population growth rates, it is instructive to introduce our examination of the sources of economic growth by first examining the model in terms of aggregate output expansion. Here we find that technical change accounts for only about 18 percent of aggregate output growth. A decomposition of the growth of aggregate output yields

$$\frac{\dot{G}(t)}{G(t)} = R(t) + v(t)\frac{\dot{P}(t)}{P(t)} + v(t)\alpha_1(t)\frac{\dot{K}_1(t)}{K_1(t)}$$

$$+ [1 - v(t)]\alpha_2(t)\frac{\dot{K}_2(t)}{K_2(t)} + v(t)[1 - \alpha_2(t)]\frac{\dot{L}_1(t)}{L_1(t)}$$

$$+ [1 - v(t)][1 - \alpha_2(t)]\frac{\dot{L}_2(t)}{L_2(t)}.$$

Although the data are not reported here, the contribution of $v(t)\dot{P}(t)/P(t)$ is negligible, mainly because of the very slow rate of change in the terms of trade. Thus, factor accumulation accounts for about 80 percent of the growth of aggregate output in our economy. A similar picture emerges when we consider separately the situation in each sector: during the first five decades technical progress accounts for about 12 percent of the industrial output growth, while in agriculture it accounts for about 24 percent. The growth of sectoral output can be decomposed to

$$\frac{\dot{Q}_i(t)}{Q_i(t)} = R_i(t) + \alpha_i(t)\frac{\dot{K}_i(t)}{K_i(t)} + [1 - \alpha_i(t)]\frac{\dot{L}_i(t)}{L_i(t)}.$$

In industry, for example, capital accumulation accounts for about 63 percent of the growth in output and labor the remaining 25 percent during the first half-century.

But as already noted, the sources-of-growth literature focuses on average labor productivity growth rather than total output growth. The growth of sectoral average labor productivity can be decomposed into

$$\frac{\dot{Q}_i(t)}{Q_i(t)} - \frac{\dot{L}_i(t)}{L_i(t)} = R_i(t) + \alpha_i(t)\left\{\frac{\dot{K}_i(t)}{K_i(t)} - \frac{\dot{L}_i(t)}{L_i(t)}\right\}.$$

In our model the average growth in labor productivity in industry is approximately 1 percent a year in the first decade of growth (table 4.1), of which the residual "accounts for" about 0.7 percentage points. Thus, we have recaptured the fundamental paradox of the literature on sources of growth: the major part of average labor productivity growth is "explained by" technical progress.

Criticism of this methodology has been extensive, but for our present purposes we shall focus on the following five points:

1. The sources-of-growth model assumes perfectly competitive product and factor markets. This condition, it has been persuasively argued, is not satisfied in low-income economies. Yet, this is not a relevant concern to us here, since we have the opportunity to explore the impact of capital formation in a system we know with *certainty* satisfies the competitive assumptions.

2. The model involves the aggregation of inputs and outputs producing a potentially serious measurement problem.[41] Again, this qualification will not modify our analysis, since we are examining an economy for which prices are known with complete certainty and inputs and outputs are assumed homogeneous.

3. The model has normally been applied under the assumption of fully disembodied and neutral technical progress.

4. A Cobb-Douglas specification has typically been assumed.

5. The approach ignores potential "interaction effects," for

41. The most recent attempt to confront these measurement problems with a "price dual" approach can be found in D. W. Jorgenson and Z. Griliches, "The Explanation of Productivity Change."

example, the cumulative interaction of endogenous variables in the system.

The last three criticisms must be considered at some length, since our interest is in assessing the quantitative significance of the various qualifications to the methodology of sources of growth within the framework of our dualistic economy.

It was Solow who first directed interest to the embodiment issue. Under full embodiment, "improvements in technology affect output only to the extent that they are carried into practice either by net capital formation or by the replacement of old-fashioned equipment by the latest models, with a consequent shift in the distribution of equipment by date of birth."[42] This view of investment apparently put capital formation back into a prominent position as a vehicle for growth: it rejected the earlier view that little of output growth could be explained by capital accumulation. The position was further supported by Nelson,[43] who showed that the effective stock of capital, $J(t)$, could be approximated by a function of the gross capital stock, its average age, $a(t)$, and the historical rate of productivity improvement of *new* capital goods, λ:

$$J(t) = B(1 + \lambda)^t K(t) \{ 1 + \lambda[a(t - 1) - a(t)] \}.$$

Although Nelson found that the behavior of the "residual" in the American case could be effectively explained by variations in $a(t)$ (rather than by variations in λ), this has not been true of the model's application to Asia. Williamson has found for the Philippines that very little of the variation in the rate of total factor productivity growth would have been attributable to trends in the average age of the capital stock.[44] In any case, since the model underlying our simulated economy assumes disembodied technical progress, this issue can be circumvented.

According to the sources-of-growth calculation using the Cobb-Douglas specification, $\hat{R}(t)$ accounts for all of the growth

42. R. M. Solow, "Investment and Technical Progress."

43. R. R. Nelson, "Aggregate Production Functions and Medium Range Growth Projections."

44. Williamson, "Postwar Economic Progress," pp. 93–109.

in GNP per capita in the first decade but only 38 percent by the fifth decade. In the simulation, however, technical progress actually accounts for 88 percent in the first decade and 44 percent in the fifth decade. We find in the first decade that $\hat{R}(t)$ overstates $R(t)$ by about 15 percent but by the fifth decade it is understated by about 14 percent. We feel that these discrepancies are large enough to justify greater concern about the usefulness of decomposing the growth of GNP per capita with an aggregate Cobb-Douglas function.

Nevertheless, with technical progress accounting for about 60 percent of the growth in GNP per capita in the first five decades, our model does replicate the paradox of the literature on sources of growth in average labor productivity. Does it therefore follow that capital formation, and thus the savings effort, is unimportant in our approximation of a low-income economy?

The assumption that a Cobb-Douglas function describes the production technology introduces a potentially important bias into the estimate of the rate of technical progress. As Nelson has indicated, output growth in the CES case can be approximated by

$$\frac{\dot{Q}_1(t)}{Q_1(t)} = R_1(t) + \alpha_1(0)\frac{\dot{K}_1(t)}{K_1(t)} + [1 - \alpha_1(0)]\frac{\dot{L}_1(t)}{L_1(t)} + \frac{1}{\alpha}$$

$$\alpha_1(0)[1 - \alpha_1(0)]\frac{[\sigma_1 - 1]}{\sigma_1}\left\{\frac{\dot{K}_1(t)}{K_1(t)} - \frac{\dot{L}_1(t)}{L_1(t)}\right\}^2.$$

By estimating $R_1(t)$ with a Cobb-Douglas function,

$$\hat{R}_1(t) = R_1(t) + \frac{1}{\alpha}\alpha_1(0)\,[1 - \alpha_1(0)]\frac{[\sigma_1 - 1]}{\sigma_1}$$

$$\left\{\frac{\dot{K}_1(t)}{K_1(t)} - \frac{\dot{L}_1(t)}{L_1(t)}\right\}^2.$$

If $\sigma_1 < 1$ then $\hat{R}_1(t)$ will underestimate $R_1(t)$. The extent of the underestimation will depend largely on the value of $(\sigma_1 - 1)/\sigma_1$ and the growth rate of the capital-labor ratio. Clearly as σ_1 approaches zero, and therefore $(\sigma_1 - 1)/\sigma_1$ approaches $-\infty$, the degree of underestimation may become very large indeed. In the case of the simulation model, however, $(\sigma_1 - 1)/\sigma_1 = -1.0$ so the bias from this source is unlikely to be significant: any discrepancies that occur are therefore largely attributable to the temporal behavior of the capital-labor ratio.

We find that $\hat{R}_1(t)$ declines steadily from about 0.7 percent a year in the first decade to 0.2 percent a year in the fifth decade, whereas $R_1(t)$ was relatively stable at 0.54 percent a year throughout the five decades. Thus, in the first decade $R_1(t)$ is overestimated by about 25 percent, but by the fifth decade it is underestimated by some 70 percent because of the increasingly rapid growth of $\hat{k}_1(t)$.

Using a Cobb-Douglas function to describe the growth of aggregate per capita output, we find that the bias is a combination of the misspecification of the production functions and the aggregation error that results from approximating the growth of national product with an aggregate production function. For the economy as a whole, the true rate of technical progress is given by

$$R(t) = v(t)R_1(t) + [1 - v(t)]R_2(t),$$

where

$$R_i(t) = \lambda_K \alpha_i(t) + \lambda_L[1 - \alpha_i(t)].$$

By estimating aggregate output with a Cobb-Douglas function we have

$$\frac{\dot{G}(t)}{G(t)} = \hat{R}(t) + \alpha \frac{\dot{K}(t)}{K(t)} + (1 - \alpha) \frac{\dot{L}(t)}{L(t)}.$$

From our earlier expression for $\dot{G}(t)/G(t)$ we can see that the error between $R(t)$ and $\hat{R}(t)$ now involves $v(t)\dot{P}(t)/P(t)$ as well as a discrepancy term comparable to that derived by Nelson. In passing we note that by definition we have

$$\alpha(t) = v(t)\,\alpha_1(t) + [1 - v(t)]\,\alpha_2(t),$$

but it is not the case that

$$\alpha(t)\,\frac{\dot{K}(t)}{K(t)} = v(t)\alpha_1(t)\,\frac{\dot{K}_1(t)}{K_1(t)} + [1 - v(t)]\alpha_2(t)\,\frac{\dot{K}_2(t)}{K_2(t)}$$

and similarly for $[1 - \alpha(t)]\,\dfrac{\dot{L}(t)}{L(t)}$.

6.2.4.2. *Savings Behavior, Capital Formation, and Growth in the Dualistic Economy.* Just how significant capital formation is in influencing the growth path of the economy can be seen from the sensitivity analysis with the savings parameter. The elasticities are reported in tables 6.10 and 6.11. Here we see that capital stock and GNP growth rates are profoundly influenced by a 1 percent increase in the savings parameter. A 1 percent increase in the savings parameter produces a 2.5 percent increase in economy-wide growth rates of capital stock by the end of the first decade. This result may at first seem puzzling. Given the capital-output ratio, the nonlabor share, and $\delta = 0$, we might expect a 1 percent change in s to produce a like change in the rate of capital formation. This comparative static result need not conform to a comparative dynamic result; that is, it need not yield the same expansion in rates of capital formation at some point in the future (say, a decade hence). *In fact, the initial rise in s produces an accelerated increase in $\alpha(t)$ and thus even higher rates of accumulation at the end of the first decade of development.* These cumulative effects are ignored in the literature on sources of growth. (This literature also ignores the impact of increased savings propensities, and thus investment demand, on capital goods prices. This offsetting influence on capital goods accumulation is discussed at greater length below).

In any case, the resulting impact on output growth is almost 0.7 percent. With an economy-wide capital share of a little less than 50 percent and with constant rates of (disembodied) technical progress, this result is consistent with *both* the sources-of-growth literature and the emphasis which savings behavior receives from development economists. Note, however, that

TABLE 6.10 Structural elasticities (capitalists' savings rate, $\Theta = s$)

Variable	$\epsilon_t^*(\Theta)$: Value of elasticity at year				
	10	20	30	40	50
GNP growth rate	+0.684	+0.501	+0.431	+0.081	+0.027
Per capita GNP growth rate	+3.022	+2.040	+1.709	+0.612	+0.472
Level of urbanization	+0.409	+0.777	+1.017	+1.160	+1.216
Industrial output share	+0.191	+0.322	+0.382	+0.392	+0.373
Capital-labor ratio (overall)	+0.701	+1.349	+1.868	+2.265	+2.539
Capital-labor ratio (urban)	+0.313	+0.592	+0.844	+1.059	+1.234
Capital-labor ratio (rural)	+0.834	+1.685	+2.425	+3.068	+3.590
Capital stock growth (overall)	+2.433	+1.767	+1.246	+0.786	+0.458
Capital stock growth (urban)	+2.040	+1.528	+0.974	+0.605	+0.258
Capital stock growth (rural)	+3.340	+2.334	+1.977	+1.327	+1.109
Labor factor share (overall)	-0.057	-0.105	-0.116	-0.098	-0.056
Labor factor share (urban)	+0.163	+0.351	+0.518	+0.666	+0.778
Labor factor share (rural)	-0.082	-0.183	-0.265	-0.343	-0.410
Rate of labor absorption	+1.284	+0.897	+0.415	+0.113	-0.186
Terms of trade	+0.152	+0.338	+0.503	+0.644	+0.736

TABLE 6.11 Structural elasticities (depreciation, $\theta = \delta$)

Variable	$\epsilon^*_t(\theta)$: Value of elasticity at year				
	10	20	30	40	50
GNP growth rate	−0.467	−0.340	−0.284	−0.135	−0.050
Per capita GNP growth rate	−2.030	−1.343	−1.081	−0.593	−0.339
Level of urbanization	−0.260	−0.470	−0.574	−0.630	−0.645
Industrial output share	−0.115	−0.222	−0.213	−0.210	−0.196
Capital-labor ratio (overall)	−0.414	−0.776	−1.047	−1.238	−1.354
Capital-labor ratio (urban)	−0.168	−0.354	−0.460	−0.565	−0.649
Capital-labor ratio (rural)	−0.506	−0.910	−1.380	−1.704	−1.956
Capital stock growth (overall)	−1.537	−0.806	−0.637	−0.323	−0.171
Capital stock growth (urban)	−1.290	−1.835	−0.521	−0.217	−0.158
Capital stock growth (rural)	−2.154	+1.971	−0.970	−0.662	−0.247
Labor factor share (overall)	+0.034	+0.070	+0.060	+0.050	+0.028
Labor factor share (urban)	−0.110	−0.177	−0.300	−0.370	−0.421
Labor factor share (rural)	+0.055	+0.095	+0.151	+0.192	+0.224
Rate of labor absorption	−0.799	−0.817	−0.241	−0.013	+0.018

per capita income growth is raised by 3 percent! The significance of Nelson's remarks regarding interaction effects now
becomes strikingly apparent. *What the sources-of-growth literature does not fully reveal is precisely how increased savings
rates foster industrialization-urbanization and a more rapid
decline in population growth.* Although such interaction effects
may be ignored in a mature, fully industrialized economy, they
can hardly be overlooked in the dualistic low-income economy.

In relation to the neoclassical growth literature on speed of
adjustment, it is of considerable interest to note how rapidly
the effect of a rise in s diminishes over time. The effect on
both the capital stock and the GNP per capita growth rates
declines sharply during these decades of development: by the
end of a half-century of development, the structural elasticities
of GNP per capita growth have declined from 3.0 to 0.5.

Finally, it would appear that the economy is relatively more
sensitive to the savings than to the demand parameters (see
section 6.2.2. above). This result is hardly surprising, but we
should emphasize again that experiments in this section only
consider once-and-for-all parameter changes. Judging from the
research of Parks and Stone, we can reasonably expect continued decreases in β_{2j} over time. As a result, the historical
impact of changes in consumer tastes on industrialization and
growth is far greater than these sensitivity experiments reveal,
based, as they are, on once-and-for-all changes in demand
parameters. Note that over time the importance of changes in
the demand parameter *increases,* compared with that of changes
in the savings parameter (tables 6.3 and 6.10). Indeed, we
noted above that the long-run sensitivity of the industrialization
rate to increased demand for urban consumption goods is
roughly equivalent to that for alterations in the savings propensity (0.392 vs. 0.373 in the fifth decade of simulation). In
the long run the "importance" of shifts in this demand behavior
may be as significant as that of shifts in savings behavior although the latter has certainly attracted more attention in the
literature.

A final comment deserves reporting before we leave this section. An increase in the savings parameter, s, implies an increase in the demand for capital goods. The ability of the industrial sector to respond to that demand is crucial. In the foreign aid literature[45] this point has received detailed attention where the capacity of the capital goods sector, or the foreign exchange earnings capacity of the export sector if capital goods are imported, becomes critical. Thus far we have assumed an elastic supply response in the domestic capital goods sector so that the price of capital goods does not rise sufficiently to offset significantly the increased savings. This, of course, need not be the case for a low-income developing economy. In chapters 7 and 8, specifications about factor immobility are introduced so as to constrain these supply elasticities. We then find that the impact of an increased savings parameter, s, on capital accumulation is significantly reduced.

6.2.5. Production Dualism, Leading Export Sectors, and the Export Technology Hypothesis

To what extent does a greater degree of "production dualism" imply growth paths different from those obtained by a low-income economy with a less striking divergence between sectoral factor intensities and possibilities of factor substitution? This is one form of the question raised by the development and the historical literature dealing with the "export technology" hypothesis and by the literature emphasizing leading export sectors in early growth phases.[46] While ours is a closed economy to be sure, and while, as a result, a comprehensive analysis of these hypotheses is not possible, selected elements of this literature can effectively be explored with our model.

45. H. B. Chenery and A. M. Strout, "Foreign Assistance and Economic Development."

46. R. E. Baldwin, *Economic Development and Export Growth: A Study of Northern Rhodesia, 1920–1960*; D. C. North, "Location Theory and Regional Economic Growth"; idem, *The Economic Growth of the United States: 1790–1860*; Tsiang, "Economic Growth in Rostovian Stages"; and W. W. Rostow, *The Stages of Economic Growth*.

The traditional comparative statics in trade theory views export expansion essentially as equivalent to an outward shift in the production frontier through increased specialization. "In this essential aspect, improvement in trade opportunities is equivalent to improvement in technology, and its effect on the growth of the economy should be the same. . . . Improvement in trade opportunities is, however, very unlikely to be neutral with respect to its effect on the marginal productivities of factors."[47] Trade expansion shifts the composition of (aggregate) commodity demand in the system, and thus both the output mix and income distribution. The technological characteristics of the "leading export sector" are obviously critical in influencing the growth pattern of the system. The importance of the demand analysis in section 6.2.2 once again becomes relevant. If the expansion takes place in a sector which is relatively labor intensive, for example, our rural-agricultural sector, we know that growth will be hampered. In section 6.2.2, it was shown that a shift in demand toward the labor-intensive commodity (either an increase in γ or β_{2j}) tends to stimulate population growth, suppress capital accumulation, and, as a result, diminish per capita GNP growth. If, instead, the leading export sector is capital intensive, the opposite results obtain. Furthermore, these dynamic effects are *quantitatively* very important influences on the growth path of the low-income economy. Thus, our dualistic model provides a simple explanation of why the emergence of leading export sectors may have played a potentially important role in early development phases for some economies (e.g., Sweden, Denmark, England, and the American Northeast) and not for others (e.g., the American South, Southeast Asia).

The export technology hypothesis raises a related but somewhat different issue and emphasizes comparative analysis low-income economies producing primary products. Yet this literature still appeals to the variation in production technologies among alternative export commodities in explaining the char-

47. Tsiang, "Economic Growth in Rostovian Stages," p. 639.

acter and pace of growth. Baldwin, for example, emphasizes the importance not only of the wide disparities in the level of technology employed in the various sectors but also of changes in the nature of the production relationships. Indeed, "a study of the factors that determine the extent and speed of adoption of new techniques and skills is a key topic of development theory."[48] While he argues that initially "the elasticity of substitution of unskilled labor for capital goods and for skilled labor was relatively high" in the developing economies,[49] the development of new export industries, with imported production techniques, may significantly alter this relationship. The key linkages between the export sector and the remainder of the economy lie in the nature of the export sector's production technology; in particular, the impact of the sector in training skilled labor, in creating demand for indigenous commodity production, and in generating pecuniary externalities. Our dualistic model is much too limited to explore all these elements in the export technology hypothesis, but at least we can investigate the sensitivity of our economy's growth path to one critical production parameter, the elasticity of substitution.

Up to this point we have assumed fixed sectoral elasticities of substitution; the export technology hypothesis, however, offers a justification for changes in σ_i over time. Additionally one might hypothesize the existence of *systematic* long-run changes in σ_i for other reasons. Our sectors are highly aggregated over a large number of commodities. Surely the "observed" elasticity of substitution is not independent of the level of sectoral aggregation. Indeed, for a given process relevant to a unique industrial or agricultural product, the production function may be best described by fixed input coefficients. To the extent that unsophisticated low-income economies are characterized by "industrial" or "commercial" sectors producing only a limited number of goods, the observed elasticity of substitution for sector aggregates may be much closer to zero than one.

48. Baldwin, *Economic Development and Export Growth*, p. 59.
49. Ibid., p. 62.

As the output mix of each sector increases, measured substitution possibilities may increase markedly. The argument here suggests that σ_1 may increase systematically with industrialization. On the other hand, as agriculture becomes more specialized in the course of development, one could argue that σ_2 might be expected to decline. Although the evidence is limited, our predictions on the secular behavior of σ_i appear to be confirmed by recent empirical studies.[50] The most detailed evidence relates to σ_1. Chetty's research is summarized in table 6.12. In the majority of two-digit industry groups, the relatively low-income countries exhibit lower elasticities of substitution. In summary, it appears plausible that production dualism, as specified in our model, may diminish as development takes place.

From chapter 3 we know that changes in σ_i not only influence the static equilibrium solution for the economy but also enter directly into the determinants of the bias of technical progress. Consider first the impact of increases in the efficiency capital-labor ratio on labor redistribution in our economy given, for example, a *decline* in σ_2. A decrease in the ease of substitution of capital for labor in agriculture implies that the agricultural sector substitutes relatively less capital for labor than before. For a given increase in the efficiency capital-labor ratio, less labor will be transferred out of agriculture for a new equilibrium to be reached. Thus the rate of urbanization is inhibited, which implies a less rapid decline in population growth and a less rapid increase in per capita income growth. The influence on structural change is *negative*. To the extent that early development is associated with export specialization in primary products, and a decline in σ_2, the effects on structural change are negative. However, the analysis ignores the further impact of technological progress. Our economy is characterized by a labor-saving bias in industry and a labor-

50. P. Zarembka, "Basic Dual Economy Model"; V. K. Chetty, "International Comparison of Production Functions in Manufacturing."

TABLE 6.12 Recent estimates of the elasticity of substitution in industry from developed and underdeveloped economies

	Elasticity of substitution: $\hat{\sigma}_i$	
i = SIC	Developed	Underdeveloped
20	0.778	0.510
21	0.852	0.796
23	0.750	0.833
24	0.743	0.863
25	0.775	0.736
26	1.055	0.763
27	0.788	0.790
28	0.978	0.776
29	0.940	0.866
30	0.982	0.866
31	0.880	0.860
33	0.788	0.790
34	0.750	0.770
35	0.994	0.643
36	0.934	0.790
37	1.101	1.000
38	0.777	0.415

SOURCE: V. K. Chetty, "International Comparison of Production Functions in Manufacturing," tables 1–19.

NOTE: The values reported above are unweighted averages of Chetty's country estimates. Included in the "underdeveloped" category are Columbia, Turkey, and the Dominican Republic. Included in the "developed" category are the United States, Japan, United Kingdom, Canada, Finland, Sweden, New Zealand, Yugoslavia, and Hungary. Chetty's estimation equation is

$$\log V/L = a + \sigma \log W + \lambda_L (1 - \sigma) t + u.$$

using bias in agriculture. As a result, technical progress alone tends to cause the transfer of labor from industry to agriculture. Any tendency for σ_1 to increase and σ_2 to decrease over time will reduce the tendency for technical change to retard urbanization as $k(t)$ increases. Because the two effects discussed above are mixed, no unambiguous prediction of the impact of a rise in σ_1 and a decline in σ_2 on urbanization is possible.

The key question in the comparative statics, however, is the sign of the impact of changes in σ_i on income distribution and, thus, on investment demand. We know that for our CES production function, where $\omega = k_i^{1/\sigma_i}$, that

$$\frac{dk_i(t)}{d\sigma_i} = \sigma_i \omega(t)^{\sigma_i - 1} \frac{d\omega(t)}{d\sigma_i};$$

therefore, sign $dk_i(t)/d\sigma_i =$ sign $d\omega(t)/d\sigma_i$. The simulation results (for initial periods not reported in tables 6.13 and 6.14) suggest that, for any given $k(t)$, an increase in σ_1 lowers $\omega(t)$. That is, an increase in the ease with which capital is substituted for labor in industry tends to lower the wage-rental ratio. It follows that the fall in $\omega(t)$ produces lower $k_i(t)$, a higher $P(t)$, a decline in per capita consumption levels, but a rise in capital's share and thus in $\phi(t)$. In effect, a more "austere" growing economy results in lower consumption and higher investment levels. Whether at the same time this produces higher rates of per capita income growth is uncertain, since population growth may also receive a stimulus. The issue here is what happens to urbanization in response to a rise in σ_1. With the resulting decline in the wage-rental ratio, investment demand increases, but consumption demand for urban goods declines. Thus, the change in labor requirements via demand may not be sufficient to offset the reduced labor demand via increased substitution possibilities in industry. Indeed, the net effect on urbanization may be strongly negative, and, as a result, population growth rates may increase significantly.

The simulation results presented in table 6.13 yield the following conclusions: a rise in σ_1 tends to accelerate growth and structural change in the economy; labor's share declines, capital accumulation is fostered, and more rapid growth and structural change results. Furthermore, the size of the elasticities reported in tables 6.13 and 6.14 suggest the profound importance of such changes. Our numerical analysis therefore confirms the critical importance of production parameters in the growing dualistic economy.

To the extent that the composition of agricultural output shifts significantly and becomes more highly concentrated with the expansion of exports of primary products, experiments with

TABLE 6.13 Structural elasticities (elasticity of factor substitution in industry, σ_1)

Variable	$\epsilon_t^*(\Theta)$: Value of elasticity at year				
	10	20	30	40	50
GNP growth rate	+1.070	+0.688	+0.367	+0.361	+0.242
Per capita GNP growth rate	+4.546	+2.669	+1.495	+1.465	+1.113
Level of urbanization	+0.571	+1.041	+1.331	+1.500	+1.575
Industrial output share	+0.278	+0.487	+0.532	+0.542	+0.512
Capital-labor ratio (overall)	+0.948	+1.843	+2.567	+3.122	+3.512
Capital-labor ratio (urban)	+0.428	+0.871	+1.210	+1.521	+1.774
Capital-labor ratio (rural)	+1.116	+2.166	+3.232	+4.093	+4.808
Capital stock growth (overall) ...	+3.650	+2.426	+1.628	+1.087	+0.636
Capital stock growth (urban)	+3.031	+1.999	+1.317	+0.816	+0.448
Capital stock growth (rural)	+5.011	+3.337	+2.382	+1.833	+1.213
Labor factor share (overall)	−0.109	−0.192	−0.209	−0.193	−0.147
Labor factor share (urban)	+0.203	+0.402	+0.651	+0.840	+1.000
Labor factor share (rural)	−0.135	−0.245	−0.369	−0.465	−0.559
Rate of labor absorption	+1.866	+1.102	+0.670	+0.255	+0.007

NOTE: The $\epsilon_t^*(\Theta)$ in this table are based upon an increase in σ_1.

TABLE 6.14 Structural elasticities (elasticity of factor substitution in agriculture, σ_2)

Variable	$\epsilon_t^*(\Theta)$: Value of elasticity at year				
	10	20	30	40	50
GNP growth rate	−0.593	−0.149	+0.003	+0.030	+0.137
Per capita GNP growth rate	−3.893	−1.748	−1.098	−0.944	−0.574
Level of urbanization	−0.282	−0.473	−0.537	−0.530	−0.449
Industrial output share	−0.049	−0.019	+0.160	+0.350	+0.519
Capital-labor ratio (overall)	−0.681	−1.311	−1.785	−2.107	−2.265
Capital-labor ratio (urban)	−0.179	−0.438	−0.624	−0.803	−0.979
Capital-labor ratio (rural)	−0.681	−1.311	−1.785	−2.107	−2.265
Capital stock growth (overall)	−2.316	−1.364	−0.762	−0.298	−0.011
Capital stock growth (urban)	−0.839	−0.299	+0.151	+0.393	−0.413
Capital stock growth (rural)	−3.675	−2.338	−2.010	−1.426	+1.938
Labor factor share (overall)	+0.114	+0.168	+0.121	+0.018	−0.121
Labor factor share (urban)	−0.171	−0.317	−0.531	−0.705	−0.810
Labor factor share (rural)	+0.138	+0.242	+0.354	+0.442	+0.478
Rate of labor absorption	−0.021	+0.582	+0.967	+1.215	+1.293

NOTE: The $\epsilon_t^*(\Theta)$ in this table are based upon a *lowering* of σ_2.

the reduction in σ_2 are relevant to the export technology hypothesis. The results of this experiment are summarized in table 6.14. If a wider interpretation of Baldwin's thesis—that there is a tendency for the long-run disparities between sectoral production parameters and technologies to diminish—is employed, a *joint* examination of the results of tables 6.13 and 6.14 appears appropriate. Finally, if the primary impact of trade lies less in *changing* production technologies and more in export-stimulated sectoral expansion with largely *existing* technologies, Tsiang's interpretation would imply a reinterpretation of the findings in table 6.5. There, "tastes" shifted in favor of rural goods, a trend which could plausibly be attributed to foreign demand.

While several of the influences highlighted by Baldwin and Tsiang cannot be examined in our model, the frameworks are sufficiently similar for a comparison of their key predictions. For example, whether one considers a diminishing σ_2 or a rising γ, the net impact on per capita GNP growth is negative. This occurs not only because of the diminished demand for capital goods (a linkage highlighted by Baldwin) but also because of the increase in labor's share and the resulting reduction in capital formation (highlighted by Tsiang). In addition, we find lower rates of urbanization and, as a result, higher aggregate rates of population growth. Our results tend to confirm that the choice of production activities, and their production parameters, is important in influencing the trajectory of the dualistic economy. The literature on the export technology hypothesis focuses on the implications of such choices for income distribution, demand composition, the international flow of technology, factor prices, and factor supply response. Although our dualistic economy is closed, and thus ignores the possibility of international capital flows,[51] our results em-

51. The literature on export technology emphasizes the importance of profit repatriation when the export firms are foreign owned. Since we find efficiency rental rates rising in the simulation, our economy would be characterized by high and increasing rein-

phasize the difficulties with an enclave export-oriented development. However, to the extent that early development is characterized by a narrowing of $(\sigma_2 - \sigma_1)$, growth and structural change may receive a positive stimulus.

---

vestment rates in the local economy, were it open. This may appear inconsistent with the emphasis of the literature but the reader will recall that we are dealing with a *growing* economy. Much of the literature focuses on stagnant systems exporting primary products. This blurs issues considerably.

7

Dualistic Development as a Disequilibrium Process: Adding a Spatial Dimension

7.1. GROWTH AS A DISEQUILIBRIUM PROCESS

In constructing a theory of economic development our strategy thus far has been to view growth as a movement by the economy through a sequence of short-run equilibrium positions in which sectoral wages, rental rates, and per capita labor income are equated. Yet economic history is replete with evidence of persistent sectoral differentials in labor incomes, wages, and rental rates.[1] The models developed in the preceding chapters are unable to capture such differentials and hence are incapable of providing an explanation for and appraisal of this facet of the growth process. Moreover, the persistence of spatial inequalities in factor returns and productivities has become an increasingly important element in growth analysis as governments attempt to cope with burgeoning urban populations that are associated with large rural-urban income differentials and high rates of internal labor migration.

The persistence of such differentials has led Higgins, Bruton, and others to argue that economic development is not an equilibrium process, but rather a process of change that is subject to continuous disequilibrating forces.[2] A variety of hypotheses have been advanced to explain why discrepancies in sectoral incomes and factor prices may exist over extended

1. G. H. Borts and J. L. Stein, *Economic Growth in a Free Market*; T. Watanabe, "Economic Aspects of Dualism in the Industrial Development of Japan"; and J. G. Williamson, "Regional Inequality and the Process of National Development."
2. B. Higgins, *Economic Development*; H. J. Bruton, *Principles of Development Economics.*

234

periods. Most of these are based on the notion of sluggish adjustments in factor allocation in response to changes in the industrial output mix and labor demand.[3] The slow adjustment of the capital and labor markets is attributed to a variety of factors that include the existence of high transactions costs, imperfect information, risk and uncertainty, and sectoral capital specificity.

This chapter presents an attempt to take explicit account of the phenomena of continuing disequilibria, at least in factor markets. It integrates the regional and dualistic elements of our model by adding to the economic framework developed in previous chapters several hypotheses relating to intersectoral factor movements. This prior framework provides a suitable basis for capturing the notions of regionalism and flows of spatial factors, since it is based on hypotheses relating to region-specific differentials in production technique, demand, and demographic behavior. All the previous specifications about production, technological progress, and consumption are retained. By relaxing the assumptions of instantaneous and costless adjustments to differentials in factor prices, and by incorporating limitations on the movement of factors between region-specific production sectors, we provide an analytical framework that is particularly useful for capturing regional disparities in factor prices and for analyzing structural change under conditions of disequilibrium growth. In sections 7.2 and 7.3, alternative specifications of the capital and labor markets are developed; the nature of the commodity market is discussed in section 7.4, and in section 7.5 some of the properties of the static model are compared with those of the previous models.

7.2. AN ALTERNATIVE VIEW OF THE CAPITAL MARKET

7.2.1. Capital Ownership and the Notion of Capital Specificity
One reason sometimes given for the persistence of differentials in rental rates is that, once an investment is made, the installed

3. H. O. Nourse, *Regional Economics: A Study in the Economic Structure, Stability, and Growth of Regions.*

capital stock is specific to that production process; it cannot easily be utilized in the production of an unrelated commodity (or group of commodities). In the short run, the ability of entrepreneurs to reallocate capital in response to changes in relative prices is therefore limited. While reallocation can occur in the sense that the depreciating stock of capital need not be replaced and depreciation funds can be reinvested in alternative lines of production where returns to capital appear more attractive, the burden of adjustment shifts to new investment funds. Of course, even in the short run there may be considerable scope for changing the product mix within a sector where production processes are similar. In agriculture, for example, there is considerable opportunity for varying the composition of output through use of the same stock of land, machinery, and structures.

In order to capture the idea of capital specificity in the production process we now relax our previous assumption about capital mobility and assume that, once in place, the capital stock is perfectly *immobile*; only new investment goods can be allocated between sectors. It is also assumed that the ownership of capital used in each sector is divided between urban and rural capitalists. With $K_{ij}(t)$ defined as the current stock of capital used in the ith sector and owned by capitalists residing in the jth sector,[4] it follows that

$$K_i(t) = K_{i1}(t) + K_{i2}(t). \tag{7.1}$$

The rate of increase in $K_{ij}(t)$ is given by

$$\dot{K}_{ij}(t) = I_{ij}(t) - \delta K_{ij}(t), \tag{7.2}$$

where $I_{ij}(t)$ is the gross investment in the ith sector by capitalists in the jth sector. The rates of depreciation are identical between sectors, and there is no requirement to replace sectoral capital stocks depreciated over the period; that is, $\dot{K}_{ij}(t)$ is not necessarily restricted to positive values.

4. Since we assume that there is no intersectoral migration of capitalists, the interpretation of sectoral capital ownership remains unambiguous.

7.2.2. Financial Intermediation in the Capital Market

There has been considerable discussion of the role of financial intermediation in the development process. Fei, Ranis, Cameron, Gurley, Shaw, and others have emphasized the underdeveloped character of financial intermediation in low-income economies and the contribution of financial markets to overall rates of capital accumulation.[5]

Listed below are several ways in which the financial system can influence growth through its effect on the capital stock.

1. Financial institutions can encourage a more efficient allocation of a given amount of wealth (capital) by effecting changes in its ownership and its composition through intermediation among asset holders. The composition of individual holdings of real wealth in underdeveloped countries typically consists of land and land improvements, simple tools, livestock, inventories (notably foodstuffs), traditional valuables, and durable consumer goods (especially housing), while the share of producer durables is relatively low.[6] Thus, a considerable portion of tangible wealth in low-income economies is held in forms whose contribution to sustained growth may be rather limited. By effecting shifts to more productive forms of wealth, financial institutions can influence the course of growth, although such changes in the composition of a given stock of wealth presumably yield a once-over effect on the growth path of the economy. In our model, of course, we admit only one kind of asset. We are, therefore, unable to take account of such effects, although it could be argued that the efficiency variable, $x(t)$, captures systematic improvements in the composition of the capital stock.

2. Financial institutions can encourage a more efficient allocation of new investment by intermediation between savers

---

5. J. C. Fei and G. Ranis, *Development of the Labor Surplus Economy: Theory and Policy*; R. Cameron, *Banking in the Early Stages of Industrialization: A Study in Comparative Economic History*; J. G. Gurley and E. S. Shaw, "Financial Aspects of Economic Development"; and idem, "Financial Intermediaries and the Savings-Investment Process."
6. R. W. Goldsmith, "The Formation of Savings in the U.S."

and investors. They effect this transfer by issuing their liabilities to savers in exchange for real savings or monetary claims upon such assets and by assigning the assets so accumulated to investors by purchasing their securities. The financial system can create a wide variety of claims to serve as assets for savers and thereby improve the efficiency of the savings transfer to investors. The effect of this aspect of financial intermediation on growth and structural change has received a great deal of attention in the literature. Fei and Ranis, for example, stress the allocation of agricultural surplus and "the availability of the institutional arrangements through which savings decisions can be implemented." Without an intersectoral financial market, potential agricultural savers cannot purchase claims on newly created industrial goods.[7] Nicholls highlights the impact of urbanization on agricultural productivity through "improved" capital markets.[8]

3. Financial institutions can augment the rate of capital accumulation by providing increased incentives to save and invest. The standard approach here has been to point out that more efficient financial intermediation narrows the differential between the interest rates savers receive and investors pay. The reduction in the effective interest rate reduces the cost of investments. Gurley and Shaw suggest that by offering a wide array of financial assets financial institutions stimulate saving.[9] Presumably, financial institutions in their model are able to create new assets that have a higher yield, a lower risk, or other desirable characteristics to raise the return on savings. Stigler, on the other hand, has argued persuasively that so-called capital market imperfections reflect nothing more than positive information costs. These costs are likely to be very significant for low-income societies where the economic distance between regions and sectors is large.[10]

7. Fei and Ranis, *Labor Surplus Economy*, p. 32.
8. W. H. Nicholls, "Industrialization, Factor Markets, and Agricultural Development."
9. J. G. Gurley and E. S. Shaw, *Money in a Theory of Finance*.
10. G. J. Stigler, "The Economics of Information"; and "Imperfections in the Capital Market."

We shall assume that costs are incurred in the process of investing savings in each period, and we define τ as a constant transaction cost per unit of assets (capital stock in efficiency units) held outside the sector of residence. The *net* rental rate received on urban assets owned by agricultural "capitalists," $x(t)K_{12}(t)$, is the prevailing urban rate minus transaction costs; that is, $r_1(t) - \tau$. Similarly, assets used in the agricultural sector but owned by urban capitalists, $x(t)K_{21}(t)$, yield a *net* rental rate, $r_2(t) - \tau$, which excludes the per unit payment to intermediaries. We assume that intermediation is performed by financial institutions owned by urban capitalists so that $\tau x(t)K_{12}(t)$ appears as a component in urban property income. For the same reason, $x(t)r_2(t)K_{21}(t)$, which is a component of urban property income, includes *both* the net rental rate on agricultural assets held by urban capitalists *and* intermediation services performed by urban capitalists. Since capital tends to flow from rural to urban areas, τ can in effect be interpreted as a brokerage fee on industrial capital owned by capitalists in the agricultural sector. To the extent that the fee is levied solely to offset the costs of search, information, and transactions associated with the intersectoral savings transfer, τ would apply to the initial asset purchase, to the annual flow of rental payments on the asset stock, or to both. However, we have elected to treat these costs as an annual "tax" on assets held outside the sector of residence. While this particular formulation has been selected primarily for analytical convenience, it does capture the additional possibility that intermediaries dealing in portfolio management may assess a service charge on nonresident capital. This charge encompasses fees for earnings transfers, earnings reinvestment, analysis reports, legal services, and the costs of switching between alternative forms of sectoral assets.

7.2.3. The Savings Allocation Decision

We define $Y_j(t)$ to be the nonwage income of capitalists in the jth sector. Property income is therefore given by

$$Y_1(t) = x(t)[r_1(t)K_{11}(t) + r_2(t)K_{21}(t) + \tau K_{12}(t)], \quad (7.3)$$

$$Y_2(t) = x(t)\{r_2(t)K_{22}(t) + [r_1(t) - \tau]K_{12}(t)\}. \quad (7.4)$$

Nonwage income is assumed to be divided in fixed proportions between savings and consumption. It follows that the capitalists' savings in the *j*th sector are given by

$$S_j(t) = s_j \, Y_j(t), \quad (7.5)$$

where $0 \leqq s_j \leqq 1$ is the fixed savings rate from nonwage income in the *j*th sector. In each period the aggregate gross savings of capitalists are used to purchase new investment goods which, in turn, are allocated to agriculture and industry for replacement and expansion. As a result, the following relationship between savings and investment holds:

$$S_j(t) = P(t) \, [I_{1j}(t) + I_{2j}(t)]. \quad (7.6)$$

Now consider the manner in which the savings (or new investment goods) are allocated between sectors. There are several possibilities. Luxemberg, for example, assumed that rental income in each sector is always reinvested in the same sector—certainly an unrealistic assumption.[11] In introducing the assumption of perfect immobility of capital into Uzawa's two-sector model, Inada has considered another polar case in which all rental income is invested in the sector with the higher rental rate.[12] We adopt a more general formulation that encompasses both of these cases.

We begin by defining

$$i_{ij}(t) = \frac{I_{ij}(t)P(t)}{S_j(t)} \quad (7.7)$$

to be the share of gross savings of capitalists in the *j*th sector that is invested in the *i*th sector. At the beginning of each period capitalists form an expectation, on the basis of past experience, about the rental rates on efficiency capital that

11. R. Luxemberg, *Social Reform or Revolution.*
12. K. I. Inada, "Investment in Fixed Capital and the Stability of Growth Equilibrium."

· will prevail in the current period. This expectation provides the basis for allocating new investment goods between sectors. We define $r^*(t)$ to be the differential between sectoral rental rates expected to prevail in period t. When $|r^*(t)| \leqq |\tau|$, capitalists reinvest all their earnings in their sectors of residence, since the expected earnings differential by comparison with the transfer cost is not sufficiently large to justify intersectoral investment. In this case,

$$i_{12}(t) = 0 = i_{21}(t) \quad \text{if} \quad |r^*(t)| \leqq |\tau|. \tag{7.8}$$

When $|r^*(t)| > |\tau|$, the portion of capitalists' savings invested in the nonresident sector is a monotonic function of the extent to which the expected rental rate differential diverges from the unit transactions costs. In particular, taking $r^*(t) = r_1^*(t) - r_2^*(t)$, we assume

$$i_{12}(t) = 1 - e^{-\mu[r^*(t)-\tau]} \text{ if} \quad r^*(t) > \tau, \tag{7.9}$$

$$i_{21}(t) = 1 - e^{\mu[r^*(t)+\tau]} \text{ if} \quad r^*(t) < -\tau, \tag{7.10}$$

where $\mu > 0$ is a parameter whose value is constant over time. As $r^*(t)$ increases without limit, $i_{12}(t)$ approaches one; as $|r^*(t)|$ approaches $|\tau|$, $i_{12}(t)$ and $i_{21}(t)$ approach zero (figure 7.1).

It might be argued that $i_{ij}(t)$ will not respond continuously to expected rental rate differentials and that $i_{ij}(t) = 1$ at some finite expected differential. It seems to us more appropriate to recognize implicitly the heterogeneity of assets. The recipient of property income in sector j may respond to an *average* expected rental rate in sector i, but the variance in rental rates within each sector is surely significant; there will always be profitable investments in the sector of residence, but their number diminishes with an increasing average rental rate in the nonresident sector of potential investment.

An explicit statement involving the formation of "price" expectations is required. There is an extensive theoretical and econometric literature to draw upon for this purpose. The work on distributed lags suggests a number of fruitful hypoth-

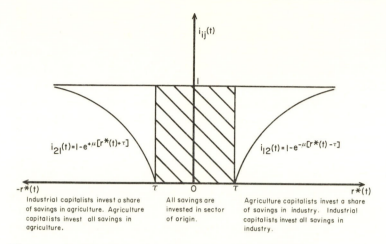

Fig. 7.1. The Sectoral Allocation of Current Investment

eses, one of which postulates that the currently held expectation about future intersectoral rental rate differentials is a weighted average of the expectations held during the last period and the current value of $r^*(t)$.[13] An equivalent form of this hypothesis is

$$\frac{dr^*(t)}{dt} = \epsilon[r(t) - r^*(t)], \qquad 0 \leqq \epsilon \leqq 1, \qquad (7.11)$$

where $r(t) = r_1(t) - r_2(t)$ is the current differential; ϵ measures the speed of response of $r^*(t)$ to past values of $r(t)$. Alternatively, we can write $T = 1/\epsilon$, where T is the time constant of the lag. Capitalists adjust their expectations so as to eliminate the current difference, $r(t) - r^*(t)$, over T periods. Presumably, the "less well developed" the capital market, the smaller ϵ is likely to be and hence the larger the period required for adjustment. Most of the quantitative evidence, however, suggests that Asian households and firm units adjust rapidly to price changes.[14]

By differentiating equations (7.9) and (7.10) with respect

13. C. F. Christ, *Econometric Models and Methods*, pp. 204–8.
14. J. G. Williamson, "Relative Price Changes, Adjustment Dynamics, and Productivity Growth: The Case of Philippine Manufacturing."

to time, equating each of these results with equation (7.11), and rearranging, we obtain

$$\frac{di_{12}(t)}{dt} = \begin{cases} \mu\epsilon[1-i_{12}(t)]\{r(t)-\tau+\mu^{-1}\log[1-i_{12}(t)]\} \\ \qquad\qquad\qquad \text{if } r^*(t) > \tau, \\ 0 \text{ if } r^*(t) \leqq -\tau; \end{cases} \qquad (7.12)$$

and

$$\frac{di_{21}(t)}{dt} = \begin{cases} -\mu\epsilon[1-i_{21}(t)]\{r(t)+\tau-\mu^{-1}\log[1-i_{21}(t)]\} \\ \qquad\qquad\qquad \text{if } r^*(t) < -\tau, \\ 0 \text{ if } r^*(t) \geqq \tau. \end{cases} \qquad (7.13)$$

These differential equations describe the way in which the allocation of investment goods between sectors changes over time. It is seen that $di_{ij}(t)/di \geqq 0$ for all t and that in each period $i_{ij}(t)$ is predetermined. The change in $i_{ij}(t)$ from the previous period is a function of the rental rate differential and the actual investment share prevailing in that period.

Although we continue to assume that efficiency capital is paid its marginal value product, for any given allocation of labor, rental rates may not be equated. In each period the stock and sectoral allocation of capital is predetermined by past behavior; the new allocation of investment, which is also based on past experience, may not bring about equality in the rental rates. Thus, in our treatment of the capital market, the possibilities for persistent intersectoral differences in rental rates are captured through the effects of disequilibrating forces in three separate ways. First, by introducing the notion of capital stock immobility, we have prevented rental rate equalization through capital stock reallocation. Second, the notion of costs associated with the intersectoral transfer of savings is introduced. Even if there were sufficient savings to equalize rental rates, the appropriate allocation may not be made because of the costs of intersectoral savings transfers. While this admittedly simplistic treatment of capital market costs may influence the extent of the intersectoral savings transfer and rental rate differential, it is unlikely to have a significant effect on the overall level of savings and, hence, on capital accumulation in the economy. A fixed share of income is saved by capitalists in each sector, so that the costs represent an income transfer between the two groups of savers. It is only when s_1 is significantly different from s_2 that the income transfer is likely to have a substantial impact; under the not unreasonable assumption that $s_1 > s_2$, the transfer would lead to a higher level of savings in the economy. Finally, we have introduced the notion of basing decisions on investment allocation only on a knowledge of past differentials in interest rates between sectors, which, of course, may be a poor guide to the present. Moreover, by utilizing an expectations adjustment mechanism, we have incorporated into the framework a lag in the rate at which capitalists adjust their expectations to realized differentials in rental rates.

This formulation of intersectoral capital migration appears capable of generating trajectories consistent with economic history. While nonproportional sectoral output and labor force growth are typical of early phases of dualistic development, these shifts frequently take place in the face of high rental rates on capital in the urban sector and low rates of investment in urban industry by landlords. With significant information costs, interregional rental rate differentials in such a model may be large: in fact, high rates of accumulation in the urban sector may prevail for some time before $i_{12}(t)$ becomes at all significant. Efforts to reduce τ will surely increase the intersectoral flow of savings, but the sensitivity of response is uncertain. In Japan and New England, this was often achieved through the development of rural industries. A general improvement in the efficiency and availability of financial institutions has long been urged by economic historians as a prime vehicle for economic change. But even if $\tau = 0$, the extent of intersectoral savings flows depend critically upon μ and ϵ. Rapid growth may also have profound effects upon the behavior of the rental rate differentials over time. Intersectoral factor price differentials are likely to remain a permanent feature in the low-income economy as long as technological improvements are centered on the urban sector and lower rates of labor force growth are obtained there.

7.3. MIGRATION AND THE LABOR MARKET

Intersectoral migration has been highlighted by many as a critical feature in the development process. According to Fei and Ranis, migration of labor from the agricultural to the industrial sector in an economy with an initial "unfavorable" factor endowment and population pressure is central to hastening economic growth. In the model analyzed in chapter 4, growth was accompanied by a continuous flow of labor from agriculture to industry under the assumption of perfect labor mobility at zero cost. The introduction of labor market imperfections, and a behavioral hypothesis to determine the migration rate, will now provide an opportunity to isolate the extent to which less than instantaneous adjustment to wage differentials affects the growth of the dualistic economy. A slower rate of out-migration from agriculture, for example, will raise the overall rate of population growth and, hence, retard the growth of per capita income. Yet with a higher wage in industry and a lower wage in agriculture, labor's share is reduced, and thereby capital formation and the ability of the industrial sector to absorb more labor are stimulated. Which force dominates growth in the dualistic economy? With a more realistic treatment of the migration decision we are in a better position to evaluate the sensitivity of migration rates to the key behavioral and technical parameters of the system.

7.3.1. The Supply of Labor

Define $m_i(t)$ to be the current rate of migration from the ith sector; that is,

$$m_i(t) = \frac{M_i(t)}{L_i(t)},$$

where $M_i(t)$ is the number of laborers that migrate from the ith sector at time t. The increase in the sectoral labor force consists of the natural increase plus the net change due to migration; that is,

$$\frac{\dot{L}_1(t)}{L_1(t)} = n_1 + \frac{1}{u(t)}\{m_2(t)[1 - u(t)] - m_1(t)u(t)\},$$

(7.14)

$$\frac{\dot{L}_2(t)}{L_2(t)} = n_2 + \frac{1}{1 - u(t)}\{m_1(t)u(t) - m_2(t)[1 - u(t)]\}.$$

(7.15)

The growth rate of the total labor force is then given by

$$\frac{\dot{L}(t)}{L(t)} = n_1u(t) + n_2[1 - u(t)],$$

(7.16)

while the rate of change in the level of urbanization is

$$\frac{\dot{u}(t)}{u(t)} = (n_1 - n_2)u(t) + \frac{1}{u(t)}$$

$$\{m_2(t)[1 - u(t)] - m_1(t)u(t)\}.$$

(7.17)

We continue to assume that migrants immediately adopt the demographic characteristics of their new sectors of residence. In reality, however, recent urban migrants should tend to have higher rates of family formation; they are younger and they adjust to urban "family patterns" only after a lag.

7.3.2. Determinants of Migration

The theoretical research into the determinants of rural-urban labor transfer in developing economies has proceeded along two lines. The first extends the classical treatment of the migration decision either to include an urban unemployment variable, and thus focuses on expected annual earnings differentials,[15] or to utilize a capital theoretic framework which explicitly introduces calculations of present values and migration costs.[16] As

15. M. P. Todaro, "A Model of Labor Migration and Urban Unemployment in Less Developed Countries"; P. Zarembka, "Labor Migration and Urban Unemployment: Comment."

16. L. A. Sjaastad, "The Costs and Returns of Human Migration"; D. J. DeVoretz, "A Programming Approach to Migration in a Less Developed Economy."

yet there has been almost no attempt to introduce these hypotheses into a dynamic intersectoral framework.[17]

The second line of theoretical research has as its source the formal dualistic models of labor transfer. However, the treatment of the migration decision in the dualistic literature has typically been at a very simplistic level. Central to the Lewis, Fei-Ranis, and Jorgenson models is the hypothesis that the current wage differential causes labor to transfer between sectors.[18] The significance of current wage differentials as a determinant of migration is well documented.[19] It is widely recognized, however, that the current wage differential is not the only determinant of migration, and that all determinants are not necessarily economic. Other variables suggested include expected income or wages, costs of migration, age, education, information, urbanization, population density, and distance.

We shall assume that the decision to migrate is based upon the difference between the income differential expected to prevail in the forthcoming period and the costs of migration—that is that the aggregate rate of migration is an increasing monotonic function of the expected net income differential. We do not attempt to develop our theory in terms of individual behavior. In view of the selectivity of migration, considerable variation may exist among individuals with respect to migration costs and expected returns. Older workers, for example, may be less disposed to move because the expected lifetime

17. See, however, V. Galbis, "Dualism and Labor Migration in the Process of Economic Growth: A Theoretical Approach."

18. Fei and Ranis, *Labor Surplus Economy*; D. W. Jorgenson, "The Development of a Dual Economy."

19. F. A. Hanna, *State Income Differentials, 1919–1954*; G. S. Sahota, "An Economic Analysis of Internal Migration in Brazil." There has been considerable debate in the literature whether observed intersectoral wage differentials are, in fact, representative of real income differentials. Recent studies confirm the hypothesis of real income differentials (see L. G. Reynolds, "Wages and Employment in a Labor Surplus Economy"; B. F. Johnston and S. T. Nielsen, "Agricultural and Structural Transformation in a Developing Economy"; J. K. Hellemer, "Agricultural Export Pricing Strategy in Tanzania"; and W. M. Warren, "Urban Real Wages and the Nigerian Trade Union Movement, 1939–1960").

earnings are smaller for them than for younger workers. Thus, for any given expected income differential, not all the labor will migrate, but as the differential increases a larger share of the sector's labor force will be inclined to move.

As in the previous models, efficiency labor is paid its marginal value product. We assume that there are no remittances of income by migrant laborers to their sectors of origin, so that $y(t)w_i(t)$ is the current income per laborer.[20] According to Sjaastad the costs of migration comprise money elements—increased expenditures of food, lodging, and transportation; foregone earnings during the period of transfer and while locating new employment—and psychic costs.[21] Since direct migration costs are relatively small in many developing regions, the major determinant of costs is the loss of income during the migration process itself. This suggests that $\theta(t)$, the current costs of migration, may be a function of the income in the sector from which the migrant departed. In fact, we shall assume that the cost of migrating from rural to urban areas is a linear function of income per laborer in agriculture but that there is no cost associated with movement in the opposite direction. An implication of this hypothesis is that, if the rural wage rises, wage differentials may increase as development takes place. Thus, we have

$$\theta(t) = ay(t)w_2(t) - c, \qquad (7.18)$$

where $a \geqq 0$ and $c \geqq 0$ are parameters whose values are fixed over time. When c = 0, the costs of migration are proportional

---

20. In many low-income economies the notion that migrants retain their ties to the rural sector is quite common and is manifested by a flow of remittances to rural relatives. The reverse flow is also common in cases where the migrants are temporarily unemployed and therefore must be supported by rural relatives. The main effect of introducing income transfers into our models would be to alter the composition of consumption demand among laborers and, therefore, to affect the terms of trade. A transfer of income to the rural population, ceteris paribus, would raise the demand for agricultural output and therefore lower the price of industrial goods relative to the price of agricultural goods.

21. Sjaastad, "Costs and Returns of Human Migration."

to the rural wage; when $a = 0$, the migration costs are constant over time.

The expected income differential to which laborers respond is the differential expected to prevail in the current period, that is,

$$w^*(t) = y(t)[w_1^*(t) - w_2^*(t)].$$

Although migrants are assumed to respond to income differentials expected to prevail in the current period, our formulation could easily be extended to allow for the decision to be based in the present value of the expected gain for some finite number of future periods.[22] Assuming that the rate of migration from each sector is related monotonically to the net income gain, we have

$$m_1(t) = \begin{cases} 1 - e^{\rho w^*(t)} & \text{if} \quad w^*(t) < 0, \\ 0 & \text{if} \quad w^*(t) \geq 0, \end{cases} \quad (7.19)$$

$$m_2(t) = \begin{cases} 1 - e^{-\rho[w^*(t)-\theta(t)]} & \text{if} \quad w^*(t) > \theta(t), \\ 0 & \text{if} \quad w^*(t) \leq \theta(t), \end{cases} \quad (7.20)$$

22. Ibid.; J. R. Harris and M. P. Todaro, "Migration, Unemployment, and Development: A Two-Sector Analysis"; and Galbis, "Dualism and Labor Migration." Define the present value of the future net income expected to be gained from migration as

$$V^*(t) = \int_t^{t+n} [w^*(t) - \theta(t)]e^{-n(s-t)}ds \ ,$$

where $s = t+n$, r is the discount rate, and n is the time horizon of migrants. If we assume, for example, that migrants expect $w^*(t) - \theta(t)$ to remain constant over time, the expected net gain is given by

$$V^*(t) = \frac{1-e^{rn}}{r} [w^*(t) - \theta(t)] \ .$$

We can now restate $m_2(t)$, for example, as

$$m_2(t) = 1 - e^{-\rho V^*(t)} \ .$$

The advantage of this specification is that we introduce two more parameters of interest into the migration decision: the migrant's time preference rate, and his time horizon, n. Galbis (ibid.) argues that both of these parameters may be important determinants of migration.

where $\rho > 0$ is a parameter that is fixed over time. The resulting migration pattern is illustrated in figure 7.2.

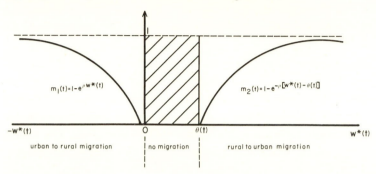

Fig. 7.2. The Rate of Intersectoral Migration

We postulate that the laborer ascertains the expected wage differential by reference to past wage differentials about which he has complete knowledge. In particular, $w^*(t)$ is determined by a simple exponential lag function, from which we obtain

$$\frac{dw^*(t)}{dt} = b[w(t) - w^*(t)], \qquad (7.21)$$

where $w(t) = y(t)[w_1(t) - w_2(t)]$ and the parameter $0 \leqq b \leqq 1$ is the speed of response of $w^*(t)$ to past values of $w(t)$. The interpretation of b is similar to that of ϵ in the equation (7.11).

By differentiating equations (7.18) and (7.19) with respect to t, substituting equations (7.20), (7.18), and (7.19) into the results, and rearranging, we obtain

$$\dot{m}_1(t) = -\rho b[1 - m_1(t)]$$
$$\{y(t)w(t) - \rho^{-1} log\,[1 - m_1(t)]\}, \qquad (7.22)$$

$$\dot{m}_2(t) = \rho[1 - m_2(t)]$$

$$[b\,\{y(t)w(t) - \theta(t) + \rho^{-1} \log\,[1 - m_2(t)]\} - \dot{\theta}(t)], \qquad (7.23)$$

and

$$\dot{\theta}(t) = ay(t)w_2(t) \left\{\lambda_L + \frac{\dot{w}_2(t)}{w_2(t)}\right\}. \qquad (7.24)$$

Thus, the rate of migration in any period is determined by conditions prevailing in the previous period and, in particular, by the previous rate of migration, the labor income differential between the two sectors, and the cost of migration. Because the rate of migration is predetermined, it is clear that there will not necessarily be an amount of migration sufficient to equalize the wage rates and close the income gap between the sectors. In fact, because of the migrant's lagged response in adjusting the expectations about income differentials and the existence of migration costs, income differentials, or a "wage gap," may persist as development takes place.

7.3.3. Migration as an Equilibrium Process

Our present treatment of the migration process is in sharp contrast to the view developed in the earlier models. There migration was considered an equilibrium process, since there was always enough agricultural labor willing to migrate to industry to close the wage gap. Moreover, the migrant's response to an emerging wage gap was sufficiently rapid, relative to the forces causing the divergence in wages, to permit a convergence to short-run equilibrium in every period. This view of migration is basically the same as that of Fei-Ranis and Jorgenson. In formulating his theory of migration, Jorgenson assumes that agricultural labor moves in response to a wage differential. He argues that "the differential which is necessary to cause movement of agricultural labor force into the industrial sector is roughly proportional to the industrial wage rate."[23] He then assumes that in

$$w_1(t) - w_2(t) = \phi w_1(t),$$

where $\phi > 0$ is a parameter that is fixed over time.[24]

23. Jorgenson, "Development of a Dual Economy," p. 313.
every period there would be sufficient migration to ensure that

24. It would have been a simple matter to introduce a similar specification for equilibrium in the labor market in the model developed in chapter 2. A specification such as $w_1(t) - w_2(t) = \phi w_2(t)$, which is equivalent to Jorgenson's ($\phi = \theta/(1 + \theta)$), would not have altered any of the conclusions about the behavior of the model.

According to Harris and Todaro, it is more realistic to consider labor migration in a low-income economy as a two-stage process.[25] In the first stage the unskilled rural worker migrates to an urban area and initially spends a period of time in the "urban traditional" sector. The second stage is reached when the migrant obtains a more permanent job in the modern sector. In Harris and Todaro's view the decision to migrate from rural to urban areas is a function of the urban-rural differential in real income and the probability of obtaining urban employment. Thus, it is the "expected" income differential rather than the prevailing real income differential that is the relevant determinant of migration. Harris and Todaro recognize the existence of a politically determined minimum wage at levels substantially higher than those of agricultural earnings. In effect, they assume that the expected real wage in the urban sector is equal to the average urban wage, which, in turn, is equal to the fixed real minimum wage adjusted for the proportion of the total urban labor force actually employed. Nevertheless, migration is still viewed as an equilibrium process in their model, since labor migration continues in each period until the expected income differential is zero. With the production functions and with a fixed minimum wage, it is possible to solve for sectoral employment, the equilibrium unemployment rate, and, therefore, the equilibrium expected wage, relative output, and the terms of trade. A further limitation of their model is the assumption of fixed stocks of capital in both sectors and no technical progress of any kind. The ability of the economy to absorb an increasing labor force depends solely on the substitution possibilities in industry relative to those in agriculture.

7.4. The Commodity Markets

If there is no change in the assumptions about the nature of the production process, the supply of output in each sector is given by

$$Q_i(t) = F^i[x(t)K_i(t), y(t)L_i(t)], \qquad (7.25)$$

25. Harris and Todaro, "Migration, Unemployment, and Development."

as before. Consumption demand for the ith good by recipients of property income in the jth sector, $D_{1j}{}^k(t)$, is given by

$$D_{1j}{}^k(t) = \frac{\pi_{1j}}{P(t)} \left[(1 - s_j)\,Y_j(t) - \gamma\phi_j L_j(t)\right], \qquad (7.26)$$

$$D_{2j}{}^k(t) = \pi_{2j}(1 - s_j)Y_j(t) + (1 - \pi_{2j})\gamma\phi_j L_j(t), \qquad (7.27)$$

where $\phi_j L_j(t)$ is the total number of property income recipients in the jth sector.

Furthermore, we continue to assume that all wage income is consumed and that migrants immediately adopt the consumption characteristics of the sector of residence. Thus,

$$D_{1j}{}^l(t) = \frac{1}{P}\,\beta_{1j}(y(t)w_j(t) - \gamma)L_j(t), \qquad (7.28)$$

$$D_{2j}{}^l(t) = \left[\beta_{2j}y(t)w_j(t) + (1 - \beta_{2j})\gamma\right]L_j(t). \qquad (7.29)$$

In this model the economy is defined to be in static equilibrium when the quantity supplied is equal to the quantity demanded in each commodity market. As in the previous models, in static equilibrium there is no excess demand in any market, and all prevailing market prices are nonnegative.

$$Q_1(t) = \sum_{j=1}^{2} \left[D_{1j}{}^l(t) + D_{1j}{}^k(t) + I_j(t)\right], \qquad (7.30)$$

$$Q_2(t) = \sum_{j=1}^{2} \left[D_{2j}{}^l(t) + D_{2j}{}^k(t)\right]. \qquad (7.31)$$

Additionally, the neoclassical factor pricing system is the same as in the equilibrium model, and is presented in equations 7.32a, 7.32b, 7.33a, 7.33b in Appendix D; full employment is ensured by equations 7.36 and 7.37, also in Appendix D.

7.5 THE STATIC ECONOMY

The static model is described by a system of 27 equations, 26 endogenous variables, and 12 exogenous variables. In the present model, the solution to the static model depends on the values of the exogenous variables $(x, y, K_i, L_i, K_{ij}, i_{21}, i_{12})$. If a solution exists, it is obtained in the following way (see App. D for equations cited): The stocks and the sectoral allocation of efficiency capital and labor are given. Thus, both the output and the marginal physical products of efficiency factors are determined by the sectoral production functions. The marginal physical products $F^2{}_1$ and $F^2{}_2$ permit the determination of the wage and rental rates in agriculture from equations (7.32b) and (7.33b) respectively. By substituting (7.25), (7.29), (7.27), (7.3), (7.4), (7.32b), (7.33b), into (7.31), we obtain a solution for P of the form

$$P = P(K_1, K_2, L_1, L_2, x, y, K_{11}, K_{22}). \qquad (7.35)$$

This then permits us to obtain r_1 from (7.33), w_1 from (7.32), Y_1 from (7.3), Y_2 from (7.4), I_j from (7.5), I_{12} from (7.7a), I_{21} from (7.7b), I_{11} I_2 and $_2$ from (7.6), and I_i from (7.34).

It is not essential to the present objectives to demonstrate rigorously the conditions under which a solution exists and is unique. Nevertheless, it should be clear that expression (7.35) is fundamental to the solution of the static model in much the same way that (3.13) was fundamental to the analysis of the static economy in chapter 3.

A further contrast between the model analyzed in chapter 3 and the present one relates to our conception of short-run equilibrium and the growth process. In the previous models growth was viewed as a movement by the economy through a sequence of short-run equilibria in both the factor and the commodity markets. It was shown that plausible conditions existed for a stable adjustment to short-run equilibrium. In the present model, we require only that there be equilibrium in commodity markets.[26] Growth is therefore viewed as a sequence of short-run adjustments in which the commodity market attains a new equilibrium, while in the factor markets, on the other hand, there is no equilibrium condition for wage and rental rates, only the full-employment condition. There is no short-run adjustment mechanism to be described for the factor market. All migration proceeds according to a specific decision rule while the capital stock is immobile, and new investment goods are allocated in a predetermined way.

26. In Appendix E it is shown that this short-term adjustment process is stable.

From this brief explanation of alternative approaches to factor market behavior, we can see that it is a relatively easy matter to extend the theoretical framework of our models. Of course, these gains come only at the expense of having to deal with an increasingly complex system of interdependent relationships. What is of interest in our extension of equilibrium treatment of factor markets used in earlier chapters is whether the introduction of costs and rigidities has a quantitatively significant effect on the rate and pattern of growth within a plausible range of parameter values, and it is to this question that we now turn in chapter 8.

8

Disequilibrium Growth
in the Dualistic Economy

8.1. INTRODUCTION

Having developed an alternative specification of the factor market, we now explore its effect on our dualistic economy. The disequilibrium model is simulated and compared with the equilibrium model by the use of similar initial conditions and parameter values. While the disequilibrium model is capable of generating persistent rental rate differentials and wage "gaps," it remains to be seen whether the simulated development pattern provides a more accurate description of the "stylized facts" of growth in low-income economies than that provided by the equilibrium model and in particular, whether it improves our ability to reproduce the Japanese economic history as reported in chapter 5.

Even if the patterns of growth and structural change in the two systems are the same, differences may occur with respect to each model's sensitivity to changes in comparable parameters. Significant differences in response to changes in the population, technical progress, and production and consumption parameters may require a modification of our conclusions regarding their influence on the pattern of growth and structural change that were derived from the analysis in chapter 6. At the same time, the disequilibrium model affords us an opportunity to extend the analysis of chapter 6 by examining the impact of the new parameters relating to factor market behavior. Moreover, by explicitly introducing behavioral assumptions that make possible continued differentials in factor price and productivity between sectors, we can now consider why low-income developing economies exhibit interregional factor price differentials in spite of significant factor transfers.

Because of the added complexity of the model, our analysis is based largely on numerical techniques. The procedure has been to maintain wherever possible the same parameter values and initial conditions specified in the equilibrium model. The differences between the two systems, however, made some compromises necessary. These and other matters relating to the choice of parameter values and initial conditions are discussed in Appendix G. Briefly, the economy again starts out as predominantly agricultural with two-thirds of the population in rural areas, more than half of GNP produced by the agricultural sector, a gross savings rate of about 15 percent, an annual population growth rate of 2.7 percent, industrial output per laborer almost twice that of agriculture, and the industrial capital-output ratio 1.7 times that in agriculture (table 8.1).

8.2. THE PATTERN OF GROWTH AND STRUCTURAL CHANGE

It is useful to summarize briefly the main features of the simulation before turning to a detailed discussion of the pattern of growth and structural change. The disequilibrium model exhibits patterns that in many respects are similar to those described by the equilibrium model. The rate of increase in GNP is fairly stable at about 4 percent per year during an entire century of growth, and the industrial output share tends to level off at 70 percent toward the end of the century. As expected, the gap between urban and rural factor prices not only persists but widens during the first half-century of growth. In response, there is a steady flow of labor from rural to urban areas and a consequent decline in the population growth as the economy becomes more urbanized. The rate of capital formation rises slightly during the first half-century of growth and then declines, but only minor increases in the economy's savings rate are required for the initial acceleration. Once again the efficiency capital-labor ratio falls slightly in the first two decades, when the effects

TABLE 8.1 Comparison of initial conditions in the equilibrium (E)
and disequilibrium (D) models

Indicator	E	D	D/E (100)
Urbanization level	0.300	0.319	106.3
Industrialization level	0.429	0.472	110.0
Gross savings rate	0.150	0.153	102.0
Population growth rate	0.270	0.268	99.3
Output per laborer (valued)			
Aggregate	1.663	1.903	114.4
Industry	2.375	2.815	118.5
Agriculture	1.354	1.479	109.2
Efficiency capital-output ratio			
Aggregate	1.854	1.826	98.5
Industry	2.455	2.349	95.7
Agriculture	1.402	1.358	96.9
Capital-labor ratio[a]			
Aggregate	0.302	0.319	105.6
Industry	0.571	0.607	106.3
Agriculture	0.186	0.184	98.9
Capital's share			
Aggregate	0.481	0.491	102.1
Industry	0.636	0.642	100.9
Agriculture	0.364	0.356	97.8

a. Net of efficiency factors.

of biased technical progress outweigh the effects of increases
in the capital stock relative to additions to the labor force. After
the second decade, however, capital accumulation dominates,
and the efficiency capital-labor ratios rise steadily. Labor's overall share in GNP falls steadily for much of the first century of
growth, and the phases of sectoral income share movements
found in the equilibrium model reappear.

8.2.1. Output and Population Growth
As already noted, the rate of GNP growth exhibits remarkable
long-run stability at about 4 percent per annum (table 8.2).
In the equilibrium model, the average annual growth rate rose
from about 3.5 percent in the first decade to about 4 percent
in the fifth. The average rate of agricultural output growth is
about 3.3 percent per year, almost exactly the same as the rate

TABLE 8.2 Average annual growth rate of output (valued) and population in the equilibrium (E) and disequilibrium (D) models

Period	Output						Population		GNP per capita	
	GNP		Industry		Agriculture					
	E	D	E	D	E	D	E	D	E	D
1–10	0.035	0.039	0.037	0.044	0.030	0.032	0.027	0.027	0.008	0.012
11–20	.037	.039	.041	.045	.031	.032	.027	.026	.010	.013
21–30	.038	.040	.044	.045	.032	.033	.027	.026	.011	.013
31–40	.039	.040	.045	.045	.032	.033	.026	.026	.012	.014
41–50	.040	.040	.046	.045	.033	.033	.026	.026	.013	.014
1–50	0.038	0.040	0.043	0.045	0.032	0.033	0.027	0.026	0.011	0.013

in the equilibrium model. The average growth rate in the industrial sector is about 4.5 percent per year as compared with 4.2 percent in the equilibrium model. We conclude that the growth rates in the two models are not very different, but that the disequilibrium model exhibits less variability over time.

The level of industrialization in the disequilibrium regime is higher at all stages of development, rising linearly from 47 percent to about 60 percent by the sixth decade and leveling off at about 70 percent by the end of the century (fig. 8.1). Apart from the first few years, the rate of industrialization declines steadily to less than 0.2 percent a year by the end of the century. In the equilibrium model the rate of industrialization rose to a peak of 0.6 percent a year by the start of the sixth decade.

There is very little difference between the two models with respect to population growth rates (table 8.2). The rate of decline is slightly more rapid in the disequilibrium regime, since the economy is more urbanized in the initial period and the rate of migration is somewhat more rapid in the first two decades. However, the annual growth rate tends to stabilize at about 2.4 percent in the latter part of the century. The level of urbanization, rising linearly from 32 percent at the outset to 47 percent by the start of the sixth decade (compared with 41 percent in the equilibrium model), reaches a plateau of about 60 percent toward the end of the century. The rate of urbanization rises during the first three decades, after which it declines steadily. In the equilibrium model, on the other hand, the rate of urbanization rose steadily during the first four decades and then stabilized at about 0.8 percent a year.

8.2.2. The Level and Distribution of Income

With the more rapid growth in GNP in the early periods and with the slightly slower growth in population, the annual rate of per capita GNP expansion in the disequilibrium model is somewhat higher in the first three decades; by the fifth decade, however, the average rate of increase is the same in both regimes, 1.4 percent (see table 8.2).

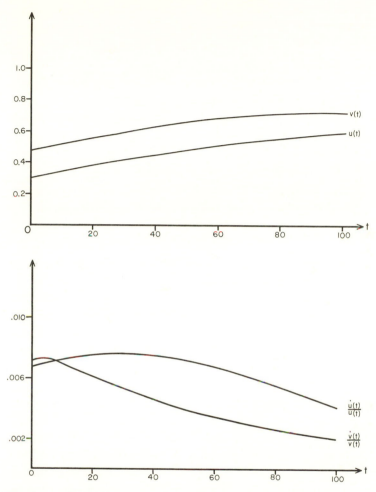

Fig. 8.1. *Above,* Level of Industrialization and Urbanization; *below* Rates of Industrialization and Urbanization

Consistent with our earlier results, labor's share in aggregate output falls steadily over five decades from 51 percent to 47 percent (compared with a fall from 52 percent to 48 percent in the equilibrium model). However, in the latter half of the century labor's share stabilizes at about 47 percent and then begins to rise again at the end of the century. Labor's share in

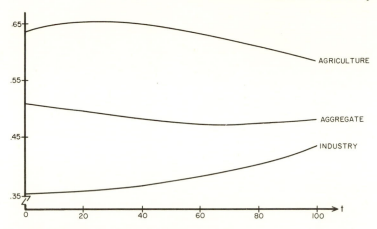

Fig. 8.2. Trends in Labor's Share of Output

industry remains stable at about 36 percent for the first three decades and then rises steadily to 43 percent by the end of the century. Thus, the disequilibrium model displays slightly less variability in factor shares over the first half-century of growth. The relatively smaller changes in labor's share reflect the greater stability of the sectoral efficiency capital-labor ratios, since the higher rate of accumulation and somewhat slower population growth offset the influence of the falling $x(t)/y(t)$.[1]

Despite the remarkable similarities with respect to the rate of per capita output growth and its aggregate distribution, the two regimes exhibit substantial differences in sectoral income per laborer and output per laborer. Sectoral wage incomes per laborer were equated by assumption in the equilibrium model, but in the disequilibrium regime industrial wage income exceeds that of agriculture. At the outset urban labor income is 6 percent higher than in rural areas, and by the fifth decade the differential rises to 15 percent. The disequilibrium model is thus able to reproduce the familiar phenomenon of an increas-

1. Recall that

$$\frac{\dot{\alpha_i}(t)}{\alpha_i(t)} = [1 - \alpha_i(t)] \frac{(\sigma_i - 1)}{\sigma_i} \frac{\dot{k_i}(t)}{k_i(t)} .$$

ing disparity between wage income per laborer in urban and rural areas, while at the same time allowing for a substantial increase in the absolute level of income per laborer in each sector. Over the first half-century, for example, wage income per laborer in industry rises by 83 percent and in agriculture by 69 percent. The reasons for the emergence of this gap will be examined when the wage behavior in the economy is considered.

Despite the differences between the two models with respect to wage income per laborer, in the behavior of output per laborer they are rather similar. The average productivity of labor in the disequilibrium regime rises substantially during the first half-century of development, although the increases are greater than in the equilibrium model (table 8.3). In industry, for ex-

TABLE 8.3 Trends in labor productivity in the equilibrium (E) and disequilibrium (D) models

Period	Sector output (valued) per laborer				Ratio of industry to agriculture	
	Industry		Agriculture			
	E	D	E	D	E	D
1	2.375	2.814	1.354	1.479	1.751	1.903
10	2.589	3.122	1.411	1.598	1.834	1.954
20	2.855	3.499	1.517	1.764	1.888	1.984
30	3.152	3.919	1.648	1.972	1.913	1.987
40	3.482	4.388	1.828	2.228	1.904	1.969
50	3.862	4.911	2.061	2.539	1.873	1.934
Average	3.053	3.776	1.636	1.930	1.861	1.955

ample, output per laborer rises by 74 percent over the first five decades (compared with 63 percent in the equilibrium model) and in agriculture by 72 percent (52 percent in the equilibrium model). In the equilibrium model the productivity of industrial relative to agricultural labor increased from an index of 1.75 at the outset to a peak of 1.91 by period 30 and fell again to 1.87 by period 50. The productivity differential is even higher in the disequilibrium framework. Although the absolute increase in productivity for both sectors is greater than in the equilibrium model and than observed for Japan, the relative sector productivities are more stable and conform with Japanese experience more closely.

Thus, the disequilibrium model confirms once again the inevitability of large sectoral differences in average labor productivity in a growing economy. As our analysis of the equilibrium model has indicated, such regional disparities are bound to exist, even when urban wage and rental rates are equalized. This is due to the differences in the nature of the production functions and the resulting differences in sectoral capital intensities. Under conditions of factor immobility, the sectoral disparity in average labor productivity is even greater.

This brief review of the key features of the disequilibrium model reveals that the patterns of output and population growth, the levels of industrialization and urbanization, and the behavior of factor shares are remarkably similar in the two regimes despite some small differences in early periods (largely as a result of differences in initial conditions). There is less variation between the models themselves than between the equilibrium model and the Japanese data examined in chapter 5. At this highly aggregate level of comparison, it is very difficult to choose between the models on the grounds of descriptive power. This observation raises an important issue relating to the empirical testing of alternative theories of economic growth. In appears that appeal to some set of minimum checks is insufficient; indeed, we must go beyond the most general "stylized facts" such as the growth and distribution of output and population if we are to formulate judgments about the usefulness of the two models. One such extension relates to the somewhat different behaviors of prices in the two systems.

8.3. BEHAVIOR OF PRICES

8.3.1. Terms of Trade

There is remarkably little difference between the two models in the temporal behavior of the terms of trade (fig. 8.3). The

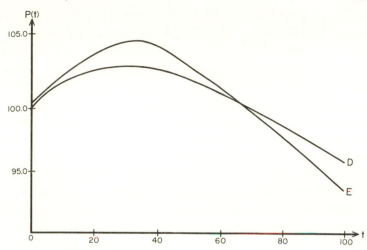

Fig. 8.3. Terms of Trade Index

mild upward trend during the first three decades and the steady
decline thereafter appear once again.

8.3.2. Rents and Wages
One of the shortcomings of the equilibrium model was its inability to capture the commonly observed differentials in factor
prices that persist in a growing economy. The disequilibrium
model is superior in this respect. It reproduces differentials in
wage and rental rates that remain throughout the entire history
of the economy; these are illustrated in figure 8.4. As expected,
industrial factor prices (*both* wages and rental rates) exceed
those in agriculture.

Rental rates in each sector rise during the first two decades
and fall steadily thereafter. This phase of increasing rental rates
is produced by the falling sectoral efficiency capital-labor ratios
(the rate of decrease in $x(t)/y(t)$ exceeds the rate of increase
in $k_i(t)$ during this period). But the positive effects of capital
accumulation begin to outweigh the negative influence of technical progress by the latter part of the second decade. As a
result, the marginal productivity of efficiency capital falls in
each sector throughout most of this economy's growth experi-

ence. The decline in $r_i(t)$ is delayed somewhat by the positive influence of the increasing terms of trade during the initial two decades of development.[2]

The absolute and relative rental rate gaps display rather interesting behavior in the disequilibrium model. The absolute gap increases slowly during the first four decades, stabilizes, and then declines steadily. In relative terms the industrial rental rate is about 4 percent higher than the rate in agriculture at the outset, and this differential increases slowly to a little more than 7 percent by the end of the seventh decade, after which it falls slightly. Thus, the disequilibrium model suggests that, under conditions of sustained output growth, intersectoral (and interregional) rental rate differentials will not only persist but in fact widen (both in absolute and relative terms). This result is consistent with Watanabe's documentation of Japanese twentieth-century experience. Watanabe found that agriculture had a far lower profit rate than all other sectors over the period 1923–39. He also found that profit rate differentials had not diminished and furthermore, were much larger than wage differentials over these decades of rapid growth. As we shall see shortly, this last characteristic is absent from the simulation.[3] In a similar study of American industry, Stigler focused on the dispersion of industrial rates of return as a measure of current disequilibrium.[4] Stigler's study suggests that the forces initiating disequilibrium are relatively weak in American manufacturing. As a result, intersectoral capital flows in any current time period, which are responding to previous differentials in rate of return, are sufficient to offset the disequilibrating influences also

2. Recall that

$$\frac{\dot{r}_1(t)}{r_1(t)} = \frac{\dot{P}(t)}{P(t)} - \frac{1 - \alpha_1(t)}{\sigma_1} \frac{\dot{k}_1(t)}{k_1(t)}$$

and

$$\frac{\dot{r}_2(t)}{r_2(t)} = - \frac{1 - \alpha_2(t)}{\sigma_2} \frac{\dot{k}_2(t)}{k_2(t)}.$$

3. T. Watanabe, "Industrialization, Technological Progress, and Dual Structure."

4. G. J. Stigler, *Capital and Rates of Return in Manufacturing Industries.*

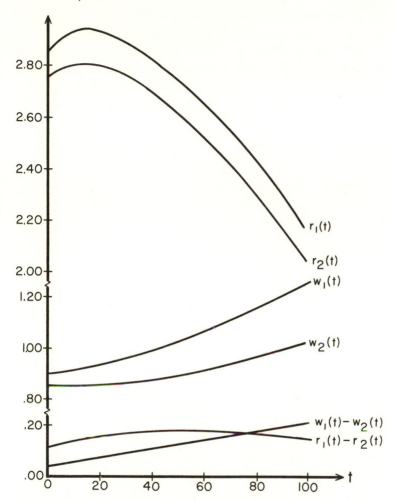

Fig. 8.4. Trends in Efficiency Wages and Rents

occurring in the current time period. For Stigler's view to hold
in our model, the relative rental rate differentials should decline
as growth occurs. That this does not occur during a century of
growth in our low-income economy is not surprising, since the
disequilibrating forces may be greater in a country undergoing
continual structural change.

As we shall now see, once the possibility of *changes* in
parameter values over time are introduced, the historical be-

havior of the rental rate differentials may be quite difficult to interpret because of the conflicting influences of several key parameters. The rental rate differential is particularly sensitive to exogenous shocks such as changes in the rate and bias in technical progress, the elasticity of factor substitution, the propensity to save, and changes in consumer tastes (table 8.4).

TABLE 8.4 Structural elasticities for change in rental rate differential in response to increases in selected parameter values

Parameter	Value of elasticity at year				
	10	20	30	40	50
Technical change					
Bias constant	+1.480	+1.296	+1.088	+0.721	+0.227
Rate constant	+0.997	+1.395	+1.776	+2.172	+2.595
Elasticity of substitution[a]					
σ_1	+0.679	−0.216	−0.682	−1.082	−1.450
σ_2	+17.810	−5.491	−3.256	−2.691	−2.250
Savings					
$s_1 = s_2 = s$ ..	−0.102	−0.388	−0.666	−0.924	−1.159
s_1	−2.822	−3.700	−4.651	−5.604	−6.112
s_2	+2.721	+3.335	+4.016	+4.723	+5.505
Consumption					
$\beta_{11} = -\beta_{21}$ ..	+0.554	−2.654	−2.515	−2.554	−2.617
$\beta_{12} = -\beta_{22}$ ..	−0.068	−0.522	−0.481	−0.455	−0.430
γ	−0.628	+1.093	+0.789	+0.574	+0.403

a. Measures an increase in σ_1 and a decrease in σ_2.

The more rapid the rate of technical progress, the more pronounced are rental rate differentials. This result makes intuitive sense, since rapid technical progress represents a strong force in generating factor market disequilibrium. Interestingly, development economists have tended to view such differentials in the rate of return as evidence of market "failure" in the low-income economy. It may be more appropriate to view these differentials as indicative of successful dynamic performance! The effect of a change in the savings propensities is also predictable, but here perhaps the *magnitude* of the effect would not have been fully anticipated. In our growing dualistic economy, the industrial sector is continually "starved" for financing, and excess demands are a consistent feature of the industrial capital market. As a result, an increase in the urban capitalists' savings propensity has an impressive effect in reducing those excess demands, as reflected in sharply declining differentials between sectors in the rate of return. Further on in this chapter we shall compare these results with those focusing on the capital market parameters themselves. There we shall discover that changes in parameters describing capital market imperfections have a negligible effect on both savings transfers and rental rate differentials. Generally we shall conclude that in a putty-clay world parameters exogenous to the capital market exert a far greater influence on resource flows and rental rate differentials than parameters *endogenous* to the capital market itself.

Consider now the wage behavior of the economy. It appears that the agricultural wage is very stable over the first half-century of growth (it rises by only 3.5 percent during the first five decades, and much of this increase is recorded in the fifth decade), but in the second half of the century there is an increase of 17 percent. The industrial wage, on the other hand, rises steadily from the outset (with a 13 percent increase in the first half-century and a further 22 percent increase in the second half). These results contrast sharply with the relatively stable wage in the equilibrium model. Nevertheless, it is of some interest to discover that stability in the agricultural wage and rapid growth in the industrial wage are forthcoming in a simple neoclassical model. This important result again supports the conclusion that historically stable wage rates in agriculture can be readily explained without invoking the concepts of wage fixing and surplus labor. The explanation of the behavior of sectoral wages parallels that for rental rates.[5] A falling $k_1(t)$ in the early periods is offset by a rising terms of trade, with a

5. Recall that

$$\frac{\dot{w}_1(t)}{w_1(t)} = \frac{\dot{P}(t)}{P(t)} + \frac{\alpha_1(t)}{\sigma_1}\frac{\dot{k}_1(t)}{k_1(t)}$$

and

$$\frac{\dot{w}_2(t)}{w_2(t)} = \frac{\alpha_2(t)}{\sigma_2}\frac{\dot{k}_2(t)}{k_2(t)}.$$

resultant increase in $w_1(t)$. But when $k_1(t)$ begins to increase, the effects of the then falling terms of trade are countered so that $w_1(t)$ rises increasingly rapidly. In the agricultural sector, the initial fall in $w_2(t)$ reflects the decline in $k_2(t)$; when $k_2(t)$ begins to increase, $w_2(t)$ also reverses its trend. The relative "stability" in agriculture's efficiency capital-labor ratio is therefore responsible for the stable agricultural wage in the early periods of growth.

Much has been made of the "wage gap" between agriculture and industry in the development literature. Note that the absolute and relative wage gaps both rise in the disequilibrium model. The urban wage was 6 percent higher than the agricultural wage at the outset; after a century of growth this difference widens to 20 percent. The appearance of a wage gap in the disequilibrium model is in contrast to both Jorgenson's framework and the equilibrium model analyzed in earlier chapters. Jorgenson assumes that the absolute differential is constant over time so that wages grow at the same rate in each sector.[6] Thus, he implicitly assumes that the rate of migration is sufficiently responsive, for any rate of technical progress and capital accumulation, to prevent a widening of the wage gap in a developing economy. Our results not only contrast sharply with his view of wage behavior; they are also consistent with the empirical evidence from Japan and other countries. The discussion in chapter 5 on Japanese wage trends noted that the agricultural wage was relatively stable over the period 1890–1910, with perhaps a mild upward trend while the manufacturing wage rose by some 40 percent. The disequilibrium model therefore appears to yield a more accurate description of wage behavior in Meiji Japan than the equilibrium model, where sectoral wages were equalized by assumption.

While the present focus is on the differential between agriculture and industry, it is worth noting that the analysis of

6. Jorgensen assumed that for all t
$$\frac{w_1(t)}{w_2(t)} = \frac{1}{1 - \phi},$$
where ϕ is constant over time.

interindustry wage differentials has received increased attention in recent years. That literature, however, has not arrived at a general conclusion regarding the relationship between the industrial wage structure and the level of economic development. Defining a theoretical relationship between wage rates for homogeneous labor employed in different industries is easy enough. Expanding industries in which profits and productivity are higher than normal also pay higher than average wages to attract the required labor. Interindustry differentials serve this allocation function. But the actual differentials are complicated by the existence of continuously high-paying industries. In many less developed countries there may be a small group of industries dominated by export giants and local monopolies willing to pay high wages to attract the best labor, for example, petroleum economies of North Africa or the heavily protected Philippine manufacturing sector. The analytical distinction here is the heterogeneity of labor. Nevertheless, several major propositions have been advanced in the literature. Reynolds and Taft have suggested that interindustry wage dispersion tends to reach a maximum sometime during the early stages of industrialization and to diminish gradually after that point.[7] Newly industrializing economies show a widening tendency in their wage structure, while the wage structure of an advanced industrialized economy has a tendency toward contraction. The long-term validity of the "contraction" hypothesis is sometimes doubted, however, since some studies have revealed that the differentials have more often increased or stayed constant.[8] Borts, for example, found that during twentieth-century American history regional wage differentials increased in spite of heavy interregional migration.[9] He attributes this result in large part to the higher rates of population reproduction rate in low-wage areas.

7. L. G. Reynolds and C. H. Taft, *The Evolution of Wage Structure.*
8. D. E. Cullen, "The Inter-industry Wage Structure: 1899–1950"; OEDC, *Wages and Labour Mobility.*
9. G. H. Borts, "The Equalization of Returns and Regional Economic Growth."

Another hypothesis of interest is the supposed existence of a systematic relationship between the wage *level* and the wage structure. According to Reis, when a secular rise in wages takes place, percentage differentials persist and the absolute differential widens.[10] Papola and Bhenodway have suggested that in recent years there has been a general tendency toward the narrowing of interindustry relative wage differentials in most countries, irrespective of their levels of industrialization.[11] The absolute differentials have had a tendency to widen in all countries. They find that an increase in the wage level is generally accompanied by a widening of absolute differentials; the relative differentials may increase at a slower pace or even decline. The behavior of wages in our model is not inconsistent with their findings, but we find no tendency for the relative gap to diminish.

What are the determinants of the so-called gap (table 8.5)? The development literature stresses the constraints on migration in low-income economies. Further on in this chapter it will be emphasized that, with the exception of migration costs, migration flows are quite insensitive to the migration parameters themselves. This result is consistent with the findings on rental rate differentials. However, the wage gap is sensitive to parameters exogeneous to the labor market itself: for example, changes in the parameters of technical progress, savings, and the elasticity of substitution all play important roles in influencing the magnitude of the wage gap. Indeed, the structural elasticity for the rate of technical progress is approximately two, which indicates a very sensitive response of the wage gap to economy-wide rates of technical change. A similar result is obtained for increases in savings propensities. In short, the wage gap may be less an index of market failure and more a measure of dynamic performance in the developing economy. Note, however, that the wage differential is relatively insensitive to demand and demographic parameters. The relative unimportance of

10. A. M. Reis, *Trade Union Wage Policy.*
11. T. S. Papola and V. P. Bhenodway, "Dynamics of Industrial Wage Structure: An Inter-country Analysis."

TABLE 8.5 Structural elasticities for change in wage rate differential in response to increases in selected parameter values

Parameter	Value of elasticity at year				
	10	20	30	40	50
Technical change					
Bias constant	+1.747	+2.149	+2.504	+2.789	+3.040
Rate constant	−0.397	−0.632	−0.822	−1.023	−1.227
Elasticity of substitution[a]					
σ_1	+1.368	+2.215	+2.250	+2.213	+2.163
σ_2	+5.308	....	−8.411	−7.623	−7.015
Savings					
$s = s_1 = s_2$ ..	+1.845	+1.888	+1.824	+1.754	+1.686
s_1	+0.872	+1.088	+1.053	+1.012	+0.969
s_2	+0.964	+0.793	+0.759	+0.727	+0.699
Consumption					
$\beta_{11} = -\beta_{21}$ ..	+0.345	−0.544	−0.439	−0.438	−0.434
$\beta_{12} = -\beta_{22}$ ..	−0.039	−0.097	−0.076	−0.070	−0.066
γ	−0.180	+0.060	+0.047	+0.063	+0.072
Migration					
ρ	−0.400	−0.339	−0.281	−0.236	−0.198
b	−0.010	−0.011	−0.007	−0.005	−0.003
a	−2.833	−2.327	−1.948	−1.641	−1.512
c	−2.356	−1.756	−1.317	−1.017	−0.803

a. Measures an increase in σ_1 and a reduction in σ_2.

demographic forces is interesting and certainly at variance with the traditional literature.[12]

To return to the simulation itself, it appears that our disequilibrium specification does not suffer in a comparison with the equilibrium model. It also satisfies a minimum set of empirical checks in describing growth and structural change. Furthermore, it represents an improvement in describing sectoral wage behavior, at least for the case of Meiji Japan.

8.4. CAPITAL ACCUMULATION, SAVINGS, AND THE CAPITAL MARKET
8.4.1. Capital Accumulation and Productivity
One of the reasons for the somewhat more rapid early growth

12. See, for example, Borts, "Equalization of Returns."

in the disequilibrium model is the higher rate of capital accumulation in the first two decades, which, in turn, is largely the result of the differences in initial conditions between the two models. In the disequilibrium model the unaugmented capital stock grows by more than 3.5 percent a year in the first two decades, compared with 2.7 percent in the equilibrium model (table 8.6). For the remainder of the first half-century, the

TABLE 8.6 Trends in rates of capital accumulation

Period	Aggregate		Industry		Agriculture	
	E	D	E	D	E	D
1	0.024	0.034	0.030	0.040	0.016	0.024
10	.029	.036	.034	.041	.020	.028
20	.033	.038	.038	.043	.024	.031
30	.037	.040	.041	.043	.028	.033
40	.040	.041	.043	.044	.032	.035
50	.041	.041	.044	.044	.035	.037
Average (1–50)	0.034	0.038	0.038	0.043	0.026	0.031

NOTE: Net of the efficiency factor, $x(t)$.

rate of accumulation in the disequilibrium model increases only moderately and levels off at about 4 percent a year by the start of the fifth decade, a rate identical with that of the equilibrium model. In the latter half of the century, the rate of accumulation declines to slightly below 4 percent.

The aggregate capital-output ratio is relatively stable at about 1.8 in the first half-century of growth. (It actually declines from 1.83 to 1.79, whereas in the disequilibrium model the ratio falls from 1.85 to 1.66 over the same period.) The efficiency capital-output ratio rises steadily, reflecting the continuous decline in the average productivity of efficiency capital in both sectors. The behavior of the unaugmented capital-output ratio in the industrial sector is very similar to that of the equilibrium model (table 8.7) but the ratio is more stable in the agricultural

TABLE 8.7 Trends in capital-output ratios

Period	Aggregate		Industry		Agriculture		Ratio of industry to agriculture	
	E	D	E	D	E	D	E	D
1	1.853	1.826	2.455	2.349	1.402	1.358	1.751	1.730
10	1.765	1.801	2.352	2.282	1.286	1.317	1.829	1.733
20	1.704	1.786	2.259	2.219	1.198	1.290	1.886	1.720
30	1.671	1.782	2.183	2.167	1.144	1.283	1.908	1.689
40	1.657	1.784	2.122	2.124	1.117	1.292	1.900	1.644
50	1.656	1.791	2.072	2.087	1.111	1.313	1.865	1.589

NOTE: Capital is net of the efficiency factor, $x(t)$.

sector and is somewhat higher for most of the period.[13] A comparison of this experience with the historical data presented in chapter 5 shows that the disequilibrium model does not predict the extent of the increase in Japanese capital-productivity as well as the equilibrium regime.

8.4.2. The Level and Sources of Savings
Like that of the equilibrium model, the aggregate gross savings rate of the disequilibrium model does not change dramatically as the economy grows but instead rises slowly from an initial value of 15.3 percent to 16.4 percent by the start of the sixth decade (compared with 16.2 percent in the equilibrium model; see table 8.8). However, the allowance for replacement investment is constant at about 9 percent of GNP; in the equilibrium model this ratio declined steadily. The ratio of replacement allowances to GNP was constant in Meiji Japan as well.

13. Recall that the behavior of the efficiency capital-output ratios is given by

$$\frac{\dot{k_1}(t)}{k_1(t)} - \frac{\dot{q_1}(t)}{q_1(t)} = [1 - \alpha_1(t)] \frac{\dot{k_1}(t)}{k_1(t)}$$

and

$$\frac{\dot{k_2}(t)}{k_2(t)} - \frac{\dot{q_2}(t)}{q_2(t)} = \frac{\dot{P}(t)}{P(t)} + [1 - \alpha_2(t)] \frac{\dot{k_2}(t)}{k_2(t)}.$$

TABLE 8.8 Share of savings in aggregate output

Period	Gross savings		Replacement		Net savings	
	E	D	E	D	E	D
1	0.150	0.153	0.093	0.091	0.063	0.068
10	.151	.156	.088	.090	.069	.072
20	.154	.158	.085	.089	.075	.076
30	.157	.161	.084	.089	.080	.079
40	.160	.163	.083	.089	.084	.081
50	0.162	0.164	0.083	0.090	0.087	0.082

The results presented in table 8.9 permit a more detailed examination of the sources of savings. The share of total savings provided by urban capitalists rises from 57 percent to 71 percent over five decades in the equilibrium model. In the disequilibrium regime, urban capitalists provide 62 percent of total savings at the outset, but their share rises to 73 percent by the start of the sixth decade. Thus, the share of total capital formation financed by industrial capitalists rises in both models, but in the disequilibrium economy the share increases more slowly. It is difficult to judge the historical accuracy of this result. Most data documenting sources of savings deal only with savings by income source (from wage and property income) or savings made by the public sector and corporate and noncorporate private sectors. There is very little historical in-

TABLE 8.9 Sources of saving in the equilibrium (E) and disequilibrium (D) models

Period	Aggregate	Industrial capitalists		Agricultural capitalists			
				Total		Retained	Transferred
		E	D	E	D	D	D
1	1.000	0.566	0.614	0.434	0.386	0.328	0.058
10	1.000	.597	.646	.403	.354	.287	.067
20	1.000	.631	.675	.369	.325	.253	.072
30	1.000	.661	.698	.339	.302	.228	.074
40	1.000	.688	.717	.312	.283	.209	.074
50	1.000	0.710	0.733	0.290	0.267	0.196	0.071

formation on urban and rural savings and, in particular, on savings out of urban and rural property income. It is generally believed that rural savings are small in most of today's low-income countries—the peasants have a high propensity to hoard, and a significant proportion of the agricultural surplus is skimmed off in the form of rents to landlords, interest to money lenders, or profit margins by merchants. These entrepreneurial classes frequently have been characterized as having a high propensity for conspicuous consumption, the result of which is to starve agriculture of investment funds. Nevertheless, the relative importance of landlords' attitudes toward accumulation in explaining successful or unsuccessful growth performance in developing economies has attracted considerable attention.[14] In Meiji Japan, for example, the system of feudalistic tributary payments was replaced by a system of land ownership, farm rental, and land taxes. Landowners accumulated wealth by receiving farm rents from the tenants and, in turn, by investing these funds in various enterprises or depositing them with banks which channeled savings into industries.

While the behavior of the aggregate savings rate is the same in the two models, they differ with respect to sensitivity to changes in urban and rural savings parameters. When $s_1 = s_2 = s$ is increased in the disequilibrium system, there is a much smaller positive stimulus to GNP and per capita GNP growth in early periods, although the effect in the latter part of the first half-century of growth is similar to that in the equilibrium model; for example, in period 10 the structural elasticity on per capita GNP growth rates is 3.022 in the equilibrium model (table 6.9) and 0.753 in the disequilibrium model (table 8.10). A striking difference indeed! Moreover, there is a smaller positive impact on the level of industrialization, although the stimulus to urbanization is similar. The smaller impact of changes in savings propensities on growth and industrialization when

14. W. A. Lewis, "Development with Unlimited Supplies of Labour"; J. C. Fei and G. Ranis, *Development of the Labor Surplus Economy: Theory and Policy*; and idem, "Agrarianism, Dualism, and Economic Development."

TABLE 8.10 Elasticities of various performance indicators to changes in savings parameters

Variable	Value of elasticity at year				
	10	20	30	40	50
	Increase in $s = s_1 = s_2$				
GNP growth rate	+0.208	0.498	0.304	0.165	+0.055
Per capita GNP growth rate	+0.753	1.669	1.117	0.750	+0.470
Level of urbanization	+0.412	0.699	0.881	0.979	+1.015
Industrial output share	+0.031	0.129	0.170	0.177	+0.165
Capital stock growth (aggregate)	+1.891	1.383	0.950	0.600	+0.317
	Increase in s_1				
GNP growth rate	+0.147	0.263	0.146	0.060	−0.010
Per capita GNP growth rate	+0.519	0.890	0.562	0.339	+0.162
Level of urbanization	+0.237	0.406	0.517	0.581	+0.606
Industrial output share	−0.003	0.054	0.076	0.079	+0.070
Capital stock growth (aggregate)	+1.163	0.862	0.614	0.411	+0.244
	Increase in s_2				
GNP growth rate	+0.058	0.231	0.152	0.099	+0.062
Per capita GNP growth rate	+0.226	0.776	0.535	0.391	+0.295
Level of urbanization	+0.174	0.291	0.358	0.390	+0.397
Industrial output share	+0.034	0.074	0.092	0.095	+0.090
Capital stock growth (aggregate)	+0.721	0.506	0.317	0.169	+0.053

market imperfections exist is the result of a substantially lower increase in the rate of capital accumulation, particularly in the agricultural sector. For example, in period 10 the structural elasticity on aggregate capital stock growth is 2.433 in the equilibrium model and 1.891 in the disequilibrium regime. The slower rate of accumulation is explained by supply elasticities and price behavior. An increase in savings implies a shift in demand for industrial (capital) goods. With restrictions on re-source reallocation, and with low supply elasticities compared with the equilibrium model, a sharp rise in the prices of industrial goods occurs. As a result, the physical rate of accumulation is stifled by rising prices of capital goods in much the same way that foreign exchange availability inhibits capital formation in models of open economies (this result is discussed at greater length in section 8.6.3). Thus, with factor market imperfections the stimulating effect of an increase in savings parameters is dampened because of the adverse effects on the sectoral terms of trade.

Despite the smaller short-run effects of increases in the saving propensity, the presence of factor market imperfections does not reverse our analysis of the long-run effects generated by the equilibrium model. That is, the disequilibrium specification reaffirms our previous conclusion that simple one-sector models normally underestimate the cumulative impact of changes in savings propensities, since one-sector models ignore the interaction between capital accumulation, urbanization, and population growth when sectoral differences in demographic behavior and in factor shares are present.

8.4.3. Allocation of Investment
One of the key issues in development economics has been the allocation of investment between competing activities and it is of interest to explore the question in our models. In the disequilibrium model the share of gross investment allocated to the industrial sector rises from 67 percent in the initial period to about 80 percent by the beginning of the sixth decade. In the equilibrium model, on the other hand, the share of invest-

ment allocated to industry rises from 57 percent at the outset to 73 percent by period 50.

Most of the investment in each sector is financed from savings generated within the sector itself. The agricultural sector finances only about 9 percent of industrial investment throughout the first five decades in the disequilibrium model. About 15 percent of total rural savings are transferred at the outset; by the end of the first half-century the figure is 27 percent but by the end of the century it falls to 21 percent.

These results from the disequilibrium model appear to be roughly consistent with contemporary Asian data. According to a study of savings behavior in the ECAFE region,[15] in all countries except Japan at least one-half of household savings is utilized within the sector, while half or less is transferred to other sectors. In Japan, households devoted less than one-third of their savings to self-use and transferred the balance to other investors. This may reflect, in part, the sophistication of Japanese financial intermediaries (especially the banking system) and the corresponding low level of development of these institutions in other ECAFE countries. However, the share of household savings transferred by direct means is small in all countries, which indicates the uniformly low level of development of markets for financial instruments. The growth of the financial structure has been a recent phenomenon in most of Asia, and the channeling of household savings into financial institutions is still relatively retarded. Even in Japan, where the financial structure was more highly developed at the time of the ECAFE study, the banking system dominated, so that savings transferred indirectly (through banks) greatly exceeded savings transferred directly through public security markets.

Not only is the amount of agricultural savings transferred relatively unimportant in financing industrial investment in our disequilibrium model, but, more interesting, the share of agricultural savings transferred is insensitive, with one exception,

15. ECAFE, "Measures for Mobilizing Domestic Savings for Productive Investment."

to changes in *all* parameter values. Even the capital market parameters have little impact on the savings transfers. This generalization includes τ, our measure of transaction costs. The exception is the rural capitalist's propensity to save. As would be expected, an increase in the rural savings propensity leads to an increase in the share of agricultural savings transferred (table 8.11).

TABLE 8.11 Structural elasticities for change in share of rural savings transferred in response to increases in selected parameter values

Parameter	Value of elasticity at year				
	10	20	30	40	50
Technical change					
Bias constant	+0.010	+0.007	−0.001	−0.013	−0.028
Rate constant	+0.012	+0.025	+0.039	+0.052	+0.064
Savings					
$s = s_1 = s_2$ ..	+1.980	+1.966	+1.954	+1.945	+1.939
s_1	−0.013	−0.024	−0.035	−0.044	−0.051
s_2	+1.993	+1.990	+1.988	+1.989	+1.990
Capital market					
τ	+0.001	+0.001	+0.001	+0.001	+0.001
μ	−0.001	−0.002	−0.002	−0.002	−0.002
$1 - \epsilon$	+0.000	+0.000	+0.000	+0.000	+0.000

This result is somewhat at variance with much of the literature dealing with the role of the capital market in development, where great stress has been placed on the advantages to be gained from "improved" capital markets. In fact, a general improvement in the efficiency and availability of financial institutions has long been urged by economic historians as a prime vehicle for economic change. Efforts to reduce the costs associated with undertaking industrial investments are presumed to lead to an increase in the intersectoral flow of savings. However, we find that it is the absolute level of rural savings that is important in influencing the extent of the intersectoral transfer rather than the capital market parameters. The finding that reductions in τ have an insignificant effect on savings performance, capital accumulation, and growth is not surprising. Costs of capital market intermediation do not *directly* influence saving (and, hence, investment) in our model. The specification serves only to transfer income from one group of savers (landlords) to another (urban capitalists). If the urban capitalists' propensity to save were greater than their rural counterparts', the presence of the transactions costs could result in a higher level of savings. Furthermore, since interest rates have no influence on savings rates in our model, we do not directly confront the question to what extent the savings propensity is influenced by the costs of investing funds outside a given sector. The introduction of a mechanism by which costs in the capital market have a direct influence on the savings decision, and not just in the level of income from which a fixed share is saved and then allocated, would provide a more interesting framework within which to investigate the importance of capital market imperfections on growth. If, as a result of cost reductions in financial intermediation, the effective return on investments outside of agriculture is raised, there may be some additional incentive to increase the share of income saved. Since, as we know from the sensitivity analysis, a 1 percent increase in the propensity to save has a significant impact on growth and structural change, the effect of changes in capital market costs, operating through the propensity to save, may also have a significant impact on the system. Relaxing the assumption that the savings propensity is fixed over time goes beyond the scope of this study, but it does seem a fruitful area for further theoretical research into the influence of capital market imperfections on growth.

8.5. LABOR SUPPLY, MIGRATION, AND LABOR ABSORPTION
8.5.1. Labor Supply
As already indicated, the labor supply grows more slowly in the disequilibrium model. Yet the effect of variations in the "natural" rates of population growth on output expansion, output per capita, the level of industrialization, and urbanization is similar to that of the equilibrium model (table 8.12). Note,

283

TABLE 8.12 Structural elasticities: increase in population growth rates

Variable	Value of elasticity at year				
	10	20	30	40	50
	Urban Population Growth (n_1)				
GNP growth rate	+0.127	+0.146	+0.169	+0.191	+0.213
Per capita GNP growth rate	− .150	− .126	− .096	− .079	− .064
Level of urbanization	− .012	− .033	− .048	− .059	− .066
Industrial output share	− .015	− .020	− .023	− .024	− .023
Capital-labor ratios (overall)	− .043	− .086	− .123	− .153	− .179
Capital-labor ratios (urban)	− .032	− .054	− .072	− .088	− .103
Capital-labor ratios (rural)	− .048	− .105	− .160	− .212	− .259
	Rural Population Growth (n_2)				
GNP growth rate	+ .335	+ .387	+ .409	+ .420	+ .426
Per capita GNP growth rate	− .522	− .340	− .206	− .111	− .036
Level of urbanization	− .099	− .165	− .200	− .213	− .211
Industrial output share	− .034	− .054	− .060	− .058	− .053
Capital-labor ratios (overall)	− .165	− .301	− .394	− .450	− .476
Capital-labor ratios (urban)	− .065	− .129	− .178	− .212	− .233
Capital-labor ratios (rural)	−0.217	−0.412	−0.561	−0.667	−0.733

however, the smaller negative effect on GNP per capita growth
and on the levels of urbanization and industrialization, especially in the first two decades. Our previous comments on the
possible exaggeration of the long-run deleterious effects of rapid
population growth are still valid, since the presence of constrained factor mobility does not seriously modify the effect of
changes in population growth rates on the pattern of growth
and structural change. Rapid increases in population growth
may still have significant short-run effects, but it is interesting
to note that the short-run impact does not appear to be as
severe as in the equilibrium model.

8.5.2. Migration

The determinants of migration are very different in the two
models, and, a priori, one might expect a substantial difference
in the patterns of migration. In the equilibrium model, for example, the rate of migration is such that sectoral wage rates are
equated at all times. From this requirement and the expressions
for labor force growth in each sector, the following expression
is obtained for the rate of migration from agriculture to industry:

$$m_2(t) = u(t) \frac{\dfrac{\dot{P}(t)}{P(t)} + \dfrac{\alpha_1(t)}{\sigma_1} V_1 - \dfrac{\alpha_2(t)}{\sigma_2} V_2}{\dfrac{\alpha_1(t)}{\sigma_1} [1 - u(t)] + \dfrac{\alpha_2(t)u(t)}{\sigma_2}}$$

where $V_i = \dfrac{\dot{K}_i(t)}{K_i(t)} + \lambda_K - \lambda_L - n_i$.

On the other hand, the current rate of migration in the disequilibrium model is predetermined by past rates of migration,
current wage rates, and migration costs. An expression for this
migration rate could be obtained as the integral of equation
(7.23).[16]

16. Our migration specifications contrast with that developed by
Jorgenson. Using his formulation one can solve for the "equilibrium" rate of migration, that is, that rate of migration required to
maintain his equilibrium wage differential condition. V. Galbis

There are only very small differences between the two simulations in the rate of migration despite the differences in labor
migration specifications. The rate of migration in the disequilibrium regime is 0.6 percent a year at the outset (0.4 percent in
the equilibrium regime), but by the end of the fifth decade the
rate is about 1 percent in both models (table 8.13). In the

TABLE 8.13 Trends in labor migration and absorption

Period	Rate of migration[a]		Rate of absorption[b]	
	E	D	E	D
1	0.004	0.006	0.029	0.033
10	.005	.007	.031	.034
20	.006	.008	.033	.034
30	.008	.009	.034	.034
40	.009	.010	.035	.033
50	0.010	0.010	0.034	0.032

a. The rate of migration is defined as the ratio of the net number
of laborers moving into industry to the total agricultural labor force.
b. The rate of growth of industrial employment.

second half-century the migration rate rises steadily to reach
1.3 percent after 100 simulation periods.

The rate of migration is most sensitive to changes in the
parameters of technical progress, savings, population, elasticity
of substitution, and consumption demand (table 8.14). It is not
influenced in any significant way by a 1 percent change in the
parameters relating to migration behavior or costs. An increase
in the rate of technical progress (with the bias held constant)

("Dualism and Labor Migration in the Process of Economic
Growth: A Theoretical Approach"), showed this to be $m(t) =
(\alpha - \beta\epsilon)/(1 - \beta)$, where α is the rate of technical change in
agriculture, ϵ is the population growth rate, and $1-\beta$ is the elasticity of agricultural output with respect to agricultural labor.
Now $m(t) > 0$ when $\alpha-\beta\epsilon > 0$ is also the condition required for
the emergence of an agricultural surplus. In contrast to the rate of
migration in our model, the rate of migration in Jorgenson's specification is unaffected by the rate of growth of the capital stock, by
technical change in the industrial sector, and by changes in the
terms of trade.

TABLE 8.14 Structural elasticities for change in rate of migration in response to increases in selected parameter values

Parameter	Value of elasticity at year				
	10	20	30	40	50
Technical change					
Rate constant	−0.909	−1.224	−1.461	−1.659	−1.818
Bias constant	+2.035	+2.709	+3.261	+3.682	+3.977
Population					
n_1	−1.093	−1.069	−1.038	−1.021	−1.016
n_2	+0.661	+0.787	+0.886	+0.981	+1.077
Savings					
$s = s_1 = s_2$ ..	+3.353	+2.567	+2.217	+1.881	+1.579
s_1	+1.903	+1.530	+1.343	+1.154	+0.980
s_2	+1.442	+1.022	+0.850	+0.696	+0.562
Factor substitution[a]					
σ_1	+5.517	+3.268	+2.711	+2.304	+1.944
σ_2	−7.937	−3.741	−2.518	−1.931	−1.420
Consumption					
$\beta_{11} = -\beta_{21}$ ..	−5.541	−1.687	−2.029	−2.075	−2.124
$\beta_{12} = -\beta_{22}$ ..	−1.080	−0.337	−0.374	−0.349	−0.322
γ	+4.025	+0.283	+0.427	+0.308	+0.212
Migration					
a	+0.010	−0.224	−0.225	−0.202	−0.182
b	+0.004	+0.002	+0.001	+0.001	+0.000
c	−0.063	+0.123	+0.107	+0.074	+0.046
ρ	+0.001	+0.034	+0.031	+0.025	+0.018

a. Increase in σ_1 and a decrease in σ_2.

tends to raise the rate of migration because of the resulting increased rate of capital accumulation. On the other hand, with a more serious labor-saving bias in industry and labor-using bias in agriculture, the rate of migration is retarded. The negative effect on the rate of migration of an increase in n_1 is also to be expected. In partial equilibrium, the rise in n_1 would reduce the required volume of urban in-migration, while a rise in n_2 would have the opposite effect. The sensitivity analysis confirms this response in a dynamic framework as well.

We find that a 1 percent increase in the savings parameters produces a 3–4 percent increase in the rate of migration in the first decade, after which the impact gradually decreases. Again, the direction of change would have been predicted by partial equilibrium analysis, but perhaps the magnitude of the response might not have been anticipated. The development literature seems to be unanimous in its emphasis on demographic factors as the prime cause of current urban explosions in low-income nations. Yet the results of table 8.14 suggest this effect to be relatively minor compared with, say, the increase in capital accumulation through more aggressive development efforts. Note too that the very high migration response to increases in the savings parameter does not produce an equally impressive increase in the rate of labor absorption (see table 8.15)!

TABLE 8.15 Structural elasticities for change in rate of labor absorption in response to increases in selected parameter values

Parameter	Value of elasticity at year				
	10	20	30	40	50
Technical change					
Rate constant	− 0.326	− 0.378	− 0.376	− 0.344	− 0.290
Bias constant	+ 0.738	+ .838	+ .836	+ .746	+ .599
Population					
n_1	+ 0.149	+ .165	+ .199	+ .235	+ .271
n_2	+ 0.326	+ .428	+ .493	+ .536	+ .561
Savings					
$s = s_1 = s_2$ ..	+ 1.151	+ .631	+ .332	+ .086	− .100
s_1	+ 0.649	+ .381	+ .210	+ .066	− .046
s_2	+ 0.495	+ .241	+ .111	+ .011	− .062
Factor substitution[a]					
σ_1	2.167	+ .977	+ .537	+ .222	− .016
σ_2	− 1.459	+ .121	+ .634	+ .828	+ .944
Consumption					
$\beta_{11} = -\beta_{21}$ ..	− 1.822	− .123	− .171	− .094	− .022
$\beta_{12} = -\beta_{22}$ ..	− 0.352	− .021	− .019	+ .006	+ .026
γ	1.287	− .274	− .202	− .229	− .239
Migration					
a	+ 0.062	− .019	− .008	+ .009	+ .022
b	+ 0.001	+ .000	+ .000	+ .000	+ .000
c	− 0.075	− .007	− .017	− .030	− .038
ρ	− 0.008	+ 0.003	+ 0.001	− 0.003	− 0.006

a. Increase in σ_1 and a decrease in σ_2.

It is interesting to find that an increase in b (the speed of potential migrant response to wage changes) has only a negligible positive effect on the rate of migration and that an increase in migration costs as a result of an increase in a, or a reduction in c, also has an insignificant negative effect on the migration rate. We noted earlier that the parameters of migration cost had a substantial impact on the wage gap (particularly in the first four decades). But the fact that the migration decision is based on a weighted average of past wage differentials apparently is sufficient to dampen the effects of a once-over change in the parameters of migration cost on the rate of migration. One interpretation of this result is that potential migrants may regard such a once-over change in costs as transitory and that therefore only a few migrants at the margin will be induced to move. Of course, we should not be too hasty in rejecting the migration parameters as being relatively unimportant, since they may change markedly in a rapidly growing economy. It is possible, for example, that $b = 1/T$ may rise substantially in an economy undergoing rapid growth in which there are persistent wage gaps; a reduction in T from three years to two years over a short period of time may not be unusual, in which case the influence of b could be much greater. We have been content to explore the sensitivity of our economy to once-over changes in key parameters. In fact, the rate at which these migration parameters actually do change over time is an empirical question about which we know very little at this stage.

8.5.3. Labor Absorption

With the relatively stable and low rates of migration from agriculture, the annual rate of labor absorption in industry is also stable at about 3.4 percent for most of the first half-century of growth (table 8.13). Nevertheless, the labor absorption rate is "disappointingly low" in *both* models during the first decade. Although the contemporary rates of labor absorption in Latin America and Southeast Asia are somewhat lower than those reported here,[17] our models closely reproduce early years of rapid growth yet low rates of labor absorption in manufacturing. It seems inevitable, even in a rapidly growing neoclassical model, that labor absorption rates will be initially disappointing, and thus that low productivity employment will dominate in our economy over protracted time periods. The tendency for the rate to fall in the latter part of the period is continued in the second half-century. After a full century of growth the rate of labor absorption is 2.8 percent a year. In short, there is very little difference between the two models with respect to the rate of labor absorption.

An expression for the rate of growth of the industrial labor force can be derived from the expression for the industrial wage rate:

$$\frac{\dot{L}_1(t)}{L_1(t)} = \frac{\dot{K}_1(t)}{K_1(t)} + \lambda_K - \lambda_L + \frac{\sigma_1}{\alpha_1(t)}\left\{\frac{\dot{P}(t)}{P(t)} - \frac{\dot{w}_1(t)}{w_1(t)}\right\}.$$

This expression is an alternative form of the familiar labor absorption equation used by Fei and Ranis. (Recall that Fei and Ranis assumed a constant real wage; the last term does not appear in their labor absorption equation.) Interest in labor absorption and unemployment in developing nations has been active since Ricardo and Marx. In the Fei and Ranis approach, for example, it is the comparison between the rate of growth of the industrial demand for labor and the population growth for the economy as a whole that determines whether the existing labor surplus will tend to disappear or whether unemployment will increase. The work of Fei and Ranis and others has helped focus attention on the effect of capital accumulation and the labor-saving bias in industry on labor absorption. In this debate, however, there has been little discussion of the role of other key variables such as the ease of factor substitution.[18]

17. W. Baer and M. Hervé, "Employment and Industrialization in Developing Countries"; J. G. Williamson, "Capital Accumulation, Labor Saving, and Labor Absorption Once More."
18. Williamson, "Capital Accumulation, Labor Saving, and Labor Absorption Once More."

While our sensitivity analysis confirms the importance of capital accumulation (through changes in the savings parameters) and technical progress, we also find that changes in the elasticity of factor substitution and in consumer tastes have a significant effect on the rate of absorption.

As expected, an increase in the rate of technical progress raises labor absorption, and an increase in the labor-augmenting bias reduces labor absorption. Similarly, increases in the savings propensities and, hence, in capital accumulation, also raise the rate of absorption. Note, however, that the impact diminishes very rapidly and is concentrated in the first two decades. The sensitivity analysis also reveals that an increase in σ_1 has a large positive effect on the rate of labor absorption similar to that found in the equilibrium model, while a decrease in σ_2 has a large negative effect on absorption in the first decade, and thereafter an increasingly positive effect. Equally interesting is the finding that a shift in consumer tastes toward industrial goods produces a positive effect on labor absorption. The impact is quite large in the first decade; in fact, larger than in the equilibrium model. However, there has been only a limited discussion of the role of demand in influencing labor absorption in the literature. Our results suggest this to be a fruitful line of research.[19]

8.6. SOURCES OF GROWTH AND STRUCTURAL CHANGE:
A RECONSIDERATION

To complete the analysis of growth and structural change in an economy characterized by imperfect factor markets, it remains only to review the role of technical progress, factor intensity and substitution, and consumer demand.

---

19. Some empirical research on Latin America and Asia has been done in a comparative static framework which combines the impact of changing investment demand as well as the composition of household consumption expenditures (see S. A. Morley and G. W. Smith, "The Effect of Changes in the Distribution of Income on Labor, Foreign Investment, and Growth in Brazil"; and Williamson, "Capital Accumulation, Labor Saving, and Labor Absorption Once More").

8.6.1. The Role of Technical Progress Once Again

The rate of technical progress in the disequilibrium model is quite stable during the first half-century of growth at about

TABLE 8.16 Average annual rate of technical progress

Period	Aggregate		Industry		Agriculture	
	E	D	E	D	E	D
1–10	0.0066	0.0065	0.0055	0.0055	0.0075	0.0075
11–20	.0066	.0065	.0054	.0055	.0076	.0075
21–30	.0065	.0064	.0054	.0055	.0076	.0075
31–40	.0064	.0064	.0054	.0056	.0076	.0075
41–50	0.0064	0.0063	0.0054	0.0056	0.0076	0.0074

0.6 percent per year and is very similiar to that in the equilibrium model. Nevertheless, when the sources-of-growth methodology is applied to the disequilibrium model, a much smaller discrepancy is found between the true and estimated rates of technical change in the economy than was the case in the equilibrium model. This result is somewhat surprising, but it will perhaps serve to illustrate vividly the capriciousness of the sources-of-growth methodology.

Recall from chapter 6 that an increased labor-augmenting bias in technical change reduced the rate of capital formulation, the rate of urbanization, and, to a lesser extent, the rate of per capita income growth. In contrast, an increased rate (intensity) of technical change had the opposite effect. Furthermore, an increased labor-augmenting bias inhibited industrialization, while an increase in the economy's intensity of technical change stimulated industrialization. In the disequilibrium model, the direction of response to increases in the bias and in the rate of technical change is the same as in the equilibrium regime except that industrialization now receives a positive stimulus in both cases (table 8.17). However, there are significant differences between the two models with respect to the *magnitudes* of the impacts, particularly to those of changes in the rates of technical progress. Consider first the

TABLE 8.17 Technical progress structural elasticities

Variable	Value of elasticity at year				
	10	20	30	40	50
Bias constant: increase in rate					
GNP growth rate	+1.037	+1.226	+1.309	+1.342	+1.332
Per capita GNP growth rate	+3.291	+3.764	+3.952	+4.047	+4.065
Level of urbanization	+0.178	+0.454	+0.755	+1.050	+1.316
Industrial output share	+0.196	+0.370	+0.510	+0.610	+0.674
Capital-labor ratio (overall)	+0.074	+0.375	+0.853	+1.453	+2.119
Capital-labor ratio (urban)	+0.015	+0.131	+0.345	+0.642	+1.001
Capital-labor ratio (rural)	−0.041	+0.223	+0.803	+1.651	+2.707
Capital stock growth (aggregate)	+0.500	+1.009	+1.324	+1.488	+1.531
Rate constant: increase in bias					
GNP growth rate	+0.121	+0.124	+0.120	+0.128	+0.143
Per capita GNP growth rate	+0.359	+0.314	+0.249	+0.219	+0.207
Level of urbanization	−0.087	−0.212	−0.347	−0.479	−0.602
Industrial output share	+0.023	+0.033	+0.036	+0.034	+0.031
Capital-labor ratio (overall)	−0.013	−0.062	−0.131	−0.205	−0.269
Capital-labor ratio (urban)	+0.148	+0.304	+0.442	+0.567	+0.687
Capital-labor ratio (rural)	−0.187	−0.486	−0.846	−1.246	−1.661
Capital stock growth (aggregate)	−0.089	−0.145	−0.158	−0.133	−0.076

effects of an increase in the rate while the bias is held constant. The impact on GNP and GNP per capita growth rates is more pronounced in the disequilibrium model. A 1 percent increase in the rate of technical progress induces a 3–4 percent increase in the growth of GNP per capita. This compares with a 1 percent increase in the equilibrium model. In the disequilibrium model, capital's share, and thus the rate of capital accumulation, receives a much stronger positive stimulus (by a factor of five!) following an increase in the rate of technical change. As a result, the capital-labor ratio rises more rapidly and output growth responds accordingly. Thus, our comparison suggests that with imperfections in the capital market an increase in the rate of technical progress provides an even greater stimulus to growth and structural change than the stimulus found in the equilibrium model.

When the bias of technical progress is increased but the rate is held constant the impact on the GNP and GNP per capita growth is somewhat larger than in the equilibrium model. There is a larger negative impact on urbanization but a positive impact on the level of industrialization.

8.6.2. Factor Intensity and Substitution in an Imperfect Market Despite their differences in the way in which the capital-labor ratios are determined the two models are not markedly different in behavior over time. (table 8.18). With its more

TABLE 8.18 Trends in capital-labor ratios

Period	Aggregate		Industry		Agriculture	
	E	D	E	D	E	D
1	0.302	0.319	0.571	0.607	0.186	0.184
10	.300	.344	.582	.643	.174	.190
20	.312	.392	.605	.693	.170	.203
30	.339	.434	.641	.756	.177	.225
40	.382	.501	.690	.832	.191	.257
50	0.438	0.584	0.754	0.923	0.217	0.300

NOTE: Net of efficiency factors.

rapid capital accumulation and slightly slower labor force growth, the disequilibrium model's aggregate capital-labor ratio (unaugmented) is, at all times, higher than the equilibrium model's. The initial decrease in the capital intensity of agricultural production observed in the equilibrium model is not reproduced in the disequilibrium regime.

The behavior of the sectoral augmented capital-labor ratios over time, when $w^*(t) > \theta(t)$ and $r^*(t) > \tau$, is given by:

$$\frac{\dot{k_1}(t)}{k_1(t)} = \phi_1(t) - m_2(t)\frac{1-u(t)}{u(t)} - (\delta + n_1 + \lambda_L - \lambda_K),$$

and

$$\frac{\dot{k_2}(t)}{k_2(t)} = \phi_2(t) + m_2(t) - (\delta + n_2 + \lambda_L - \lambda_K),$$

where $\phi_i(t) = I_i(t)/K_i(t)$ is the gross rate of accumulation in the ith sector. The behavior of the economy-wide efficiency capital-labor ratio is given by

$$\frac{\dot{k}(t)}{k(t)} = \frac{u(t)k_1(t)\phi_1(t)}{k(t)} + \frac{[1-u(t)]k_2(t)\phi_2(t)}{k(t)}$$

$$+ (n_2 - n_1)u(t) - (\delta + n_2 + \lambda_L - \lambda_K). \quad (8.1)$$

Define

$$\phi(t) = \frac{u(t)k_1(t)\phi_1(t)}{k(t)} + \frac{[1-u(t)]k_2(t)\phi_2(t)}{k(t)},$$

to be the weighted sum of $\phi_i(t)$; then equation (8.1) reduces to an expression comparable to that describing the growth of $k(t)$ in the equilibrium model.

In a qualitative investigation of the behavior of $k_i(t)$ and $k(t)$ over time, we face again a problem raised in chapter 3: namely, is the positive impact of $\phi(t)$ and $(n_2 - n_1)u(t)$ sufficient to outweigh the negative impact of the constant term? As table 8.19 suggests, with the exception of the stronger positive stimulus toward capital intensity when the rate of technical progress is raised, and the greater negative influence when σ_2 is reduced, the two models are very similar in the sensitivity of the capital-labor ratios to changes in parameters. This result suggests that factor intensity is not particularly sensitive to the presence of imperfections in the factor markets, *and indeed that the presence of capital specificity in the production process does not materially affect the pattern of growth and structural change in a growth-oriented economy.*

TABLE 8.19 Structural elasticities for change in the capital-labor ratio in response to increases in selected parameter values.

Parameter	Value of elasticity at year				
	10	20	30	40	50
Technical change					
Rate constant	−0.013	−0.062	−0.131	−0.205	−0.269
Bias constant	+ .075	+0.375	+0.853	+1.453	+2.119
Savings					
$s = s_1 = s_2$ ..	+ .641	+1.237	+1.690	+2.014	+2.227
s_1	+ .387	+0.755	+1.042	+1.257	+1.406
s_2	+ .254	+0.481	+0.643	+0.748	+0.805
Population					
n_1	− .043	−0.086	−0.123	−0.153	−0.179
n_2	− .165	−0.301	−0.394	−0.450	−0.476
Consumption					
$\beta_{11} = -\beta_{21}$ ..	− .045	+0.110	+0.243	+0.361	+0.462
$\beta_{12} = -\beta_{22}$ ..	− .009	+0.023	+0.050	+0.074	+0.093
γ	+0.038	−0.087	−0.170	−0.226	−0.249

The differences between the two models with respect to changes in the elasticities of substitution deserve some comment. It was argued in chapter 6 that systematic long-run changes in σ_i are to be expected with σ_1 rising and σ_2 falling with industrial and output expansion. In the equilibrium model an increase in σ_1 strongly stimulated growth in per capita output, the level of urbanization, and industrialization. Moreover, a decrease in σ_2 exerted a strong negative effect on the growth of per capita output, and a mild negative effect on the level of urbanization and industrialization. This result was due to the equilibrium model's requiring less labor to be transferred out of agriculture to attain equilibrium in the factor markets;

with the higher overall population growth rates in the equilibrium model, the growth of output per capita was retarded. In the disequilibrium model (table 8.20), however, the negative effects of a decrease in σ_2 are greatly magnified, especially with respect to the level of urbanization and industrialization: a 1 percent decrease in σ_2 results in a 4 percent decrease in the level of industrialization and a 2 percent reduction in the level of urbanization (compared with a decrease of less than 0.5 percent in both cases in the equilibrium model). At the same time, the positive effects of an increase in σ_1 are substantially smaller than in the equilibrium model.

8.6.3. The Role of Consumption Demand Revised
The most striking difference between the two models in interpretation lies in the role of consumption demand. For this reason it might be useful to review the results in chapter 6. The comparative static analysis revealed that an increased preference for urban consumption goods raised the price of industrial goods but, more important, reduced the labor share (since urban goods are assumed to be more capital intensive). The dynamic effect was, therefore, to increase the aggregate savings rate and to reduce rates of population growth in response to the relative expansion in the urban labor force. Numerical analysis indicated that the effect of the increased savings rate exceeded the impact of rising industrial goods (capital goods) prices; the rate of accumulation of physical assets therefore received a strong positive stimulus. When this result was combined with the declining rate of labor force growth through increased urbanization, the aggregate growth performance of the dual economy was augmented. The key to this result is the relatively small initial increase in the relative price of capital goods. Supply elasticities were high enough to minimize the price rise. The increased cost of capital goods only marginally diminished the stimulatory impact of increased savings.

Can the same result be expected in the disequilibrium model? By the introduction of a putty-clay specification and the re-

TABLE 8.20 Elasticity of substitution structural elasticities

Variable	Value of elasticity at year				
	10	20	30	40	50
	Increase in σ_1				
GNP growth rate	+0.791	+0.691	+0.451	+0.263	+0.111
GNP per capita growth rate	+2.518	+2.212	+1.528	+1.031	+0.643
Level of urbanization	+0.217	+0.596	+0.856	+1.010	+1.083
Level of industrialization	+0.218	+0.330	+0.372	+0.369	+0.343
Capital-labor ratio (aggregate)	+0.922	+1.747	+2.382	+2.843	+3.150
Capital-labor ratio (urban)	+0.861	+1.263	+1.568	+1.802	+1.971
Capital-labor ratio (rural)	+0.759	+1.862	+2.834	+3.646	+4.284
Capital stock growth rate (aggregate)	+2.630	+1.903	+1.321	+0.853	+0.474
	Decrease in σ_2				
GNP growth rate	−7.385	+0.122	−0.104	+0.066	+0.193
Per capita GNP growth rate	....	−0.338	−0.999	−0.508	−0.143
Level of urbanization	−2.822	−2.546	−2.466	−2.312	−2.118
Level of industrialization	+4.498	+4.015	+3.967	+3.949	+3.956
Capital-labor ratio (aggregate)	+0.302	−0.379	−0.867	−1.192	−1.375
Capital-labor ratio (urban)	+1.146	+0.678	+0.371	+0.123	−0.067
Capital-labor ratio (rural)	+2.268	+1.063	+0.194	−0.533	−1.077
Capital stock growth rate (aggregate)	−3.400	−1.257	−0.819	−0.401	−0.073

striction of the intersectoral flow of labor, the short-run supply elasticities in the economy have been markedly diminished. As a result, there is now the possibility of more pronounced increases in the relative prices of industrial goods in response to demand changes. Will this price effect be strong enough to offset the increase in aggregate savings so that the rate of accumulation of capital goods is *diminished*? To put it differently, given the resource stock in industry and inelastic supply, the competition between consumers and investors for industrial output is more critical than the price effect in influencing the behavior of accumulation and growth. Although an increased relative demand for urban consumption goods may stimulate industrialization and urbanization in the short run, does it restrict the availability (price) of capital goods to the point of inhibiting growth? The results presented in table 8.21 generally indicate an affirmative answer to this question. Ignoring the atypical results for period 10, we generally find labor's share reduced and the industrial output share increased by a shift in tastes toward urban consumption goods. As in the equilibrium model, labor's share is diminished, since urban goods are capital intensive and the industrial output share is increased (in part because the prices of industrial goods rise). But in the disequilibrium regime, the terms of trade is *very* sensitive to taste changes. Given the small increase in capital's share, *the rate of capital accumulation is always diminished because of the large rise in capital goods' prices.*

This interesting result is consistent with the findings in section 8.4.2. There we discovered that an increase in the savings parameter had a much smaller impact on capital accumulation and per capita GNP growth in the disequilibrium model. The explanation is clear enough. Supply elasticities were assumed to be elastic in the equilibrium model. As a result, a rise in the demand for capital goods generated only a small increase in capital goods' prices. In the disequilibrium model, industrial goods' supply is more inelastic, and the *availability* of capital goods play a more important role. The increased rate of savings is largely, although not entirely, dissipated by the rise in capital goods' prices.

These results confirm once again the complexity of the growth process. They certainly emphasize how little we know about demand in relation to economic change. Although much more theoretical research remains to be done, our investigation of demand alone suggests the potential productivity of moving toward disequilibrium specifications of the growth process. While parameter changes in demand were shown to play a critical role in development, viewed as an equilibrium process, the added dimensions of factor immobility and disequilibrium growth reveal an even more complex, yet important, role for demand.

TABLE 8.21 Elasticities of various performance indicators to changes in demand parameters

Variable	Value of elasticity at year				
	10	20	30	40	50
		Increase in β_{11} (= decrease in β_{21})				
GNP growth rate	+4.120	−0.337	−0.072	−0.046	−0.002
Per capita GNP growth rate	+12.715	−1.243	−0.480	−0.442	−0.358
Level of urbanization	−0.757	−0.878	−0.980	−1.062	−1.127
Industrial output share	1.110	+0.916	+0.792	+0.692	+0.612
Capital-labor ratio	0.045	−0.110	−0.243	−0.361	−0.462
Terms of trade	3.481	+3.346	+3.360	+3.389	+3.436
Labor's share	−0.316	−0.266	−0.248	−0.239	−0.240
Rate of capital accumulation	−0.147	−0.301	−0.232	−0.170	−0.107
		Increase in β_{12} (= decrease in β_{22})				
GNP growth rate	+0.801	−0.068	−0.011	−0.004	+0.007
Per capita GNP growth rate	+2.468	−0.252	−0.089	−0.075	−0.047
Level of urbanization	−0.157	−0.183	−0.200	−0.210	−0.214
Industrial output share	+0.213	+0.177	+0.156	+0.141	+0.133
Capital-labor ratio (overall)	+0.010	−0.023	−0.050	−0.074	−0.093
Terms of trade	+0.678	+0.660	+0.664	+0.672	+0.684
Labor's share	−0.061	−0.051	−0.049	−0.049	−0.052
Rate of capital accumulation	−0.027	−0.064	−0.048	−0.033	−0.017

Decrease in γ

GNP growth rate	+3.927	−0.252	+0.015	+0.034	+0.058
Per capita GNP growth rate	+12.143	−0.917	−0.115	−0.056	+0.017
Level of urbanization	−0.612	−0.598	−0.558	−0.507	−0.453
Industrial output share	+1.118	+1.064	+1.048	+1.040	+1.037
Capital-labor ratio	+0.038	−0.087	−0.170	−0.223	−0.249
Terms of trade	+3.261	+3.209	+3.238	+3.280	+3.328
Labor's share	−0.320	−0.319	−0.342	−0.369	−0.397
Rate of capital accumulation	−0.087	−0.226	−0.121	−0.047	+0.011

Joint increase in β_{11}, β_{12} (= decrease in β_{21}, β_{22})

GNP growth rate	+5.007	−0.408	−0.083	−0.051	+0.005
Per capita GNP growth rate	⋯	−1.503	−0.569	−0.519	−0.406
Level of urbanization	−0.915	−1.062	−1.181	−1.273	−1.341
Industrial output share	+1.328	+1.095	+0.950	+0.836	+0.748
Capital-labor ratio	+0.053	−0.135	−0.295	−0.437	−0.556
Terms of trade	+4.194	+4.035	+4.053	+4.091	+4.150
Labor's share	−0.377	−0.318	−0.297	−0.289	−0.293
Rate of capital accumulation	−0.172	+0.364	−0.279	−0.202	−0.123

9

Progress and Problems: The Legacy of the Dualistic Framework

9.1. AN OVERVIEW

The time has come to take stock. This study has examined several old questions in economics. What are the causes and consequences of growth and structural change? In what ways can a formal model of economic dualism add insight into these critical problems? Which of the many dualistic attributes of the low-income economy are most important to understanding the process of modern economic growth? We have argued that because growth and structural change are influenced by both supply and demand characteristics of factor and product markets, it is only within an interdependent framework that the relative importance of these influences can be ascertained. Building on the contributions of Jorgenson and Fei and Ranis, this book has made considerable progress in producing tentative answers to some of these questions. In the process, however, analytical difficulties have been encountered: these difficulties must be resolved if further progress is to be made with theories of dualistic development.

Our methodology is at variance with that found in most of the literature on growth and development; a review of our approach is presented in section 9.1.1. Section 9.1.2 presents the key qualitative and quantitative results of the study. Several suggestions for revising the dualistic model are then made in section 9.2. These represent potential avenues not only for an extension of the theory of the growth process, but also for directions for confronting the problems the dualistic model has bequeathed as a legacy. Section 9.2 raises issues which, of necessity, must lie outside the scope of this study. These include the treatment of surplus labor, underemployment and intersectoral labor migration when an urban service sector is appended to the traditional specification, the short-run labor supply function and the work-leisure choice, and the small economy model with external migration. The focus of that discussion underscores the importance we attach to the demographic dimension of the growth process. Furthermore, the role of the public sector is examined in some detail at the end of that section. The chapter concludes with a theme central to this study: the critical need for bridging the ever widening gap between growth and development theory, empirical analysis, and economic history.

9.1.1. The Methodology

9.1.1.1. *Short-run Versus Long-run Equilibrium.* Over the past decade, the conventional approach to analyzing the long-run dynamic properties of growth models has been to inquire whether a steady-state, or balanced, growth solution exists, and then to determine its properties. Balanced growth is typically defined as the state where all relevant endogenous variables grow at a constant rate. Thus, in the steady state, relative prices are constant, and each sector grows at the same fixed rate; therefore, the level of industrialization is constant. There has been increased uneasiness among growth theorists over the indiscriminant use of the steady-state concept. This has been manifested by an increased interest in the speed with which the growing economy adjusts to balanced growth after the system has been disturbed by some exogenous force. Quite apart from the speed of adjustment issue, it seems inappropriate to use the notion of balanced growth given our interest in explaining structural change. To our knowledge, no developing economy has exhibited a long-run pattern of growth consistent with the properties of steady-state growth.[1]

1. As a descriptive and analytical device, balanced growth may be "sufficiently" representative of the growth pattern of present-day

Because *non*proportional growth is a pervasive characteristic of developing economies, the exploration of the steady-state properties of the dualistic model may be of limited value. This methodology abstracts from a key analytical issue: isolating the determinants of structural change.

We have instead initially viewed the economy as moving through a sequence of *short-run* equilibrium positions where the period between these positions has a calendar-year interpretation. This approach analyzes the behavior of the economy in long-run disequilibrium. Later in the study, even the conception of short-run equilibrium is challenged when the traditional assumptions of instantaneous adjustment in factor markets are relaxed. The impact of short-run factor market disequilibrium is then assessed to ascertain the extent to which short-run adjustments influence the long-run growth path. Our numerical experiments confirm the critical importance to be attached to further research on the issue of speed of adjustment. Indeed, the empirical results reveal that balanced growth may have little relevance to the analysis of the dualistic economy as it passes through many decades of disproportional growth.

9.1.1.2. *A Separate Theory for Developing Economies?* There is no "general theory" of development contained in the present study. Economists wisely discarded this goal some time ago. On the other hand, if progress is to be made in analyzing the developing economies, relatively simply and analytically tractable models must be developed. An inevitable decision must therefore be confronted: which aspects of the developing economy should we highlight, thereby distinguishing it from the industrialized, high-income economy?

First, what level of disaggregation is most appropriate for examining the nature of structural change in the developing economy? Surely, at a minimum two sectors must be specified. Furthermore, a widely documented growth characteristic of

---

developed economies, in much the same way that the assumption of perfect conditions is used as a "norm" for the study of market behavior.

low-income nations is the decline in the relative importance of agricultural-rural activity and the corresponding rise in industrial-urban activity associated with this redistribution. For our purposes the two-sector models developed by Uzawa and others do not provide an appropriate framework for examining the issue of rural-urban structural change. Moreover, since these models specify an investment and consumption goods sector, they abstract from Engel effects. Our study attempts to fill this gap by examining an economy characterized by agricultural-rural and industrial-urban dichotomies. However, even on this point our interpretation is somewhat at variance with the formal dualistic models which abstract from locational considerations.

The second issue involves the interpretation of dualism in the low-income economy. While dualistic features of the developing economy have been emphasized at length in the descriptive literature, the difficulty is to select those features that are empirically relevant and are capable of being translated into a formal model. The features we have chosen distinguish in *degree* the low-income economy from the advanced economy; they are sectoral differences in demographic behavior, consumption behavior, and production conditions. The first two features have received little attention in the formal literature. Our analysis indicates their importance for understanding development from low-income levels. While the third feature, dualism in production, has constituted a standard concern in multisectoral models, our treatment of it differs sharply from the conventional approach. Production dualism can appear in three forms: (1) sectoral parameter differences (for example, bias in technological change, elasticities of substitution), (2) sectoral differences in production arguments (e.g., capital and labor in industry, labor and land in agriculture), (3) sectoral differences in observed ratio variables. The latter form of dualism is pervasive: any model of the low-income economy must generate ratio variables consistent with such evidence. Our model meets this minimum test. Of the remaining two forms of production dualism, our theory has emphasized parameter variation. Three reasons form the primary basis for this choice. First, agriculture becomes "commercialized" over time: it increases its capital intensity and purchases increasingly large amounts of capital and intermediate inputs from the industrial sector. A model structure which abstracts from this historical evolution may be inapplicable to a very wide range of developing economies. Second, labor-saving biases in new industrial technology and labor-using biases in new agricultural technology are widely documented features of the developing economy. We approach this issue by postulating differing parameters of sectoral production. Finally, dualistic models typically rely heavily on *exogenous* determinants of agricultural labor productivity (e.g., land endowment and exogenously determined efficiency levels). In contrast, in our model capital goods can be accumulated in agriculture, albeit at very low levels; average labor productivity is therefore determined endogenously. To put the matter another way: dualistic models must explicitly confront the issue of investment allocation between agriculture and industry. Our inclusion of capital in agriculture may in part explain why our model has many feasible growth paths while those of Jorgenson and Fei-Ranis generate changes along a single time path. The success or failure of the development effort in the Fei and Ranis models depends critically on the size of parameter values rather than on endogenously determined forces in the model, while the Jorgenson model relies on the concept of balanced growth by considering a growth path along which the capital-labor ratio is constant over time. Constancy of the capital-labor ratio does not appear to be a feature of Japanese growth over the period that Jorgenson was interested in explaining.

9.1.1.3. *Qualitative Versus Quantitative Analysis.* Modern growth theorists normally avoid quantitative analysis. When analytical difficulties arise, the usual procedure is to revise and simplify the model structure rather than restrict the values which parameters and initial conditions may assume. The present study departs from this convention. Maintaining what

may be excessively restrictive assumptions in the interests of
obtaining unambiguous mathematical results may represent
too great a cost. The basic dualistic model in this study incorporates as many concessions to abstraction as we feel acceptable.
To simplify the model still further would suppress some of the
most interesting and relevant development problems we wish
to confront. This preference for mathematical determinacy
may be one of the reasons why formal models of dualistic development have excluded capital goods from agricultural activity. However, by making fewer concessions to abstraction
we find that qualitative analysis yields ambiguous results about
patterns of growth and structural change. The qualitative analysis of the dynamic behavior of our model, which centered on
the temporal behavior of $k(t)$, led to the conclusion that there
are several feasible growth paths for our low-income economy;
moreover, one is no more likely a priori than another. While
this result may, in fact, be consistent with the varied experience
of developing (and regressing) economies, most simple dynamic models make unambiguous (although frequently historically inaccurate) predictions about the temporal behavior of
the efficiency capital-labor ratio.

In general, we find that $k(t)$ may increase or decrease without limit or may enter into some irregular cyclical pattern.
What feature is contained in our theoretical specifications that
produces this variety? Recall that the time path of the efficiency capital-labor ratio is described by

$$\frac{\dot{k}(t)}{k(t)} = x(t)f'_1[k_1(t)] + (n_2 - n_1)u(t) - (\delta + n_2).$$

The assumption of diminishing marginal productivity of capital
means that $f'_1[k_1(t)]$ decreases when $k(t)$ is increasing. But
we do not know whether the increasingly positive effect of
$x(t)$ is sufficient to offset the decreasing positive influence of
$f'_1[k_1(t)]$ when $k(t)$ is increasing; that is, the behavior of
$x(t)f'_1[k_1(t)]$ is ambiguous. Our difficulty does not stop there,
however, for when $k(t)$ is rising, $u(t)$ is also rising and therefore exerting a positive influence on the growth of $k(t)$ because

we assume that $n_2 - n_1 > 0$. Thus, it is not possible to deter-mine the conditions under which $x(t)f'_1[k_1(t)] + (n_2 - n_1)u(t)$ will exceed $(\lambda_L - \lambda_K + \delta + n_2)$ and hence, ensure continuous growth of the capital-labor ratio. If, in fact, $f'_1[k_1(t)]$ decreases sufficiently rapidly, it is possible that the growth of $k(t)$ may be reversed. When $k(t)$ declines, however, $x(t)f'_1[k_1(t)]$ increases; if it increases at a sufficiently rapid rate, it may offset the decreas-ing positive effect of $(n_2 - n_1)u(t)$—$u(t)$ decreases when $k(t)$ falls—and also offset the negative impact of $(n_2 + \delta + \lambda_L - \lambda_K)$. In this case $k(t)$ would begin to rise again. On the other hand, $k(t)$ may continue to decrease until the lower bound on the marginal product of efficiency labor is violated, at which point the model is undefined. However, because the lower bound is itself declining, there is the possibility that $k(t)$ could decrease without limit.

The qualitative analysis also indicates that even if $k(t)$ grows over time, GNP growth is not assured, although GNP does increase if property income rises relative to wage income. This latter phenomenon has been documented for developing econ-omies and it *is* consistent with the empirically relevant case where per capita income increases with $k(t)$. The ambiguity is also removed when the elasticity of factor substitution in each sector is equal to one or if the capital intensities are always the same in the two sectors. But in our view such restrictive assumptions overlook some of the important dualistic charac-teristics of low-income economies. However, qualitative anal-ysis of our model has revealed one restriction—that the income elasticity of demand for agricultural products is positive but less than one—which is sufficient to ensure GNP growth, industrialization, and urbanization when there is an increase in $k(t)$. This quite plausible restriction therefore permits us to derive unambiguous qualitative relationships between growth and structural change in our model. On the other hand, for any given set of parameter values and initial conditions, $k(t)$ may generate a variety of time paths, and thus the possibilities for exploring further the qualitative properties of our system are limited.

To move forward in the analysis of this modeled economy, we have therefore turned to numerical analysis rather than simplify the model structure. The parameters and initial conditions have been taken as representative of contemporary Southeast Asia. We have argued that the generality lost in the process is not great. Because the objective of this study is to examine growth and structural change in an economy that is successfully developing from low-income levels, we are not concerned with all conceivable growth paths, but only with those which have historical relevance. The quantitative representation of the dualistic economies presented in this study comprises a significant portion of that relevant set. Our numerical analysis suggests that from these initial conditions positive and accelerating rates of $k(t)$ growth are likely and these results are consistent with the commonly cited evidence of "takeoff."

It has also been common in growth and development theory to treat lightly the descriptive power of the modeled economy. Economic theory can be viewed as a set of paradigms for evaluating the behavior of complex social systems. Yet the theoretical permutations are indefinite, and at some point the models' predictions must be confronted with historical evidence. Formal model construction (chaps. 2 and 7), qualitative analysis (chap. 3), simulation (chaps. 4 and 8), sensitivity analysis (chaps. 6 and 8), *and* empirical testing (chap. 5) are equally important elements in gaining analytical insight into the growth process. This study is not only concerned with the development and analysis of theoretical structures; it also provides models which describe the development process. Japanese data drawn from the Meiji period have been used to evaluate the degree to which the simulated growth trajectories broadly conform to one well-documented, non-Western pattern of historical growth. Not only has our neoclassical dualistic model replicated history well, but in some dimensions it appears to perform better than other models of economic dualism.

There is yet another compelling reason for quantitative analysis. Theorists are usually content to evaluate the sign of a variable's response to parameter shifts. Yet the problems

raised by development economists are largely *quantitative* in
nature. To take an example from the sources-of-growth literature, it may not be startling to learn that capital accumulation
positively affects per capita output expansion, but the overriding issues of resource allocation require more knowledge of
the relative *importance* of various factors influencing growth
and structural change, including the aggregate savings rate.
While rigorous theoretical analysis is required to untangle complex interactions, quantification is mandatory if progress is to
be made toward developing simple multisectoral models useful
in formulating economic policy. This book has attempted to
bridge the very large gap between empirical analysis (including
economic history) and abstract growth theory.

9.1.2. Growth and Structural Change in the Dual Economy
The central focus of theories of growth and development is
the path of per capita output growth. The rapid and sustained
character of economic growth in Meiji Japan, for example,
has been cited by many as perhaps her most distinguishing
feature. The same is true of the simulated economy. Further,
per capita income growth *accelerates* in the simulated economy
as in fact it does in Japanese economic history. A partial explanation for this trend is found in the accelerating rate of capital
formation. But this acceleration occurs in the *absence* of abrupt
increases in aggregate savings rates and with constant parameters; that is, a dramatic upward shift in the savings function
is not required for "takeoff" either in our economy or in
Japan. Rates of capital formation are explained by the joint
movements in factor shares, the capital-output ratio, and the
savings parameter. Stability in savings parameters does not
imply stability in either aggregate national savings rates or
the rate of capital formation.

One of the key historical aspects of structural change that
has been widely associated with growth in income per capita
is the redistribution of labor from agriculture to industry.
Moreover, the causes of labor redistribution in the dual economy have received considerable attention in the development

theory literature: Fei and Ranis, for example, believe it to be the prime concern of development theory. Urbanization always increases in our economy when the overall efficiency capital-labor ratio rises, and with the increase in $k(t)$ in the simulation, we find that after five decades the level of urbanization stabilized at about 70 percent, having risen from an initial level of about 30 percent. This result is, of course, consistent with the historically observed patterns of most of the present-day higher-income economies. In passing, however, we should note that among the developing economies, rapid urbanization often occurs under conditions of little or no per capita GNP growth. This finding is fully consistent with our theoretical framework since urbanization does not necessarily coincide with growth in per capita income. (Income per capita growth does not necessarily occur when $k(t)$ is rising.)

The response of urbanization to changes in the capital-labor ratio is determined in part by relative sectoral capital intensities. Given a higher capital intensity in industry and the relative ease of factor substitution in agriculture, an increase in $k(t)$ results in a labor transfer from agriculture. While this is a replication of the standard result of the simple dual economy where capital is used only in "modern" activities, note that in our model the increase in $k(t)$ leads to a *decline* in relative sectoral capital intensities. Thus, the impact of growth on urbanization diminishes at higher levels of economic development. In fact, urbanization ceases at the point of factor reversal (if it exists). In summary, acceleration in the rate of capital formation in early growth phases produces an acceleration in urbanization. At high levels of development, two forces dampen the rate of urbanization: (1) the rate of $k(t)$ growth may diminish; (2) the impact of a given rise in $k(t)$ on urbanization declines. As a result, the simulated economy passes from a phase of increasing rates of urbanization to stability.

While the level of urbanization increases during the first five decades of growth, this occurs despite the fact that the rate of growth of the industrial labor force, or the rate of labor absorption, is unimpressive and is barely above the overall rate of labor force growth. The reasons for this result are the low rates of labor migration in the face of relatively rapid rates of labor-saving technical progress and low initial rates of capital accumulation in industry. These trends are consistent with observed low rates of labor absorption and urban "unemployment" in much of Asia, Latin America, and Africa. However, we do find that the rate of labor absorption increases over time in spite of the relative stability of the aggregate savings rate.

Industrialization represents another key aspect of structural change. A common explanation for the relative decline in agricultural output is the influence of consumption demand as described by Engel's law. Because demand elasticities and the level of industrialization are endogenously determined in the model, we cannot say that Engel effects are a "cause" of industrialization in our economy. Indeed, without restrictions in the model, the rate of industrialization cannot be determined from qualitative analysis, even when per capita income growth is taking place. By imposing behavior consistent with Engel's hypothesis, however, we may be able to ensure a positive association between income growth and industrialization.

In fact, we find that the existence of Engel effects is neither a necessary nor a sufficient condition for industrialization to occur in the simple model developed and analyzed in chapters 2 and 3. Engel effects, together with the tendency for demand elasticities to converge toward one as development takes place, will always be forthcoming from the simple model for any theoretically possible set of demand parameters. However, when we modify the simple model to allow consumption from both wage and rental income, the existence of Engel effects is a sufficient condition to ensure an increase in the level of industrialization when the efficiency capital-labor ratio is rising. Thus, we reaffirm the importance of Engel's law in the process of growth and industrialization. But the difference between the two models leads us to conclude that at least in the context of dualistic two-sector models, the extreme assumption of consumption only from wage income can result in a rather misleading interpretation of the role of demand elasticities. We should note, however, two other restrictions where industrialization always occurs with rising per capita income: these are the case of Cobb-Douglas production functions, and the case where purchased capital inputs are excluded from production activities in agriculture. Jorgenson imposes these two restrictions on his model of a dual economy.

In the simulations, where we do not impose any of these restrictions, the qualitative ambiguities between industrial growth rates and capital deepening are resolved; moreover, we find the empirically relevant result that growth and industrialization are positively associated. Indeed, the dual economy produces phases of industrial development reminiscent of Rostovian stages, but it does not rely on parameter shifts or changes in model structure to yield such historical behavior.

The ambiguity between industrialization and the capital-labor ratio in the case where restrictions are not imposed on income elasticities may at first seem inconsistent with trade theory and the so-called Rybczynski effect. The Rybczynski theorem states that increases in the capital-labor ratio should generate a relative expansion in that sector which utilizes capital the most intensively. The apparent conflict can be easily resolved. The Rybczynski theorem is derived assuming "small-country" conditions, that is, constant and exogenously determined commodity prices. (In our model commodity prices are determined endogenously.) With the small-country assumption, commodity prices *and* the wage-rental rate are assumed constant; the latter result is more familiarly known as the "factor price equalization" theorem. As we noted in chapter 3, this strong assumption, normally made by trade theorists, implies that $v(t)$ increases because the growth of industrial output exceeds that of agriculture. As long as commodity prices are determined endogenously, as they are in our model, industrialization is not assured by increases in $k(t)$, because when $k(t)$ increases $P(t)$ decreases. Thus, we cannot determine whether the price or the quantity effects dominate. Furthermore, it is not unambiguously the case that with increases in $k(t)$ the rate of industrial output growth will exceed that in agriculture. Comparative static theorems from trade theory may be inapplicable to the broader problems of the sources of industrialization in low-income societies.

Another of the well-documented empirical characteristics of the developing economy is the persistent and wide productivity differentials between agriculture and industry. This characteristic is often cited as another aspect of dualism. Furthermore, regional disparities in income per capita or labor productivity frequently increase during early development phases. Does the simulated economy conform to this evidence? Does agricultural development precede modern industrial growth, or does it occur simultaneously? In the simulations the sectoral productivity differentials persist into late phases of growth. Yet, while the growth of industrial productivity outstrips that of agriculture in the early periods, this pattern is subsequently reversed, since agricultural productivity growth accelerates more rapidly throughout. Observed levels and trends in regional productivity disparities can be readily explained. The reversal in relative growth rates in later phases results from the combined effects of more rapid increases in capital intensity (mechanization) in agriculture during late development phases—the opposite is true in early growth phases—and from the differential rates of technical progress throughout. If an "agricultural revolution" is to be characterized by rapid increases in the accumulation of working and fixed capital (that is, commercialization) in our model, it is to be found in late rather than early growth phases. This result does not imply that agriculture is "backward"; it is enjoying more rapid rates of technical progress than industry and thus can hardly be viewed as a drag on development in spite of sluggish initial productivity growth. Finally, agriculture should not be characterized as passing into a new *stage* of commercialization; the process is instead cumulative and gradual.

These results relating to relative productivity growth and sectoral productivity dualism are also generated by the disequilibrium economy presented in chapter 7. Because restrictions are placed on intersectoral factor mobility, the capital-labor ratio in agriculture is adversely affected and sectoral productivity differentials widen all the more rapidly—dualism and regional inequalities are even more pronounced. Average labor productivity in both sectors increases, almost without exception, in response to relatively rapid rates of capital accumulation and technical change. In agriculture, however, early phases of industrialization are characterized by mild *relative* declines in labor productivity in spite of significant technological improvements. This result is also forthcoming from the equilibrium economy. Moreover, it confirms the importance placed by Asian economists on agriculture as a potential labor-absorbing sector. While part of the increasing regional "dualism" is due to factor immobilities, our analysis of the dualistic model with perfect factor mobility shows that disparities will normally exist given the differing sectoral production functions.

In the simulated economy the efficiency wage-rental ratio *declines* in early growth phases. This reflects the lower rate of capital accumulation and the high rate of population growth, coupled with significant rates of labor augmentation through technical change. In spite of the early decline in the efficiency wage-rental ratio, the substitution of capital for labor continues unabated in manufacturing as labor-saving technical change takes place. This result is consistent with Asian experience, where persistent increases in industrial capital intensity have occurred in concert with low and stable per unit labor costs (and even *declining* efficiency wage-rental ratios), a trend that has been of great concern to development economists. It has already been noted that "disappointingly low" rates of labor absorption occur in the simulated economy, at least in early phases of growth.

Agricultural experience with capital intensity is quite different. Early growth produces a slight *reduction* in the capital-labor ratio. This confirms the importance which those concerned with "unemployment" place on agriculture as a potential labor-absorbing sector. With rapid rates of labor-using technical change in agriculture, increases in labor intensity may play a major role in absorbing labor force increments in early growth phases when capital accumulation is less rapid. This pattern is even more pronounced when factor mobility is constrained.

Debate over the existence, nonexistence, or degree of surplus labor in the dual economy has continued unabated for almost two decades. One of the elements of confirming evidence for the labor-surplus postulate is the existence of the stability of real wages over long periods of industrial growth. But perhaps these trends in factor prices and real wages can be produced by a full-employment neoclassical model as well!

The emphasis which the behavior of real wages has received in the literature has been in response to an attempt to discriminate between alternative theories of factor pricing. Yet we found that efficiency wages consistently decline, though modestly, over three to four decades of impressive growth in our simulated economy. This result also holds for the disequilibrium economy, although the time period is shorter. Like the labor-surplus model, the neoclassical economy is fully capable of generating stable (or declining) real wages for even a growing economy. We cannot therefore discriminate between the two models on these grounds. Moreover, declining efficiency wages do not necessarily imply that workers' living standards are declining. In the simulated economy real wages (as opposed to real *efficiency* wages) *do* improve, as they also did in Japan. In the dual economy the explanation lies with efficiency improvements in labor; in the Japanese case the explanation lay with more intensive labor utilization.

Much has been made of the "wage gap" between agriculture and industry (or between peasant and capitalist agriculture). The disequilibrium framework is quite capable of producing wage gaps that persist over time. The more important question, at least in this study, is whether the factor immobility restrictions influence in any significant way the aggregate growth path and the course of structural change. While the answer is not unambiguous, we shall suggest below that our preliminary assessment does not favor incorporating complex factor mobility specifications in two-sector models.

A final result from the numerical analysis which merits some emphasis relates to the behavior of factor shares. One-sector growth models typically make somewhat uninteresting predictions regarding factor shares: in most cases the property income share is constant. These predictions have generated considerable debate over the alleged stability of labor's share during the twentieth century. But the so-called Great Ratio Debate is irrelevant for the present study, since our interest is the low-income, not the advanced, economy. Those economists concerned with development from low-income levels have reached a quite different position on the behavior of factor shares. Marx, Lewis, Fei and Ranis, Jorgenson, and even Kaldor predict rising profit shares in manufacturing. Furthermore, a labor-surplus model generates a rising profit share in manufacturing, and then stability after the turning point where neoclassical conditions are satisfied. Jorgenson's framework predicts an improvement in the overall property income share even in the neoclassical case, since the larger output share of manufacturing produces an overall increase as industrialization takes place. Although our model is far more general, our results are consistent with the fragments of historical evidence relevant to early development. The economy-wide labor share declines throughout, while in industry it first declines and then rises. The significant feature of our model, in contrast to the labor-surplus formulations or Kaldor's framework, is that the results are generated under assumptions of parameter stability. Most other models rely either on changing the specifications of wage determination or on sectoral divergence in output growth.

9.1.2.1. *Quantitative Analysis of the Dual Economy.* We turn now to a summary of the parametric experiments. Seven key development issues have been confronted. (1) The role of changes in demand parameters on economic growth is investigated. Also explored is the relevance of "demonstration effects" and changes in subsistence requirements. (2) We evaluate the impact of a labor force explosion on the dual economy. (3) The nature and significance of changing factor-saving biases

318 *Progress and Problems*

are analyzed. (4) The sensitivity of the economy to shifts in the savings parameter is explored in detail. (5) We reexamine the sources-of-growth methodology within the framework of a dynamic interdependent system. (6) An interpretation of the export technology hypothesis and production dualism is provided. (7) We examine the role of capital market imperfections and constrained labor migration in the process of growth and structural change.

Each of these issues has been analyzed under two quite different supply specifications. The first invokes the conventional assumptions of perfect factor mobility. The second introduces restrictions on supply elasticities by relying on a putty-clay treatment of capital goods and by a more realistic specification of the intersectoral labor and capital markets. In only a few cases did the introduction of less elastic short-run supply conditions change our conclusions.

The study offers somewhat interesting findings regarding the role of demand in growth. Not only does the existence of Engel effects influence the pattern of growth and industrialization when we allow consumption from both wage and rental income, but demand also plays a pervasive and important role through *changes* in consumer tastes (i.e., in parameter values). The numerical analysis has illustrated the sensitivity of the economy to shifts in tastes, but our supply specifications play a critical role in determining the direction of effect. In the equilibrium regime, where short-run supply elasticities are high, shifts in tastes toward urban goods may be as stimulatory to structural change in the long run as alterations in savings behavior, the variable of traditional focus. Demonstration effects, commonly villains in descriptive analyses of growth and development, may have an important positive influence on growth. Furthermore, it has long been recognized that increases in subsistence requirements have a depressing influence on growth in the dual economy. In labor-surplus models, for example, a key analytical focus is the impact of wage setting on the surplus available for accumulation. In our model the subsistence parameter enters only into the decision on expenditure composition. Even here the results are consistent with those of the labor-surplus models: a rise in the subsistence parameter depresses growth in the overall expansion of capital intensity, urbanization, and per capita output.

Are the same results forthcoming in the disequilibrium model? Through the introduction of a putty-clay specification and the restriction of intersectoral labor migration, short-run supply elasticities are diminished in the dual economy, and much more pronounced variations in commodity prices may result from shifts in consumer demand. We have found the price effect to be sufficiently powerful to offset the increased aggregate savings rate resulting from the decline in labor's share. With the rise in the sectoral terms of trade and the restriction on capital goods' availability, the rate of accumulation of physical assets is, in fact, diminished. These conflicting results show how little economists know about the role of demand in growth and emphasize the need for future research in this area.

The findings that increased rates of labor force growth exert a negative impact on per capita output expansion is hardly surprising. Of much greater interest is the possibility that this negative influence may be attenuated through time as the result of the impact of labor force growth on factor shares and capital accumulation. A notable feature of our dualistic model, under either supply specification, is that a rise in labor force growth also *increases* the rate of accumulation and, as a result, the capital-labor ratio growth. These findings underscore the utility of the methodology employed in this study; we have been able to evaluate the *quantitative* dimensions of the population problem as well as to distinguish explicitly between long- and short-run effects. If the quantitative analysis is accurate, the short-run disadvantage of more rapid population growth rates in Southeast Asia may be dissapated in later growth stages. However, the role of population growth will still be felt on lower levels of per capita output. It is not at all obvious that any plausible discounting of future consumption would compensate for the current costs to the material welfare of large families. Finally, the importance of demographic factors are brought into sharpest focus by an application of the model to Japanese experience. Here we have argued that the "Japanese miracle," commonly analyzed in terms of productivity patterns and linkages between agriculture and industry, may be more simply explained: labor force growth rates were less than half of those at present prevailing in Southeast Asia.

Experiments with the parameters of technical progress and their resulting biases have been related to the debate over investment criteria of the 1950s. The contributors to that debate were critically aware of the potentially important feedback effects of current techniques on income distribution and factor prices, and thus on future rates of capital formation and population growth. The simulation results in both models reveal that an increased labor-augmenting bias can reduce the rate of capital formation, urbanization, and, to a lesser extent, per capita income growth. Given the intensity of technical progress, higher labor-augmenting biases are a disadvantage to developing economies; moreover, this disadvantage increases as the degree of production dualism increases. On the other hand, the advantage of rapid rates of technical change in developing economies now becomes much clearer than has been apparent in the sources-of-growth literature. Using our model as the norm, the analysis suggests how and to what extent the contribution of technical progress may have been underestimated. This is because technical progress in our system may raise achievable rates of capital formation and lower population growth rates in the future. This result does *not* imply that capital formation contributes little to output growth, the conventional result from sources of growth analysis.

While criticisms of the sources-of-growth methodology have been legion, none of this research has attempted an evaluation of the methodology within a dynamic interdependent framework where the properties of the system are known with certainty. Our equilibrium model by assumption satisfies

competitive conditions of product and factor markets, aggregates perfectly, and is truly described by disembodied technical
progress. Thus, in comparing our model predictions with those
obtained by use of the sources-of-growth methodology, observed
differences must be attributed to two factors: (1) the importance of departures from the Cobb-Douglas specification, and
(2) the role of "interaction effects." The numerical experiments quantify the possible magnitude of the divergence
attributable to the assumed Cobb-Douglas specification. This
difference is not great. Yet the magnitude of interaction effects
is large enough to suggest that the application of the sources-
of-growth methodology to low-income economies may be
plagued with error. Paradoxically, our numerical analysis also
replicates a fundamental finding of the sources-of-growth literature: 70 percent of the average growth of industrial labor
productivity is "explained by (?)" technical progress. But a
more relevant result is that, by the end of a decade, a 1 percent
increase in the economy's savings parameter raises capital
stock growth rates by 2.5 percent and output per capita growth
rates by 3 percent! What the sources-of-growth literature ob-
scures is how increased savings rates foster industrialization-
urbanization, more rapid rates of capital accumulation, and
diminished population growth rates. These effects may be
relatively unimportant for advanced economies; they cannot
be ignored for the low-income dual economy.

These results are not reversed in the disequilibrium model,
but the impact on growth and industrialization from increased
savings rates is considerably reduced. The explanation, once
again, is to be found in short-run supply inelasticity and price
behavior. With restrictions on resource reallocation, a shift
in industrial (capital) goods demand produces a rise in capital
goods prices, and the positive stimulus to the physical rate of
accumulation is suppressed as a result.

The quantitative analysis provides some support for the
relevance of the export technology hypothesis. The export
sector, either as a source of relative expansion or through its
production parameters, may be important in influencing the

growth trajectory. The export technology hypothesis explores the impact of technical parameters on income distribution, demand composition, the international flow of technology, factor prices, and factor supply. Even though our model is closed, the results provide some insight into the possible difficulties of an enclave, export-oriented development. To the extent that early development is characterized by diminishing production dualism, growth and structural change may be significantly stimulated.

9.1.2.2. *Disequilibrium Growth in the Dual Economy.* It has been commonly observed that economic development is not an equilibrium process but rather a sequence of short-run adjustments. In this respect, factor market disequilibria have been highlighted in the literature as a key element in the developing economies. To capture this characterization we have introduced into the model factor immobilities based on migration and transaction costs, sluggish factor movements arising from risk and uncertainty, and sectoral capital specificity (putty-clay). A comparison of the pattern of growth and structural change in the equilibrium and disequilibrium models reveals that the two regimes generate similar growth paths as judged by economy-wide rates of capital accumulation, observed capital-labor ratios, and output growth per capita. The literature has emphasized the importance of inequality in factor prices and factor market fragmentation, and our revised model successfully replicates these phenomena. The behavior of factor prices in each sector does represent an improved description of the historical movements in factor prices. With these exceptions, however, we have not uncovered any significant insights beyond those obtained from a more naïve interpretation of capital as "putty-putty" and from instantaneous adjustment of factor markets. There is less variability between the two simulation models with respect to the rate and pattern of growth and structural change than between either model and the data reported in chapter 5 describing Japanese development during the period 1885–1915. Moreover, the rates of change in the key structural variables of the two models are not significantly different. It could be argued, for example, that while the presence of market imperfections does not substantially alter the broad pattern of growth and structural change, such imperfections may have a significant effect on the rate of structural transformation in an economy. Thus, we might have reasonably expected a retardation in the rate of structural transformation even though the same pattern is observed. While the rate of industrialization and urbanization is somewhat slower, in general differences between the two models are not significant.

The sensitivity analysis suggests that the pattern of growth and structural change is almost totally insensitive to a once-over change in the parameters relating to migration and transaction costs and rates of change in expectations about factor prices. Great stress has been placed on the advantages to be gained from "improved" capital markets through increased rates of accumulation and improved resource allocation. These arguments may appear plausible, but our analysis suggests that their quantitative importance may not be significant. While it is tempting to conclude from this that market imperfections of the kind introduced here have little effect on growth and structural change, it should be noted that the presence of such imperfections does significantly alter the sensitivity of the economy to changes in the parameters of production, technical change and savings. Compared with the equilibrium model, the economy is in general more sensitive to changes in production parameters and to the rate and bias of technical progress, and less sensitive to changes in savings parameters. Furthermore, our concern has been with growing dual economies; we ignore the cases of stagnation or sluggish growth. In a rapidly growing economy with positive depreciation rates, the requirement for intersectoral resource transfers are minimized. For an economy with much lower initial income and industrialization levels and with lower accumulation rates, the putty-clay and migration specifications might be more important.

Finally, not only does the disequilibrium formulation alter the sensitivity of the dual economy to changes in consumption parameters; it also changes the *sign* of the effects. From results such as these, a strong case has been made for greater attention to the theory of growing disequilibrium systems.

9.2. DIRECTIONS FOR FUTURE RESEARCH

Theorizing is an unending process. Of necessity, the hypotheses explored in this study represent only a subset, albeit an important one, of those we would have liked to explore. On the other hand, our findings, a reading of the literature on development and growth, and insights gained from this study suggest several relatively productive extensions of the formal model of dualism.

9.2.1. Adding an External Sector

What is to be gained by opening up the system to external trade? The answer depends on how we view the role trade plays in growth. If export expansion is seen simply as a source of demand (and a vent for surplus), we suspect that very little is to be gained in the way of greater insights into the forces contributing to growth and structural change since identical insights are forthcoming from an analysis of "domestic" demand shifts. Some progress in identifying the impact of foreign trade has been made in this study by interpreting the changes in production parameters (and production dualism) in the context of selected elements in the export technology hypothesis. Alternatively, if trade is viewed as an opportunity to export a product in which there is comparative advantage in return for imported capital goods and/or raw materials, its major contribution may be considered the releasing of production constraints on capital accumulation and short-run capacity. An alternative way of introducing this specification is to create an independent indigenous capital (raw material) goods sector. But whatever the device for introducing supply constraints, numerous other issues are raised in developing meaningful specifications for the foreign trade sector. What is the consumption-savings behavior of the recipients of export income? Is it appropriate to maintain marginal productivity distribution with laborers consuming income fully and capitalists saving a fixed share of rental income? Under what conditions are capitalists "conspicuous consumers" or investors? Finally, how are relative prices to be treated in the system? The small-country assumption in trade theory has a venerable tradition. We are not convinced of its general relevance; moreover, it may eliminate not only the role for demand but other important elements of theoretical interest as well.

9.2.2. Land as an Input

How should land be introduced as an input into the agrarian sector? While the quality and stock of land may have an important effect on the pattern of production and the rate of per capita output growth, economic theory offers few guidelines explaining the rate of land expansion and its quality improvement as distinct from capital improvements to land. Furthermore, inclusion of land can influence savings and consumption patterns if they are specific to this form of property income. Yet the available empirical evidence to guide the development of meaningful specifications is meager. It has been noted, for example, that in low-income economies "savings motives are satisfied by land holdings (and the increase in real land prices) rather than by capital accumulation."[2] If land is introduced into the dualistic model, it is imperative that its role should, at a minimum, be exercised through relevant hypotheses relating to its rate of improvement and expansion, its differential impact on income distribution or saving, or both. Otherwise the inclusion of land may represent little more than a superficially plausible production argument of relatively little analytical importance.

9.2.3. Technical Progress Once Again

In a model where capital goods are not sector specific, and

2. D. A. Nichols, "Land and Economic Growth," p. 332.

thus need not be equally augmented by technical change, what hypotheses might be employed to capture a more realistic specification of technical progress and its biases? The addition of neutral disembodied technical change would yield far greater discrepancies on the *intensity* of sectoral rates of technological improvement, but neither this specification nor a learning-by-doing formulation adds flexibility in varying the *bias* by sector. Further work on these issues could be fruitfully pursued with the objective of developing more meaningful specifications of *sector-specific* changes in factor-augmenting biases to technical progress, and perhaps with endogenous determination of the rate and bias in technical progress that isolates the movements in relative factor prices.

9.2.4. Unemployment and the Demographic Specification
This study has developed a model of economic dualism which has the neoclassical attributes of marginal product pricing and full employment. Several considerations influenced this decision. First, the empirical evidence has not discredited the neoclassical hypothesis, and alternative formulations have not commanded clear empirical support. Second, marginal product pricing is founded on well-established postulates of economic behavior. In contrast, hypotheses of institutional wage setting, which are well founded in theory, are notably absent from the economic literature. Third, by assuming this form of factor pricing we are better able to evaluate the importance of our other dualistic specifications in comparison with the conventional growth literature. Finally, the key evidence supporting the existence of labor-surplus conditions—constant real agricultural wages—has been shown in this study to be fully consistent with periods of neoclassical growth.

Even with neoclassical conditions assumed, an interpretation of our framework is available which could effectively capture the existence of "unemployment." Suppose it were assumed that efficiency factors were paid their marginal value products *provided* they were sufficient to allow each member of the labor force to consume a minimum-subsistence bundle of agricultural goods, γ. This bundle is considered by society to be essential and is above the caloric level at which starvation occurs. The *variable* minimum wage per efficiency labor unit can then be defined as $w_i(t) = \gamma/y(t)$. When the minimum-subsistence wage-fixing mechanism is operating, $r_i(t)$ is less than the shadow price of capital services since factor payments must exhaust output; that is, there is an implicit tax on capitalists' earnings. The tax is required to insure labors' full employment at the minimum wage. Without a tax, profit-maximizing behavior would dictate that capitalists hire efficiency labor only up to the point where the shadow price equals the minimum wage. But this would introduce overt unemployment. If all members of the population must consume at least γ, a subsidy must be paid to the unemployed workers. The burden of the tax must therefore fall on the capitalists.[3]

While an extension of this approach might be pursued, perhaps a more productive approach would be one which focuses on urban *underemployment* in the service sector. The urban economy may be decomposed into two sectors: the modern industrial sector and the low-productivity "traditional" urban service sector. This traditional urban service sector is an important source of employment in developing economies. Its output may be described by a simple linear technology and as a function of labor inputs alone. As a first approximation, the marginal physical product of labor in that sector may be considered fixed. The real wage would then be determined by the fixed technology in the traditional service sector and the price of agricultural wage goods. This formulation would shift the focus toward the problem of urban *under*employment. It would also allow for a differentiation between urbanization measures and industrial employment measures of structural change. It also offers a potentially fruitful approach to the rural-urban migration problem.

This study has emphasized the importance of the economic-

3. The remarks in this paragraph are amplified in R. J. Cheetham, "Growth and Structural Change in a Two-Sector Economy," pp. 48–57.

demographic interdependence in influencing growth in the dual economy. A convenient simplification has been employed: labor force and population variables possess the same properties. There are at least three avenues for introducing more realistic demographic specifications. First, a short-run labor supply function, which highlights the work-leisure choice, might be incorporated into the model. Second, the age structure of the population might be explicitly introduced. This approach, however, would present serious technical problems in the analysis if demographic-specific consumption and savings patterns were to be meaningfully examined. Third, the model may be applied to the small economy case (Puerto Rico, Hong Kong, the American North) where external migration is, or has been, significantly large.

9.2.5. Consumption and Savings Behavior
Alternative hypotheses about both demand and savings behavior could readily be introduced into the dual economy. Our treatment of savings behavior, for example, does not explain the motivation for capital accumulation. Alternative approaches could consider the rate of return on assets, wealth effects, and the impact of capital gains on the propensity to save. One such approach may be to formulate the savings decision from the basic behavior of utility maximization over time. Srinivasan, for example, has shown that a savings function such as ours can be derived by maximizing a rather simple intertemporal utility index.[4] A more general approach would be to assume that at each point in time capitalists purchase both agricultural goods (for consumption) and industrial goods (for consumption and/or investment purposes). Each capitalist possesses a utility function which depends on the consumption of both types of goods. Rational behavior implies that each capitalist maximizes an intertemporal utility function subject to an intertemporal expected income constraint. By assuming that the capitalist's utility function possesses the property of strong

4. T. N. Srinivasan, "On a Two-Sector Model of Growth."

separability, the process of utility maximization may be viewed as a two-stage procedure. In each period capitalists decide first on the proportions of their incomes to consume and save, and second on the proportions of agricultural and industrial output to consume.[5] Given the optimal consumption plan for each capitalist, his current savings (investment) would be derived as a residual from his current income.

Another area of considerable interest is the influence of demographic variables on demand. In our model, population growth enters into the consumption decision indirectly through its effect on incomes, relative prices, and by the presence of a minimum-consumption requirement in the demand specification. Family size effects might be introduced explicitly into the household consumption decision, although this would be most fruitful if introduced with a complementary theory of family size determination, an issue about which economists know relatively little. Alternatively, demographic effects could be introduced directly into the model in quite a different way. A large share of population-sensitive consumption is provided by the public sector: for example, education, health, and housing. One approach to capturing these population-sensitive demand effects would be to introduce explicitly a public sector into the model.

9.2.6. The Urban Service Sector and the Provision of
Public Goods

In view of the importance of the urban service sector as an employer in developing economies and of government in providing investment in social overhead, it seems remarkable that few development economists have seriously attempted to introduce this sector into their analyses. The analytical problems are numerous but hardly insurmountable. The first conceptual issue relates to specifying the nature of the product. This heterogeneous service flow may, for example, be broken down into two basic types: (1) education, medical care, and other social

5. L. R. Christensen, "Savings and the Rate of Return."

services, which frequently are relatively labor intensive; and (2) transportation and public utilities, which tend to be very capital intensive. Aggregation of these two services into a single output produced by a single production function appears to be unrealistic. For simplicity, it may be most productive to begin by suppressing type 2 by including urban investment in social overhead in the industrial capital stock and thereby focusing on labor-intensive public services.

A second problem relates to the way in which these public services are utilized in the economy. The simplest approach is to treat them as satisfying final demand; they cannot then be inputs into other production processes. To the extent that they *are* inputs into other production activities, the production functions must be expanded to include them.

The introduction of public services into the model introduces another investment allocation decision. To what extent should resources flow into the production of government services for consumption, or if public services entered into other production processes, to raise the capacity of the capital and the industrial consumer goods sectors rather than to augment the private capital stock in these two sectors? This investment decision is brought into sharper focus if we consider the way in which capital accumulation might be determined in the public sector. One approach would be to apply a tax to wage and rental income in the urban private sector (total taxes are identical to public revenue; i.e., the prices of public services are set at zero). Public expenditures are the wage payments plus depreciation allowances on capital stock in the public sector. Given exogenous tax rates, the differences between public revenues and expenditures then represents net savings on current account in the public sector and determines capital accumulation. Variations in the tax rate will yield differing net savings rates in the public sector. The aggregate national savings rate would depend on the level and functional distribution of income, the tax rate, and labor intensity in the public sector.

Many refinements could be readily introduced here; for example, a minimum bundle of public services might be consumed by all members of the urban labor force; the growth of technical efficiency of the labor force could be determined by the per capita consumption of public services (human capital accumulation). In any case, the rural-urban migration decision will need considerable revision for the low-income economy, where cheap (free?) urban public services may loom large in the effective real income received in urban employment. Needless to say, much work remains in this potentially fruitful area of theoretical development.

9.3. CONCLUDING REMARKS

This study has set out to demonstrate the usefulness of a genre of general equilibrium and disequilibrium models in interpreting the interrelationships between growth and structural change in a growing economy. These models, built around the notion of dualism in the production, consumption, and demographic characteristics of low-income economies, have provided significant qualitative and quantitative insights into the nature of the economic forces at work during sustained growth. And a comparison with Meiji Japan has confirmed the empirical validity of the models. However, far more research remains to be done on the dual-economy model. Not only can the model be extended in the directions indicated, but there is also a need for more empirical research to develop a better knowledge of the relevant parameter values. A greater effort is required to bridge the gap between growth theory and empirical analysis of observed experience. Because of the severe limitations of qualitative analysis, our study urges the greater use of numerical analysis in analyzing the properties of dynamic models of growth and change. This effort could yield richer insights into the long-run problems facing contemporary developing nations.

Appendix A

Existence, Uniqueness, and Stability of the Basic Dualistic Model

A.1. EXISTENCE

It follows by definition that the wage-rental rate, ω_i, is equal to the marginal rate of substitution of efficiency labor for efficiency capital in the ith sector; that is,

$$\omega_i = \frac{\omega_i}{r_i} = \frac{F_L{}^i}{F_K{}^i} = \frac{f_i(k_i)}{f'_i(k_i)} - k_i. \tag{A.1}$$

It follows from equation (A.1) that

$$\frac{d\omega_i}{dk_i} = -\frac{f_i(k_i)f''_i(k_i)}{[f'_i(k_i)]^2}, \tag{A.2}$$

and if $f_i(k_i) > 0$, $f'_i(k_i) > 0$, and $f''_i(k_i) < 0$ for all $k_i > 0$, it further follows that $d\omega_i/dk_i > 0$, or that $\omega_i(k_i)$ is a strictly increasing function of k_i.

Let

$$\underline{\omega}_i = \lim_{k_i \to 0} \bar{\omega}_i(k_i), \qquad \bar{\omega}_i = \lim_{k_i \to +\infty} \underline{\omega}_i(k_i),$$

$$\underline{\omega} = \max(\underline{\omega}_1, \underline{\omega}_2) \quad \text{and} \quad \bar{\omega} = \min(\bar{\omega}_1, \bar{\omega}_2).$$

Clearly, $0 \leqq \underline{\omega}_i \leqq \bar{\omega}_i \leqq +\infty$. We assume that f_i are such that $\underline{\omega} < \bar{\omega}$ holds. Then, for any positive ω, we can solve $\omega_i(k_i)$ for a unique positive capital-labor ratio $k_i = k_i(\omega)$ in each sector, provided that $\underline{\omega} < \omega < \bar{\omega}$.

Since marginal product pricing prevails only when $y\omega_1 f'_1(k_1)P \geqq \gamma$ and $y\omega_2 f'_2(k_2) \geqq \gamma$, we assume that γ/y is such that there is some $\omega \in \{\underline{\omega}, \bar{\omega}\}$ for which marginal product pricing operates. In the limiting case, $y_\omega f'_2[k_2(\omega)] = \gamma$, and therefore

$$\frac{d\gamma}{d\omega} = y\alpha_2(\omega)f'_2[k_2(\omega)] > 0,$$

where

$$\alpha_2(\omega) = \frac{k_2(\omega)f'_2[k_2(\omega)]}{f_2[k_2(\omega)]}$$

is the elasticity of output with respect to the input of capital in the agricultural sector. Thus, in this limiting case, γ is a strictly increasing funtion of ω. It follows, therefore, that, for any given γ/y, there is only one $\omega = \omega^*$ that satisfies this limiting wage condition; if it is assumed that γ/y is such that $\omega^* \in \{\underline{\omega}, \bar{\omega}\}$, the marginal productivity version of the model is defined for all ω such that

$$\omega^* \leqq \omega < \bar{\omega}. \tag{A.3}$$

Thus, for any positive wage-rental ratio which satisfies equation (A.3), equation (A.1) can be solved for a unique positive capital-labor ratio $k_i = k_i(\omega)$ in each sector.

From substitution of $k_1 = k_1(\omega)$ into equation (3.7) it follows that $\phi(\omega) = xf'_1[k_1(\omega)]$, from which we obtain

$$\frac{d\phi}{d\omega} = -\frac{x\{f'_1[k_1(\omega)]\}^2}{f_1[k_1(\omega)]} < 0, \tag{A.4}$$

because

$$f''_i[k_1(\omega)]\frac{\partial k_1(\omega)}{\partial \omega} = -\frac{\{f'_1[k_1(\omega)]\}^2}{f_1[k_1(\omega)]}.$$

Thus, $\phi(\omega) > 0$ is a strictly decreasing function of ω, and therefore $\phi = \phi(\omega)$ can be solved for a unique positive ϕ.

It follows from equation (3.10) that $P(\omega) > 0$ because $f'_i(k_i) > 0$. Differentiating $P(\omega)$ with respect to ω and rearranging, we obtain

$$\frac{dP}{d\omega} = \frac{P(\omega)[k_2(\omega) - k_1(\omega)]}{[\omega + k_1(\omega)][\omega + k_2(\omega)]}. \tag{A.5}$$

Therefore, since P is a strictly decreasing (increasing) function of ω, $P = P(\omega)$ can be solved for a unique positive P when the capital intensity in industry is greater than (less than) that in agriculture.

Now consider the relationship between z_{ij} and ω. It follows from equation (3.5) that, when $k_1(\omega) - k_2(\omega)$ is positive, z_{ij} is an increasing monotonic function of ω because

$$\frac{dz_{1j}}{d\omega} = \frac{\beta_{1j}y}{P(\omega)} \alpha_2(\omega) f'_2[k_2(\omega)] + \frac{z_{1j}[k_1(\omega) - k_2(\omega)]}{[\omega + k_1(\omega)][\omega + k_2(\omega)]}.$$
(A.6)

Simarilarly, z_{2j} is a strictly increasing function of ω because

$$\frac{dz_{2j}}{d\omega} = \beta_{2j}y\alpha_2(\omega) f'_2[k_2(\omega)] > 0.$$
(A.7)

Thus, z_{ij} is an increasing function of ω when $k_1(\omega) - k_2(\omega) > 0$; $z_{ij} = z_{ij}(\omega)$ can be solved for a unique positive z_{ij}.

From expression (3.2) the level of urbanization is determined by

$$u(\omega) = \frac{k - k_2(\omega)}{k_1(\omega) - k_2(\omega)};$$
(A.8)

after substituting for $u(\omega)$ and $z_{2j}(\omega)$ in equation (3.9) and rearranging, we have

$$k = \psi(\omega) \equiv k_2(\omega) + $$
$$\frac{\{ yf_2[k_2(\omega)] - z_{22}(\omega) \} [k_1(\omega) - k_2(\omega)]}{yf_2[k_2(\omega)] + z_{21}(\omega) - z_{22}(\omega)}.$$
(A.9)

Now, $yf_2[k_2(\omega)] - z_{22}(\omega)$ and $yf_2[k_2(\omega)] + z_{21}(\omega) - z_{22}(\omega)$ are both positive because

$$yf_2[k_2(\omega)] - z_{22}(\omega) = yf_2[k_2(\omega)] - \beta_{22}y\omega f'_2[k_2(\omega)] - $$
$$[1 - \beta_{22}]\gamma = [1 - \beta_{22}]\{ yf_2[k_2(\omega)] - \gamma \}$$
$$+ \beta_{22}yk_2(\omega)f'_2[k_2(\omega)].$$

But by assumption wage earnings per laborer are at least sufficient to meet subsistence requirements; that is,

$$y\{ f_2[k_2(\omega)] - k_2(\omega)f'_2[k_2(\omega)] \} \geqq \gamma,$$

so that $yf_2[k_2(\omega)] - \gamma \gtreqless k_2(\omega)f'_2[k_2(\omega)] > 0$. Thus, when $k_1(\omega) \neq k_2(\omega)$, it follows that $\psi(\omega) > 0$ for all $\omega \in \{\omega^*, \overline{\omega}\}$, which, in turn, implies that $k = \psi(\omega)$ has a solution for any k such that

$$\inf_{\omega \in \{\omega^*, \overline{\omega}\}} \psi(\omega) < k < \sup_{\omega \in \{\omega^*, \overline{\omega}\}} \psi(\omega). \tag{A.10}$$

Furthermore $k - k_2(\omega) \lesseqgtr 0$ when $k_1(\omega) - k_2(\omega) \gtreqless 0$, so that $u = u(\omega)$ can be solved for a positive u. Indeed, $u(\omega)$ is a decreasing function of ω when $k_1(\omega) - k_2(\omega)$ is greater than zero, for differentiation of equation (A.8) yields

$$\frac{du}{d\omega} = \frac{-1}{k_1(\omega) - k_2(\omega)}$$
$$\left\{ u(\omega) \frac{\partial k_1(\omega)}{\partial(\omega)} + [1 - u(\omega)] \frac{\partial k_2(\omega)}{\partial \omega} \right\}, \tag{A.11}$$

so that $du/d\omega \lesseqgtr 0$ as $k_1(\omega) - k_2(\omega) \gtreqless 0$.

We conclude that for any k satisfying equation (A.10) there exists at least one solution to $\psi[\mathbf{X}; k] = 0$, provided that $k_1(\omega) \neq k_2(\omega)$.

A.2. UNIQUENESS

We have already shown that for any given wage-rental ratio the endogenous variables are uniquely determined when $k_1(\omega) - k_2(\omega) > 0$. We now wish to obtain plausible sufficient conditions for the monotonicity of $\psi(\omega)$. By differentiating equation (A.9) with respect to ω, substituting

$$u(\omega) = \frac{yf_2[k_2(\omega)] - z_{22}(\omega)}{yf_2[k_2(\omega)] + z_{21}(\omega) - z_{22}(\omega)}$$

from equations (3.1) and (3.9), and rearranging the result, we have

$$\frac{dk}{d\omega} = u(\omega) \frac{\partial k_1(\omega)}{\partial \omega} + [1 - u(\omega)] \frac{\partial k_2(\omega)}{\partial \omega} +$$
$$\frac{[k_1(\omega) - k_2(\omega)]H(\omega)}{yf_2[k_2(\omega)] + z_{21}(\omega) - z_{22}(\omega)}, \tag{A.12}$$

where

$$H(\omega) = [1 - u(\omega)]yf'_2[k_2(\omega)]\frac{\partial k_2(\omega)}{\partial \omega} -$$

$$u(\omega)\frac{\partial z_{21}(\omega)}{\partial \omega} - [1 - u(\omega)]\frac{\partial z_{22}(\omega)}{\partial \omega}. \quad \text{(A.13)}$$

From the definition of σ_i it follows that $\partial k_2(\omega)/\partial \omega = \sigma_2(\omega)k_2(\omega)\omega^{-1}$; and from equation (3.6) we have $\partial z_{2j}(\omega)/\partial \omega = \beta_{2j}y\alpha_2(\omega) f_2[k_2(\omega)]$. Substitution of these expressions into equation (A.13) gives

$$H(\omega) = f'_2[k_2(\omega)]\Big([1 - u(\omega)]y\sigma_2(\omega)$$

$$\frac{k_2(\omega)}{\omega} - y\alpha_2(\omega)\Big\{\beta_{21}u(\omega) + \beta_{22}[1 - u(\omega)]\Big\}\Big). \quad \text{(A.14)}$$

But from equation (3.9),

$$[1 - u(\omega)]y = \frac{1}{f_2[k_2(\omega)]}\Big(\Big\{u(\omega)z_{21}(\omega) +$$

$$[1 - u(\omega)]z_{22}(\omega)\Big\}\Big) = \frac{1}{f_2[k_2(\omega)]}\Big(\Big\{\beta_{21}u(\omega) + \beta_{22}[1 -$$

$$u(\omega)]\Big\}y\omega f'_2[k_2(\omega)] + \gamma\Big\{\beta_{11}u(\omega) + \beta_{12}[1 - u(\omega)]\Big\}\Big).$$

$$\text{(A.15)}$$

Substituting equation (A.15) into (A.13) and rearranging, we obtain

$$H(\omega) = \alpha_2(\omega)\Big(\Big\{[\beta_{21}u(\omega) + \beta_{22}[1 - u(\omega)]\Big\}$$

$$\Big\{\sigma_2(\omega) - 1\Big\}yf'_2[k_2(\omega)] + \frac{\gamma\sigma_2(\omega)}{\omega}$$

$$\Big\{\beta_{11}u(\omega) + \beta_{12}[1 - u(\omega)]\Big\}\Big). \quad \text{(A.16)}$$

Thus, when $\sigma_2(\omega) - 1 \geqq 0$, it follows that $H(\omega) > 0$, and therefore $dk/d\omega > 0$ when $k_1(\omega) - k_2(\omega) > 0$. It is clear from equation (A.12) that the sign of $dk/d\omega$ is ambiguous when $k_1(\omega) - k_2(\omega) < 0$.

A.3. STABILITY

The excess demand per capita for the agricultural good is

$$E_A = z_{21}u + z_{22}(1 - u) - (1 - u)yf_2(k_2)$$

$$= E_A[\omega; k], \qquad (A.17)$$

since $u = u(\omega)$, $z_{2j} = z_{2j}(\omega)$, and $k_2 = k_2(\omega)$. Similarly, the excess demand per capita for the industrial good is

$$E_I = z_{11}u + z_{12}(1 - u) + ykf'_1(k_1) - yuf_1(k_1)$$

$$= E_I[P, \omega; k]. \qquad (A.18)$$

In view of our definition of static equilibrium for a given $k = k°$, the equilibrium values of ω and P, say $\omega°$ and $P°$, are obtained as the solutions of

$$E_A[\omega] = 0 = E_I[P, \omega]. \qquad (A.19)$$

Given Walras's law, we need not consider the market for capital per capita.

Following Arrow and Hurwicz,[1] we assume an instantaneous adjustment process so that the dynamic assumptions may be expressed as

$$\frac{d\omega}{dt} = h_A[E_A], \qquad h_A(0) = 0, h'_A > 0, \qquad (A.20a)$$

$$\frac{dP}{dt} = h_I[E_I], \qquad h_I(0) = 0, h'_I > 0. \qquad (A.20b)$$

If h_A and h_I are expanded around $\omega°$ and $P°$ and units are chosen such that $h'_A(0) = 1 = h'_I(0)$, the following system of differential equations will hold in the neighborhood of equilibrium:

$$\frac{d\omega}{dt} = \frac{\partial E_A}{\partial \omega}(\omega - \omega°), \qquad (A.21a)$$

$$\frac{dP}{dt} = \frac{\partial E_I}{\partial P}(P - P°) + \frac{\partial E_I}{\partial \omega}(\omega - \omega°). \qquad (A.21b)$$

1. K. J. Arrow and L. Hurwicz, "On the Stability of Competitive Equilibrium, I."

The necessary and sufficient conditions for the stability of equations (A.20a) and (A.20b) are:

$$\frac{\partial E_A}{\partial \omega} + \frac{\partial E_I}{\partial P} < 0, \tag{A.22a}$$

$$\frac{\partial E_A}{\partial \omega} \frac{\partial E_I}{\partial P} > 0. \tag{A.22b}$$

These conditions are also sufficient for the local stability of equation (A.19). It is only when $\partial E_A/\partial \omega < 0$ and $\partial E_I/P < 0$ that these conditions are satisfied.

It follows from (A.15) that

$$\frac{\partial E_A}{\partial \omega} = -H(\omega) + \frac{\partial u(\omega)}{\partial \omega}$$
$$\{ yf_2[k_2(\omega)] + z_{21}(\omega) - z_{22}(\omega) \}, \tag{A.23}$$

where $H(\omega)$ is the function defined in (A.15). Since $H(\omega) > 0$ when $k_1(\omega) - k_2(\omega) > 0$ and $\sigma_2(\omega) \geqq 1$, and since, as shown earlier, $\partial u(\omega)/\partial \omega < 0$ when $k_1(\omega) - k_2(\omega) > 0$, it follows that $\partial E_A/\partial \omega < 0$. Furthermore, from (A.18) we have

$$\frac{\partial E_I}{\partial P} = \frac{-1}{P^2} \left\{ \beta_{11}u(\omega) + \beta_{12}[1 - u(\omega)] \right\}$$
$$\left\{ yf'_2[k_2(\omega)] - \gamma \right\}. \tag{A.24}$$

But our model is defined such that $yf'_2 k_2(\omega) - \gamma > 0$, so that $\partial E_I/\partial P < 0$.

In summary, the sufficient conditions for the local stability of a static equilibrium are that $k_1(\omega) - k_2(\omega) > 0$ and $\sigma_2(\omega) \geqq 1$. As we have already shown, when these restrictions prevail there is only one static equilibrium solution to $\psi[\mathbf{X}; k] = 0$ for any given k.

Appendix B

Estimation of Parameter Values

B.1. PRODUCTION FUNCTIONS AND PARAMETER VALUES

We postulate CES production functions in both sectors. With constant returns to scale assumed, $Q_i(t)$ is now written as

$$Q_i(t) = A_i \left\{ [x(t)K_i(t)]^{(\sigma_i - 1)/\sigma_i} + \right.$$
$$\left. [y(t)L_i(t)]^{(\sigma_i - 1)/\sigma_i} \right\}^{\sigma_i/(\sigma_i - 1)}. \quad \text{(B.1)}$$

Econometric results by Sicat and Williamson on production conditions in the Philippines[1] lend support to the assumptions that the elasticity of factor substitution is less than one in the industrial sector and greater than one in the agricultural sector. These results have been confirmed for a larger sample of countries in a detailed investigation by Chetty.[2] We begin by arbitrarily setting $\sigma_1 = 0.5$, $\sigma_2 = 1.5$.

Independent estimates or empirical evidence on the values of the A_i are not available. As a result, A_1 is derived indirectly by use of current Philippine evidence relating to sectoral capital-output ratios and output elasticities relating to capital.

The marginal product of capital in the industrial sector is given by

$$F_1^1 = A_1^{(\sigma_1 - 1)/\sigma_1} Q_1(t)^{1/\sigma_1} [x(t)K_1(t)]^{-1/\sigma_1}. \quad \text{(B.2)}$$

1. G. Sicat, "Economic Incentives, Industrialization, and Employment in the Developing Economies"; J. G. Williamson, "Relative Price Changes, Adjustment Dynamics, and Productivity Growth: The Case of Philippine Manufacturing"; and J. G. Williamson and G. Sicat, "Technological Change and Resource Allocation in Philippine Manufacturing: 1956–1967."
2. V. K. Chetty, "International Comparison of Production Functions in Manufacturing."

It follows that the output elasticity for industrial capital is

$$\alpha_1(t) = A_1^{(\sigma_1 - 1)/\sigma_1} \left\{ x(t) \frac{K_1(t)}{Q_1(t)} \right\}^{(\sigma_1 - 1)/\sigma_1}. \quad \text{(B.3)}$$

An estimate of A_1 can therefore be obtained from knowledge of $\alpha_1(0)$, σ_1, $x(0)$, and $K_1(0)/Q_1(0)$. Utilizing Sicat's estimates of output elasticities in manufacturing,[3] we assume $\alpha_1(0) = 0.60$.

Asian macro models commonly assume the capital-output ratio in nonagricultural production to be approximately three and the economy-wide figure to be two. The work of Sicat and Tidalgo, Lampman, and others on the Philippines lends support to these assumptions.[4] For the purpose of establishing plausible values for A_1, we arbitrarily set

$$x(0) \frac{K_1(0)}{Q_1(0)} = 2.6 \quad \text{(B.4)}$$

and $x(0) = 1$. Substituting this expression into equation (B.3) gives $A_1 = 0.641$. For the purposes of simulation, we set $A_1 = 0.640$.

Use of the above procedure to derive a value for A_2 is complicated by the presence of $P(t)$ in the expression for the capital-output ratio in agriculture, namely, $P(t)x(t)[K_2(t)/Q_2(t)]$. While the value of this expression must be less than the corresponding figure for industry—recall, $k_1 > k_2$ by assumption— the actual capital-output ratio may be very small. We found it necessary at this point to pursue an operational alternative by assuming the following initial values for labor and the agricultural output: $Q_2(0) = 100$, $L_1(0) = 30$, $L_2(0) = 70$. These values are consistent with the requirement that the economy begin at a relatively low level of economic development. Since the *scale* of $L(0)$ does not materially influence the simulation analysis, a value of A_2 is derived by solving

3. Sicat, "Economic Incentives."
4. G. Sicat and R. Tidalgo, "Output, Capital, Labor, and Population: Projections from the Supply Side"; R. J. Lampman, "The Sources of Post-war Economic Growth in the Philippines."

$$\alpha_2(0) = A_2^{(\sigma_2 - 1)/\sigma_2} \left\{ x(0) \frac{K_2(0)}{Q_2(0)} \right\}^{(\sigma_2 - 1)/\sigma_2}$$

and equation (B.1) for A_2 and $K_2(0)$ under the assumption that $\alpha_2(0) = 0.36$. The resultant value for A_2, after rounding, was 0.350.

B.1.1. TECHNOLOGICAL PROGRESS PARAMETERS

There are very few estimates of the rate and bias of technical change for the developing countries. Rough orders of magnitude for rates of factor augmentation may be obtained by examining Philippine experience. From the estimates of total factor productivity growth by Lampman and Williamson, an empirical description of recent Philippine experience with technological change can be deduced. Lampman and Williamson independently find overall rates of technical change (total factor productivity improvement) of approximately 1 percent a year from 1956.[5] For more recent years, Williamson identifies rates in manufacturing (as opposed to industry) averaging around 1.10 percent a year.[6] However, the Philippine record of technical change in the postwar period can be considered somewhat atypical of the long-run historical experience in the developing countries for at least two reasons. First, the overall rate of technical change has been exceptionally high, partly because of postwar reconstruction. Second, the replacement of war-destroyed capital, together with the major influx of foreign manufactured capital goods, has resulted in the growth of industrial capacity with a particularly strong labor-saving bias. In both overall rates of technical change and labor-saving bias, the Philippine record must therefore be considered as representing an outer bound on the estimates plausible for the typical developing economy. Accordingly, a more acceptable rate of technical change for $t = 0$ may be around 0.0075.

5. R. J. Lampman, "Sources of Post-war Economic Growth"; J. G. Williamson, "Dimensions of Philippine Post-War Economic Progress."
6. Williamson, "Case of Philippine Manufacturing."

Utilizing the equations

$$R(t) = v(t)R_1(t) + [1 - v(t)]R_2(t)$$

and

$$R_i(t) = \alpha_i(t)\lambda_K + [1 - \alpha_i(t)]\lambda_L,$$

and the values

$$R(0) = 0.0075, \qquad \alpha_1(0) = 0.640,$$

$$v(0) = 0.430, \qquad \alpha_2(0) = 0.360,$$

we can derive an expression for λ_L in terms of λ_K:

$$\lambda_L = .0144 - .934\lambda_K, \quad \lambda_L > \lambda_K \geqq 0.$$

From the feasible set (λ_L, λ_K) implied by this expression, we selected magnitudes of λ_K and λ_L which appeared to us reasonable: $\lambda_L = 0.010$, $\lambda_K = 0.003$. It follows from equation (2.5) that $B_1 = 0.007$ and $B_2 = -0.002$. Although we believe that these estimates of the technical progress parameters are reasonably typical of the low-income economies, they may be subject to somewhat larger errors than the other parameters in our model. In any case, the available evidence is not sufficient to develop more precise estimates at this time.

B.1.2. CONSUMPTION AND INVESTMENT DEMAND PARAMETERS
The estimates of the demand parameters are based on an econometric analysis of the behavior of Philippine household expenditure. By utilizing the sectoral household budget shares for 1965, $P_j z_{ij}/w_i y$, the estimates of sectoral expenditure elasticities, η_{ij}, and the fact that in the modified Stone-Geary linear expenditure system

$$\eta_{ij}(t) = \beta_{ij} \left\{ \frac{w_j(t)y(t)}{P_i(t)z_{ij}(t)} \right\},$$

we can derive consistent estimates for β_{ij}. The linear Engel curves estimated for Philippine food consumption permitted us to calculate, for a given expenditure level, both the sectoral budget shares and the corresponding expenditure elasticities. In equilibrium our model requires that sectoral wage income per worker be equalized; thus, the functions of estimated urban and rural expenditures must be evaluated at a common income level. The estimates utilized the 1965 Philippine average rural income per household, since this figure more closely approximates per capita labor income than urban household income, where property income forms a more significant portion of factor returns. While it is likely that the rural wage is understated because of undermeasurement of income in kind, it most closely approximates the measure consistent with the underlying theoretical framework of our model. In 1965, 62 percent of Philippine rural household expenditures was devoted to food; the elasticities were those valued at this budget share. The resulting β_{ij}'s are

$$\beta_{11} = 0.80, \qquad \beta_{21} = 0.20,$$
$$\beta_{12} = 0.50, \qquad \beta_{22} = 0.50.$$

These parameter values are consistent with the common observation that $\eta_{1j}(t) > 1$, $\eta_{2j}(t) < 1$, and $\eta_{21}(t) < \eta_{22}(t)$. The estimated β_{ij}'s are also consistent with a recent econometric study of Indonesian households which has estimated the linear expenditure system for 1959–68.[7]

Estimates of γ are much more difficult to obtain. We rely on the prevailing assumption of low rural living standards in the developing countries; this implies that γ comes close to exhaust-

7. Paul Deuster, "The Effects of Indonesian Inflation in the Rural Areas: Case Study of the Jogjakarta Region." Using survey data drawn from Jogjakarta, Deuster estimates parameters for the Stone-Geary system. Expenditures are broken down into thirteen groups, of which nine are food products. If we include housing and services, the $\sum_{i=1}^{11} \beta_i = 0.81$, which is almost identical with our assumed value of β_{11}. Furthermore, the value of γ (including these eleven products and aggregated by 1959 rupiah prices) is about 80 percent of the average income of "farmer-laborers" and "small farmers." The income of "small farmers" is exhausted by γ.

ing agricultural income. In particular, we have assumed that, in the *initial* period, when the economy is at a relatively low level of economic development (70 percent of the population live in the agricultural sector), three-quarters of agricultural income is devoted to meeting minimum-subsistence requirements. Thus, we set $\gamma = 0.75[w(0)y(0)]$. As the economy grows the proportion of income required to meet subsistence demands declines.

Urban capitalists and rural landlords, receiving $r_1(t)x(t)K_1(t)$ and $r_2(t)x(t)K_2(t)$, respectively, allocate their incomes between urban goods for investment and urban and rural goods for consumption. Securing a value for s is complicated by the fact that there are very few econometric studies of savings behavior in the developing countries which provide estimates of the required parameter. Given this observation, and our desire to maintain comparability in the key initial conditions of the various simulation models—an initial urbanization rate of 30 percent and economy-wide average gross savings of 15 percent—we have elected to derive the savings parameter implied by these initial conditions. The resulting figure, approximately 0.31, appears consistent with the few qualitative and quantitative descriptions of savings behavior available on the developing economies. For example, an upper boundary on savings rates might be represented by the Philippine corporate manufacturing sector, where Hooley finds retention rates of around 60 percent for the 1960s; additional savings out of distributed corporate income will push this figure somewhat higher.[8] In contrast, the savings behavior of both farm owner-operators and unincorporated urban firms might be taken as the lower boundary on savings rates. In a study of Indonesian savings behavior, Kelley and Williamson find savings rates of these two groups ranging from 0.10 to 0.30.[9] Finally, in a

8. R. Hooley, *Saving in the Philippines, 1951–1960.*
9. A. C. Kelley and J. G. Williamson, "Household Saving Behavior in the Developing Economies: The Indonesian Case."

macroeconomic study, Williamson has identified marginal savings rates out of nonwage income varying from 0.45 to 0.50 in
the Philippines and Taiwan during the postwar period.[10] Both
countries are relatively advanced. Since our interest is to explore
a trajectory of growth rising from relatively low levels of economic development, the somewhat lower savings rate implied
by the initial conditions in the simulations appears to be reasonable.

We know of no studies relevant to the consumption behavior
of recipients of property income in the developing economies.
However, it is not uncommon to find owners of a large share
of rural assets living in urban centers, and in the absence of
empirical evidence, it seems plausible to assume that the recipient of property income allocates the remainder of his
income among consumption goods according to the demand parameters estimated for urban wage-earning households. Therefore, we set $\pi_1 = 0.80$, $\pi_2 = 0.20$ and $\gamma = 0.75[y(0)w(0)]$.

The final parameter to be established in the demand system
is Φ, the proportion of the work force that owns assets. While
direct estimates of this parameter are not available for the
developing countries, it is quite evident that the per capita
income of property income recipients is considerably greater
than that of the laborer in many low-income agrarian economies. In the absence of more concrete evidence, we have
assumed as a first approximation that the capitalist's income
is about five times that of the laborer's wage in the initial
period; the implied value of Φ is 0.20. This specification, together with the expression above relating to the minimum-
subsistence bundle, results in the plausible hypothesis that the
subsistence consumption requirements are a much smaller proportion of capitalists' income than that of workers. For capitalists as well as workers, of course, the fraction of income
devoted to subsistence declines as economic progress takes
place.

10. J. G. Williamson, "Personal Savings in Developing Nations:
An Intertemporal Cross-section from Asia."

B.1.3. THE DEPRECIATION PARAMETER

Our evidence on δ is primarily indirect. The approach has been to use the share of depreciation requirements to GNP as the key variable for selecting an appropriate depreciation rate, given the size and allocation of the capital stock in the initial period. In examining the ratio of depreciation requirements to GNP, Kuznets finds ratios ranging from 0.066 for countries with very low incomes to 0.080 for countries with per capita income (in 1958) exceeding $574 a year.[11] When $\delta = 0.05$, our model predicts the share of capital consumption, $P(t)\delta K$, in GNP to be 0.087 in the initial period. In our model almost 58 percent of gross savings is required to replace the capital stock depreciated in the first time period. Thus, the indirect evidence appears to support our choice of $\delta = 0.05$.

B.1.4. LABOR SUPPLY PARAMETERS

The values of n_j depend on sectoral mortality rates, birth rates, age and sex distribution, and rates of labor force participation. If it is assumed that mortality rates are invariant to sector and that the age distribution will not change markedly in the simulation period, the primary factor explaining the demographic characteristics of the two sectors is a differential birth rate.

Overall rates of population growth in the developing economies range from around 2 percent a year in parts of Africa to over 3 percent in much of Latin America and in major parts of Asia.[12] Since our model in the initial period is rural in character, an aggregate population growth rate in the upper range of experience for the developing countries would appear relevant. Accordingly, we have arbitrarily assumed annual rates of 2 percent and 3 percent in the urban and rural sectors, respectively. This results in an aggregate rate of 2.7 percent in the initial period.

Turning to the labor force participation rates, we see that the impact of urbanization and the changing age distribution

11. S. Kuznets, *Modern Economic Growth*, pp. 248–56.
12. United Nations, *Demographic Yearbook*, 1962, p. 124.

between sectors on the growth of the labor force in rural and urban areas is clearly of importance. We shall consider here only the impact of urbanization on the growth of the female labor force. The changing sectoral age distribution, and its resulting influence on aggregate participation rates, will exert an extremely small impact on labor force growth, since the age-specific participation rates of males do not materially vary between sectors. It is well known that the rates of participation of females in the labor force vary directly with the level of urbanization. This relationship, in terms of "activity rates,"[13] reveals rates for ages fifteen to twenty-four of about 50 percent in industrialized countries and 30 percent in agricultural countries.[14] The relevant question is whether, with this pattern of activity, the urbanization taking place during the simulation period will affect significantly the values of n_1 and n_2. The answer is no. Assuming an unchanging age distribution of the

13. "Economically active populations" are "all those who contribute to the supply of labor for the production of economic goods and services, including not only those employed at the time of the investigation, but also those unemployed but available for work" (United Nations, *Demographic Aspects of Manpower*, p. 1). As noted elsewhere, the problems arising from the measurement of "economically productive" populations plague statisticians in arriving at a consistent and theoretically meaningful estimate. The difficulties in measurement are greatest for women and children. Women and children are typically excluded unless they are working for wages or salaries, or unless, as in rural family work, the duties exceed those attributable to family obligations, the latter determined by the number of hours worked in farming or pastoral activities (A. C. Kelley, "Demographic Change and Economic Growth: Australia, 1861–1911," p. 228).

14. The definitions of "industrialized" and "agricultural" countries correspond closely to the measures of urbanization. The former, composed of Argentina, Australia, Belgium, Canada, Denmark, England, Wales, France, Israel, Netherlands, New Zealand, Norway, Sweden, Switzerland, and the United States, have less than 35 percent of active males engaged in agriculture and related activities. The latter, which employ more than 60 percent of active males in agriculture, include Algeria, Brazil, Columbia, Costa Rica, Equador, El Salvador, Guatemala, India, Morocco, Paraguay, the Philippines, and Tunisia.

population over the period 1961–81, an age-specific pattern of participation rates as reflected in the United Nations study, and a rate of urbanization consistent with recent past trends in the Philippines, the average female participation rate would increase by only 1.032 percent over the simulation period. In view of the length of the period, and the fact that females constitute less than a quarter of the entire urban labor force, the impact of urbanization on the total growth of the labor force in the urban sector is extremely small. Thus, the impact of urbanization on the differential growth rates of the labor force in the rural and urban areas, through the differential sex-specific participation rates, will not materially affect our choice of n_1 and n_2.

B.2. SUMMARY STATEMENT OF PARAMETER VALUES AND INITIAL CONDITIONS

B.2.1. Parameter Values

Production
functions:
$$A_1 = 0.640$$
$$A_2 = 0.350$$
$$\sigma_1 = 0.500$$
$$\sigma_2 = 1.500$$

Technical change:
$$\lambda_K = 0.003$$
$$\lambda_L = 0.010$$

Labor supply:
$$n_1 = 0.020$$
$$n_2 = 0.030$$

Capital
depreciation:
$$\delta = 0.050$$

Laborers'
commodity demand:
$$\beta_{11} = 0.800$$
$$\beta_{12} = 0.500$$
$$\beta_{21} = 0.200$$
$$\beta_{22} = 0.500$$
$$\gamma = 0.648$$

Capitalists' $s = 0.312$
commodity demand: $\beta_{11} = \Pi_1 = 0.800$
$\beta_{21} = \Pi_2 = 0.200$
$\Phi = 0.200$

The procedure adopted to obtain a set of parameter values necessarily required rather arbitrary choices of initial values for some key variables endogenous to the system. One consequence was that, once the complete set of parameters was obtained, the initial values of the endogenous variables did not then represent an equilibrium solution to the static model. By retaining our assumptions about the values of $u(0) = 0.30$, $v(0) = 0.43$, and $s^*(0) = 0.15$, we were able to obtain an equilibrium solution for the above set of parameters.

The resulting initial conditions are given below.

B.2.2. Initial Conditions

Factor efficiency
units: $x(0) = y(0) = 1.000$

Factor stocks: $K(0) \ \ = \ \ 30.174$
$K_1(0) = \ \ 17.135$
$K_2(0) = \ \ 13.039$
$L(0) \ \ = 100.000$
$L_1(0) = \ \ 30.008$
$L_2(0) = \ \ 69.992$

Terms of trade: $P(0) \ \ = \ \ 10.215$

Output: $Q_1(0) = \ \ \ 6.979$
$Q_2(0) = \ \ 94.990$

B.2.3. Initial Conditions on Key Statistics

Urbanization level: $u(0) \ \ = 0.300$

Industrialization
level: $v(0) \ \ = 0.429$

Gross savings
rate: $\qquad s^*(0) = 0.150$

Factor shares: $\qquad \alpha_1(0) = 0.636$
$\alpha_2(0) = 0.364$
$\alpha(0) = 0.481$

Capital-labor
ratios: $\qquad k_1(0) = \hat{k}_1(0) = 0.571$
$k_2(0) = \hat{k}_2(0) = 0.186$
$k(0) = \hat{k}(0) = 0.302$

Capital-output
ratios: $\qquad K_1(0)/Q_1(0) = 2.455$
$P(0)K_2(0)/Q_2(0) = 1.402$
$P(0)K(0)/P(0)Q_1(0)+Q_2(0) = 1.854$

Economy-wide
population growth: $\quad n(0) = 0.027$

Sectoral labor
productivity
differential: $\qquad \left\{\dfrac{P(0)Q_1(0)}{L_1(0)}\right\}\left\{\dfrac{Q_2(0)}{L_2(0)}\right\}^{-1} = 1.751$

Appendix C

Simulation Results of the Equilibrium Model

	Factor Stocks			Output			
				Per Capita Income			
	Capital	Labor		Urban Work-	Rural Work-	Urban Capi-	Rural Capi-
Period	$K(t)$	$L(t)$	GNP	ers	ers	talists	talists
1..	30.173	100.00	166.31	0.864	0.864	7.562	2.467
2..	30.894	102.70	171.92	0.869	0.869	7.652	2.467
3..	31.650	105.47	177.75	0.874	0.874	7.740	2.468
4..	32.442	108.32	183.83	0.880	0.880	7.829	2.470
5..	33.273	111.24	190.15	0.885	0.885	7.919	2.473
10..	38.066	127.06	225.93	0.916	0.916	8.375	2.502
20..	51.670	165.60	323.38	0.990	0.990	9.333	2.627
30..	72.998	215.40	469.40	1.085	1.085	10.354	2.824
40..	106.340	279.44	687.67	1.202	1.202	11.417	3.164
50..	158.290	361.43	1012.80	1.345	1.345	12.539	3.606

		Prices			
		Efficiency Factor Prices			
		Wages		Rents	
Period	Terms of Trade	Indus-trial	Agri-cultural	Indus-trial	Agri-cultural
1....	10.215	0.864	0.864	2.649	2.649
2....	10.248	.860	.860	2.668	2.668
3....	10.279	.857	.857	2.687	2.687
4....	10.310	.854	.854	2.705	2.705
5....	10.339	.851	.851	2.723	2.723
10....	10.474	.837	.837	2.803	2.803
20....	10.663	.820	.820	2.914	2.914
30....	10.774	.813	.813	2.960	2.960
40....	10.714	.815	.815	2.944	2.944
50....	10.594	0.826	0.826	2.874	2.874

Ratios

Period	Urban-ization	Industrial Output Share	Investment Share		
			Gross	Net	Replace-ment
1....	0.300	0.429	0.150	0.0632	0.0927
2....	.301	.431	.150	.0639	.0921
3....	.301	.433	.150	.0646	.0915
4....	.302	.435	.150	.0653	.0910
5....	.303	.437	.151	.0660	.0905
10....	.308	.449	.151	.0693	.0882
20....	.326	.477	.154	.0751	.0852
30....	.350	.507	.157	.0799	.0835
40....	.379	.537	.160	.0838	.0828
50....	0.412	0.567	0.162	0.0868	0.0828

Ratios

Period	Efficiency Capital/Labor Ratio			Unaugmented Capital/Output Ratio		
	Indus-trial	Agri-cultural	Total	Indus-trial	Agri-cultural	Total
1..	0.571	0.186	0.302	2.455	1.402	1.853
2..	.572	.184	.301	2.443	1.387	1.842
3..	.573	.183	.300	2.430	1.372	1.830
4..	.574	.181	.300	2.418	1.358	1.820
5..	.575	.179	.299	2.407	1.345	1.809
10..	.582	.174	.300	2.352	1.286	1.765
20..	.605	.170	.312	2.259	1.198	1.704
30..	.641	.176	.339	2.183	1.144	1.671
40..	.690	.191	.381	2.122	1.117	1.657
50..	0.754	0.217	0.438	2.072	1.111	1.656

Ratios

Period	Labor's Share			Budget Shares (Laborers)		
	Indus-trial	Agri-cultural	Total	Indus-trial	Agri-cultural	Total
1..	0.364	0.636	0.519	0.200	0.125	0.147
2..	.362	.638	.519	.204	.127	.150
3..	.361	.639	.519	.207	.129	.153
4..	.360	.640	.518	.211	.132	.156
5..	.359	.642	.518	.214	.134	.158
10..	.353	.647	.515	.234	.146	.173
20..	.347	.653	.507	.277	.173	.206
30..	.344	.656	.498	.322	.202	.244
40..	.345	.655	.488	.369	.230	.283
50..	0.349	0.651	0.480	0.414	0.259	0.323

			Growth Rates		
				Technical Change	
Period	Urban-ization	Popu-lation	Indus-trial	Agri-cultural	Total
1..	0.00151	0.0000	0.00554	0.00746	0.00664
2..	.00207	.0270	.00554	.00746	.00663
3..	.00241	.0270	.00553	.00747	.00663
4..	.00275	.0270	.00552	.00748	.00663
5..	.00307	.0270	.00551	.00749	.00662
10..	.00423	.0269	.00547	.00753	.00660
20..	.00643	.0268	.00543	.00757	.00655
30..	.00770	.0265	.00541	.00759	.00649
40..	.00828	.0262	.00541	.00759	.00642
50..	0.00831	0.0259	0.00544	0.00756	0.00636

			Growth Rates		
	Unaugmented Capital Stock			Output (Valued)	
Period	Indus-trial	Agri-cultural	Total	Indus-trial	Agri-cultural	Total
1..	.0000	0.0000	0.0000	0.0000	0.0000	0.0000
2..	.0301	.0158	.0239	.0352	.0301	.0337
3..	.0306	.0163	.0244	.0357	.0302	.0339
4..	.0312	.0168	.0250	.0362	.0303	.0342
5..	.0317	.0172	.0256	.0367	.0303	.0344
10..	.0342	.0196	.0283	.0388	.0308	.0355
20..	.0383	.0242	.0331	.0422	.0315	.0373
30..	.0412	.0281	.0368	.0445	.0321	.0385
40..	.0431	.0317	.0395	.0458	.0325	.0392
50..	0.0441	0.0346	0.0413	0.0464	0.0328	0.0396

	Growth Rates		Sectoral Flows	
Period	GNP Per Capita	Industrial-ization	Labor Migration Rate	Marketed Agricultural Surplus
1..	0.00000	0.00000	0.00000	20.738
2..	.00655	.00465	.00367	21.357
3..	.00675	.00483	.00392	22.012
4..	.00699	.00497	.00408	22.697
5..	.00723	.00510	.00424	23.412
10..	.00836	.00564	.00499	27.509
20..	.01020	.00612	.00640	38.716
30..	.01160	.00607	.00768	55.395
40..	.01270	.00564	.00888	80.467
50..	0.01340	0.00506	0.00998	117.400

	Sectoral Flows	
	---	---
Period	Share of Agricultural Surplus Marketed	Labor Absorption Rate in Industry
1......	0.218	0.0000
2......	.218	.0286
3......	.218	.0291
4......	.219	.0295
5......	.219	.0298
10.....	.221	.0313
20.....	.229	.0334
30.....	.239	.0344
40.....	.253	.0347
50.....	0.267	0.0344

Appendix D

A Restatement of the Static Model

The static model is completely described by the following system of 27 equations and 26 endogenous variables: Q_i, w_i, r_i, P, Y_i, D_{ij}^e, D_{ij}^k, S_j, I_i, I_{ij}, θ, and by 12 exogenous variables: K_i, L_i, x, y, K_{ij}, i_{12}, i_{21}. (See chapter 7 for a full discussion of the model and for the original statements of the equations.)

Production

$$Q_i = F^i[xK_i, yL_i] \tag{7.25}$$

Factor Prices

$$w_1 = PF_2^1 \tag{7.32a}$$

$$w_2 = F_2^2 \tag{7.32b}$$

$$r_1 = PF_1^1 \tag{7.33a}$$

$$r_2 = F_1^2 \tag{7.33b}$$

Capitalists' Income

$$Y_1 = x(r_1 K_{11} + r_2 K_{21} + \tau K_{12}) \tag{7.3}$$

$$Y_2 = x[r_2 K_{22} + (r_1 - \tau) K_{12}] \tag{7.4}$$

Consumption Demand

$$D_{1j}^l = \frac{\beta_{1j}}{P} (y w_j - \gamma) L_j \tag{7.28}$$

$$D_{2j}^l = [\beta_{2j} y w_j + (1 - \beta_{2j}) \gamma] L_j \tag{7.29}$$

$$D_{1j}^k = \frac{\pi_{1j}}{P} [(1 - s_j) Y_j - \gamma \phi_j L_j] \tag{7.26}$$

356

$$D_{2j}{}^k = \pi_{2j}(1 - s_j)Y_j + (1 - \pi_{2j})\gamma\phi_j L_j \tag{7.27}$$

Investment Demand

$$S_j = s_j Y_j \tag{7.5}$$

$$S_j = P(I_{1j} + I_{2j}) \tag{7.6}$$

$$I_i = I_{i1} + I_{i2} \tag{7.34}$$

$$i_{12} = \frac{I_{12}P}{S_2} \tag{7.7a}$$

$$i_{21} = \frac{I_{21}P}{S_1} \tag{7.7b}$$

Market Clearance Conditions

$$Q_1 = \sum_{j=1}^{2} (D_{1j}{}^l + D_{1j}{}^k + I_j) \tag{7.30}$$

$$Q_2 = \sum_{j=1}^{2} (D_{2j}{}^l + D_{2j}{}^k) \tag{7.31}$$

Migration Costs

$$\theta = ayw_2 - c \tag{7.18}$$

In addition, the following identities hold among the exogenous variables:

$$K = K_1 + K_2 \tag{7.36}$$

$$K_i = K_{i1} + K_{i2} \tag{7.1}$$

$$L = L_1 + L_2 \tag{7.37}$$

Appendix E

Nature of Short-run Adjustment in Factor and Commodity Markets

Given Walras's law, we need to consider the adjustment mechanism in only one of the two commodity markets, say for agricultural output, in exploring the question of stability. The excess demand for agricultural goods is given by

$$E_A = \phi_1 u z_{21}{}^k + \phi_2(1 - u)z_{22}{}^k + uk_{21}{}^l +$$
$$(1 - u)z_{22}{}^l - y(1 - u)f_2(k_2) = E_A[P].$$

If we assume that the excess demand for agricultural goods causes the terms of trade to fall,

$$\dot{P} = g_A[E_A] \text{ where } g'_A < 0.$$

Expanding about $[P = P^0]$ yields

$$\dot{P} = g'_A \frac{\partial E_A}{\partial P} [P - P^0].$$

Necessary and sufficient conditions for stability are given by $g'_A(\partial E_A/\partial P) < 0$. Since $g'_A < 0$ and $\partial E_A/\partial P > 0$ stability is assured. In contrast to the short-run stability analysis of chapter 3, this result was obtained *without* the previous restriction that $(k_1 - k_2) > 0$ *or* $\sigma_2 \geqq 1$.

Appendix F

A Restatement of the Dynamic Model

For the case in which $w^*(t) > \theta(t)$ and $r^*(t) > \tau$, the dynamic model can be restated as a system of sixteen differential equations involving $x(t)$, $y(t)$, $K_i(t)$, $L_i(t)$, $L(t)$, $K_{ij}(t)$, $u(t)$, $m_2(t)$, $i_{12}(t)$, $w_2(t)$ and $\theta(t)$, as well as $I_i(t)$, $I_{ij}(t)$, $w(t)$, $r(t)$ and $\alpha_2(t)$ from the static model.

$$\frac{\dot{K}_i(t)}{K_i(t)} = \frac{I_i(t)}{K_i(t)} - \delta$$

$$\frac{\dot{K}_{ij}(t)}{K_{ij}(t)} = \frac{I_{ij}(t)}{K_{ij}(t)} - \delta$$

$$\frac{\dot{L}_1(t)}{L_1(t)} = n_1 + \frac{m_2(t)}{u(t)}[1 - u(t)]$$

$$\frac{\dot{L}_2(t)}{L_2(t)} = n_2 - m_2(t)$$

$$\frac{\dot{L}(t)}{L(t)} = n_1 u(t) + n_2[1 - u(t)]$$

$$\frac{\dot{u}(t)}{u(t)} = [n_1 - n_2]u(t) + m_2(t)\frac{[1 - u(t)]}{u(t)}$$

$$\frac{\dot{x}(t)}{x(t)} = \lambda_K$$

$$\frac{\dot{y}(t)}{y(t)} = \lambda_L$$

$$\dot{m}_2(t) = \rho[1 - m_2(t)]\{ b[y(t)w(t) - \theta(t) + \rho^{-1} \log$$
$$[1 - m_2(t)]] - \dot{\theta}(t) \}$$

$$\dot{\theta}(t) = ay(t)w_2(t) \left\{ \lambda_L + \frac{\dot{w}_2(t)}{w_2(t)} \right\}$$

$$\dot{i}_{12}(t) = \mu\epsilon[1 - i_{12}(t)]\{r(t) - \tau + \mu^{-1} \log [1 - i_{12}(t)]\}$$

$$\frac{\dot{w}_2(t)}{w_2(t)} = \frac{\alpha_2(t)}{\sigma_2} \left\{ \lambda_K - \lambda_L + \frac{\dot{K}_1(t)}{K_1(t)} - \frac{\dot{L}_1(t)}{L_1(t)} \right\}$$

Appendix G

Initial Conditions and Parameter Values for the Disequilibrium Model

G.1. INITIAL CONDITIONS

Because of our interest in comparing the trajectories of the two models, a primary consideration in the choice of initial conditions for the disequilibrium model was the need for comparability with those used in the equilibrium model. An exact replication of the initial conditions was impossible because, for any given set of exogenous variables and parameter values, the solution to the disequilibrium model differs from that for the equilibrium model. As a result, observed differences in the variable trajectories of the two economies may be attributed to differences either in initial conditions or in model specifications. Moreover, the importance of one potential source of different growth performance relative to the other could not be ascertained.

After some experimentation we found that the most practical approach was to use the initial conditions from the equilibrium model as a starting point. The barriers to rural-urban factor migration are such that for several periods no intersectoral factor flows take place until factor price differentials are large enough to overcome the initial barriers to movement. Given the wide variation in factor prices, once factor adjustment is initiated an overcompensation in intersectoral factor movements occurs such that initial growth is characterized by cyclical behavior in migration, prices, and key indexes of economic activity. From theory alone we cannot predict whether the cycles will be damped, self-sustaining, or explosive. On the other hand, given the empirical values of the behavioral adjustment lags characteristic of the functions of both the capital and the labor migration, stability is ensured, and within a short period of time a smooth growth path is obtained. By period 12, cyclical behavior is terminated in the simulated values of all key series. Clearly the initial simulation periods of the disequilibrium system do not reflect "typical" long-run growth but rather "artificial" short-run adjustments to a somewhat arbitrary set of initial conditions. A comparison of the two models during this period is meaningless. A relevant comparison can be made only when both economies are on a stable growth path. Thus, we chose the simulation values from period 12 as the "initial" conditions for the disequilibrium model, and it is these values that are discussed, in chapter 8, as initial conditions for period 0.

The following is a comparison of initial values for key variables for the disequilibrium (i.e., output from period 12, renamed period 0 in chap. 8, in the experimental simulation) and equilibrium models. For convenience the time subscript has been omitted. A comparison of key ratio variables is given in table 8.1, while table G.1 reports the absolute values of some key variables.

TABLE G.1 Values of key variables in the simulation ($t = 0$)

Variable	E	D
Factor efficiency unit		
x	1.000	1.037
y	1.000	1.127
Factor stock		
K	30.174	43.920
K_1	17.135	26.660
K_2	13.039	17.260
L	100.000	137.560
L_1	30.008	43.910
L_2	69.992	93.650
Terms of trade		
P	10.215	10.892
Output		
Q_1	6.979	11.340
Q_2	94.990	138.490
PQ_1	71.290	123.600

G.2. PARAMETER VALUES

For those parameters common to both models, identical numerical values were used in the simulation. Our choice of values for the new parameters in the labor and capital market is discussed below.

G.2.1. Labor Market

Consider, first, plausible values for the parameter for speed of response, $b = 1/T$, which measures the rate at which potential migrants adjust their expected wage differentials to changes in the actual wage differentials. Since we are not aware of any empirical studies that would give a guide to the speed of response of potential migrants, the choice of T must, of necessity, be somewhat arbitrary. In keeping with the objective of selecting initial conditions and parameter values that portray a low-income economy with substantial constraints on factor mobility, we have chosen $T = 3$ so that $b = 0.333$.

In considering suitable parameter values from the migration cost function

$$\theta(t) = ay(t)w_2(t) - c,$$

we were guided by the observation that, in countries such as the Philippines, transportation costs are relatively small and the major determinant of $\theta(t)$ is the loss of farm income during the migration process itself. If we assume a period of three to four months for employment search in the urban labor market, the initial value for $\theta(t)$ may be taken to be 25–33 percent of the actual agricultural wage. Thus, relative to the initial wage levels used for simulation we have specified

$$\theta(t) = 0.250y(t)w_2(t) - 0.216.$$

The value of ρ was then selected such that, for an expected wage differential approximately 10 percent above the equilibrium wage differential, 0.5 percent of the rural labor force would migrate to the urban sector. From postwar Philippine experience, this seemed to be a realistic response pattern. After testing the sensitivity of the migration function around this point, we selected $\rho = 0.2$.

G.2.2. Capital Market

Given the almost complete lack of financial flow and portfolio data for Asian economies, it is not possible to verify parameter estimates for our intersectoral savings allocation rules. Since there is some quantitative evidence to suggest that firm units adjust rather rapidly to changes in factor prices,[1] we have set

$$b < 1 - \epsilon = 0.666.$$

Although there is little or no evidence as yet on differentials of the rental rate (or rate of return) for the Philippines or other Asian nations, there are scattered observations on $i_{ij}(t)$. We have attempted to select parameter values that yield initial conditions on $i_{ij}(t)$ consistent with the ECAFE data discussed earlier. According to these data and the work of Bauer,[2] as much as 80 percent of agricultural savings is retained within the sector. After some testing of the sensitivity of the expression for $i_{ij}(t)$, we chose values of $\tau = 0.05$ and $\mu = 2.50$.

1. J. G. Williamson, "Relative Price Changes."
2. The ECAFE data is taken from ECAFE, "Measures for Mobilizing Domestic Savings for Productive Investment," pp. 1–26; see also E. Bauer, *Proceedings of the International Conference on Agricultural and Cooperative Credit.*

Appendix H

Simulation Results of the Disequilibrium Model

	Factor Stocks			
			Efficiency	
Period	Capital $(K(t))$	Labor $(L(t))$	Capital $(x(t)K(t))$	Labor $(y(t)L(t))$
1..	43.925	137.560	45.533	155.000
10..	59.914	174.400	63.804	214.930
20..	86.580	226.510	95.005	308.360
30..	127.430	293.420	144.080	441.230
40..	189.870	379.010	221.200	629.560
50..	284.840	488.100	341.950	895.590

	Output			
	Per Capita Income			
Period	GNP	Urban Workers	Rural Workers	Urban Capitalists	Rural Capitalists
1..	262.09	1.008	0.952	9.031	2.635
10..	368.97	1.115	1.032	10.038	2.827
20..	543.27	1.254	1.140	11.225	3.119
30..	803.79	1.420	1.270	12.495	3.512
40..	1,191.70	1.617	1.424	13.854	4.020
50..	1,766.30	1.849	1.606	15.311	4.667

NOTE: As indicated in chapter 8, period 1, the first entry of each of the tables in Appendix H, corresponds to the twelfth period of simulation from the initial conditions employed in the equilibrium model. The variables are grouped into six categories: factor stocks, output, prices, ratios, growth rates, and sectoral flows.

| | Prices | | | | |
| | Sectoral Price Differentials | | | Efficiency Wages | |
Period	Terms of Trade	$w_1 - w_2$	$r_1 - r_2$	Indus-trial	Agri-cultural
1..	10.892	0.0503	0.113	0.895	0.844
10..	11.088	.0663	.137	0.904	0.838
20..	11.205	.0835	.153	0.921	0.838
30..	11.238	.1002	.164	0.945	0.844
40..	11.199	.1165	.171	0.973	0.857
50..	11.108	0.1325	0.174	1.008	0.875

| | Prices | | | |
| | Efficiency Rents | | Sectoral Ratios | |
Period	Industrial	Agricultural	w_1/w_2	r_1/r_2
1..	2.87	2.76	1.060	1.041
10..	2.93	2.80	1.079	1.049
20..	2.95	2.80	1.100	1.055
30..	2.92	2.76	1.119	1.060
40..	2.86	2.69	1.136	1.064
50..	2.76	2.59	1.152	1.067

| | Ratios | | | | |
| | | Industrial | Investment Share | | |
Period	Urban-ization	Output Share	Gross	Net	Replace-ment
1..	0.319	0.472	0.153	0.0682	0.0913
10..	.339	.501	.155	.0721	.0900
20..	.365	.533	.158	.0758	.0893
30..	.394	.563	.161	.0786	.0890
40..	.424	.592	.163	.0806	.0892
50..	0.455	0.617	0.164	0.0818	0.0895

	Ratios					
	Efficiency Capital/ Labor Ratios			Unaugmented Capital/ Output Ratios		
Period	Indus-trial	Agri-cultural	Total	Indus-trial	Agri-cultural	Total
1..	0.607	0.184	0.319	2.349	1.358	1.826
10..	0.642	.190	0.344	2.282	1.317	1.801
20..	0.693	.203	0.382	2.219	1.290	1.786
30..	0.756	.225	0.434	2.167	1.283	1.782
40..	0.832	.257	0.501	2.124	1.292	1.784
50..	0.922	0.300	0.584	2.087	1.313	1.791

	Ratios					
	Labor's Share			Nonfood Budget Shares (Laborers)		
Period	Indus-trial	Agri-cultural	Total	Indus-trial	Agri-cultural	Total
1..	0.358	0.644	0.509	0.286	0.160	0.202
10..	.357	.646	.501	.334	.186	.239
20..	.358	.646	.493	.387	.216	.282
30..	.362	.644	.485	.435	.245	.324
40..	.369	.639	.479	.479	.272	.367
50..	0.376	0.632	0.474	0.516	0.296	0.402

	Growth Rates				
			Technical Change		
Period	Urban-ization	Popu-lation	Indus-trial	Agri-cultural	Total
1..	0.00639	0.0268	0.00551	0.00751	0.00656
10..	.00708	.0266	.00550	.00752	.00651
20..	.00752	.0264	.00551	.00752	.00645
30..	.00753	.0261	.00554	.00751	.00640
40..	.00727	.0258	.00558	.00747	.00635
50..	0.00683	0.0254	0.00563	0.00742	0.00632

Growth Rates

Period	Unaugmented Capital Stock			Output (Valued)		
	Indus-trial	Agri-cultural	Total	Indus-trial	Agri-cultural	Total
1..	0.0398	0.0242	0.0336	0.0432	0.0316	0.0374
10..	.0411	.0277	.0362	.0442	.0323	.0391
20..	.0425	.0306	.0384	.0452	.0327	.0397
30..	.0433	.0331	.0400	.0456	.0330	.0401
40..	.0436	.0351	.0411	.0455	.0333	.0402
50..	0.0435	0.0366	0.0416	0.0452	0.0334	0.0401

Period	Growth Rates		Sectoral Flows	
	GNP Per Capita	Industrial-ization	Labor Migration Rate	Marketed Agricultural Surplus
1..	0.0103	0.00637	0.00620	46.529
10..	.0122	.00659	.00707	65.079
20..	.0130	.00596	.00802	95.183
30..	.0136	.00529	.00887	139.810
40..	.0140	.00460	.00964	205.570
50..	0.0142	0.00395	0.01030	301.850

Sectoral Flows

Period	Share of Agricultural Surplus Marketed	Labor Absorption Rate in Industry	Share Rural Savings Allocated to Industry
1..	0.336	0.0333	0.151
10..	.353	.0339	.188
20..	.375	.0341	.222
30..	.398	.0339	.245
40..	.423	.0332	.260
50..	0.446	0.0324	0.266

Bibliography

Abramovitz, M. A. "Resource and Output Trends in the United States since 1870." *American Economic Review* 46 (May 1956):5–23.

Ahmed, S. "On the Theory of Induced Invention." *Economic Journal* 76 (June 1966):344–57.

Amano, A. "Neoclassical Biased Technological Progress and a Neoclassical Theory of Economic Growth." *Quarterly Journal of Economics* 70 (February 1964):129–38.

Arrow, K. J.; Chenery, H. B.; Minhas, B. S.; and Solow, R. M. "Capital Labour Substitution and Economic Efficiency." *Review of Economics and Statistics* 43 (1961):225–50.

Arrow, K. J., and Hurwicz, L. "On the Stability of Competitive Equilibrium, I." *Econometrica* 26 (October 1958): 522–52.

Baba, B., and Tatemoto, M. "Foreign Trade and Economic Growth in Japan: 1858–1937." In *Economic Growth: The Japanese Experience since the Meiji Era,* edited by L. Klein and K. Ohkawa. Homewood, Ill.: Richard D. Irwin, 1960.

Baer, W., and Hervé, M. "Employment and Industrialization in Developing Countries." *Quarterly Journal of Economics* 82 (July 1968):88–107.

Baldwin, R. E. *Economic Development and Export Growth: A Study of Northern Rhodesia, 1920–1960.* Berkeley and Los Angeles: University of California Press, 1966.

Barten, A. "Consumer Demand Functions under Conditions of Almost Additive Preferences." *Econometrica* 32 (January 1964):1–38.

Bauer, E., ed. *Proceedings of the International Conference on Agricultural and Cooperative Credit.* Berkeley and Los Angeles: University of California Press, 1952.

Bean, L. H.   *International Industrialization and Per Capita Income.* Studies in Income and Wealth, vol. 8. New York: National Bureau of Economic Research, 1946.

Boeke, J. H.   *Economics and Economic Policy of Dual Societies.* New York: International Secretariat, Institute of Pacific Relations, 1953.

Borts, G. H.   "The Equalization of Returns and Regional Economic Growth." *American Economic Review* 50 (June 1960):319–47.

Borts, G. H., and Stein, J. L.   *Economic Growth in a Free Market.* New York: Columbia University Press, 1964.

Bowles, S.   "Sources of Growth in the Greek Economy, 1951–61." Memorandum No. 27, Project for Quantitative Research in Economic Development. Mimeographed. Cambridge, Mass.: Harvard University, 1966.

Brown, M.   *On the Theory and Measurement of Technical Change.* Cambridge: Cambridge University Press, 1966.

Bruton, H. J.   *Principles of Development Economics.* Englewood Cliffs, N.J.: Prentice-Hall, 1965.

————.   "Productivity Growth in Latin America." *American Economic Review* 57 (December 1967):1099–1163.

Budd, E. C.   "Factor Shares, 1850–1910." In *Trends in the American Economy in the Nineteenth Century: Studies in Income and Wealth,* vol. 24. Princeton, N.J.: Princeton University Press, 1960.

Cameron, R.   *Banking in the Early Stages of Industrialization: A Study in Comparative Economic History.* New York: Oxford University Press, 1967.

Cheetham, R. J.   "Growth and Structural Change in a Two-Sector Economy." Ph.D. dissertation, University of Wisconsin, 1970.

Chenery, H. B.   "Patterns of Industrial Growth." *American Economic Review* 50 (September 1960):624–54.

————.   "The Use of Interindustry Analysis in Development Programming." *In Structural Interdependence and Economic Development,* edited by T. Barna. New York: Macmillan Co., 1963.

Chenery, H. B.; Shishido, S.; and Watanabe, T.   "The Patterns of Japanese Growth, 1914–1954." *Econometrica* 30 (January 1962):98–138.

Chenery, H. B., and Strout, A. M.   "Foreign Assistance and Economic Development." *American Economic Review* 56 (September 1966):679–733.

Chenery, H. B., and Taylor, L. J. "Development Patterns: Among Countries and over Time." *Review of Economics and Statistics* 50 (November 1968):391–416.

Chetty, V. K. "International Comparison of Production Functions in Manufacturing." Mimeographed. New York: National Bureau of Economic Research, August 1969.

Christ, C. F. *Econometric Models and Methods.* New York: Wiley, 1966.

Christensen, L. R. "Savings and the Rate of Return." SFM 6706, Social Systems Research Institute. Mimeographed. Madison, Wis.: University of Wisconsin, 1968.

Clark, C. *Conditions of Economic Progress.* 3rd ed. New York: Macmillan Co., 1957.

———. Review of *Agricultural Production and the Economic Development of Japan, 1873–1922,* by James I. Nakamura. *Journal of Agricultural Economics* 18 (January 1967):428–30.

Coale, A. J., and Hoover, E. M. *Population Growth and Economic Development in Low-income Countries.* Princeton, N.J.: Princeton University Press, 1958.

Conlisk, J. "Unemployment in a Neoclassical Growth Model: The Effect on Speed of Adjustment." *Economic Journal* 76 (September 1966):550–66.

———. "A Neoclassical Growth Model with an Endogenously Positioned Technical Change Frontier." *Economic Journal* 78 (June 1968):348–62.

———. "Non-constant Returns to Scale in a Neoclassical Growth Model." *International Economic Review* 9 (October 1968):369–73.

Crawcour, E. S. "The Tokagawa Heritage." In *The State and Economic Enterprise in Japan,* edited by W. W. Lockwood. Princeton, N.J.: Princeton University Press, 1965.

Cullen, D. E. "The Inter-industry Wage Structure: 1899–1950." *American Economic Review* 46 (June 1956): 353–69.

David, P. A. "The Growth of Real Product in the United States before 1840: New Evidence, Controlled Conjectures." *Journal of Economic History* 27 (June 1967): 151–97.

Denison, E. F. *The Sources of Economic Growth in the United States.* New York: Committee for Economic Development, 1962.

372 *Bibliography*

Deuster, P. "The Effects of Indonesian Inflation in Rural Areas: Case Study of the Jogjakarta Region." Ph.D. dissertation, University of Wisconsin, 1971.

DeVoretz, D. J. "A Programming Approach to Migration in a Less Developed Economy." Mimeographed. Nigeria: University of Ibadan, October 1969.

Diamond, P. A., and McFadden, D. "Identification of the Elasticity of Substitution and the Bias of Technical Change: An Impossibility Theorem." Working Paper no. 62. Mimeographed. Berkeley: University of California, March 1965.

Dixit, A. "Growth Patterns in a Dual Economy." Technical Report no. 25, Project for the Explanation and Optimization of Economic Growth. Mimeographed. Berkeley: University of California, 1968.

————. "Theories of the Dual Economy: A Survey." Mimeographed. Berkeley: University of California, 1969.

Dobb, M. *Economic Growth and Planning.* New York: Monthly Review Press, 1960.

Drandakis, E. M. "Factor Substitution in the Two Sector Growth Model." *Review of Economic Studies* 30 (October 1963):217–28.

Drandakis, E. M., and Phelps, E. S. "A Model of Induced Invention, Growth, and Distribution. *Economic Journal* 76 (December 1966):832–40.

Dusenberry, J. S. *Business Cycles and Economic Growth.* New York: McGraw-Hill Co., 1958.

Eckaus, R. S. "The Factor Proportions Problem in Underdeveloped Areas." *American Economic Review* 45 (September 1955):539–65.

Economic Commission for Asia and the Far East. "Measures for Mobilizing Domestic Savings for Productive Investment." *Economic Bulletin for Asia and the Far East* 13, no. 3 (December 1962):1–26.

Encarnación, J. "Two-Sector Models of Economic Growth and Development." *Philippine Economic Journal* 4 (1965): 533–65.

Fei, J. C., and Ranis, G. "A Theory of Economic Development." *American Economic Review* 51 (September 1961): 533–65.

————. "Innovation, Capital Accumulation, and Economic Development." *American Economic Review* 53 (June 1963):283–313.

————. *Development of the Labor Surplus Economy: Theory and Policy.* Homewood, Ill.: Richard D. Irwin, 1964.

————. "Agrarianism, Dualism, and Economic Development." In *The Theory and Design of Economic Development,* edited by I. Adelman and E. Thorbecke. Baltimore: Johns Hopkins Press, 1966.

Ferguson, C. E., and Moroney, J. R. "The Sources of Change in Labor's Relative Share: A Neoclassical Analysis." *Southern Economic Journal* 35 (April 1969):308–22.

Furnivall, J. S. *Colonial Policy and Practice.* Cambridge: Cambridge University Press, 1948.

Galbis, V. "Dualism and Labor Migration in the Process of Economic Growth: A Theoretical Approach." EDIE 7011, Social Systems Research Institute. Mimeographed. Madison, Wis.: University of Wisconsin, February, 1970.

Galenson, W., and Leibenstein, H. "Investment Criteria and Economic Development." *Quarterly Journal of Economics* 69 (August 1955):343–70.

Geary, R. C. "A Note on a Constant-Utility Index of the Cost of Living." *Review of Economic Studies* 18 (1950–51): 65–66.

Goldberger, A. S. "Functional Form and Utility: A Review of Consumer Demand and Theory." SFM 6703, Social Systems Research Institute. Mimeographed. Madison, Wis.: University of Wisconsin, November 1967.

Goldberger, A. S., and Gamaletsos, T. "A Cross Country Comparison of Consumer Expenditure Patterns." SFM 6706, Social Systems Research Institute. Mimeographed. Madison, Wis.: University of Wisconsin, November 1967.

Gordon, R. A. "Differential Changes in the Prices of Consumers' and Capital Goods." *American Economic Review* 51 (December 1961):937–57.

Griliches, Z. "Research Expenditures, Education, and the Aggregate Agricultural Production Function." *American Economic Review* 54 (December 1964):961–75.

Gurley, J. G., and Shaw, E. S. "Financial Aspects of Economic Development." *American Economic Review* 45 (September 1955):515–38.

————. "Financial Intermediaries and the Saving-Investment Process." *Journal of Finance* 2 (March 1956):257–76.

————. *Money in a Theory of Finance.* Baltimore: Lord Baltimore Press, 1960.

Habakkuk, H. J. *American and British Technology in the Nineteenth Century*. Cambridge: Cambridge University Press, 1962.

Hahn, F. H. "The Share of Wages in the National Income." *Oxford Economic Papers* 3 (June 1951):147–57.

Hahn, F. H., and Matthews, R. C. O. "The Theory of Economic Growth: A Survey." *Economic Journal* 74 (December 1964):781–902.

Hanna, F. A. *State Income Differentials, 1919–1954*. Durham, N.C.: Duke University Press, 1959.

Haley, B. F. "Changes in the Distribution of Income in the United States." In *The Distribution of National Income*, edited by J. Marchal and B. Ducros. New York: St. Martin's Press, 1968.

Hansen, B. "The Distributive Shares in the Egyptian Agriculture, 1897–1961." *International Economic Review* 9 (June 1968):175–94.

———. "Employment and Wages in Rural Egypt." *American Economic Review* 59 (June 1969):298–313.

Harberger, A. C., and Selowsky, M. "Key Factors in the Economic Growth of Chile: An Analysis of the Sources of Past Growth and of Prospects for 1965–1970." Paper presented at the Next Decade of Latin American Economic Development, 20–22 April 1966, at Cornell University.

Harris, J. R., and Todaro, M. P. "Migration, Unemployment, and Development: A Two-Sector Analysis." *American Economic Review* 60 (March 1970):126–42.

Harrod, R. F. *Towards a Dynamic Economics*. 1948. Reprint ed., London: Macmillan & Co., 1956.

Hartwell, R. M. "The Standard of Living." *Economic History Review* 16, no. 2 (August 1963):135–46.

Hayami, Y. "Demand for Fertilizer in the Course of Japanese Agricultural Development." *Journal of Farm Economics* 46 (November 1964):766–79.

Hayami, Y., and Ruttan, V. "Factor Prices and Technical Change in Agricultural Development: The United States and Japan, 1880–1960." Staff Paper 69-19, Department of Agricultural Economics. Mimeographed. Minneapolis, Minn.: University of Minnesota, July 1969.

———. "Induced Innovation in Agricultural Development: The United States and Japan." Mimeographed. Minneapolis, Minn.: University of Minnesota, Economics Development Center, 28 October 1970.

Hayami, Y., and Yamada, S. "Technological Progress in Agriculture." In *Economic Growth: The Japanese Experience since the Meiji Era,* edited by L. Klein and K. Ohkawa. Homewood, Ill.: Richard D. Irwin, 1968.

————. "Agricultural Productivity at the Beginning of Industrialization." In *Agriculture and Economic Growth: Japan's Experience,* edited by K. Ohkawa, B. F. Johnston, and H. Kaneda. Princeton, N.J.: Princeton University Press, 1970.

Hellemer, J. K. "Agricultural Export Pricing Strategy in Tanzania." *East African Journal of Rural Development* 1 (January 1968):1–18.

Hicks, J. R. *The Theory of Wages.* London: MacMillan & Co., 1932.

————. *A Contribution to the Theory of the Trade Cycle.* Oxford: Oxford University Press, 1950.

————. *Capital and Growth.* New York: Oxford University Press, 1965.

Higgins, B. J. "The 'Dualistic Theory' of Underdeveloped Areas." *Economic Development and Cultural Change* 4 (January 1956):99–115.

————. *Economic Development.* London: Constable, 1959.

Hirschman, A. O. *The Strategy of Economic Development.* New Haven, Conn.: Yale University Press, 1958.

Ho, Y. *Agricultural Development of Taiwan, 1903–1960.* Nashville, Tenn.: Vanderbilt University Press, 1966.

Hobsbawm, E. "The Standard of Living during the Industrial Revolution: A Discussion." *Economic History Review* 16, no. 2 (August 1963):119–34.

Hooley, R. *Saving in the Philippines, 1951–1960.* Quezon City: Institute of Economic Development and Research. Mimeographed. University of the Philippines, 1963.

Houthakker, H. S. "An International Comparison of Household Expenditure Patterns, Commemorating the Centenary of Engel's Law." *Econometrica* 25 (October 1957): 532–51.

————. "The Influence of Prices and Income on Household Expenditures." *Bulletin de L'Institute International de Statistique* 37 (1960):9–22.

————. "The Present State of Consumption Theory." *Econometrica* 29 (October 1961):705–40.

Hymer, S., and Resnick, S. "A Model of an Agrarian Economy with Non-agricultural Activities." *American Economic Review* 59 (September 1969):493–501.

Inada, K. I. "On a Two-Sector Model of Economic Growth: Comments and a Generalization." *Review of Economic Studies* 30 (June 1963):119–27.

————. "Investment in Fixed Capital and the Stability of Growth Equilibrium." *Review of Economic Studies* 33 (January 1966):19–30.

Johansen, L. *A Multi-sectoral Study of Economic Growth.* Amsterdam: North-Holland Publishing Co., 1964.

Johnston, B. F. "Agricultural Productivity and Economic Development in Japan." *Journal of Political Economy* 59 (December 1951):498–513.

Johnston, B. F., and Cownie, J. "The Seed-Fertilizer Revolution and Labor Force Absorption." *American Economic Review* 59 (September 1969):519–82.

Johnston, B. F., and Mellor, J. "The Role of Agriculture in Economic Development." *American Economic Review* 51 (September 1961):566–93.

Johnston, B. F., and Nielson, S. T. "Agricultural and Structural Transformation in a Developing Economy." *Economic Development and Cultural Change* 14 (April 1966):279–301.

Johnston, B. F., and Tolley, G. S. "Strategy for Agriculture in Development." *Journal of Farm Economics* 47 (May 1965):365–83.

Jorgenson, D. W. "The Development of a Dual Economy." *Economic Journal* 71 (June 1961):309–34.

Jorgenson, D. W. "Testing Alternative Theories of the Development of a Dual Economy." In *The Theory and Design of Economic Development,* edited by I. Adelman and E. Thorbecke. Baltimore: Johns Hopkins Press, 1966.

————. "Surplus Agricultural Labor and the Development of a Dual Economy." *Oxford Economic Papers* 19 (November 1967):288–312.

Jorgenson, D. W., and Griliches, Z. "The Explanation of Productivity Change." *Review of Economic Studies* 34 (July 1967):249–84.

Jorgenson, D. W., and Stephenson, J. A. "Investment Behavior in U.S. Manufacturing, 1947–1960." *Econometrica* 35 (April 1967):169–220.

Kaldor, N. "Alternative Theories of Distribution." *Review of Economic Studies* 23 (1955–56):83–100.

————. "Capital Accumulation and Economic Growth." In *The Theory of Capital,* Proceedings of a Conference held by the International Economic Association, ed. Friedrich I. Lutz and Douglas Chalmers Hague. London: Macmillan, 1963.

———. "A Model of Economic Growth." *Economic Journal* 67 (December 1957):591–624.

Kaneda, H. "Long-Term Changes in Food Consumption Patterns in Japan, 1878–1964." *Food Research Institute Studies* 7 (1968).

Kelley, A. C. "Demographic Change and Economic Growth: Australia, 1861–1911." Explorations in Entrepreneurial History 5, no. 3 (Spring–Summer 1968):209–77.

——— "Demand Patterns, Demographic Change, and Economic Growth." *Quarterly Journal of Economics* 83 (February 1969):110–26.

Kelley, A. C., and Williamson, J. G. "Household Saving Behavior in the Developing Economies: The Indonesian Case." *Economic Development and Cultural Change* 16 (April 1968):385–403.

Kenen, P. B. "Nature, Capital, and Trade." *Journal of Political Economy* 73 (October 1965):437–60.

Kennedy, C. "Induced Bias in Innovation and the Theory of Distribution." *Economic Journal* 74 (September 1964): 541–47.

Kotowitz, K. "On the Estimation of a Non-neutral CES Production Function." *Canadian Journal of Economics* 1, no. 2 (May 1968):429–39.

Kuznets, S. "Quantitative Aspects of the Economic Growth of Nations, II: Industrial Distribution of National Product and Labor Force." *Economic Development and Cultural Change* 5 (suppl.) (July 1957).

———. *Six Lectures on Economic Growth*. Glencoe, Ill.: Free Press, 1959.

———. *Modern Economic Growth*. New Haven, Conn.: Yale University Press, 1966.

Lampman, R. J. "The Sources of Post-war Economic Growth in the Philippines." *Philippine Economic Journal* 6, no. 2 (1967):170–88.

Lau, L., and Yotopolous, P. "Micro-functions in a Macro Model: An Application to Agricultural Employment and Development Strategies." Paper read at Conference on Micro Aspects of Development, 19–21 November 1970, at University of Illinois, Chicago Circle.

Lebergott, S. *Manpower in Economic Growth: The American Record since 1800*. New York: McGraw-Hill Co., 1964.

Leibenstein, H. *Economic Backwardness and Economic Growth*. New York: Wiley, 1957.

————. "Technical Progress, the Production Function, and Dualism." *Banca Nazionale Del Lavoro Quarterly* 55 (December 1960):13–15.

Leontief, W. W.   *Essays in Economics: Theories and Theorizing.* New York: Oxford University Press, 1966.

Lewis, W. A.   "Development with Unlimited Supplies of Labour." *Manchester School of Economics and Social Studies* 20 (May 1954):139–92.

————. "Unlimited Labour: Further Notes." *Manchester School of Economics and Social Studies* 26 (1958):1–32.

————. *The Theory of Economic Growth.* London: Allen & Unwin, 1960.

Liu, T. C.   "The Tempo of Economic Development of the China Mainland, 1945–1965." In *An Economic Profile of Mainland China.* Joint Economic Committee, Congress of the United States, February 1967.

Lockwood, W. W. ed.,   *The Economic Development of Japan.* Princeton, N.J.: Princeton University Press, 1954.

Luxemberg, R.   *Social Reform or Revolution.* Tr. Integer. Colombo, Ceylon: Integer, 1969.

Marglin, S.   "Comment." In *The Theory and Design of Economic Development*, edited by I. Adelman and E. Thorbecke. Baltimore: Johns Hopkins Press, 1966.

Massel, B. F.   "A Disaggregated View of Technical Change." *Journal of Political Economy* 69 (December 1961):547–57.

Minami, R.   "Population Migration Away from Agriculture in Japan." *Economic Development and Cultural Change* 16 (January 1967):183–201.

————. "The Turning Point in the Japanese Economy." *Quarterly Journal of Economics* 82 (August 1968):380–402.

Morley, S. A., and Smith, G. W.   "The Effect of Changes in the Distribution of Income on Labor, Foreign Investment, and Growth in Brazil." Mimeographed. Madison, Wis.: University of Wisconsin, 1971.

Nakamura, J. I.   "Growth of Japanese Agriculture, 1875–1920." In *The State and Economic Enterprise in Japan*, edited by W. W. Lockwood. Princeton, N.J.: Princeton University Press, 1965.

————. *Agricultural Production and the Economic Development of Japan, 1873–1922.* Princeton, N.J.: Princeton University Press, 1966.

————. "The Nakamura vs. the LTES Estimates of the Growth Rate of Agricultural Production." *Keizai Kenkyu* 19 (October 1968):358–61.

Nelson, R. R. "A Theory of the Low-level Equilibrium Trap in Underdeveloped Economies." *American Economic Review* 46 (December 1956):894–908.

————. "Aggregate Production Functions and Medium Range Growth Projections." *American Economic Review* 54 (September 1964):575–606.

Nerlove, M. "Recent Empirical Studies of the CES and Related Production Functions." In *The Theory and Empirical Analysis of Production*, edited by M. Brown. New York: National Bureau of Economic Research, 1967.

Nicholls, W. H. "Industrialization, Factor Markets, and Agricultural Development." *Journal of Political Economy* 69 (August 1961):319–40.

————. "An 'Agricultural Surplus' as a Factor in Economic Development." *Journal of Political Economy* 71 (1963): 1–29.

Nichols, D. A. "Land and Economic Growth." *American Economic Review* 60 (June 1970):332–40.

North, D. C. "Location Theory and Regional Economic Growth." *Journal of Political Economy* 63 (June 1955): 243–58.

————. *The Economic Growth of the United States: 1790– 1860.* Englewood Cliffs, N.J.: Prentice-Hall, 1961.

Nourse, H. O. *Regional Economics: A Study in the Economic Structure, Stability, and Growth of Regions.* New York: McGraw-Hill Co., 1968.

Nurkse, R. *The Problems of Capital Formation in Underdeveloped Countries.* Oxford: Oxford University Press, 1957.

Organization for Economic Cooperation and Development. *Wages and Labour Mobility.* Paris, 1966.

Ohkawa, K. Review of *Capital Formation in Japan* by Henry Rosovsky. *Economic Development and Cultural Change* 12 (October 1963):99–103.

————. "Changes in National Income Distribution by Factor Share in Japan." In *The Distribution of National Income*, edited by J. Marchal and B. Ducros. New York: St. Martin's Press, 1968.

Ohkawa, K., and Rosovsky, H. "The Role of Agriculture in Modern Japanese Economic Development." *Economic*

Development and Cultural Change 9, no. 2 (October
1960):43–67.

―――. "A Century of Japanese Economic Growth." In *The
State and Economic Enterprise in Japan*, edited by W. W.
Lockwood. Princeton, N.J.: Princeton University Press,
1965.

―――. "Postwar Japanese Growth in Historical Perspective:
A Second Look." In *Economic Growth: The Japanese
Experience since the Meiji Era*, edited by L. Klein and K.
Ohkawa. Homewood, Ill.: Richard D. Irwin, 1968.

Ohkawa, K.; Shinohara, M.; and Umemura, M. *Estimates of
Long Term Economic Statistics of Japan since 1868.*
Tokyo: Toyo Keizai Shinpo Sha, 1966.

Ohkawa, K. (in association with Shinohara, M.; Umemura, M.;
Ito, M.; and Noda, T.). *The Growth Rate of the Japa-
nese Economy since 1878.* Tokyo: Kiholuniya Bookstore
Co., 1957.

Oshima, H. T. "Survey of Various Long-Term Estimates of
Japanese National Income." *Keizai Kenkyu* 4 (July 1953):
243–51.

―――. Review of *The Growth Rate of the Japanese Economy since 1878* by Kazushi Ohkawa and Associates.
American Economic Review 48 (September 1958):685–
87.

―――. "A Strategy for Asian Development." *Economic
Development and Cultural Change* 11 (April 1962):
294–316.

―――. "The Meiji Fiscal Policy and Agricultural Progress."
In *The State and Economic Enterprise in Japan*, edited by
W. W. Lockwood. Princeton, N.J.: Princeton University
Press, 1965.

Papola, T. S., and Bhenodway, V. P. "Dynamics of Industrial
Wage Structure: An Inter-country Analysis." *Economic
Journal* 80 (March 1970):72–90.

Parks, R. "Systems of Demand Equations: An Empirical
Comparison of Alternative Functional Forms." *Econometrica* 37 (October 1969):629–50.

―――. "Price Responsiveness of Factor Utilization in Swedish Manufacturing, 1870–1950." Report no. 6981, Center
for Mathematical Studies in Business and Economics.
Mimeographed. Chicago: University of Chicago, 1969.

Phelps, E. "Models of Technical Progress and the Golden
Rule of Research." *Review of Economic Studies* 33 (April
1966):133–45.

Reis, A. M. *Trade Union Wage Policy*. Berkeley and Los Angeles: University of California Press, 1948.

Reynolds, L. G. "Wages and Employment in a Labor Surplus Economy." *American Economic Review* 55 (March 1965): 19–39.

Reynolds, L. G., and Taft, G. H. *The Evolution of Wage Structure*. New Haven, Conn.: Yale University Press, 1956.

Robinson, J. *The Accumulation of Capital*. London: Macmillan & Co., 1956.

Rosenstein-Rodan, P. N. "Problems of Industrialization of Eastern and South-Eastern Europe." *Economic Journal* 53 (June–September 1943).

Rosovsky, H. *Capital Formation in Japan, 1868–1940*. Glencoe, Ill.: Free Press, 1961.

————. "Japan's Transition to Modern Economic Growth, 1868–1885." In *Industrialization in Two Systems: Essays in Honor of Alexander Gerchenkron*, edited by H. Rosovsky. New York: Wiley, 1966.

————. "Rumbles in the Ricefields: Professor Nakamura vs. the Official Statistics." *Journal of Asian Studies* 27 (February 1968):347–60.

Rostow, W. W. *The Stages of Economic Growth*. Cambridge: At the University Press, 1961.

Roy, R. "La hierarchie des besoins et la notion de groupes dans l'economie de choix." *Econometrica* 11 (January 1943):13–24.

Ruebens, E. P. "Capital Labor Ratios in Theory and History: Comment." *American Economic Review* 54 (December 1964):1052–62.

Sahota, G. S. "An Economic Analysis of Internal Migration in Brazil." *Journal of Political Economy* 76 (March/April 1968):218–45.

Samuelson, P. A. *Foundations of Economic Analysis*. Cambridge, Mass.: Harvard University Press, 1947.

————. "A Theory of Induced Innovation along Kennedy Weisacker Lines." *Review of Economics and Statistics* 47 (November 1965):343–56.

————. "Rejoinder: Agreements, Disagreements, Doubts, and the Case of Induced Harrod-Neutral Technical Change." *Review of Economics and Statistics* 48 (November 1966): 444–48.

Schultz, T. W. *Economic Growth and Agriculture*. New York: McGraw-Hill, 1968.

Scitovsky, T. "Two Concepts of External Economies." *Journal of Political Economy* 62 (April 1954):143–51.

Sen, A. K. *Choice of Techniques: An Aspect of the Theory of Planned Economic Development.* Oxford: Basil Blackwell, 1960.

————. "Peasants and Dualism with or without Surplus Labor." *Journal of Political Economy* 74 (October 1966): 425–50.

Shionoya, Y. "Patterns of Industrial Development." In *Economic Growth: The Japanese Experience since the Meiji Era*, edited by L. Klein and K. Ohkawa. Homewood, Ill.: Richard D. Irwin, 1968.

Shukla, T. *Capital Formation in Indian Agriculture.* Bombay: Vora, 1965.

Sicat, G. "Economic Incentives, Industrialization, and Employment in the Developing Economies." IEDR, Discussion Paper no. 68–30. Mimeographed. Quezon City: University of the Philippines, 29 September 1968.

Sicat, G. and Tidalgo, R. "Output, Capital, Labor, and Population: Projections from the Supply Side." In *First Conference on Population*, edited by M. Concepción. Quezon City: University of the Philippines Press, 1966.

Sinha, R. P. "Unresolved Issues in Japan's Early Economic Development." *Scottish Journal of Political Economy* 16 (June 1969):109–51.

Sjaastad, L. A. "The Costs and Returns of Human Migration." *Journal of Political Economy* 70 (Suppl.) (October 1962):80–93.

Smith, T. C. *The Agrarian Origins of Modern Japan.* Stanford, Calif.: Stanford University Press, 1959.

Solow, R. M. "A Contribution to the Theory of Economic Growth." *Quarterly Journal of Economics* 70 (February 1956):65–94.

————. "Technical Change and the Aggregate Production Function." *Review of Economics and Statistics* 39 (August 1957):312–20.

————. "Investment and Technical Progress." In *Mathematical Models in the Social Sciences*, edited by K. Arrow et. al. Stanford, Calif.: Stanford University Press, 1959.

Srinivasan, T. N. "On a Two-Sector Model of Growth." Cowles Foundation Discussion Paper, no. 139 (revised). New Haven, Conn.: 1962.

Stigler, G. J. "The Economics of Information." *Journal of Political Economy* 69 (June 1961):213–25.

———. *Capital and Rates of Return in Manufacturing Industries.* Princeton, N.J.: Princeton University Press, 1963.

———. "Imperfections in the Capital Market." *Journal of Political Economy* 75 (June 1967):287–92.

Stiglitz, J. E. "A Two Sector Two Class Model of Economic Growth." *Review of Economic Studies* 34 (April 1967): 227–38.

Stone, R. "Linear Expenditure Systems and Demand Analysis: An Application to the Pattern of British Demand." *Economic Journal* 64 (September 1964):511–27.

Stone, R. *Mathematics in the Social Sciences and Other Essays.* London: Chapman & Hall, 1966.

Stone, R., ed. *A Programme for Growth,* vol. 1, *A Computable Model of Economic Growth.* London: Chapman & Hall, 1962.

———. *A Programme for Growth,* vol. 5, *The Model in Its Environment: A Progress Report.* Oxford: Chapman & Hall, 1965.

Stone, R., and Brown, A. "Behavioral and Technical Change in Economic Models." In *Problems in Economic Development,* edited by E. A. G. Robinson. London: Macmillan & Co., 1965.

Swan, T. W. "Economic Growth and Capital Accumulation." *Economic Record* 32 (November 1956):334–61.

Taeuber, I. *The Population of Japan.* Princeton, N.J.: Princeton University Press, 1958.

Tang, A. M. "Research and Education in Japanese Educational Development, 1880–1938." *Economic Studies Quarterly* (February 1963; May 1963):27–41; 91–99.

Theil, H. "The Information Approach to Demand Analysis." *Econometrica* 33 (January 1965):67–87.

———. *Economics and Information Theory.* Chicago: Rand McNally & Co., 1967.

Todaro, M. P. "A Model of Labor Migration and Urban Unemployment in Less Developed Countries." *American Economic Review* 59 (March 1969):138–48.

Tsiang, S. C. "A Model of Economic Growth in Rostovian Stages." *Econometrica* 32 (October 1964):619–48.

Tussing, A. R. "The Labor Force in Meiji Economic Growth: A Quantitative Study of Yamanashi Prefecture." In *Agri-*

culture and Economic Growth: Japan's Experience, edited by K. Ohkawa, B. F. Johnston, and H. Kaneda. Tokyo: University of Tokyo Press, 1969.

Ueno, H., and Kinoshita, S. "A Simulation Approach with a Modified Long-Term Model of Japan." *International Economic Review* 9 (February 1968):114–48.

United Nations. *Demographic Aspects of Manpower.* New York: United Nations, 1962.

United Nations. *Demographic Yearbook.* New York: United Nations, 1962.

United Nations. *The Determinants and Consequences of Population Trends.* New York: United Nations, 1953.

Uzawa, H. "On a Two-Sector Model of Economic Growth, I." *Review of Economic Studies* 29 (October 1961): 40–47.

———. "On a Two-Sector Model of Economic Growth, II." *Review of Economic Studies* 30 (June 1963):105–18.

Vanek, J. *Estimating Foreign Resource Needs for Economic Development.* New York: McGraw-Hill Co., 1967.

Warren, W. M. "Urban Real Wages and the Nigerian Trade Union Movement, 1939–1960." *Economic Development and Cultural Change* 15 (October 1966):21–36.

Watanabe, T. "Industrialization, Technological Progress, and Dual Structure." In *Economic Growth: The Japanese Experience since the Meiji Era*, edited by L. Klein and K. Ohkawa. Homewood, Ill.: Richard D. Irwin, 1968.

———. "Economic Aspects of Dualism in the Industrial Development of Japan." *Economic Development and Cultural Change* 14 (April 1965):293–312.

Wellisz, S. "Dual Economies, Disguised Unemployment, and the Unlimited Supply of Labour." *Economica* 35 (February 1968):22–51.

Williams, J. E. "The British Standard of Living, 1750–1850." *Economic History Review* 19 (December 1966):581–89.

Williamson, J. G. "Regional Inequality and the Process of National Development." *Economic Development and Cultural Change* 13, no. 4. pt. 2 (suppl.) (July 1965):1–84.

———. "Personal Savings in Developing Nations: An Intertemporal Cross-section from Asia." *Economic Record* 44 (June 1968):194–210.

———. "Dimensions of Philippine Postwar Economic Progress." *Quarterly Journal of Economics* 83 (February 1969):93–109.

————. "Capital Accumulation, Labor Saving, and Labor Absorption, A New Look at Some Contemporary Asian Evidence." EDIE 6932, Social Systems Research Institute. Mimeographed. Madison, Wis.: University of Wisconsin, February 1969.

————. "Capital Accumulation, Labor Saving, and Labor Absorption Once More." *Quarterly Journal of Economics* 85 (February 1971):40–65.

————. "Relative Prices Changes, Adjustment Dynamics, and Productivity Growth: The Case of Philippine Manufacturing." *Economic Development and Cultural Change* 19 (July 1971):507–26.

————. "Production Functions, Technological Change, and the Developing Economies: A Review Article." *Malayan Economic Review* 13, no. 2 (October 1968):8–21.

Williamson, J. G., and Sicat, G. "Technological Change and Resource Allocation in Philippine Manufacturing: 1956–1967." IEDR, Discussion Paper no. 58–21. Mimeographed. Quezon City: University of the Philippines, 15 June 1968.

Yoshihara, K. "Demand Functions: An Application to the Japanese Expenditure Pattern." *Econometrica* 37 (April 1969):257–74.

Zarembka, P. "Introduction and a Basic Dual Economy Model." Technical Report no. 8. Project for the Explanation and Optimization of Economic Growth, Berkeley: University of California, April 1968.

————. "On the Empirical Relevance of the C.E.S. Production Function." *Review of Economics and Statistics* 52 (February 1970):47–53.

————. "Labor Migration and Urban Unemployment: Comment." *American Economic Review* 60 March 1970): 184–86.

Index

Abramovitz, M. A., 214
Adjustment, speed of, 223, 303
Agricultural goods: composition of, 82; demand for, 5, 35, 65, 101, 189; price of, 68
Agricultural sector: capital accumulation in, 155; capital intensity, 110, 161, 164, 294, 315–16; commercializing of, 10, 26, 53, 57, 72, 306, 314; factor substitution in, 12, 25, 64, 68, 80, 202; productivity of, 12, 23, 83, 134–35, 155n, 163–65, 258, 306, 314–15; role of capital in, 12, 24–25, 27, 53, 57, 96; share of labor force, 12, 82–83, 117, 125–26; technical progress in, 31–32, 111, 164–67, 205, 225–26, 232
Ahmed, S., 204
Argentina, 107, 108
Arrow, K. J., 6
Assets, composition of, 237, 241

Baldwin, R. E., 9, 226, 232
Barten, A., 44
Basic model, 22–57. *See also* Model
Bhenodway, V. P., 272
Bias, in technical progress, 29, 30–32, 70, 82–83, 110–11, 153, 164–65, 204–5, 207–10, 227, 285–86, 291, 306, 320, 325–26

Birth rates. *See* Population growth
Boeke, J. H., 9
Borts, G. H., 271
Brazil, 107, 108
Brown, A., 188, 191
Bruton, H. J., 15, 234
Budd, E. C., 118
Business cycle, 75

Calorie consumption, 136n, 139n
Cameron, R., 237
Capital: in agricultural sector, 12, 24–25, 27, 53, 57, 96, 110, 155, 160, 161, 164, 237, 294, 315–16; economizing on, 158–60, 161; immobility of, 240, 243; marginal productivity of, 69, 70, 71, 74, 307; nonfarm, 12, 27, 57, 164; nonresident, 236, 239; reallocation of, 11, 16, 235–36, 240–44; traditional, 12, 27, 57, 164
Capital accumulation, 51n, 57, 161, 164, 238; and capital-output ratio, 123–24, 158–61, 213, 217; difference between models, 274–75, 279; and labor force growth, 128–29, 153–54, 199, 202, 205–7, 319; and price effect, 298; rate of, 115, 153–55, 158, 212–13; and savings rate, 66, 160–61, 212–13, 220, 224;